perspectives

Corrections

perspectives

Corrections

Academic Editor
Dennis J. Stevens
University of Massachusetts at Boston

coursewise
publishing
inc.

Bellevue • Boulder • Dubuque • Madison • St. Paul

Our mission at **Coursewise** is to help students make connections—linking theory to practice and the classroom to the outside world. Learners are motivated to synthesize ideas when course materials are placed in a context they recognize. By providing gateways to contemporary and enduring issues, **Coursewise** publications will expand students' awareness of and context for the course subject.

For more information on **Coursewise,** visit us at our web site: http://www.coursewise.com

To order an examination copy, contact: Houghton Mifflin Sixth Floor Media: 800-565-6247 (voice); 800-565-6236 (fax).

Coursewise Publishing Editorial Staff

Thomas Doran, ceo/publisher: Environmental Science/Geography/Journalism/Marketing/Speech
Edgar Laube, publisher: Political Science/Psychology/Sociology
Linda Meehan Avenarius, publisher: **Courselinks**™
Sue Pulvermacher-Alt, publisher: Education/Health/Gender Studies
Victoria Putman, publisher: Anthropology/Philosophy/Religion
Tom Romaniak, publisher: Business/Criminal Justice/Economics
Kathleen Schmitt, publishing assistant
Gail Hodge, executive producer

Coursewise Publishing Production Staff

Lori A. Blosch, permissions coordinator
Mary Monner, production coordinator
Victoria Putman, production manager

Note: Readings in this book appear exactly as they were published.
Thus, inconsistencies in style and usage among the different
readings are likely.

Reading 10, "The World of the Career Criminal" by Frank Schmalleger
from *Human Nature Magazine,* March 1979,
copyright © 1979 by Human Nature, Inc.,
reprinted by permission of the publisher.

Cover photo: Copyright © 1997 T. Teshigawara/Panoramic Images, Chicago, IL. All Rights Reserved.

Interior design and cover design by Jeff Storm

Printed in the United States of America by Coursewise Publishing, Inc.
7 North Pinckney Street, Suite 346, Madison, WI 53703

10 9 8 7 6 5 4 3 2 1

from the
Publisher

Tom Romaniak

Coursewise Publishing

After reading many of the articles in this volume along with other educational materials for the corrections course, it dawned on me. I am a correctional officer. Now I don't have any formal training. I don't carry a gun or a baton, and I don't work in a jail or a prison. But I still practice corrections.

You see, I am a parent of three. Every day, I make decisions, along with my spouse, regarding the behavior of my children. By making these decisions, I either reinforce good conduct, or identify and stamp out bad conduct. Accidentally knock over a chair out of carelessness, and you might get off with a verbal warning. Intentionally hit your sister for teasing you, and you are definitely going to be incarcerated!

I know that it's a stretch to compare my role as a parent to the role of a true professional correctional officer. Correctional officers are well trained and are often placed in dangerous and even life-threatening situations. I certainly don't want to make light of that, but the general concepts applied to each role are the same.

As a parent, I must decide what type of behavior is rewarded and what type of behavior is punished. I must decide the severity of the punishments, making sure that the punishment fits the crime. I also must decide what the goals of each punishment should be. Should I try to rehabilitate, or simply punish, the offender? What type of counseling do I need to offer to ensure that the offender doesn't become a recidivist?

I love my children dearly. I want to make sure that they grow up to become productive members of society, able to determine right from wrong and to weigh the consequences of their actions. I believe that this is my responsibility to them as individuals and to society as a whole.

Dennis Stevens, the Academic Editor of this volume of readings, is a true professional who is passionate about his work. He has spent a great deal of time in prisons working as a researcher and a counselor. He has studied and worked with prisoners, correctional officers, and prison administrators. He has drawn on his experiences to craft this volume for you.

Dennis had the assistance of a diverse Editorial Board. Members of the Editorial Board had a very active role in selecting and shaping the content of this volume. Some of them even wrote introductions and wrap-ups for some of the sections. They all did a marvelous job, and I thank them for their efforts.

This volume, along with the many resources found at our **Courselinks**™ web site for Corrections, are representative of the *connected learning tools*—tools that connect theory to practice and the classroom to the outside world—that we are creating at **Coursewise**.

Just as I have a responsibility to raise my children appropriately, **Coursewise** has a responsibility and a mission to publish appropriate learning materials. Have we succeeded? Are we behaving responsibly? Please let me know by sending me an e-mail. I'd love to hear from you.

Tom Romaniak
tomr@coursewise.com

from the
Academic Editor

Dennis J. Stevens
University of Massachusetts at Boston

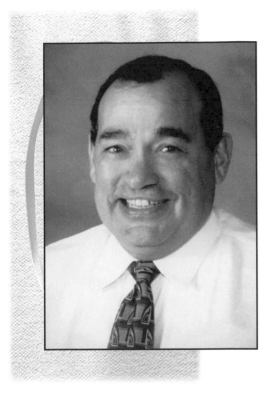

Dennis J. Stevens holds a Ph.D. from Loyola University of Chicago. He is an associate professor of criminal justice at the University of Massachusetts at Boston. Currently, he is writing a text on community policing and has recently published a book on serial rapists. In addition to developing a criminal justice program and teaching traditional university students, he has taught law enforcement officers at police academies such as the North Carolina Justice Academy and felons at maximum custody penitentiaries such as Attica in New York, Stateville and Joliet near Chicago, Eastern and NC Women's Institute near Raleigh, North Carolina, and CCI in Columbia, South Carolina. He is also a group facilitator for court-ordered sexually abusive parents. He has published many articles on corrections, policing, and prisoners in national as well as international journals and popular magazines. [dennis.stevens@umb.edu]

Perspectives: Corrections is a resource that will help any student of corrections to better understand the dynamics of correctional supervision. The focus is on the United States, with additional examples drawn from European and Canadian systems. This innovative resource joins theoretical and practical experiences of corrections to the Internet and related technologies.

This reader is organized into six sections. The readings in Section 1, "Law, Pre-Trial Issues, and Sentencing," acquaint you with decisions that members of the justice community made during police investigations, prosecution procedures, and judicial judgments. The readings highlight concerns about the reliability of criminal deterrence, judicial verdicts, and correctional supervision, including executions. The readings in Section 2, "The Correctional Client," familiarize you with some of the personal contributions and social experiences of imprisoned individuals, and they examine groups of confined individuals who are traditionally ignored, including juveniles, women, and the elderly. The readings in Section 3, "Prison Life," examine the attitudes of prisoners about their prison sentences and the effects of imprisonment both during and after incarceration. The effects of imprisonment on families of inmates are also examined. The readings in Section 4, "Rights of the Sentenced Offender," present some of the rights of confined men and women, and clarify American legal issues and misconceptions regarding prisoner litigation. The readings in Section 5, "Rehabilitation and Treatment," examine rehabilitation and treatment of men, women, and juvenile prisoners, and address public attitudes and control of sexual offenders. The readings in Section 6, "Correctional Officers and Correctional Systems," probe alternatives to traditional incarceration, such as electronic monitoring and unit management techniques, to help reduce recidivism levels and prison overcrowding. The readings also offer a window into the careers and the attitudes of male and female correctional officers in various confinement environments and suggest how those attitudes impact on other officers and offenders.

Since student development is my first concern, I accepted the challenge to be an Academic Editor for **Coursewise** to further that mission and to add integrity to the resources students use to advance themselves. I have worked and taught in both correctional and academic settings. Perhaps a little of my experience can be seen in the reading flow and in the support of the outstanding individuals who served on the Editorial Board for this project. They represent a varied assortment of practitioners, educators, and textbook authors, and all of them are experts in their particular areas and are on the cutting edge of knowledge. Their contributions have made this project possible. Clearly, **Coursewise** learning resources provide the missing link between the content that is important to discuss in class and the elements necessary to make an academic correctional course integrate practice and technology to meet the challenge of teaching both nontraditional and traditional college students.

Editorial Board

We wish to thank the following instructors for their assistance. Their many suggestions not only contributed to the construction of this volume, but also to the ongoing development of our Corrections web site.

Joanna Adler, Ph.D.
The University of Kent at Canterbury

Marie F. Ragghianti, Ph.D.
Chief of Staff, U.S. Parole Commission
Washington, D.C.

Sarah J. Brown, Ph.D.
Nene College of Higher Education

Mike Rothwell, M.A.
North Carolina Department of Corrections
Superintendent, Drug Alcohol Recovery
Treatment Center, Goldsboro, North Carolina

Jill Gordon, Ph.D.
Virginia Commonwealth University

Frank Schmalleger, Ph.D.
Director, The Justice Research Association

Kate King, Ph.D.
West Texas A&M University

Jim Thomas, Ph.D.
Northern Illinois University

Brian K. Payne, Ph.D.
Old Dominion University

Barbara H. Zaitzow, Ph.D.
Appalachian State University

ix

WiseGuide Introduction

Critical Thinking and Bumper Stickers

Question Authority

The bumper sticker said: Question Authority. This is a simple directive that goes straight to the heart of critical thinking. The issue is not whether the authority is right or wrong; it's the questioning process that's important. Questioning helps you develop awareness and a clearer sense of what you think. That's critical thinking.

Critical thinking is a new label for an old approach to learning—that of challenging all ideas, hypotheses, and assumptions. In the physical and life sciences, systematic questioning and testing methods (known as the scientific method) help verify information, and objectivity is the benchmark on which all knowledge is pursued. In the social sciences, however, where the goal is to study people and their behavior, things get fuzzy. It's one thing for the chemistry experiment to work out as predicted, or for the petri dish to yield a certain result. It's quite another matter, however, in the social sciences, where the subject is ourselves. Objectivity is harder to achieve.

Although you'll hear critical thinking defined in many different ways, it really boils down to analyzing the ideas and messages that you receive. What are you being asked to think or believe? Does it make sense, objectively? Using the same facts and considerations, could you reasonably come up with a different conclusion? And, why does this matter in the first place? As the bumper sticker urged, question authority. Authority can be a textbook, a politician, a boss, a big sister, or an ad on television. Whatever the message, learning to question it appropriately is a habit that will serve you well for a lifetime. And in the meantime, thinking critically will certainly help you be course wise.

Getting Connected

This reader is a tool for connected learning. This means that the readings and other learning aids explained here will help you to link classroom theory to real-world issues. They will help you to think critically and to make long-lasting learning connections. Feedback from both instructors and students has helped us to develop some suggestions on how you can wisely use this connected learning tool.

WiseGuide Pedagogy

A wise reader is better able to be a critical reader. Therefore, we want to help you get wise about the articles in this reader. Each section of *Perspectives* has three tools to help you: the WiseGuide Intro, the WiseGuide Wrap-Up, and the Putting It in *Perspectives* review form.

WiseGuide Intro

WiseGuide Intro

In the WiseGuide Intro, the Academic Editor introduces the section, gives you an overview of the topics covered, and explains why particular articles were selected and what's important about them.

Also in the WiseGuide Intro, you'll find several key points or learning objectives that highlight the most important things to remember from this section. These will help you to focus your study of section topics.

At the end of the WiseGuide Intro, you'll find questions designed to stimulate critical thinking. Wise students will keep these questions in mind as they read an article (we repeat the questions at the start of the articles as a reminder). When you finish each article, check your understanding. Can you answer the questions? If not, go back and reread the article. The Academic Editor has written sample responses for many of the questions, and you'll find these online at the **Courselinks**™ site for this course. More about **Courselinks** in a minute. . . .

WiseGuide Wrap-Up

Be course wise and develop a thorough understanding of the topics covered in this course. The WiseGuide Wrap-Up at the end of each section will help you do just that with concluding comments or summary points that repeat what's most important to understand from the section you just read.

In addition, we try to get you wired up by providing a list of select Internet resources—what we call R.E.A.L. web sites because they're **R**elevant, **E**nhanced, **A**pproved, and **L**inked. The information at these web sites will enhance your understanding of a topic. (Remember to use your Passport and start at http://www.courselinks.com so that if any of these sites have changed, you'll have the latest link.)

Putting It in *Perspectives* Review Form

At the end of the book is the Putting It in *Perspectives* review form. Your instructor may ask you to complete this form as an assignment or for extra credit. If nothing else, consider doing it on your own to help you critically think about the reading.

Prompts at the end of each article encourage you to complete this review form. Feel free to copy the form and use it as needed.

The Courselinks™ Site

The **Courselinks** Passport is your ticket to a wonderful world of integrated web resources designed to help you with your course work. These resources are found at the **Courselinks** site for your course area. This is where the readings in this book and the key topics of your course are linked to an exciting array of online learning tools. Here you will find carefully selected readings, web links, quizzes, worksheets, and more, tailored to your course and approved as connected learning tools. The ever-changing, always interesting **Courselinks** site features a number of carefully integrated resources designed to help you be course wise. These include:

http://www.courselinks.com

- **R.E.A.L. Sites** At the core of a **Courselinks** site is the list of R.E.A.L. sites. This is a select group of web sites for studying, not surfing. Like the readings in this book, these sites have been selected, reviewed, and approved by the Academic Editor and the Editorial Board. The R.E.A.L. sites are arranged by topic and are annotated with short descriptions and key words to make them easier for you to use for reference or research. With R.E.A.L. sites, you're studying approved resources within seconds—and not wasting precious time surfing unproven sites.

- **Editor's Choice** Here you'll find updates on news related to your course, with links to the actual online sources. This is also where we'll tell you about changes to the site and about online events.

- **Course Overview** This is a general description of the typical course in this area of study. While your instructor will provide specific course objectives, this overview helps you place the course in a generic context and offers you an additional reference point.

- **www.orksheet** Focus your trip to a R.E.A.L. site with the www.orksheet. Each of the 10 to 15 questions will prompt you to take in the best that site has to offer. Use this tool for self-study, or if required, email it to your instructor.

- **Course Quiz** The questions on this self-scoring quiz are related to articles in the reader, information at R.E.A.L. sites, and other course topics, and will help you pinpoint areas you need to study. Only you will know your score—it's an easy, risk-free way to keep pace!

- **Topic Key** The online Topic Key is a listing of the main topics in your course, and it correlates with the Topic Key that appears in this reader. This handy reference tool also links directly to those R.E.A.L. sites that are especially appropriate to each topic, bringing you integrated online resources within seconds!

- **Web Savvy Student Site** If you're new to the Internet or want to brush up, stop by the Web Savvy Student site. This unique supplement is a complete **Courselinks** site unto itself. Here, you'll find basic information on using the Internet, creating a web page, communicating on the web, and more. Quizzes and Web Savvy Worksheets test your web knowledge, and the R.E.A.L. sites listed here will further enhance your understanding of the web.

- **Student Lounge** Drop by the Student Lounge to chat with other students taking the same course or to learn more about careers in your major. You'll find links to resources for scholarships, financial aid, internships, professional associations, and jobs. Take a look around the Student Lounge and give us your feedback. We're open to remodeling the Lounge per your suggestions.

Building Better Perspectives!

Please tell us what you think of this *Perspectives* volume so we can improve the next one. Here's how you can help:

1. Visit our **Coursewise** site at: http://www.coursewise.com

2. Click on *Perspectives.* Then select the Building Better *Perspectives* Form for your book.

3. Forms and instructions for submission are available online.

Tell us what you think—did the readings and online materials help you make some learning connections? Were some materials more helpful than others? Thanks in advance for helping us build better *Perspectives.*

Student Internships

If you enjoy evaluating these articles or would like to help us evaluate the **Courselinks** site for this course, check out the **Coursewise** Student Internship Program. For more information, visit:

http://www.coursewise.com/intern.html

Brief Contents

Contents

section

2

The Correctional Client

section 3

Prison Life

section 4

Rights of the Sentenced Offender

section
5
Rehabilitation and Treatment

section 6

Correctional Officers and Correctional Systems

Topic Key

This Topic Key is an important tool for learning. It will help you integrate this reader into your course studies. Listed below, in alphabetical order, are important topics covered in this volume. Below each topic you'll find the reading numbers and titles, and R.E.A.L. web site addresses, relating to that topic. Note that the Topic Key might not include every topic your instructor chooses to emphasize. If you don't find the topic you're looking for in the Topic Key, check the index or the online topic key at the **Courselinks**™ site.

Battered Women Syndrome

4 Interviews with Women Convicted of Murder: Battered Women Syndrome Revisited

23 Legal Issues and the Female Offender

FindLaw—U.S. Supreme Court Decisions
http://www.findlaw.com/casecode/supreme.html

Death Row Inmate Web Ring
http://www.geocities.com/CapitolHill/Senate/5831/

Capital Punishment

6 College Student Attitudes about Capital Punishment: Sources of Attitudes about the Death Penalty

7 Executions in 1996 Second Highest Since 1976

Critical Criminology Division of the American Society of Criminology
http://www.soci.niu.edu/~critcrim/prisons/prisons.html

Death Penalty Links
http://www.derechos.org/dp/

The Other Side of the Wall
http://www.wco.com/~aerick/

Death Row Inmate Web Ring
http://www.geocities.com/CapitolHill/Senate/5831/

Correctional Facilities and Systems

11 Origins and Effects of Prison Drug Gangs in North Carolina

American Correctional Association
http://www.corrections.com/aca/index.html

Infrastructure Initiative
http://www.dof.ca.gov/html/budgt8-9/infrast.htm

Justice Information Center
http://www.ncjrs.org

Correctional Officers

36 Correctional Officers As Human Services Workers: The Effect on Job Satisfaction

37 Coping in Alien Territory: Corrections Officers in the AIDS Ward

38 Women Working in a Men's Jail

39 Cross Gender Supervision and Control in Male Prisons in England: A Summary of Officers' Perspectives

U.S. Government Jobs/Correctional Officers
http://www.usajobs.opm.gov/wfjic/jobs/BQ6899.HTM

International Association of Correctional Officers
http://www.acsp.uic.edu/iaco/

Criminal Life Styles

4 Interviews with Women Convicted of Murder: Battered Women Syndrome Revisited

9 A Theoretical Model for the Clinical Assessment of Dangerousness in Offender Populations

10 World of the Career Criminal

American Society of Criminology
http://www.asc41.com/

Talk Justice on the World Wide Web
http://talkjustice.com/

Effects on Families

20 The Effects of Incarceration on Families of Male Inmates

Delancey Street Foundation
http://www.igc.apc.org/justice/cjc/delancey.html

Directory of Programs Serving Families of Adult Offenders
http://www.ifs.univie.ac.at/~uncjin/famcorr/fmcordir.html

International Trends in Crime Prevention
http://www.crime-prevention-intl.org/english/index.htm

Female Prisoners

4 Interviews with Women Convicted of Murder: Battered Women Syndrome Revisited

12 Women in Prison

22 California Women Prisoners Win Improvements to Deficient Medical Care

27 Women and Fraud: Results of a Program at the Prison for Women

Bureau of Justice Statistics (BJS)
http://www.ojp.usdoj.gov/bjs/

Forum of Correctional Services of Canada
http://198.103.98.138/crd/forum/

The Other Side of the Wall
http://www.wco.com/~aerick/

Gangs

11 Origins and Effects of Prison Drug Gangs in North Carolina

RAND
http://www.rand.org/

The Redwood Highway
http://www.sonoma.edu/cja/info/infop4.html#correct

United Nations Crime and Justice Network
http://www.ifs.univie.ac.at/~uncjin/uncjin.html

Incarcerated Mothers

4 Interviews with Women Convicted of Murder: Battered Women Syndrome Revisited

19 Incarcerated Mothers and the Foster Care System in Massachusetts: A Literature Review

20 The Effects of Incarceration on Families of Male Inmates

Prison Issues Desk
http://www.prisonactivist.org/

Interrogation

1   Interrogation: Understanding the Process
3   From Police Information to Miscarriages of Justice

FindLaw—U.S. Supreme Court Decisions
http://www.findlaw.com/casecode/supreme.html

Prison Issues Desk
http://www.prisonactivist.org/

Juveniles

8   Prediction of Adult Criminal Status from Juvenile Psychological Assessment
32   The Legacy of Juvenile Corrections

National Association for Youth Justice
http://www.nayj.org.uk/links.html

National Council on Crime and Delinquency
http://solar.rtd.utk.edu/ccsi/csusa/crime/crimedel.html

Justice Information Center
http://www.ncjrs.org

Office of International Criminal Justice (OICJ)
http://www.acsp.uic.edu/index.shtml

United Nations Crime and Justice Network
http://www.ifs.univie.ac.at/~uncjin/uncjin.html

Law

4   Interviews with Women Convicted of Murder: Battered Women Syndrome Revisited
21   Update: Reversing the Pendulum of Prisoners' Rights
23   Legal Issues and the Female Offender

Legal Sites and Resources in the UK
http://www.pavilion.co.uk/legal/sites.htm

FindLaw—U.S. Supreme Court Decisions
http://www.findlaw.com/casecode/supreme.html

Law Journal Extra!
http://www.ljx.com/

School of Criminal Justice (CJ) at the University of Albany
http://www.albany.edu/scj/links.html#prison

Male Prisoners

14   Southern Prisons and Elderly Inmates: Taking a Look Inside
15   The Meaning of Punishment: Inmates' Orientation to the Prison Experience
16   The Depth of Imprisonment and Prisonization: Levels of Security and Prisoners' Anticipation of Future Violence

Bureau of Justice Statistics (BJS)
http://www.ojp.usdoj.gov/bjs/

Forum of Correctional Services of Canada
http://198.103.98.138/crd/forum/

Infrastructure Initiative
http://www.dof.ca.gov/html/budgt8-9/infrast.htm

Journal of Prisoners on Prisons
http://www.jpp.org/

The Other Side of the Wall
http://www.wco.com/~aerick/

Prison Issues Desk
http://www.prisonactivist.org/

Miscarriages of Justice

3   From Police Information to Miscarriages of Justice
4   Interviews with Women Convicted of Murder: Battered Women Syndrome Revisited

Critical Criminology Division of the American Society of Criminology (ASC)
http://www.soci.niu.edu/~critcrim/prisons/prisons.html

FindLaw—U.S. Supreme Court Decisions
http://www.findlaw.com/casecode/supreme.html

Journal of Prisoners on Prisons
http://www.jpp.org/

The Other Side of the Wall
http://www.wco.com/~aerick/

Prison Issues Desk
http://www.prisonactivist.org/

Death Row Inmate Web Ring
http://www.geocities.com/CapitolHill/Senate/5831/

Prisoner Rights

21   Update: Reversing the Pendulum of Prisoners' Rights
22   California Women Prisoners Win Improvements to Deficient Medical Care
23   Legal Issues and the Female Offender
24   Overcoming the Absurd: Prisoner Litigation As Primitive Rebellion
25   Issues and Misconceptions in Prisoner Litigation: A Critical View

Legal Sites and Resources in the UK
http://www.pavilion.co.uk/legal/sites.htm

Critical Criminology Division of the American Society of Criminology (ASC)
http://www.soci.niu.edu/~critcrim/prisons/prisons.html

FindLaw—U.S. Supreme Court Decisions
http://www.findlaw.com/casecode/supreme.html

Forum of Correctional Services of Canada
http://198.103.98.138/crd/forum/

Journal of Prisoners on Prisons
http://www.jpp.org/

Prisonization

16   The Depth of Imprisonment and Prisonization: Levels of Security and Prisoners' Anticipation of Future Violence

American Society of Criminology
http://www.asc41.com/

Probation

Delancey Street Foundation
http://www.igc.apc.org/justice/cjc/delancey.html

International Community Corrections Association
http://www.cssnet.com/icca/

National Institute of Corrections
http://www.nicic.org/inst/

The Redwood Highway
http://www.sonoma.edu/cja/info/infop4.html#correct

section 1

Law, Pre-Trial Issues, and Sentencing

Dennis J. Stevens, Ph.D.
Associate Professor of Criminal Justice, University of Massachusetts at Boston
[dennis.stevens@umb.edu]

Key Points

- In most countries, prisons are overcrowded not necessarily because there are more crimes being committed.

- One priority at a trial could be to discover the truth surrounding the evidence obtained during an investigation or interrogation which could produce a miscarriage of justice.

- The consequences of prison sentences, including capital punishment, seem to affect many offenders less often than expected.

 **WiseGuide Intro**

The United States, Canada, and the European Union are reporting an enormous growth in their prison populations, despite the notion that crime is yet to be reconciled. Nonetheless, there is a complex process prior to a new resident entering a penitentiary regardless of the country being reviewed. For instance, after a crime is reported, an investigation might be conducted by the police. Police detectives Zulawski and Wicklander explain how investigators confront a suspect without proof and how to gather the evidence for an indictment. Spears and Spohn examine the process of gathering evidence against sexual offenders in order to file charges against them. Once charges are filed against a suspect through these and other methods, van Koppen argues in the third reading that trials are designed to discover the truth of the investigation as opposed to discovering the truth about the innocence of the suspect. Therefore, it could be argued that some innocent individuals have been convicted of crimes and incarcerated.

Stevens examines the lifestyles of women prisoners prior to the event that led to their murder conviction and eventual incarceration. He concludes that many women convicted of murder describe what appears to be self-defense, but U.S. courts disagree. Lewis, in the next reading in this section, explores the relationship between long prison sentences and deterrence of crime. What college students think of the ultimate penalty and how their attitudes can be changed is the concern of Payne and Coogle in their work on capital punishment. Lastly, Dieter surveys the number of executions in the United States and evidence that shows that we may be moving toward a greater number of executions in the future.

In what ways might police investigations be arranged to produce a greater focus on innocence?

In what ways might evidence against suspected sexual offenders be inappropriate or challenge the rights of a suspect?

Under what conditions can an individual take the life of another individual without being charged with homicide?

In what ways might prison sentences and capital punishment control heinous crime?

? ? ? Questions ? ?

Reading 1. How is an official interrogation conducted? Are there legal guidelines the police should follow during an investigation?

Reading 2. What criterion is used by prosecutors to charge an individual with sexual assault?

Reading 3. In what way is a courtroom trial searching for truth? What truth?

Reading 4. What are some of the realities of battered women syndrome? In what ways might homicide laws be prejudicial?

Reading 5. In what ways do researchers differ on the deterrence effect of prison sentences?

Reading 6. In what ways might the death penalty impact the general public? Criminals? How can the ideas of the public be changed concerning capital punishment?

Reading 7. Are certain states relying more on capital punishment than they have in the past?

How is an official interrogation conducted? Are there legal guidelines the police should follow during an investigation?

Interrogation:
Understanding the Process

David E. Zulawski and Douglas E. Wicklander

David E. Zulawski and Douglas E. Wicklander are partners in the investigative and interrogation training firm Wicklander-Zulawski & Associates, Inc., Downers Grove, IL. They are also the authors of the text Practical Aspects of Interview and Interrogation, *published by CRC Press.*

Bob Jones (a pseudonym) left for work, as he did each weekday, kissing his wife of 20 years goodbye. He waved to a neighbor also beginning his day. The street was quiet, as it always was this time of morning. A nice place to live, he concluded, as he headed off.

Twelve hours later, he returned to discover that his wife had been brutally raped and murdered. Investigators noted that a package had been delivered to the home sometime during the day. The husband's whereabouts during the day were quickly confirmed and he was eliminated early in the investigation as a suspect.

Investigators focused on the package and the deliveryman, and after some difficulty they identified the deliveryman and began interviewing him at the police station. The man acknowledged that he had delivered a package and that Mrs. Jones had signed for it, but he was adamant that she was still alive when he left her. Just as the interview was concluding, one of the investigators asked the subject if he had returned to the house a second time. The subject went pale and then flushed a bright red, while he denied returning to the Jones' residence a second time.

The subject's strong reaction to the question peaked the investigator's interest in the deliveryman as a possible suspect. Why would an innocent person react that strongly to a simple inquiry?

A search was begun for the deliveryman's car. An unusual set of mismatched tire tracks had been discovered in the driveway of the victim's home and the police wondered what kind of tires were on the deliveryman's private vehicle. To no one's surprise, the tires on the deliveryman's vehicle matched those in the victim's driveway.

An interrogation of the deliveryman was concluded unsuccessfully when he asked for counsel. The deliveryman was convicted of murder/rape and is currently serving a sentence.

Confronting the target of the investigation is one of the final steps an investigator takes in concluding an inquiry. Often the ultimate outcome of the case may hinge on whether the suspect confesses. A confession is responsible for more successful case resolutions than all other forensic techniques combined.

Interviews answer the investigative questions: who, what, where, when, how and why. The interrogation of an individual is done when he becomes the target of the investigation or is suspected of withholding information crucial to the successful conclusion of the investigation.

The confrontation of a suspect is a complicated process. An individual's age, personality, education, job, experience with the criminal justice system or their awareness of the investigation are just a few of the variables an investigator must deal with when preparing to confront a subject. Confronting the reluctant witness or suspect has a process that can be applied to increase the likelihood of engaging the individual's cooperation.

Decision to Confess

The subject who elects to confess makes the decision to do so either emotionally or rationally. Emotional decisions to confess are related to the subject's guilt feelings and self-image. This type of individual needs the support of rationalization and projection to protect the framework of his or her self-image. It is not unusual for a suspect making an emotional decision to confess to have pronounced signs of submission prior to the confession. These signs of submission could progress from a head and shoulder slump, to tearing and crying.

In some situations, the interrogation of an offender making an emotional decision to confess is very much like a mother confronting a child about a misdeed. The child makes a denial to the mother's direct accusation, quiets into submission, becomes withdrawn, and then finally

Interrogation: Understanding the Process. D. Zulawski and D. E. Wicklander. *Law and Order,* July 1998, 46(7), 82–90. Reprinted by permission of the authors.

cries and admits the incident. In this type of interrogation, conflicts may arise when one party, the interrogator, tries to force a role, the child, on the other party that he or she does not wish to play. The child reacts to a mother in a similar way, "Well go ahead and send me to my room for the rest of my life and don't feed me!" The suspect responds, "Well go ahead and lock me up. I don't care!" Neither of these statements is the true desire of the speaker, but is instead an attempt to change roles in the conversation.

When the suspect makes a rational decision to confess, the interrogator and the suspect are in a complementary conversation that encourages the confession. In this approach, the interrogator takes the role of an adult speaking to an adult. The interrogator addresses the fears or hurdles the suspect may have in a rational manner allowing the suspect to feel comfortable confessing. The decision to confess means that the suspect has addressed his fears or concerns and resolved them in his mind. This is true whether the suspect has made a rational or emotional decision to confess. The fears or hurdles the interrogator must address to overcome the suspect's resistance generally fall into one of the following five categories:

Fear of termination or financial repercussions. The suspect is reluctant to make an admission because it may impact his ability to get or retain a job or pay bills and other financial obligations in his life.

Fear of arrest or prosecution. This area is often of greater concern to those suspects who have had little previous contact with the police.

Fear of embarrassment. This hurdle to a confession relates to a suspect's self-image. They fear that they will shock family, friends or co-workers and lose their respect. Some are unable to face what they have done in their own mind without destroying their own self-image.

Fear of restitution. Some suspects are resistant to a confession because they could not compensate the victim for the damage or loss their actions caused.

Fear of retaliation. An individual's fear for his safety or that of a family member can be a difficult hurdle for the interrogator to overcome. This factor is more prevalent as gang intimidation and violence increases. Child molesters are often reluctant to make an admission because of the fear of being labeled as such in the prison system.

Interrogators, through experience, recognize that some suspects confess to relieve guilt, others because of overwhelming proof of their guilt, and others because of the interrogator's persuasion. In the authors' research with convicted felons, they have all said essentially the same thing, that if an interrogator treats them as if they had value they would at least consider confessing. This seems to be true regardless of the consequences that they faced. The felons all said their resistance to a confession would increase if they were berated or looked down upon.

Suspect Denials

One of the frustrating and difficult phases of an interrogation is handling the suspect's denials. Certainly, the fears of the suspect play a role in the decision to confess, but the way a suspect is approached by the interrogator is undoubtedly a greater factor. Every individual has a predisposition to deny, which is an avoidance behavior learned as a child. This learned behavior attempts to avoid the consequences of an illegal, dishonest or shameful act. Interrogators must anticipate what actions or behaviors the suspect will engage in to counter the accusations of wrongdoing.

The role of the interrogator in the confrontation should be to avoid forcing the suspect into a position where he or she must deny. Traditionally, interrogators have been trained to do the same things each time as they confront a guilty subject, a tactic that often influences the suspect to deny, rather than make an admission of guilt.

The reasons a suspect might deny break down into three basic areas; environment, suspect and interrogator. The decision to deny is often directly influenced by the

choices the interrogator makes and the strategies chosen to engage the suspect in the confrontation.

Environment: The timing of the interview, location, room setting, witness selection and other factors all may play a role in the decision to confess. The resources and flexibility of the interrogator may dictate which of these factors may become hindrances or helps to obtaining a confession.

Suspect: Suspects often deny because of past experience with the criminal justice system. During a confrontation the suspect is making decisions about what the interrogator knows and what the evidence of his guilt may have been uncovered during the investigation. The suspect reacts to the interrogator and his strategies, either reducing resistance to his confession or increasing it. Some simply use the denial to buy time to evaluate the investigation and interrogator.

Interrogator: The interrogator is a major contributor to the suspect's decision to deny. The interrogator's confidence in the suspect's guilt, word usage and plan of attack help to define the probable response of the suspect.

The interrogator must look at the behavior of the suspect in all aspects of his daily life to be able to answer the question, "How is the suspect likely to react when told that his involvement in an illegal act has been uncovered?" The answer to this can often be found in the individual's life and personal relationships. We all tend to respond to similar problems with a preset response. The suspect's choice of a strategy will be based on what the individual has found to be successful in the past. The suspect's likely response can often be discovered by asking the question, "If the suspect has been disciplined or confronted, how did he react?"

Once the interrogator identifies the probable suspect response to a confrontation, he decides on what approach may be most effective. The approach should not encourage the suspect to use the preferred strategy. For example, if an individual is generally aggressive in confrontations, the interrogator should devise an approach that will not allow the suspect to become aggressive. This may mean that the witness selection, the location of the interview or other strategy would be used to control the subject's decision making process.

The interrogator should encourage the suspect to make a denial. Once the suspect makes a denial, he is forced to defend the lie with additional denials. This places the suspect in a position of having to continually lie to defend himself. It is often easier for an individual to make an admission if he has not been put in a position where he had to lie.

There are certain situations where the suspect's lie can work in the interrogator's favor. In fact, a lie may be as good as a confession in some instances. Encouraging a suspect to tell lies can increase the value of the evidence that was developed during the investigation. Direct contradiction of the suspect's statements with irrefutable evidence can be a powerful wedge in bringing out the truth, but it does not always result in a confession. In some instances, the presentation of overwhelming evidence may have the reverse effect, increasing the suspect's resistance to a confession. The benefit to the investigation, when a suspect lies is that the suspect must live with that lie even though it contradicts the evidence.

Four Parts of Interrogation

Reducing Resistance: The interrogator chooses some method to reduce the suspect's resistance to a confession. Depending on the style of interrogation chosen, this could be done with a systematic presentation of evidence, use of an emotional appeal, interrogator persistence or sensory depravation.

Obtaining the Admission: The second part of every interrogation is the first admission of the suspect. This is the first acknowledgement by the suspect that he is involved in the act under investigation. This is not a confession, but merely the first admission that confirms the interrogator's assertion that the suspect was involved.

Development of the Admission: This section expands the suspect's admission into a legally acceptable confession that answers the questions; who, what, where, when, how, and why. It allows the in-

terrogator to explore other areas of criminal activity in which the suspect may be involved.

Professional Close: The interrogator reduces the suspect's oral admission to a permanent form, either written or taped, and has it witnessed.

Wicklander-Zulawski Technique

To this point we have considered interrogations which encourage denials, causes of denials, fears of the suspect, and the common parts to an interrogation. Now we will focus on the construction of an interrogation designed to encourage a suspect to make a rational decision to confess, in many cases without making a denial.

Preparation and Profiling—The interrogator considers the investigation and goal of the interrogation. The elements of the crime or violation are defined and the evidence indicating the violation is clearly understood. The interrogator should understand the strengths and weaknesses of the inquiry and begin to consider whether direct evidence should be used early or late in the confrontation, or if it should be revealed at all. It is at this point that the interrogator may consider what type of enticement questions, or bluffs, might prove useful, and when they should be used.

The next consideration is special personnel or legal requirements that may be necessary to close the investigation. Is the interrogator public law enforcement, acting as an agent of the police or working independently for an organization? Is there a union? There may be legal issues that need to be addressed based on the answer to these and other questions. Different countries and even states within the United States have unique legal aspects the interrogator should consider before beginning the confrontation. The ultimate goal to prosecute, or simply terminate employment, may dictate some of the case closure methods. There are many factors to consider during the preparation phase in addition to those mentioned here.

In most investigations, there will be a time that the suspect will be more susceptible to a confession.

Unfortunately for the investigator, that time may arrive before the investigation is complete. The investigator has to make a decision whether the value of possible additional evidence will outweigh the suspect's current susceptibility to a confession. If the investigators, in the opening example, had confronted the deliveryman based on his verbal and physical responses even though the investigation was not complete; they would not have lost the subsequent evidence, and may have gained a confession because of the suspect's momentary confusion at being identified.

How can an interrogator confront someone without proof? The interrogator could not if he planned to use a factual attack, building the case for the suspect's guilt with the evidence that was accumulated during the investigation. There are several problems with a factual interrogation. First, the presentation of evidence may show the weaknesses in the investigation. Second, presenting evidence to a suspect when he is still physically and emotionally strong will often result in the suspect contradicting the evidence's meaning or relevance. Third, in the small number of cases where there might exist the possibility of a false confession, the subject's knowledge of the evidence could contribute to a convincing statement from the suspect who just repeats the facts that he was told. The WZ Technique solves these problems and allows the interrogator to confront a suspect even when the investigation is not as complete as it could have been. This gives the interrogator an opportunity to take advantage of the "optimum moment in time" when the individual is susceptible to a confession.

Reducing Resistance: The interrogator, in the first part of the interrogation has several clear goals. Establish rapport with the suspect, convince him his guilt is known, and allow him to save face, while avoiding forcing the suspect into a position where he has to deny.

After the interrogator has established rapport with the suspect, he develops the credibility of the investigation. This conveys to the suspect that his guilt is known. The interrogator accomplishes the credibility or when he talks about the work that he does. This discussion also includes the types of crimes that are investigated which include the type of crime under investigation. This allows the interrogator to introduce the topic of the investigation without making a specific accusation the suspect might deny. The second benefit that the interrogator derives from this approach is possible suspect behavioral reactions to other acts of dishonesty or criminal involvement.

Building the credibility of the investigation continues with a general discussion of investigative techniques, which if they had been used, could have developed information linking the suspect to the crime. The discussion of investigative techniques causes the suspect to consider, perhaps for the first time, that there may be evidence linking him to the crime.

The guilty suspect has been rocked by the realization that his guilt is known, but he generally does not deny because there has been no direct accusation made by the interrogator. The suspect also may withhold his denial because he hopes that perhaps he is wrong in his assessment of the situation and the interrogator is not really there to accuse him.

The second component of reducing resistance is showing understanding for the problems that people face. The interrogator begins a discussion of reasons why people might become involved in criminal acts. The interrogator offers these reasons or rationalizations to the suspect as a monologue, selecting those that match the background of the suspect. The interrogator speaks in the third person using "he", "she", "they", or "them", rather than "you" as he presents the rationalizations. This lack of personalization during the rationalizations continues the suspect's pattern of denial avoidance as he listens to the reasons why people make "errors in judgement."

The process of rationalization is perfectly suited for the criminal suspect. Above all else, criminals are rationalizers. This personality characteristic allows them to justify their actions and project their feelings onto others. These rationalizations might include; the company makes a lot of money, she was asking for it, or

he doesn't pay us enough. These are the same rationalizations that the interrogator offers the suspect to minimize the consequences to the suspect and victim, focus the suspect's attention on the resolution of the problem, and to transfer blame to his circumstances in life.

The rationalizations are selected based on the background of the suspect. For example, if a suspect is having financial problems, the interrogator might talk about the costs of raising a family and the stress of bills. The interrogator knows that the reasons he offers the suspect may not be the real reasons why the individual became involved in the criminal act, but these are simply reasons that allow the suspect to save face. The other benefit to the interrogator is rationalization allows the suspect to save face, but it does not usually affect the elements of the crime. Does it make a difference that a suspect says he stole the money to take care of his children or to buy drugs? No, what the money was used for is irrelevant, but the admission that he stole the money is not. Showing understanding allows the interrogator to continue rapport building and the interrogator becomes a mediator, rather than an opponent in the encounter. Rationalizations help the suspect overcome his fears of confessing; loss of employment, financial issues, arrest, self-image, restitution and retaliation.

While an interrogator might suggest that there are benefits to confessing, the suspect does not necessarily see these advantages. The interrogator has to deal with either perceived tangible or intangible benefits to the suspect. Tangible benefits might be the placing of only certain charges, allowing bond, charging the suspect at a later date or any of a number of other perceived benefits. More likely, the interrogator has to deal with intangible benefits. These are the suspect's perceived advantages of a confession; self-image, relieving guilt, or others understanding his plight.

One way to shorten the suspect's recognition of the benefit of confession is through the use of a role reversal with the suspect. The interrogator sets up a story where the suspect has to make a decision about

two people, one who is uncooperative and one who is not. The suspect recognizes that he would feel differently about the two people if he were in the decision-making role. This story empowers the suspect with the knowledge that he is not helpless, but can have an influence on the decision-makers, based on his actions. Behaviorally, a suspect will move through several distinct phases as the interrogator continues his monologue. The first phase is rejection as the suspect recognizes that his involvement in the criminal act has been discovered. This usually results in closed body posture, crossed arms and or a leg that provides a defensive barrier, behaviors that increase the comfort level of the suspect. The second phase of behavior, evaluation, commences after the interrogator begins the process of showing understanding and rationalization. The suspect's body will appear more open, the muscles will lose tension and the hand will often move to the face in a consideration pose. The final behavioral change is submission. The suspect's body begins to open, the arms and legs uncross and the suspect begins to withdraw mentally to consider his options. A salesman recognizes these behaviors as the "buy signs" of the customer. The interrogator comes to the same conclusion.

Obtaining the Admission: The third phase of the interrogation is obtaining the first admission from the suspect. They may be made verbally or with a head movement, either a nod or a shake. The interrogator observes the signs of submission and offers an assumptive question to the suspect that encourages an admission of guilt. The Assumptive Question is generally an extension of the rationalization the interrogator was offering to the suspect. If the interrogator was talking about the proceeds of the crime being used to pay family bills, the assumptive question might be, "Did you use the money for bills or was it for drugs?" The interrogator offers the suspect a choice, acceptable vs. unacceptable, which makes it easier for the suspect to save face. Another type of assumptive question is the Soft Accusation. This does not provide the suspect a choice, but instead asks about some aspect of the suspect's involvement in the crime. An example might be "When was the first time you broke into a vehicle no matter how long ago?" This type of question is followed immediately with a follow up question such as, "It wasn't two years ago, was it?" This exaggeration by the interrogator often brings a denial from the suspect. However, it is a denial that is really an admission of guilt. The interrogator supports this denial as an admission saying, "Great, I didn't think that it was that long ago! When was the first time?" The suspect's admission brings us to the third phase of the interrogation, Development of the Admission.

This phase of the interrogation answers the questions who, what, where, when, how and why. The suspect's involvement in the criminal act is explored fully by the interrogator who looks for confirmation of the investigative findings and the suspect's mental state at the time of the incident. A key purpose of this is to expand the admission into other areas of dishonesty or criminal activity of which the interrogator may not even be aware. The development of the admission and the expansion of the individual's involvement can have a number of obvious benefits to the investigation.

During this phase the interrogator may be faced with an absolute denial from the suspect, "That is all I did and I don't care what you or your investigation say." This is the time to present evidence that contradicts the suspect's statement. Even weaker circumstantial evidence is often enough to break these denials and gain additional admissions. Saving evidence for this phase of the interrogation often has a greater impact on the suspect than using it early in the interrogation.

Professional Close: The final phase of the interrogation is preserving the statement for future use and witnessing it. The final statement contains the subject's admission and covers the elements of the crime or policy violation to which the suspect has admitted. The language clearly details what was done; by whom and in what context it was done. The suspect's statement may be handwritten, audio/video taped, or taken by a court reporter. Regardless of the format, the information included accurately portrays the suspect's admission and its voluntary nature.

Discussion

In general, suspects decide to confess based on their own perception of the situation and their own personal needs. Few do so as a result of overpowering guilt or desire to punish themselves. Rather, the decision is probably a combination of the suspect's need to release the internal pressure of guilt by talking about the incident and rationalizing his involvement. It could also be the suspect's belief that his guilt is known, and the interrogator's persuasive arguments, or some combination of all of these reasons.

Research has attempted to quantify the reasons for a confession resulting from these internal, external or proof factors. External factors, the fear of being arrested, threats or other issues contributed to a confession less than 20% of the time. Internal factors proved to be a much stronger reason to confess. Suspects, 42%, indicated that they experienced relief after talking and explaining their side of the story. Fully a third indicated that they wanted to "get it off their chest". Proof by far was the strongest factor to encourage a confession. Some 55 percent of the suspects in the study said that they confessed because they believed that the police could prove their involvement.

The Wicklander-Zulawski Technique takes advantage of these findings by creating a strong belief that the suspect's guilt is known, credibility of the investigation.

Second, the technique offers rationalizations that allow the suspect to save face, while building a persuasive argument in favor of a confession. Finally, it creates a winning situation for the suspect by not forcing him to lie to the interrogator in the early stage of the interrogation when he is physically and emotionally strongest.

The WZ Technique also allows the interrogator to change tactics and strategies based on the type of suspect personality or their reaction to the confrontation. The interrogator who understands the suspect and his motives can create an environment and strategy that encourages a confession.

Sources

Hilgendorf, E. L. and Irving, B. (1981). A decision-making model of confessions. In: *Psychology in Legal Contexts. Applications and Limitations*, M. A. Lloyd-Bostock (ed.). Macmillan: London, pp. 67–84.

Gudjonsson, G. H. (1989b). The psychology of false confessions. *Medico-Legal J.*, 57, 93–110.

Reik, T. (1959). *The Compulsion to Confess: on the Psychoanalysis of Crime and Punishment.* Farrar, Straus and Cudahy: New York.

Jayne, B. C. (1986). The psychological principles of criminal interrogation. An Appendix. In: *Criminal Interrogation and Confession*, 3rd Edition (Eds. F. E. Inbau, J. E. Reid, and J. P. Buckley). Williams and Wilkins: Baltimore, pp. 327–347.

Moston, S., Stephenson, G. M., and Williamson, T. M. (1992). The effects of case characteristics on suspect behavior during police questioning. *Br. J. Criminol.* 32-23-39.

Zulawski, D. and Wicklander, D. (1993). *Practical Aspects of Interview and Interrogation.* CRC Press: Boca Raton.

Gudjonsson, G. H. and Petursson, H. (1991a). Custodial interrogations: why do suspects confess and how does it relate to their crime, attitude and personality? *Pers. Individ. Diff.*, 12, 295–306.

 Article Review Form at end of book.

What criterion is used by prosecutors to charge an individual with sexual assault?

The Genuine Victim and Prosecutors' Charging Decisions in Sexual Assault Cases

Jeffrey W. Spears

University of Nebraska at Omaha

Cassia C. Spohn

University of Nebraska at Omaha

Introduction

Someone walked over and asked what we were talking about. About rape, I replied; no, actually about cases that aren't really rape. The D.A. looked puzzled. That was rape, he said. Technically. She was forced to have sex without consent. It just wasn't a case you prosecute.

—Susan Estrich, *Real Rape*

Social scientists and legal scholars suggest that the factors influencing criminal justice decision making in sexual assault cases differ somewhat from the factors affecting decision making in other types of cases. More to the point, they suggest that case outcomes are affected by stereotypes about rape and rape victims, and that only "real rapes" with "genuine victims" will be taken seriously. Estrich (1987, p. 28), for example, suggests that criminal justice officials differentiate between the "aggravated, jump-from-the-bushes stranger rapes and the simple cases of unarmed rape by friends, neighbors, and acquaintances." LaFree (1989) asserts that nontraditional women, or women who engage in some type of "risk-taking" behavior, are less likely to be viewed as genuine victims who are deserving of protection under the law.

Studies of sexual assault case processing decisions provide support for these assertions. A number of researchers have analyzed the extent to which sexual assault case outcomes are influenced by legally irrelevant assessments of the victim's socio-economic status, character, and relationship with the defendant. Studies have demonstrated that sexual assault case outcomes are affected by the victim's age, occupation, and education (McCahill et al., 1979), by "risk-taking" behavior such as hitch-hiking, drinking, or using drugs (Bohmer, 1974; Kalven & Zeisel, 1966; LaFree, 1981; McCahill et al., 1979; Nelson & Amir, 1975), and by the reputation of the victim (Feild & Bienen, 1980; Feldman-Summers & Lindner, 1976; Holmstrom & Burgess, 1978; Kalven & Zeisel, 1966; McCahill et al., 1979; Reskin & Visher, 1986).

Research also has demonstrated that the relationship between the victim and the accused has a significant effect on decision making in sexual assault cases. These studies demonstrate that reports of rapes by strangers are investigated more thoroughly than reports of rapes involving someone the victim knows (McCahill et al., 1979). Stranger rapes also are less likely to be unfounded by the police (Kerstetter, 1990) or rejected by the prosecutor (Battelle Memorial Institute, 1977; Loh, 1980; Sebba & Cahan, 1973; Weniger, 1978; Williams, 1978). A prior relationship similarly affects the decision to dismiss the charges rather than prosecute fully (Vera Institute of Justice, 1981), the likelihood that the defendant will be convicted (Battelle Memorial Institute, 1977), and the odds of incarceration (McCahill et al., 1979).

We build on this body of research in this paper. We focus on the prosecutors' initial decision to file charges or not. Using a sample of arrests for sexual assault made by the Detroit Police Department in 1989, we test the hypothesis that charging decisions are affected by prosecutors' stereotypes concerning real rapes and genuine victims.

The Genuine Victim and Prosecutors' Charging Decisions in Sexual Assault Cases. J. W. Spears and C. C. Spohn. *American Journal of Criminal Justice*, 20(2), 1996, 183–205. Reprinted with permission.

Victim Characteristics and Sexual Assault Case Outcomes

As noted above, there is a substantial body of research examining case processing decisions in sexual assault cases. Five recent studies have attempted to untangle the effects of legal and extralegal factors in sexual assault cases. LaFree (1989) examined decisions made by police, prosecutors, judges, and jurors. He found that the strongest predictors of these decisions were legal factors such as the ability of the victim to identify the suspect, the offense type, and use of a weapon. Several extralegal variables, however, were also important. Evidence of victim misconduct, the victim's age, the promptness of the victim's report, and the racial composition of the offender-victim dyad influenced decision making. He concluded (p. 241) that while decisions in rape cases were affected by the "typifications of rape held by processing agents," they also were "influenced strongly by considerations that most observers would interpret as justified."

Another study focused on jury decision making. Reskin and Visher (1986) interviewed jurors from sexual assault trials in Indianapolis. They found that jurors' verdicts were affected by their personal evaluation of the victim's moral character and by their beliefs that the victim exercised poor judgement at the time of the assault. Reskin and Visher also found, however, that all five of the extralegal variables influenced jurors' verdicts in cases with weak evidence, but only one influenced the verdicts in cases with strong evidence. They concluded that their results provided support for Kalven and Zeisel's (1966) "liberation hypothesis"—that is, that jury nullification is most likely to occur when evidence is weak.

Spohn and Horney (1993) examined the effect of victim characteristics on the outcome of sexual assault cases in Detroit before and after rape law reforms were enacted. They found little support for their hypothesis that "the rape reform laws have resulted in less suspicion of the claims of rape victims and that this has been translated into less re- liance on legally irrelevant assessments of victim characteristics" (1993, p. 385). Most of the extralegal victim characteristics had little effect on case outcomes in either the pre-reform or the post-reform period. The authors speculated that these results reflected the fact that the attitudes of criminal justice officials in Detroit had begun to change prior to the enactment of law reforms.

A second study by Horney and Spohn (1994) focused on the effect of victim characteristics on case outcomes in aggravated and simple rapes. The authors used data on a sample of sexual assault complaints received by the Detroit Police Department in 1989 to test their hypothesis that the effect of victim characteristics would be greater in simple than in aggravated rapes. They reasoned that "because the essential features of aggravated rape cases—an attack by a stranger, multiple assailants, the use of a weapon or injury to the victim—meet the requirements of 'real rape,' there is no reason for distrust of the victim. . . ." (1994, p. 3).

Horney and Spohn's (1994) hypothesis was not confirmed; victim characteristics did not have a greater impact on case outcomes in simple than in aggravated cases. The only exception was that a prompt report to the police increased the odds of prosecution in simple rape cases but had no effect on prosecution in aggravated cases. The authors concluded that their findings indicated that criminal justice officials had adopted "more enlightened" attitudes toward rape cases than in the past. As they noted, the similarities in case outcomes suggested that criminal justice officials no longer believed that an assault has to be a " 'jump from the bushes' type in order to be a 'real rape' " (1994, p. 17).

A final study (Spohn, 1994) compared case processing decisions in sexual assault cases with child and adult victims. Legal scholars and social scientists have suggested that because sexual assault cases involving children are particularly likely to raise questions concerning victim credibility, they are more likely to be dismissed and are less likely to result in conviction or incarceration of the offender. Spohn (1994) found only limited support for this assertion. Her comparison of outcomes for sexual assault cases with child and adult victims revealed that there were no differences in the dismissal or conviction rates for the two types of cases. There were, on the other hand, large and statistically significant differences in the incarceration rate and the mean sentence. The sentences imposed on offenders convicted of assaulting children were considerably more lenient than the sentences imposed on offenders convicted of assaulting adults.

Further analysis, however, revealed that these differences in sentence severity could be attributed to factors other than the age of the victim. Cases with child victims were less likely than cases with adult victims to be aggravated sexual assaults—they were less likely to involve an offender who was a stranger to the victim, who held a knife to the victim's throat or a gun to head, or who physically injured the victim while forcing her to engage in sexual intercourse. When these differences were taken into account, offenders convicted of assaulting children faced a higher risk of incarceration than did offenders convicted of assaulting adults.

These recent studies provide mixed evidence concerning the effect of legal and extralegal characteristics on the processing of sexual assault cases. They indicate that while legal factors—particularly the strength of evidence in the case—play an important role in case processing decisions, extralegal factors—particularly the relationship between the victim and the offender and the age of the victim—also influence these decisions. These studies also demonstrate that the effect of stereotypes concerning real rapes and genuine victims may not be as pronounced as previous research has suggested. Considered together, the results of these studies suggest that additional research designed to untangle the effect of evidence factors and victim characteristics on sexual assault case processing decisions is needed.

It also seems clear that there is a need for additional research focusing explicitly on the prosecutor's initial decision to file charges. We noted earlier that this critical and highly discretionary decision has not been studied extensively. Most previous research operationalized charging as the decision to prosecute fully; this research did not differentiate between the initial charging decision and the subsequent decision to dismiss filed charges. These studies seemed to assume that the variables that affect dismissals also affect rejections. This is problematic, given that one study (Spohn et al., 1987) found that defendant race had an effect on the decision to reject charges at the initial screening, but had no effect on the subsequent decision to dismiss the charges. The authors suggested that this reflected the fact that dismissals were more visible and thus were more subject to scrutiny. They concluded that "previous studies which found no discrimination at the dismissal stage may have overlooked discrimination at the earlier screening" (Spohn et al., 1987, p. 187). . . .

Findings
Sexual Assault Cases with Child and Adult Victims

An underlying assumption of this study is that cases with child victims are qualitatively different from cases with adolescent/adult victims. The data presented in Table 1* indicate that this assumption is warranted. Cases involving children were much less likely than cases involving adults to result in the filing of charges; only 49.2% of the suspects arrested for assaulting children were charged, compared to 77.8% of those arrested for assaulting adults.

There are other important differences between the two types of cases. Cases with child victims were much less likely than cases with adult victims to involve a victim and a suspect who were strangers. Cases with child victims also were significantly less likely to involve suspects who threatened or physically restrained their victims, suspects who used weapons, or suspects who injured their victims. These differences suggest that cases involving children are much less likely to be aggravated sexual assaults (Estrich, 1987; Kalven & Zeisel, 1966).

Victims in cases involving children also differed in important ways from victims in cases involving

*Not included in this publication.

adults. None of the cases with victims under age 13 involved questions concerning the victim's moral character, and only six of these cases involved allegations of risk-taking behavior. Neither of these findings is surprising; we would not expect children under age 13 to have a history of drug/alcohol abuse, a prior criminal record, or a history of working as a prostitute or go-go dancer; similarly, we would not expect young children to be walking alone late at night, in a bar alone, or hitch-hiking. Child victims were also significantly less likely to have screamed, physically resisted, or reported the crime within one hour. Again, these results are not surprising. Sexual assaults of children are more likely to involve verbal, as opposed to physical, coercion; they also are often not reported immediately.

Considered together, these differences suggest that the factors affecting prosecutors' decisions to file charges in cases involving children may differ significantly from those influencing their decisions in cases involving adults. It thus seems appropriate to analyze the two types of cases separately.

Genuine Victims, Evidence Factors and Charging Decisions

The first hypothesis tested in this study focuses on the effect of victim characteristics on charging decisions. As explained above, we combined six victim characteristics to create a genuine victim scale. We hypothesized that the more closely the sexual assault victim conforms to the image of a genuine victim, the more likely it is that the prosecutor will decide to file charges against the suspect.

If the victim is at least 13 years old, the likelihood of charging increases as the number of characteristics associated with the genuine victim increases. Prosecutors filed charges in only 57% of the cases with a score of 1 on the scale, compared to 70% of the cases with a score of 2, 85% of the cases with a score of 3 or 4, and 100% of the cases with a score of 5. Charging decisions in cases involving children, on the other hand, did not vary along the genuine victim scale.

The findings discussed above, while suggestive, do not prove that prosecutors take victim characteristics into account in deciding whether to charge or not. The differences uncovered thus far might disappear once controls for case characteristics and suspect characteristics are taken into account. More to the point, these differences might disappear once controls for the four evidence factors are added to the model. In line with previous research demonstrating that strength of evidence is an important predictor of prosecutors' charging decisions, we hypothesized that the four evidence factors included in this study would affect charging decisions in sexual assault cases.

The data suggest that victim characteristics, but not evidence factors, affect prosecutors' charging decisions. In fact, the only significant predictors of charging in these types of cases are the age of the victim and the genuine victim scale. Prosecutors in Detroit are much less likely to file charges if the victim is under age 13. They are more likely to file charges if the victim conforms more closely to the image of the genuine victim.

The results of our analyses of cases involving adult and child victims demonstrate that victim characteristics affect charging decisions only in cases in which the victim is at least 13 years old. In fact, in these cases the genuine victim scale is the only significant predictor of prosecutors' charging decisions. In cases involving children, on the other hand, the likelihood of charging is enhanced if there was a witness to the incident and if the suspect had a prior felony conviction; the genuine victim scale is not a predictor of charging in these cases.

The results discussed thus far indicate that prosecutors' charging decisions are affected by stereotypes concerning genuine victims, at least in cases with adolescent or adult victims. These results, however, do not indicate which of the six individual victim characteristics affect the decision to charge or not. To determine this, we re-ran the analysis on cases with adult victims, substituting the six victim characteristics for the genuine victim scale. We found that prosecutors were less likely to file charges if there were questions about the victim's moral character or concerns about her behavior at the time of the incident; they were more likely to charge if the victim reported the crime to the police within one hour. The relationship between the victim and the offender, whether the victim screamed, and whether the victim physically resisted the attack, on the other hand, did not influence the decision to charge or not.

We noted earlier that our measures of the victim's moral character and risk-taking behavior incorporate several individual items. MORALS, for example, was coded 1 if any of six different types of information about the victim's moral character were included in the police file; RISK was coded 1 if the police file contained information about any of eight separate types of "risky" behavior.

To obtain a clearer understanding of the victim characteristics that prosecutors consider in making charging decisions, we examined the frequency distributions for each of the individual items comprising the MORALS and RISK variables. We also compared the charging rate for cases with and without each of these types of information. Because so few of the cases with child victims involved questions about the victim's moral character or allegations of risk-taking behavior, we only examined cases with adolescent or adult victims.

There were 26 cases with evidence questioning the victim's moral character. Most of these involved a pattern of alcohol or drug abuse (N=9) or evidence that the victim had a prior criminal record (N=8). In addition, there were three cases involving victims who allegedly were prostitutes; in each of these three cases the prosecutor declined to file charges.

Eighty-three of the cases with adult victims involved an allegation that the victim engaged in some type of risk-taking behavior at the time of the incident. Most of these cases involved a victim who willingly accompanied the suspect to his home (N=32), used alcohol or drugs at the time of the assault (N=23), or was walking alone late at night (N=21). Charging was significantly less likely if the victim voluntarily went to the suspect's home or apartment; prosecutors also were less willing to file charges if the victim was drinking or using drugs at the time of the assault[1]. . . .

This hypothesis was confirmed. The genuine victim scale did not influence charging decisions in cases with child victims but was the only significant predictor of charging in cases involving adolescent or adult victims. Further analysis of the cases with adult victims revealed that the odds of charging were reduced if there were questions about the victim's moral character or allegations that the victim had engaged in risk-taking behavior at the time of the incident; the likelihood of charging was increased if the victim made a prompt report to the police.

We also hypothesized that evidence factors would influence prosecutors' charging decisions in sexual assault cases. We found very limited support for this hypothesis. None of the four evidence factors had an effect on the prosecutor's decision to charge, either in the analysis using all of the cases or in the analysis using only adults. Among cases involving children, only one of the evidence factors—whether there was a witness to the assault—was related to charging.

Several of these findings merit elaboration. First, our finding that the four individual evidence factors did not influence charging is surprising. A number of scholars (Albonetti, 1987; Jacoby et al., 1982; Miller, 1969; Nagel & Hagan, 1983) have suggested that strength of evidence is one of the major predictors of convictability, and thus of prosecutorial decision making. Albonetti (1987, p. 311), for example, argues that prosecutors attempt to avoid uncertainty and that "uncertainty is significantly reduced with the introduction of certain legally relevant evidence." Nagel and Hagan (1983) similarly assert that strength of evidence probably accounts for most of the variance in charging decisions.

The results of this study call these general assertions into question and challenge Estrich's (1987, p. 21) more specific contention that because police and prosecutors are initially more skeptical of rape victims, corroborative evidence "is therefore that much more important to begin with." At least in sexual assault cases involving adults, Detroit prosecutors are not routinely deterred from filing charges by a lack of witnesses or by the fact that there is not a recovered weapon or other physical evidence to corroborate the victim's testimony.

Detroit prosecutors are, on the other hand, deterred from filing charges in cases in which the victim's background or behavior conflicts with the image of a genuine victim. In deciding whether to proceed in cases with adult victims, prosecutors consider the victim's moral character, the victim's behavior at the time of the incident, and the promptness of the victim's report to the police.

A major objective of this study was to test the validity of assertions that only real rapes with genuine victims are taken seriously. Estrich (1987) maintains that criminal justice decision makers differentiate between cases involving strangers and cases involving acquaintances; she also suggests that they distinguish between cases in which the victim verbally and/or physically resisted and cases in which she did not. Estrich (1987, p. 5) further asserts that these distinctions are even more obvious "where there was 'contributory behavior' on the part of the woman—where she was hitchhiking, or dating the man, or met him at a party. . . ."

Our findings suggest that criminal justice decision makers, including prosecutors, believe that the genuine victim of a sexual assault is a woman whose background and behavior conform to traditional gender-role expectations. The more closely the victim conforms to this stereotypical image, the more likely it is she will be viewed as a genuine victim, her assault as a real rape. . . .

Prosecutors do not take the relationship between the victim and the suspect into account in deciding whether to file charges or not. Being raped by a stranger, in other words, is not a key component of Detroit prosecutors' definition of a genuine victim. A woman raped by an acquaintance will be viewed as a genuine victim if her background and behavior at the time of the incident corresponds to traditional gender-role expectations and if she made a prompt report to the police. . . .

The results of this study suggest that Detroit prosecutors believe that a prompt report is, the law notwithstanding, an important element of a sexual assault case. It suggests that prosecutors attempt to avoid uncertainty by screening out cases where the victim's allegations will be questioned because she waited a week, a month, or longer to report the crime to the police. This may not be an unreasonable strategy. If the case goes to trial, the defense attorney will use the lack of a prompt report to impeach the victim's credibility and to raise doubts in the minds of the jurors.

Our finding that the age of the victim influenced the decision to charge or not also deserves comment. It is not surprising that prosecutors were more reluctant to file charges when the victim was younger than 13. Previous research (Chapman, 1987; MacMurray, 1989; Williams & Farrell, 1990) has demonstrated that sexual assaults involving children are difficult to prosecute. As noted above, this reflects the fact that children may be unable to articulate what happened to them. It also reflects the fact that children who allege that they have been sexually assaulted are regarded as more impressionable and thus as less credible than older victims. These factors, coupled with concerns about the psychological impact of testifying at trial, apparently affect prosecutors' assessments of the probability of conviction and produce a higher rejection rate for cases with child victims.

In sum, our findings concerning the effect of victim characteristics suggest that prosecutors attempt to avoid uncertainty by screening out sexual assault cases unlikely to result in a conviction because of questions about the victim's character, the victim's behavior, and the victim's credibility. Prosecutors may assume that jurors will not regard a woman who was drinking or using drugs at the time of the incident, a woman who has numerous sexual partners, or a woman who willingly accompanied the suspect to his home or apartment as a credible or genuine victim. They may assume that jurors will question the credibility of children who claim they were raped. Again, these may not be unreasonable or unwarranted assumptions. As Reskin and Visher's (1986) study demonstrated, jurors' verdicts in sexual assault cases are af-

fected by their evaluations of the victim's moral character and by their beliefs that the victim exercised poor judgement.

Taken together, our findings imply that the warrant section of the Wayne County Prosecutor's Office utilizes a trial sufficiency policy (Jacoby, 1980) in screening sexual assault cases. Charging decisions appear to be motivated by the prosecutor's assessment of convictability at trial. This may be due, in part, to the fact that the Wayne County Prosecutor's Office has an explicit policy concerning plea bargaining in sexual assault cases (Spohn & Horney, 1992). Plea bargains must be approved by the complainant. Moreover, first degree criminal sexual conduct can only be reduced to third degree criminal sexual conduct, and third degree cannot be reduced to a less serious charge. This policy clearly limits prosecutors' options and forces them to consider the likelihood of conviction at trial.

The findings of this study add to a growing body of literature suggesting that prosecutors' charging decisions are motivated by attempts to avoid uncertainty and by predictions of convictability. These findings also confirm Albonetti's (1987, p. 311) conclusion that there are "extralegal sources of uncertainty."

This study found that prosecutors, in Detroit, consider extralegal victim characteristics in making their initial screening decisions in sexual assault cases. Prosecutorial decision making in these types of cases is influenced by stereotypes of rape and rape victims—only real rapes with genuine victims will be taken seriously. This is a cause for concern. As LaFree (1989, p. 239) noted, "if women who violate traditional gender roles and are raped are unable to obtain justice through the legal system, then the law is serving as an institutional arrangement that reinforces women's gender-role conformity."

Endnote

1. Prosecutors filed charges in 62% of the cases in which the victim willingly went to the suspect's place of residence; they filed charges in 81% of the cases where the victim did not accompany

the suspect to his home or apartment. Charges were filed in 61% of the cases in which the victim was drinking or using drugs; they were filed in 79% of the cases in which the victim was not drinking or using drugs.

References

Albonetti, C. (1987). Prosecutorial discretion: The effects of uncertainty. *Law and Society Review, 21*, 291–313.

Battelle Memorial Institute Law and Justice Study Center. (1977). *Forcible rape: A national survey of the response by prosecutors.* Washington, DC: Author.

Bohmer, C. (1974). Judicial attitudes toward rape victims. *Judicature, 57*, 303–307.

Chapman, J. (1987). *Child sexual abuse. An analysis of case processing.* Washington, DC: American Bar Association.

Estrich, S. (1987). *Real rape.* Cambridge, MA: Harvard University.

Feild, H., & Bienen, L. (1980). *Jurors and rape. A study in psychology and law.* Lexington, MA: Lexington Books.

Feldman-Summers, S., & Lindner, K. (1976). Perceptions of victims and defendants in criminal assault cases. *Criminal Justice and Behavior, 3*, 135–150.

Holmstrom, L., & Burgess, A. (1978). *The victim of rape. Institutional reactions.* New York: Wiley-Interscience.

Horney, J., & Spohn, C. (1994, March). *The processing of simple versus aggravated rape cases.* Paper presented at the meeting of the Academy of Criminal Justice Sciences, Chicago, IL.

Jacoby, J. (1980). *The American prosecutor. A search for identity.* Toronto: D.C. Heath.

Jacoby, J., Mellon, L., Ratledge, E., & Turner, S. (1982). *Prosecutorial decision making. A national study.* Washington, DC: U.S. Department of Justice.

Kalven, H., & Zeisel, H. (1966). *The American jury.* Boston: Little, Brown.

Kerstetter, W. (1990). Gateway to justice: Police and prosecutorial response to sexual assaults against women. *Criminology, 81*, 267–313.

LaFree, G. (1981). Official reactions to social problems: Police decisions in sexual assault cases. *Social Problems, 28*, 582–594.

LaFree, G. (1989). *Rape and criminal justice. The social construction of sexual assault.* Belmont, CA: Wadsworth.

Loh, W. (1980). The impact of common law and reform rape statues on prosecution: An empirical study. *Washington Law Review, 55*, 543–625.

MacMurray, B. (1989). Criminal determination for child sexual abuse: Prosecutor case-screening judgements. *Journal of Interpersonal Violence, 4*, 233–244.

McCahill, T., Meyer, L., & Fischman, A. (1979). *The aftermath of rape.* Lexington, MA: Lexington.

Miller, F. (1969). *Prosecution: The decision to charge a suspect with a crime.* Boston: Little, Brown.

Nagel, H., & Hagan, J. (1983). Gender and crime: Offense patterns and criminal court sanctions. In M. Tonry & N. Morris (Eds.), *Crime and justice: An annual review of research* (Vol. 4). Chicago: University of Chicago.

Nelson, S., & Amir, M. (1975). The hitchhike victim of rape: A research report. In I. Dropkin & E. Viano (Eds.), *Victimology: A New Focus*. Lexington, MA: Lexington.

Reskin, B., & Visher, C. (1986). The impacts of evidence and extralegal factors in jurors' decisions. *Law and Society Review, 20,* 423–438.

Sebba, L., & Cahan, S. (1973). Sex offenses: The genuine and the doubted victim. In I. Dropkin & E. Viano (Eds.), *Victimology: A New Focus*. Lexington, MA: Lexington.

Spohn, C. (1994). A comparison of sexual assault cases with child and adult victims. *Journal of Child Sexual Abuse, 3,* 59–79.

Spohn, C., Gruhl, J., & Welch, S. (1987). The impact of the ethnicity and gender of defendants on the decision to reject or dismiss felony charges. *Criminology, 25,* 175–191.

Spohn, C., & Horney, J. (1992). *Rape law reform: A grassroots revolution and its impact*. New York: Plenum.

Spohn, C., & Horney, J. (1993). Rape law reform and the effect of victim characteristics on case processing. *Journal of Quantitative Criminology, 9,* 383–409.

Vera Institute of Justice. (1981). *Felony arrests: Their prosecution and disposition in New York City's courts*. New York: Longman.

Weninger, R. (1978). Factors affecting the prosecution of rape: A case study of Travis County, Texas. *Virginia Law Review, 64,* 357–397.

Williams, K. (1978). *The role of the victim in the prosecution of violent offenses*. Washington, DC: Institute for Law and Social Research.

Williams, L., & Farrell, R. (1990). Legal response to child sexual abuse in day care. *Criminal Justice and Behavior, 17,* 284–302.

 Article Review Form at end of book.

In what way is a courtroom trial searching for truth? What truth?

From Police Information to Miscarriages of Justice

Peter J. van Koppen

Evaluation of Evidence by Fact Finders

Bennett and Feldman (1981) begin their book *Reconstructing Reality in the Courtroom* by stating that "the criminal trial is organized around story telling". The idea is that the work of the judge consists of determining the plausibility of the stories presented by the prosecution and the defence. Narrative theories, like the one proposed by Bennett and Feldman, have a long history in cognitive psychology (cf. Rumelhart, 1975). Applied to the decision making in criminal cases, these theories hold that evidence derives its meaning from a story context. Detached from a story, facts do not prove anything. A court cannot decide on mere facts, only on a story. Two aspects of a story may determine its believability: the "goodness" of the story in itself (to be defined later), and the degree to which it is supported by facts, the evidence. . . .

Good and Bad Stories

Scientists in many disciplines, such as literature, anthropology, and artificial intelligence, have tried to establish what makes a story believable. Rumelhart (1975), Robinson (1981), and Van Dijk (1980) all designed story grammars: sets of rules to which a well-formed story must

obey. The story grammar proposed by Bennett and Feldman (1981) was designed specifically for judicial contexts (cf. Jackson, 1988). The manner in which they obtained their grammar is quite interesting. They asked 58 students to tell a story; half of them were asked to tell a true story, the other half to invent a story. Every time a story had been told, the others were asked to guess whether it was true or invented. The guesses were not better than chance. But stories that were accepted as true shared some properties that the rejected stories were lacking. These properties were:

- A readily identifiable central action.

- A context (setting) that provides an easy and natural explanation of why the actors behaved in the way they did.

In a good story all elements are connected to the central action; nothing sticks out on its own. The context provides a full and compelling account of why the central action should have developed in this particular manner. If the context does not achieve that effect, then the story is said to contain ambiguities.

The analysis of what makes stories plausible was extended by Nancy Pennington and Reid Hastie in a series of subsequent publications (1986; 1988; 1991). Without going into too much detail, it can be said that, according to them, in good

stories all actions are explained by factors of three kinds: physical conditions, psychological conditions and goals. Pennington and Hastie's story grammar, and their thesis about the importance of stories, was supported by their research. In one study Pennington and Hastie (1986) showed that the order in which evidence is presented has a major influence on the judgement. Both the prosecution and the defence could present their evidence in a random order, or in story order. The combination of these two variables results in four groups. The dependent variable was the answer to the question whether the subjects thought that the defendant was guilty of first-degree murder. The results are presented in Table 1.

The data indicate that the party who presented the evidence in story order was believed more readily, even though the evidence itself was exactly the same in both conditions. The effect can be as large as changing a 31 per cent chance of conviction into a 78 per cent chance. Clever presentation of the story is half of the work. What is the other half?

Anchoring

Stories told in a criminal court must not only be good, we want them to be true. The prosecutor's story may be good, but it is not necessarily true. The truth of a story is established by means of evidence. In and of itself, however, evidence does not prove

First published in *Issues in Criminological and Legal Psychology: Rights and Risks: The Application of Forensic Psychology*, No. 21.

Table I	Effect of Presentation in Random Order or Story Order on Percentage of Convictions		
		Defence	
Prosecution	**Random Order**		**Story Order**
Random order	63%		31%
Story order	78%		59%

anything at all. Any piece of evidence only proves something if we are willing to believe in a general rule which we hold to be true most of the time. For instance, the testimony by two eyewitnesses will only prove something, i.e. support the story, if it is assumed that eyewitnesses do not lie or make mistakes. The rules that make evidence prove something should rather be phrased like: witnesses speak the truth *most of the time*, and pathologists *almost* never make mistakes. But this possibility of exceptions to rules means that on occasion we must show that a possible exception does not apply.

In a similar manner every piece of evidence needs further support, until it can be safely *anchored* in a general rule that cannot be sensibly contested because all parties acknowledge it to be true in the given case. These general rules are usually common-sense facts of life. We often accept an argument because we unwittingly believe the underlying rule which gives it an anchor, even though an explicit formulation of the rule would cause us to protest or even reject it. . . .

Where the Information Comes From

Preparing evidence to be submitted at trial is the task of police and prosecution. Not all information gathered during police investigation is suitable to become evidence at trial. The prime purpose of the police investigation is to detect crimes and to find those who committed them. Although some of the information gathered by the police during the investigation may eventually wind up as evidence at trial, the quality of information offered in evidence is usually higher than the quality of information used in the investigation.

Moreover, information valuable during the investigation may be of a different nature from that which can be submitted in evidence. For instance, an anonymous tip may provide the police with a long-hoped-for breakthrough, but as evidence this tip is at best very weak, if at all admissible. . . .

Investigation Versus Proof

When a criminal offence comes to the notice of the police, their first objective is to find a suspect. In most cases, however, it is not the police, but members of the public who report that a crime has been committed and who point out a suspect to the police (Black, 1970; Bottomley and Coleman, 1976; Erickson, 1981; Greenwood et al., 1977; Steer, 1980; Sellin and Wolfgang, 1964). The gathering of information following such notifications is done by professional investigators, who must abide by the rules governing these investigations.

The decision that turns an ordinary citizen into a suspect of a criminal offence is taken on the basis of a narrative, in the same manner as at a later stage the decision to convict is to a large extent taken on the basis of a narrative. Many of the problems in court decision-making also apply to decisions of the police. There are, however, important differences. At an early stage of their investigation the police can probably only work from an incomplete narrative, mostly based on what was found at the scene of the crime. Some elements of the narrative are available from the start, found by accident, by reports from citizens, through combining and verifying facts, or mere guesswork. Other parts of the narrative only emerge during the investigation. From this incomplete story the investigators work their way up; ambigui-

ties or contradictions are further investigated or put aside as irrelevant. Gradually a coherent and complete story emerges.

Proving guilt, however, is something quite different. It is not done by investigators and it is not done prior to the trial. Proof of guilt is offered at trial by the prosecutor and starts with a ready-made narrative, aimed at the conviction of the defendant. . . .

The difference between the quality of investigative information and evidence offered at trial is sometimes misunderstood. I will argue below that miscarriages of justice occur when information that is perfectly sound for investigative purposes but falls short as evidence, is used to prove the guilt of the defendant. It should be noted that under each system of criminal evidence miscarriages of justice will occur, because all pieces of evidence bear a risk, although sometimes quite small, of being wrong. The investigative problems discussed below merely raise the risk of accepting unsound evidence and thus raise the risk of miscarriages of justice.

Offence-Driven and Suspect-Driven Search

The distinction between offence-driven and suspect-driven searches is related to the starting point of the investigation. In an offence-driven search the starting point is the crime and the facts related to the crime. The identity of the culprit, then, is inferred from these facts. In a suspect-driven search someone becomes a suspect for no clear reason, or at least no reason that is explained by the known facts of the crime. Only then is an attempt made at finding evidence which links this particular suspect to the crime. Such a search is limited right from the start. An example of the latter is showing photographs of known criminals to a witness; an example of the former is finding a fingerprint from the scene of the crime among the police-database.

The relevance of the distinction between offence-driven and suspect-driven investigations lies in the diagnostic value of the resulting evidence. In an offence-driven search the narrative is the product of an in-ferential process, based on information. In suspect-driven search the narrative is the starting point, and the information its product. In offence-driven search one collects so much information that the search logically excludes all possible alternative suspects. In suspect-driven search one needs only enough information to make the suspect look bad. It can even be argued that one may take any citizen, investigate him thoroughly, and connect him to one of the many unsolved crimes in the police files. This may be done by way of recognition tests, an accusation by another suspect, attributing a motive, identifying some piece of intimate knowledge, forensic analysis of traces, a report by a psychiatrist, the absence of an alibi, or even a confession obtained under prolonged interrogation.

In many of the cases discussed by Wagenaar et al. (1993) the suspects became suspects because of their criminal records. Gross (1987) reported that in 60 percent of 92 miscarriages of justice in which a suspect was incorrectly identified by eyewitnesses, the first suspicion was based on outer appearance, while nothing else related the suspect to the crime. This 60 percent is an extremely high figure, compared to Steer's (1980, Table 4:2, p. 97) finding that in of all crimes 21 per cent of the suspects are connected to crimes through suspect-driven searches. Suspect-driven searches appear to promote unsafe convictions. . . .

Verification and Falsification

Logically, hypotheses are tested by two complementary processes: verification and falsification. An attempt at verification means looking for facts that are predicted by the hypothesis; falsification means looking for facts that are excluded by the hypothesis. To test a hypothesis both processes are necessary. Falsification is not some sort of luxury, in which one only engages when there is an excess of means. As long as alternative hypotheses are not excluded, they may be more likely than the verified hypothesis (comp. Wason and Johnson-Laird, 1972). . . .

In its simplest form falsification of a criminal charge means that alternative stories of a denying suspect are checked. If the suspect's narrative appears to be false, this contributes to the proof of the charge brought against the suspect. . . .

The Trawling Method

Particularly deceptive results may be obtained by means of what is called the "trawling method". This method falls into the class of suspect-driven search methods. The term is used for police investigations which start from a generalized and little specified suspicion against a person or, more often, a group of people, in which a large police force is engaged, investigating every conceivable detail of his or its behaviour until some sort of mischief is discovered. It is like trawling a very wide net in a place where there may not be many fish, but if the net is wide enough one always may be expected to catch some fish. A good example of the method is the case against Alderman Schuddeboom.

Schuddeboom had been alderman in the municipality of Brunssum for many years. At every municipal election (every four years) politicians in this part of the country are accused by the media of swindling with proxy votes. This local custom has attracted national attention, putting pressure on the local police to investigate the practice thoroughly. Why local politicians are interested in proxy votes is obvious. Schuddeboom obtained them mostly from people in a nearby mobile home camp and from foreign labourers, who in The Netherlands are allowed to vote in municipal elections. The procedure for voting by proxy is as follows: somebody wanting to authorize another to vote on his or her behalf must say so by filling in a form to be signed by both voter and proxy. Nobody is allowed to stand proxy for more than two voters. Thus politicians must not only find voters who are willing to yield their votes, but also a sufficient number of proxies who are willing to use their proxy in the "right" way. The forms to be filled out are distributed by the township. Each form must be certified. Nobody can obtain more

than four forms. At the time of the Schuddeboom case only 27 per cent of the thousand or so forms received by the township turned out to be certified. The other forms submitted were apparently obtained from other sources. Hence the mayor sent a letter to all voters whose names appeared on uncertified forms, enquiring whether they had indeed authorized someone else and if so, who their proxy was. In the end only 35 per cent of the forms offered were accepted as legally correct. Collecting proxy votes itself is not illegal, but giving promises in return is, as is forging such forms. The police started a criminal investigation against all persons who had handed in the rejected forms. Seven of them were suspected of fraud, but in the end a criminal charge was only brought against alderman Schuddeboom.

What did he do? Schuddeboom had obtained four signed forms from four voters, who yielded their votes to unspecified proxies. To use these forms he needed two proxies. His gardener agreed to sign himself as a proxy for two voters, and to ask his wife to sign for the two other voters. In reality, however, the gardener, Mr. Hol, forged his wife's signature. Alderman Schuddeboom was accused of having provoked the forgery and of having been present when it was done. He denied this. There was no evidence other than the two forged forms, yet he was convicted by the District Court (but acquitted on appeal). The forger, Mr. Hol, was never prosecuted, although he had admitted the forgery. Apparently Mr. Hol was considered unimportant. The investigation was directed against Schuddeboom because as an alderman he had refused the police an expensive piece of speed control equipment. After a thorough investigation of hundreds of forms, finally one was discovered with a forged signature. It had nothing to do with Schuddeboom, but flimsy evidence had to do. . . .

An Example: The Dutch CID

Traditional police activities started after a crime had been committed. In the fight against organized crime, police investigations often do not start with a crime, but start from a suspicion that some individual or some group of individuals may be involved in planning crimes as drug-trafficking (see Crombag et al., 1993). In these police investigations many of the problems discussed above come together. Such "proactive" investigations are suspect-driven, are based on verification and use a trawling method. . . .

Safe Evidence

I have discussed three dichotomies: investigation versus proof, offence-driven versus suspect-driven search, and verification versus falsification. The logically soundest method to proceed in both criminal investigation and the construction of proof is offence-driven search, combined with a balanced search for verifications as well as falsifications. In practice, however, this cannot be achieved.

The construction of proof during the trial will always be suspect-driven, because there is a defendant present right from the beginning. So the question to be answered by the court is not "Who did it?", but 'Did he do it?' In other words, the objective of the trial is not to uncover the truth, but to evaluate the believability of the indictment's narrative by testing the quality of the available evidence. If in criminal proceedings there is any room for a offence-driven search, it is only in the investigative, pretrial stage.

All parties involved in criminal proceedings, with the possible exception of the defence, have a strong preference for suspect-driven search

and verification, both in the investigative stage and during the construction of proof. As a consequence, investigation and construction of proof, although essentially different, may become indistinguishable, especially after the investigation did not involve discovery of a suspect, but the construction of sufficient proof against a known suspect. In these cases the investigators become judges, although they were never meant to be so. Judges are doomed to repeat what the investigators have already done, allowing innocent defendants little hope that the outcome of the trial will be anything else than a predictable confirmation of the indictment. Thus, miscarriages of justice are best prevented by the police.

References

Bennett, W. L., and M. S. Feldman. (1981). *Reconstructing Reality in the Courtroom*. London: Tavistock.

Black, D. J. (1970). The social organisation of arrest. *American Sociological Review*, 23, 1087–1111.

Bottomley, A. K., and C. A. Coleman. (1976). Criminal statistics: The police role in the discovery and detection of crime. *International Journal of Criminology and Penology*, 4, 33–58.

Crombag, H.F.M., P.J. van Koppen, and W.A. Wagenaar. (1993). "Wandelen in strafvorderlijk niemandsland," in A.W.M. van der Heijden (ed.), *Criminele Inlichtingen: De Rol van de Criminele Inlichtingendiensten bij de Aanpak van de Georganiseerde Misdaad*. Gravenhage: Vuga.

Erickson, R.V. (1981). *Making Crime: A Study of Detective Work*. Toronto, Canada: Butterworth.

Greenwood, P.W., J.M. Chaiken, and J. Petersilia. (1977). *The Criminal Investigation Process*. Lexington: Heath.

Gross, S.R. (1987). "Loss of innocence: Eyewitness identification and proof of guilt," *Journal of Legal Studies* 16, 395–453.

Jackson, B.S. (1988). *Law, Fact and Narrative Coherence*. Liverpool, England: Deborah Charles.

Pennington, N., and R. Hastie. (1986). "Evidence evaluation in complex decision making," *Journal of Personality and Social Psychology* 51, 242–258.

Pennington, N., and R. Hastie. (1988). "Explanation-based decision making: Effects of memory and structure on judgment," *Journal of Experimental Psychology: Learning, Memory, and Cognition*, 14, 521–533.

Pennington, N., and R. Hastie. (1991). "A theory of explanation-based decision-making," in G. Klein and J. Orasanu (eds.), *Decisionmaking in Complex Worlds*. Hillsdale, N.J.: Ablex.

Robinson, J.A. (1981). "Personal narratives reconsidered," *Journal of American Folklore*, 94, 58–85.

Rumelhart, D.E. (1975). "Notes on a schema for stories," in D.G. Bobrow and A. Collins (eds.), *Representation and Understanding: Studies in Cognitive Science*. New York: Academic.

Sellin, T., and W.E. Wolfgang. (1964). *The Measurement of Delinquency*. New York: Wiley.

Steer, D. (1980). *Uncovering Crime: The Police Role*. London: Her Majesty's Stationary Service (Research study no. 7, Royal Commission on Criminal Procedure).

van Dijk, T.A. (1980). *Macrostructures: An Interdisciplinary Study of Global Structures in Discourse, Interaction, and Cognition*. Hillsdale, N.J.: Erlbaum.

Wagenaar, W.A., P.J. van Koppen, and H.F.M. Crombag. (1993). *Anchored Narratives: The Psychology of Criminal Evidence*. New York: Harvester Wheatsheaf.

Wason, P.C., and P.N. Johnson-Laird. (1972). *Psychology of Reasoning: Structure and Content*. London: Batsford.

 Article Review Form at end of book.

What are some of the realities of battered women syndrome? In what ways might homicide laws be prejudicial?

Interviews with Women Convicted of Murder:

Battered Women Syndrome Revisited

Dennis J. Stevens

In America, there were approximately 2,000 women arrested for murder and non-negligent manslaughter in 1996 (Bureau of Justice Statistics (BJS), 1997). Government statistics reveal that 15% of all females in American prisons were convicted of murder or non-negligent manslaughter as compared to 12% of all male offenders. What lacks explanation is that many female murderers are first-time offenders (Snell, 1994; BJS, 1997).[1] Why would an individual with little or no criminal history commit an extraordinary act such as homicide? Perhaps one answer lies in the knowledge that each year more than 4 million American women are injured at home, 2 million women seek medical treatment for injuries inflicted by husbands, ex-husbands, or boyfriends, and many of those women take the life of their attacker in an effort to defend themselves and/or their children (Bean, 1992; Levy, 1995; National Coalition Against Domestic Violence (NCADV), 1994).

In general, women convicted of the crime of murder tend to share similar experiences. For example, the typical female ran away from home one to three times due to feelings of

insecurity about parental acceptance and love, was easily manipulated by her peers, witnessed spousal abuse as a child, and/or was the victim of domestic abuse as an adult (Biggers, 1979; Brett, 1992; Flethcer and Moon, 1993; Sargent et al., 1993). Roberts argues that the majority of women who kill intimates are more likely than other women to have experiences that include both a[n] illicit drug dependency and/or a drug addiction, attempted suicide by drug overdosing; and to have had access to the victim's gun (1996). Furthermore, circumstances associated with these women include brutal and repeated assaults, death threats, and failures in their attempts to escape being victimized through alcohol or drug abuse (Johnson, 1996; Roberts, 1996).

Lenore Walker identifies a cluster of behavioral and emotional features that are often shaped by women who have been physically and psychologically abused over a period of time by the dominant male figure in their lives. Feelings of low self-esteem, depression, and helplessness are among the important components that frequently accompany continual domestic violence. She coined the term battered woman syn-

drome (BWS) to describe this condition (1979).

For the purposes of this paper, Patricia Easteal's (1993) updated description of BWS will be utilized. Easteal suggests that BWS refers to a certain pattern of violence and to the psychological consequences experienced by the victim. Easteal considers BWS to be a sub-type of post traumatic stress syndrome, the culmination of three stages that can recur in the domestic violent situation. The first phase of tension-building can lead to the second stage of severe physical abuse. The third stage is a time period exemplified by the batterer's contrition, promises, and temporary cessation of violence. Then, too, a psychological condition develops with the victims acquiring a learned helplessness response to most situations. The battered woman lives in a state of terror, lives in isolation, and is constantly vigilant against the ever-present but erratic threat of violence, knowing that justice agencies are largely unsuccessful at controlling both the psychological and physical violence in her life (Bean, 1992; Easteal, 1993; Hirschel and Hutchison, 1991).[2] If justice agencies inadequately protect at-risk individuals such as a woman living a victimized existence, under what

Interviews with Women Convicted of Murder: Battered Women Syndrome Revisited, D. J. Stevens. Paper presented at the annual conference of the American Society of Criminology at San Diego, Calif., November 1997. Reprinted by permission of the author.

conditions is it reasonable for her to use excessive force to protect herself?[3] That is, females tend to kill male partners to pre-empt what they perceive to be inevitable further victimization (Websdale, 1998; p. 24).[4] This comment is consistent with earlier research suggesting that, due in part to the inadequacies of law enforcement to protect at-risk community members, homicide is seen as an appropriate response by those law abiding community members (Stevens, 1997a; 1997b).

Legally, murder is the felonious killing of one human being by another with malice aforethought (Black, 1979; Nettler, 1982; p. 3).[5] Manslaughter is the unlawful killing of another without malice, either expressed or implied (Black, 1979). The test for malice is whether, under the circumstances known to a defendant, a reasonable person would have known that her intentional act created a substantial risk of death to the victim. This test has long been the rule in Massachusetts and other states. As Chief Justice Oliver Wendell Holmes noted almost a century ago, It is possible to commit murder without any actual intent to kill or to do grievous bodily harm (*Commonwealth v. Chance*, 174 Mass. 245, 252 (1899). The only intent the prosecution needs to prove is the intent to perform the act, not any particular intent as to the act's consequences.

As for self-defense, there are, broadly speaking, three components of the defense: that the threat was imminent; that the responding amount of force equivalent, and that the defendant had met the obligation to retreat or try to escape from the attack (Easteal, 1993). The perception of the imminence and the severity of the assault as well as the individual's perception of how much force is requisite to counter it, must all be reasonable. Also, juries tend to be instructed that the burden of proving the defense of self defense is upon the defendant. She must establish such defense by a preponderance of the evidence (Find Law, 1997). But, it could be said that women who suffer from BWS assault their aggressors not when they are being attacked but when their aggressors are most vulnerable. So, one could ask, where is the threat of imminent danger? Does

increased marital conflict often take the form of increased male coercion, as Wilson and Daly (1992) argue? Those researchers further suggest that marital conflict further constrains the woman's options, encouraging more drastic forms of self-defense and escape.[6]

On the other hand, Mann (1988) suggests that BWS is not a legitimate defense since many women killers have committed violent crimes previous to killing their spouses, and that the majority of these killings were premeditated. Mann's data show that women who kill are not battered women acting in self-defense; they are the victors of domestic fights. Caplan (1991) adds that the BWS is unscientific and biased against males. Public acceptance of the battered woman defense may actually increase family violence by undermining personal responsibility. That is, if battered women kill their abuse[r]s, they are guilty of murder and should be incarcerated (Peele, 1991). Women murderers are said to be responding to domestic quarrels to resolve conflicts, assert power, or to protect themselves, and see their intimates as objects to dispose of rather than real persons with a right to life (Biggers, 1979). Lastly, some experts admit that women kill abusive partners, but are quick to point out that they also kill non-abusive partners, children, and other adults in their lives (Ogle et al., 1995).

Thus, one central question is asked in this paper: is BWS a successful and reasonable defense for taking of another's life? Mark Williams (1995) [says] that the best answer to this inquiry is, no. He argues that while the state usually allows the use of expert testimony regarding BWS, that that in itself is not a reasonable defense to murder. One example might be the case of *North Carolina v. Pamela Warlick* (1996), where the defendant was shown to suffer from BWS but was found guilty of first-degree murder and sentenced to life imprisonment. When the defendant asked the Supreme Court of North Carolina[7] to review the case, the court held that while the Court understood her to be a battered woman, the arguments the defendant advances as to why evidence that she suffered from the battered woman syndrome entitles her

to a charge on self-defense were answered in another case, "and we see no reason to change our position" (*North Carolina v. Warlick*, 1996). To understand these homicides, this research went to the experts-by-experience—convicted felons in high custody penitentiaries—to ask 28 of them about their experiences prior to their prison conviction. Research design is available through the author.

Conviction History and Victims of Female Killers

Fifty-seven percent (16) of the participants were first-time convicted offenders; that is, they have never been charged with any previous criminal offensive: 32% (9) have been convicted of a felon prior to homicide, and 11% (3) have been convicted of nonviolent crimes such as breaking and entering prior to a homicide conviction. Of the first-time offenders, 69% (11) killed spouses, 13% (2) killed parents, 6% (1) killed offspring, 6% (1) killed a sibling, and 6% (1) was convicted of murder during the commission of another felony. Of the 32% (9) who have been convicted of serious crimes prior to this murder conviction, 33% (3) killed spouses, 56% (5) killed friends, and 11% (1) killed a stranger.

Research Findings

A typology was developed based on the participants' descriptions to explain the findings independent of legal dispositions. More specifically, 50% (14) of the explanations about murder will be explained as delayed murder, 25% (7) will be explained as reactive murder, and 25% (7) will be explained as intentional murder.[8] Both delayed and reactive descriptions show that the respondents experienced a continuum of victimization, and that they were not in immediate danger when they were implicated in the murder. The chief distinction between delayed murder descriptions and reactive murder descriptions is that the delayed descriptions suggested, from the perspective of the respondents, that the women were left with no choice but to end the life of another, while the reactive descriptions seem to characterize choices or alternatives to the murder act. These brief descriptions will be clarified in the specific accounts that follow.

Delayed Murder

The descriptions from 50% (14) of the respondents represent what the researcher calls delayed murder. That is, the women convicted of the crime of murder reacted to repeated attacks by their aggressors, but they had not protected themselves at the time of those attacks. At the time they took the life of their aggressor, they were not in fact in imminent danger as defined by U.S. courts and therefore were not acting, according to the court's perspective, out of a need to defend themselves. Rather, the characteristics described by the respondents show that murder was their response towards an individual who interacted with them over time, fueled by abusive progressive interactions that produced a continuum of fear reinforcing their state of helplessness; as a last resort, the respondent attacked her abuser when he was most vulnerable. That is, delayed murder descriptions are characterized by victims who were abusive antagonists, and if they had abused others as they had the respondents, they would have been arrested and convicted long before they met with their death. In this study, 14 participants offered delayed murder explanations, of which 12 murdered their spouses, one murdered her father, and one murdered both her parents.

Delayed Spouse Murder

Eleven respondents without previous police records and one with a nonviolent arrest were convicted of the crime of murdering their spouses. Their descriptions fit what the researcher calls delayed murder explanations. That is, 10 of the respondents describe their own early childhood prior to the homicide, as largely a middle-class experience, free from personal abuse or marital discord. Nine of these respondents lived at home with their respective intimates and children at the time of murder. Two were divorced. All 14 murderers describe activities charac-

terizing full-time house-keeping activities including the upkeep of their children; they also describe extreme psychological and constant physical abuse towards the offenders and their children by their intimates.

Abuse by their spouses started early in the relationship, taking the form of verbal put-downs which accelerated to physically violent assaults, producing a state of fear for both the offenders and children. These fears progressed from the fear of losing their intimate, to a fear of losing their homes and everything they worked for, hence to the fear of losing their own life and the well-beings of their children. For example, Karen said that when she dated the man of her dreams, she thought it was cute when he originally made little cutting remarks about her family. "He said things about my daddy, but it wasn't worth losing Eddy over. Little did I know! I should of stopped it." Karen and Eddy met in high school and married. She was 20, he was 21. "He became a fire-men," she said, "and I was pregnant for a living."

Most of the participants' accounts, matched Karen's descriptions, including the responsibilities of homes, children, husbands, and in some cases jobs outside their homes. Then, too, as the job responsibilities of their spouses grew, lifestyles improved, the abuse accelerated.

It was almost as if he thought that the more money he brought home, the more he could hurt me. Why was I so dumb? I thought he would change. I thought as soon as he gets over those (job) pressures, he'd stop pushing me around. Looking back, it only got worse. I couldn't see it! But I didn't want to lose our home. Hell, I worked as hard as he did for it!

Lauren.

Furthermore, as abuse grew in frequency and degree, most of the participants also described isolation. For example:

When we were struggling to make ends meet, he just screamed at me. When he was promoted to manager, he smacked me when I wouldn't tell my every move during the day. Then he threw his dinner plate at me when I told him I wasn't to be his prisoner. After that I stayed home and made sure I was there by the phone or else. After a year or two that didn't satisfy him.

Lauren.

As the abuse accelerated the reuse of isolation contributes to a continuum of imminent danger producing further helplessness. This finding is congruent with Grant and Curry's (1993) indication that abused incarcerated women convicted of murder were more often isolated from friends and relatives prior to the murder than abused women who used women shelters. Websdale (1998) also finds that abused women might be manipulated into social and physical isolation by their abuser. That is, her aggressor may move his family geographically out of reach of others or deny them transportation and/or communication privileges; when these factors are linked to an ineffective social services intervention, they can result in making it difficult for the women to escape.

Karen also reported that at her murder trial, she learned that her husband was having an affair with another woman—her best friend. Although Karen denied that she killed him, she said that the prosecutor presented her husband's affair as motive. "But I was in fear of my own life when he (her husband) was around," she argued. She said that towards the end, he demanded control of every part of her life including who she could look at. On the family's return from church, at a red light, she casually glanced at a male driver in the auto next to theirs. She recognized the driver as their pharmacist and smiled. Her husband accused her of infidelity and beat her the rest of the day.

If I ever look at another man, he'd take my children from me, throw me into the street, run me out of town, and kill me as I ran. I believed him. And he'd never be arrested cause everybody knows 'em.

The respondents similarly reported that they failed to report the abuse to anyone because they did not want to be embarrassed. Some thought their spouses would change, and some thought that if they reported it, they would abuse their children. For example

He'd come home stoned, late at night and do things to me. . . . Okay, I let it pass. He was a struggling engineer in a big company . . . transferred us around the country. Six moves in 10 years! . . . I had no friends . . . one time he came home and dragged me out of my bed in the middle of the night . . . if it weren't for my daughter he'd of strangled me to death. He had me by the throat and she jumped between us. He kicked her to the wall but she came back screaming. I passed out and when I awoke Brandon was sitting on me crying. The other kids were crying, too, but they were too small to understand . . . the room was a mess, he tore the drapes and my new dress. The first one I bought in years!

Millie said that she kept those violent attacks from others, especially her parents, because she knew what her parents would say: "We told you he was bad." As long as he wouldn't take his anger on the kids, I'd play the role of a happy wife. Millie indicated that her husband lived as long as her children were safe. When he violently beat her nine-year-old daughter from a previous marriage, Millie loaded his shotgun and took his life before he could beat her daughter for the fourth time that day.

Delayed Parent Murder

Both respondents who murdered their parents describe life-long sexual, physical, and/or psychological abuse visited on them by their victims. The respondents' ages at the time of the murders were 16 and 17; both received life sentences and the younger one, Tess, life without parole. Tess described her home an affluent middle-class environment; she was a junior at high school when she stabbed her father to death twenty-one times with the aid of her boyfriend (who also received a life sentence). When her mother tried to stop her, she stabbed her several times too. Her mother was an alcoholic who was usually in a drunken stupor when her father abused Tess. She explained that her father would abandon the family, including her two younger brothers for days, sometimes weeks on end. Tess was sexually active with many boys prior to her 16th birthday; this included sexual contact, which she instigated, with one of her brothers. Her father beat her whenever he discovered her with boys. Tess reported that she became flirtatious to make her father mad. She added:

It was the only time he spent with me. The last time, he came home unexpectedly and found me busy with Billy (boyfriend) on

the kitchen floor. The woman who gave birth to me was baked as usual and didn't know what was up. He started kick'en Billy. That's when I jumped in and cutt'en in to the fucker. I don't know what happened to me. I never thought of cutting him before, but I should of. I just went off. Once I started, I couldn't stop. I'd kill'em again. I could see some of the stuff he used to do to me with each cut!

Some of the memories Tess shares were descriptions of torture, reinforcing her belief that she lived a daily life at-risk of her father inflicting violence on her as her mother and brothers watched. For example, when Tess was 13, he found lipstick and eyeliner in her pocketbook and smeared it on her face after tying her to a broken kitchen chair in the closet. He told the family that if they released her, opened the door, or cleaned her face, he would kill them.

Vivian, the other parent murderer, revealed similar experiences. Furthermore, the corrupting experiences of both young women are shared by Brett (1992) who suggests that many women are sexually abused by their parents, but often the first indication of its existence is when the victim attacks, possibly killing her aggressor. Both women said that their abuse was introduced as part of their legal defense, but as little could be corroborated, none of it was admissible. This reinforces Kristal (1994) and Jones (1986) who argue that many females kill in self defense, but that courts see it otherwise.[9]

Reactive Murder

Twenty-five percent (7) of the participants characterized their lives as filled with constant danger, at the hands of the "victims" who exploited them. When they perceived their own helplessness, they murdered those who had exploited them, or allowed those individuals to be attacked; much like the individuals who described delayed murder, this was a last resort to end the exploitative relationship. Unlike delayed, these participants described alternatives to murder; accordingly, we refer to their explanations as reactive. Of the seven reactive murderers, two were responsible for their spouses' death, one murdered her children, three killed friends, and one killed a stranger.

Reactive Spouse Murder

The two respondents who described reactive spouse murder shared similar abuse accounts. For example,

He tried to kill me one time, he kicked me, pulled my hair out, blackened my eyes, when I tried to get away he'd come find me and beat me again. I didn't want him dead, but God knows I don't miss him (Brenda).

Both of these participants had prior violence convictions. Brenda fired her husband's service revolver at him a few years prior to killing him. He was a police officer in a mid-sized city in upper New York. She was charged with a felony. Brenda claimed she wanted to scare him into leaving her alone.

I was so stressed and hurting all the time from his constant beatings. But, the freg'gin state is run by men and when you attack one, you attack'em all, the basters!

Judy set fire to her husband's new car after he had "terribly beat" one of their three children over dropping cookies on the lawn. Judy was found guilty of a felony, and released to his custody. He had to file monthly reports to the probation department about her conduct:

Because he was financially a successful man, he knew everybody and everybody wanted to know him. Now, I was cut-off from getting help from anybody.

She and her children moved to an apartment, but she could not pay their debts. He filed a report with probation saying that she had been involved with drugs and many men. The judge made it clear to her: home or prison. She was trapped. Sometime later, her husband was shot by their daughter's boyfriend while the family members, including Judy, watched. She received a life sentence because the judge said that she could have stopped the murder, but had not. The judge called her behavior, "irresponsible and disgusting." She explained:

I could have screamed or something. I could have warned my husband. The boy isn't doing time because he turned state witness on me. I got the life sentence. He got a full pardon. He said that I told him to do this. I said I wasn't guilty. Now he admits that I didn't put him up to it but no one will listen. . . . The boy said that I told him to do it and that I would let him marry my daughter and I'd get him a condo at the beach and a car if he killed my husband. When they pulled my record about setting fire to his car and moving . . . my conviction was automatic.

Brenda, also, had a previous felony record related to activities with her abusive husband whom she had caught with a 15-year-old girl (which never came out at court, she says). Brenda watched as her police officer husband pleaded for help when he arrived home after being involved in a street fight against another officer. He bled to death. She could have prevented his death. The judged asked me what kind of an evil monster am I.

Reactive Children Murder

One of the participants killed her two children, aged five and four. Both children were mentally ill. As Martha unraveled her story, her words were slow and reminded the researcher of how a young child speaks. Bill, her husband, worked nights while she worked days as a maid. Martha came home early one morning to discover her husband and three of [his] friends high on drugs, and that one of them was fondling her daughter. Over the next few weeks Martha learned that this had been a frequent occurrence at their apartment, and that both her children were sexually abused by her husband's friends. She refused to call the police because they might hurt her husband, and she refused to call social services because they might take her children. Thus, she had alternatives to murder. Martha added:

What's I's to do? I's work'en and he's tak'en cares of my's chill'en. . . . I's has no family f'er's help. No one's to look's in on 'em. Every minutes at work, I's feel'en though my chill'en is be'in used all's over their's little bodies again. . . . I's keep com'in home early and caught's them's again and again. Cuz of t'at, I's lose my job. I's find's more work. Loses t'at one. . . . I's start's get'en folks' laundry's and such and clean'em at home. . . . When's I's sleeps, my's man's get'en high and mess'en with's'em (with my children). The po'lice was'n no help. Social services is'n nut'en. I's tires all the times. Work'en, no sleep'en, and him. I's let's my child'en be peaceful. I's let's

them's go to Sweet Jesus. My's man can's never hurt's them's ever. . . . I's get'en some poison, puts it in their's supper. . . . I held's'em the rest's of t'at night. They's with Sweet Jesus and's peaceful. I's thankful f'er tat.

While it was her hand that killed her husband, a few questions arose: had legal intervention or mandatory treatment occurred long before Martha took her husband's life, would the outcome have been different? How many female suicides in the United States might be linked to domestic violence?

Reactive Friend Murder

Three of the participants describe reactive friend murder. Two of the participants had prior violent convictions and one was previously convicted of a non-violent crime. The descriptions of their murders included a perceived state of helplessness; while the offenders had alternatives, they did nothing to hamper the offending individuals. For example, Lillian was with her live-in boyfriend and his friend when the boys committed murder. Lillian explained:

My boyfriend and his friend killed a girl and because I was present I got 30 years. I was the first woman in South Carolina to receive a life sentence and my roommate was the second woman to receive it. These boys were drunk and they just killed her. She was 28 at the time and she lived with me and my boyfriend. I don't know why they killed her, they just did.

Lillian could have stopped the murder, but had not. Beth, too, implied that she had little to do with the murder but like Lillian, had not tried to stop it. Her brother lived with her and her three children. He sold drugs. They had many arguments over drugs, and she told him that he would have to move if he would not stop.

He said he did. One night, my best friend comes to the apartment. I thought she comes to see me. She wants Jason. When he comes to the door, Olivia pulls a knife. She screams about justifiable dope (drugs) and cuts'im. My babies start cry'en. Jason scream'en. I rush to 'im. Olivia scream'en at me. I panic and draws my gun. My first shot dropped her fast. I was afraid for my children and my brother.

Intentional Murder

Twenty-five percent (7) of the participants intentionally and with malice aforethought took the lives of others. What makes these accounts fit the typology of intentional murder is that the respondents displayed manipulated events leading to murder independent of the victims' contributions. Also, only these seven participants gave accounts that fit the legal definition of murder therefore they were not included in this discussion but information is available through the author.

Conclusion

For many women, homicide is an event utilized as a last resort to end a continuity of terror with partners, parents, or others. What emerges from this study is that homicide can sometimes be seen as the culmination of progressive interchanges between an offender and a victim. The trigger for such women lies in a continuum of imminent danger, reinforcing feelings of helplessness as produced by numerous episodes of physical abuse and psychological exploitation visited upon her by her antagonist. It is more likely that the individuals categorized by the researcher as delayed murderers and reactive murderers appeared to use a reasonable amount of force to end their fear. Leaving the abusive man, because of family, economics, and concerns about retaliation, was not an option.[10] This conclusion is based on the reasonable perception of a battered woman and not the reasonable perception of a white middle-class male, a conclusion consistent with Patricia Easteal (1993). Clearly, the events leading to the crime of domestic murder were orchestrated, maintained, and intensified by the eventual victim of the homicide.

One implication is that ordinary individuals with little or no criminal history may commit extraordinary deeds in a violent environment when they perceive themselves to be in imminent danger producing their own helplessness.[11] Social events can lead some individuals to murder and others to victimization.[12] Also, emerging from this study is the idea that abusive individuals can be detected early in a relationship and that their abusive practices accelerate.[13] Clearly, it is wise to resolve a potentially abusive relationship before one of its partners becomes a killer or a victim. Aggressors who might be violent offenders tend to fear few consequences from their behavior. For example, criminally violent offenders believe they will never be apprehended and if they are, prison will only add to their reputation (Stevens, 1992b, 1994). As for capital punishment, they consider that it will never be used against them (Stevens, 1992a). So, why would someone's violent husband or father fear a vulnerable wife or child? On the other hand, a few incarcerated women convicted of the crime of murder behave in a manner similar to criminally violent men convicted of the crime of murder who are incarcerated in high custody institutions (Stevens, 1995).

The researcher asked the participants: if you were able to talk to a group of young women about your experiences, what would you tell them? Ginny's response was typical of the other women in this study.

I rid the world of a bastard who they don't want to deal with and I lose everything mostly my kids; fight to get laws to protect our homes. Build organizations that can legally help. We send military people all over the world to defend our way of life but our greatest enemies are in our own homes.

Authority and Relative Response

When husbands are murdered, the state's subsequent procedures and the in-laws' responses to wives [were] unbelievable. Karen, for example, was immediately arrested and brutally treated, her children were taken from their home, the state and her husband's parents took, without legal interference, all their possessions including their cars, clothes, bank accounts, real estate, and retirement funds. "I owned all of those things and worked damn hard for them," Karen said. However, the greatest loss for these women was the loss of their children to their in-laws who believed the women to be

"evil"; they were denied access to their children, and because most of the participants' finances were in the hands of their in-laws, they lacked the funds to defend their own murder cases. Lauren saw her children during her trial, nine years ago, and has not seen them since. She said:

I'm 28. I have 2 boys, 1 will be 12 on May the 12th and my baby . . . my little girl will be 11 in June . . . I think? In '91 and '92 I saw my sons when I went to court for 10 minutes. And my little girl I haven't seen her since I've been locked up. . . . I've never been in trouble with the law until this stuff happened. . . . I got no one except my roommate. She's a black woman and real sweet. She and her family adopted me and her sister, has power of attorney over me so if anything happens to me like I die, she takes the body and buries me.

Judy commended:

In the end, all of the things I feared losing are gone because I killed that sona-bitch, who should have [been] crucified by the state long ago. He deserved to die. I defended my children. If anyone else attacked them or me on the streets, and I killed them in self-defense, I wouldn't be here. Because my husband did it, I do time. How do they figure?

Thus, many females convicted of the crime of murder responded to a pattern of terror; now that they are incarcerated, their victimization continues at the hands of the state. My argument is that legal policy must be adjusted to meet the realities of all members of our community, especially those living in a constant state of imminent danger. I agree with Easteal (1995) who suggests that laws must be redefined, and that the judiciary must be educated as to what is reasonable behavior in the context of a battered woman. Future research is also called for to examine the relationship between mandatory arrest and domestic violence rates. References available by request from the author.

Notes

1. As compared to males convicted of the crime of murder who tend to be career criminals and engage in crime including murder as a lifestyle (BJS, 1996).
2. For an in-depth look at BWS victims in rural America, see Websdale (1998). Johnson (1996) adds to this perspective

suggesting that most domestic violence homicide occurred in the context of domestic discord, indicating that the murder was a culminating event in a long history of interpersonal violence.
3. Since the attempt to use BWS as a self defense theory ordinarily raises only the issue whether the defendant has successfully made out the elements of self defense in a given jurisdiction, the theory has not been addressed in a great many appellate opinions. But see, e.g. *Ibn-Tama v. US*, 407 A.2d626 (D.C. 1979) (discussing admissibility of expert testimony on BWS); *People v. Powell*, 102 Mics.2d 775, 424 NYS 2d 626 (1980) (same), affd. 83 App.Div. 2d 719, 442 NYS 2d 645 (1981); cf. *State v. Wanrow*, 88 Wash.2d 221, 234–241, 559 P.2d 548, 555–559 (1977).
4. Whereas, Websdale (1998) further argues that men kill their female partners after an extended period of abuse.
5. Murder and non-negligent manslaughter are both classified as criminal homicide, yet the latter suggests an absence of killer intent. Jack Katz (1988) adds that when people kill, their perspective often seems incomprehensible to others, but in examining the social events leading to homicide, offenders are defending what they see as self-righteous acts—acts which in themselves defend communal or moralistic values. Then too, Luckenbill argues (1977) that victims and offenders may act in concert with each other, until the final end—murder; thus, homicide can be a "situated transaction" and not a "one-sided event" with an unwilling victim assuming a passive, noncontributory role.
6. One study compared a group of 100 battered women who had killed their partners with 100 battered women who had not. Women who resorted to violence were usually those who were most isolated socially and economically: they had been the most badly beaten; their children had been abused; and their husbands were drug or alcohol abusers. Their common bond was circumstantial not psychological (Glick, 1995).
7. North Carolina is one of the three American states where this study was conducted.
8. The researcher must say that the taking of another's life is never as simple and as insignificant an act as this typology implies.
9. This is probably because when females engage in violence, they are considered more pathological than men, since men allegedly are violent in nature and women are not (Herrnstein, 1995). He argues further that differentiating genetic factors for men are more likely to be antisocial than women. By contrast, Johnson (1996) suggests that women who kill are not generally

emotionally charged at the time of the murder.

10. Government statistics suggest that most women who flee are beaten and/or shot down by their aggressors (BJS, 1996).

11. There is some congruence with the findings in Seligman's (1975) argument that when a woman lacks skills and strategies to modify at least part of her life, feelings of helplessness may result. Moreover, these feelings may provoke one of two responses, attack or withdraw. Most convicted of the crime of murder at first withdrew. But as the abuse accelerated, something prompted a fatal attack upon their aggressors.

12. For an in-depth look at the social events leading males to criminally violent crime see Stevens (1997c). One denominator for these offenders was early childhood experiences that included parents who quarreled a great deal with each other, leaving their children unsupervised, and producing neglect.

13. For more in-depth about the attitudes of violent offenders especially when they were younger see Stevens (1997c, 1995).

References

Bean, C.A. (1992). *Women murdered by the men they loved.* New York: Harrington Park Press.

Biggers, T.A. (1979). Death by murder: A study of women murderers. *Death-Education,* 3 (1), 1–9.

Black, H.C. (1979). *Black's law dictionary.* 5th ed., St. Paul, Minn.: West Publishing Company.

Brett, C. (1992). From victim to victimizer. *Federal Bureau of Prisons, Spring.*

Bureau of Justice Statistics (BJS), (1997). *Sourcebook of criminal justice statistics 1996.* Washington, D.C.: Office of Justice Programs, U.S. Department of Justice.

Caplan, G. (1991, February 25). Battered wives, battered justice. *National Review.*

Easteal, P. (1995). Reconstructing reality. *The Alternative Law Journal,* 20(3), 108–112.

Easteal, P.W. (1993). *Killing the beloved: Homicide between adult sexual intimates.* Australia: Australian Institute of Criminology.

Find Law. (1997). Query: battered woman syndrome. (Online). http:caselaw.findlaw.com/scripts/ case...iRestriction=battered %20woman%20syndrome

Flethcer, B., and Moon, D.G. (1993). Introduction: The population. In B.R. Flethcer, L.D. Shaver, and D.G. Moon (Eds.), *Women prisoners: A forgotten population* (pp. 5–14). Westport, Conn.: Praeger.

Glick, L. (1995). *Criminology.* Boston: Allyn and Bacon.

Gottfredson, M., and Hirschi, T. (1990). *A general theory of crime.* Stanford, Calif.: Stanford University Press.

Grant, B., and Curry, D. (1993). Women murderers and victims of abuse in southern state. *American Journal of Criminal Justice,* 17 (2), 73–83.

Herrnstein, R.J. (1995). Criminogenic traits. In J.Q. Wilson and J. Petersilia (eds.), *Crime* (pp. 39–65). San Francisco: ICS Press.

Hirschel, J.D., and Hutchison, I. (1991). Police preferred arrest policies. In Michael Steinman (ed.), *Woman battering: Police responses,* (pp. 49–70). Cincinnati, Ohio: Anderson.

Johnson, I.M. (1996). Female murders in a southern city. *American Journal of Criminal Justice,* 20(2), 207–224.

Jones, A. (1986). *Women who kill.* New York: Holt, Rinehart and Wilson.

Karmen, A. (1996, November 30). What's driving New York's crime rate down? *Law Enforcement News,* John Jay College of Criminal Justice/CUNY.

Katz, J. (1988). *Seductions of crime.* New York: Basic.

Kristal, A. (1991). You've come a long way, baby: The battered woman's syndrome revisited. *New York Law School Journal of Human Rights,* 9, 111–160.

Levy, D. (1995, June 14). Nation gets D in war on violence. *USA Today,* p. 1.

Luckenbill, D. (1977). Criminal homicide as a situated transaction. *Social Problems,* 25, 176–186.

Mann, C.R. (1988). Getting even? Women who kill in domestic encounters, *Justice Quarterly,* March.

Mills, C. Wright. (1940). Situated actions and vocabularies of motive. *American Sociological Review,* 5 (6).

North Carolina v. Pamela Warlick Grant. (1994). In The Supreme Court of North Carolina. (Online), Available: http://www.aoc.state.nc.us/www/ public/sc/slip/slip96/067a95.html

National Coalition Against Domestic Violence. (1994). Every fifteen seconds a woman is battered in this country. *Contemporary Women's Issues Collection.* (Online). Available: http://www.elibrary. com/getdoc.cgi?id=82...ctionandpuburl= http~C~~S~~S~www.rdsinc.com

Nettler, G. (1982). *Killing one another.* Cincinnati, Ohio: Anderson.

Newton, J. (1996, March 13). Number of arrests by LAPD plunges since '91. *LA Times.*

Ogle, R.S., Katkin, D.M., and Bernard, T.J. (1995). A theory of homicidal behavior among women. *Criminology,* 33 (2), 173–187.

Peele, S. (1991, August). Getting away with murder. *Reason Magazine.*

Roberts, A.R. (1996). Battered women who kill: A comparative study of incarcerated

participants with community sample of battered women. *Journal of Family Violence,* 11(3), 291–304.

Sargent, E., Marcus-Mendoza, S., and Ho Yu, C. (1993). Abuse and the women prisoner. In B.R. Flethcer, L.D. Shaver, and D.G. Moon (Eds.), *Women Prisoners: A Forgotten Population* (pp. 55–64). Westport, Conn.: Praeger.

Seligman, M.E. (1975). *Helplessness: On depression, development, and death.* San Francisco: W.H. Freeman.

Snell, T.L. (1994). Women in prison. *Bureau of Justice Statistics, Special Report.* U.S. Department of Justice.

Stevens, D.J. (1998a). The impact of time-served and regime on prisoners' anticipation of crime: Female prisonisation effects. *The Howard Journal of Criminal Justice,* 37(2), 188–205.

——— (1998b). Incarcerated women, crime, and drug addiction. *The Criminologist,* 22(1), 3–14.

——— (1997a). Urban communities and homicide: Why blacks resort to murder. *Criminologist,* 21(3), 145–158.

——— (1997b, December). What do law enforcement officers think about their jobs. *The Law Enforcement Journal,* 5(1), 60–62.

——— (1997c). Influences of early childhood experiences on subsequent criminally violent behaviour. *Studies on Crime and Crime Prevention,* 6(1), 34–50.

——— (1995). American criminals and attitudes. *International Review of Modern Sociology,* 25 (2), 27–42.

——— (1994). The Depth of Imprisonment and Prisonisation: Levels of Security and Prisoners' Anticipation of Future Violence." *The Howard Journal of Criminal Justice* 33(2): 137–157.

——— (1992a). Research note: The death sentence and inmate attitudes. *Crime and Delinquency* 38, 272–79.

——— (1992b). Examining inmate attitudes: Do prisons deter crime? *The State of Corrections—American Correctional Association: 1991.*

Walker, L.E. (1979). *The battered woman.* New York: Harper.

Websdale, N. (1998). *Rural woman battering and the justice system: An ethnography.* Thousand Oaks, Calif.: Sage Publications.

Williams, M. (1995, July 21). Court turns down battered woman syndrome defense: Case number 94APA12-1728. *The Daily Reporter.*

Wilson, M.I., and Daly, M. (1992). Who kills whom in spouse killings? On the exceptional sex ratio of spousal homicides in the United States. *Criminology,* 30(2), 189–215.

 Article Review Form at end of book.

In what ways do researchers differ on the deterrence effect of prison sentences?

The General Deterrent Effect of Longer Sentences

Donald E. Lewis

Wollongong, New South Wales

How long, if at all, should convicted offenders serve in prison? The responses to this question will depend, *inter alia,* on the type of crime committed and the previous record of the offender. Allowing for different circumstances there is still substantial variation in attitudes concerning the longevity of sentences. Opinions differ significantly among politicians, police officers, parole and probation officers, prison governors and officers, judges and magistrates, criminologists and the general public. This paper provides summary empirical evidence which may reduce these differences.

Few would deny that prisons are undesirable; they are degrading, expensive and rarely seem capable of rehabilitating prisoners. As Nigel Walker points out, "In a non-sadistic culture the deliberate infliction of death, pain or harm is seen as requiring a very strong justification if it is not to be condemned. If the benefit is doubtful or non-existent, toleration very quickly turns into censure" (Walker, 1979, p. 129). The potential benefits of longer sentences are threefold. Those serving longer sentences will not be able to commit offenses against the general public while in prison (although crimes against fel-low prisoners and prison officials can still be committed). After serving a longer sentence those released may be less likely to revert to criminal behaviour. This is referred to as the rehabilitation effect. The third possible beneficial effect of longer sentences occurs if some potential offenders are less likely to break the law when longer terms are served by others. This is commonly referred to as the general deterrent effect. We shall drop the adjective "general" and adopt the definition used by the National Panel of Research on Deterrent and Incapacitative Effects: "*Deterrence* is the inhibiting effect of sanction on the criminal activity of people *other than* the sanctioned offender." (Blumstein *et al.*, 1978, p. 3).

The premises of this article are threefold. First, the deterrent effect of longer sentences can be measured and quantified. Secondly, the knowledge and awareness of several recent attempts to measure empirically the deterrent effect is limited. Finally, an improved understanding of the empirical evidence can improve decision-making within the criminal justice system and reduce the enormous differences of opinion within society concerning sentencing. . . .

The present survey can be distinguished from earlier ones in several important respects. It incorporates several recent studies published since the earlier surveys were completed. Secondly, the only studies included are those which attempt to quantify empirically the magnitude of the deterrent effect of longer sentences while holding constant other variables which affect the crime rate. Thus the deterrent effect of other sanctions, such as the increased probability of arrest, are excluded. This is a more specialised survey which allows us to concentrate on the problems and results of attempts to measure the deterrent effect of longer sentences. It should be particularly useful to legislators, judges, members of parole boards and others whose decisions directly affect the time offenders serve in prison.

Summary of the Findings

Most studies reviewed provide evidence that is consistent with the hypothesis that longer sentences deter most types of crime. Supportive studies derive their findings from a variety of data bases representing different countries, different time periods and utilising a variety of control variables and alternative specifications.

All of the studies provide estimates for the elasticity of severity which can be defined as the percentage change in the crime rate for a specific crime divided by the percentage change in the average sentence served by prisoners convicted of that crime, other things being

The General Deterrent Effect of Longer Sentences, D. E. Lewis. *British Journal of Criminology,* 26, 1986, 47–62. By permission of Oxford University Press.

equal. An elasticity of –0·2, for example, indicates that a 10 per cent. increase in the average sentence served is associated with a 2 per cent. reduction in the crime rate. The importance of such a seemingly small elasticity can be illustrated with an example. England and Wales recorded approximately five indictable/serious crimes per 100 population in 1980. Assuming a population of 50 million, an increase in the average sentence served from four to five months would reduce the total number of indictable/serious crimes by 108,696.

The average estimates indicate that the deterrent effect is strongest for rape and assault, weakest for hijacking and fraud with robbery, burglary, auto-theft, larceny and murder in between. With the exception of murder, violent crimes tend to have larger (negative) elasticities than non-violent crimes.

Authors often report more than one estimate of elasticity for the same crime using the same basic data. Differences occur when alternative exogenous variables are included in the model, alternative specifications are estimated (linear, log-linear and so forth) and when alternative estimating techniques (simple least squares, two-stage least squares, SUR, etc.) are used. . . .

Nevertheless, the evidence is generally consistent with the existence of a substantial deterrent effect for longer sentences. In 1978 Nagin concluded, "In summary, then, analyses that have examined the association of clearance rates, arrest probabilities, or police expenditures per capita with crime rates find consistently negative and nearly always significant associations." He added, "The evidence on the association between sentence severity, primarily measured by time served, and crime rates is much more equivocal" (Nagin, 1978, p. 110). The accumulated evidence now warrants a stronger yet still guarded statement. For most crimes a substantial majority of the studies have found a negative association between crime rates and sentence severity.

Common Problems

While a negative association between sentence severity and crime rates is consistent with the deterrent hypothesis, the reported partial correlations may be spurious for several reasons. There are three major problems which necessitate caution when interpreting the elasticities: (a) measurement errors in the basic data, (b) the confounding of the deterrent and incapacitation effects, and (c) difficulties in appropriately identifying the crime supply equation within a system of simultaneous equations. These problems led the Panel on Research on Deterrent and Incapacitative Effects to conclude,

". . . we cannot yet assert that the evidence warrants an affirmative conclusion regarding deterrence . . . Our reluctance to draw stronger conclusions does not imply support for a position that deterrence does not exist, since the evidence certainly favors a proposition supporting deterrence more than it favors one asserting that deterrence is absent" (Blumstein et al., 1978, p. 7).

In a similar vein Cook concluded, "my evidence from reviewing these studies is that they have produced little persuasive evidence of the deterrence mechanism . . . these studies have not produced reliable evidence to date" (Cook, 1977, pp. 194–195). Greenberg also concluded that, "Although many of the statistical studies of deterrence report correlations consistent with a deterrence effect, many sources of bias remain to be eliminated before conclusions about the presence of deterrence can be regarded with confidence" (Greenberg, 1977, p. 290). Finally, Beyleveld asserts that "Recorded offence rates do not vary inversely with the severity of penalties (usually measured by the length of imprisonment). The homicide-severity relationship, however, is usually inverse" (Beyleveld, 1980, p. 306).

While there is no question that problems exist, it is our view that they have been exaggerated, distorted and represent only a partial analysis. Just as there are factors which may bias the studies in the direction of measuring a greater deterrent effect than actually exists, there are other factors which are operating at the same time, which are potentially just as strong and which will bias the reported findings in the opposite direction; that is, indicating a weaker deterrent effect than actually

exists. This will become apparent as we analyse each of the identified problems.

(a) Measurement Errors

Everyone agrees that basic crime data in all countries are seriously deficient. The general problems have been discussed by many writers but we are only concerned with the way in which measurement errors may bias the empirical findings which attempt to calculate the magnitude of the deterrent effect. Measurement problems may result from (i) under-reporting, (ii) artificially inflated arrest rates, (iii) leniency granted in return for admissions of unsolved crimes, (iv) variations in the extent to which police declare crimes "unfounded", and (v) plea-bargaining. The effect of measurement errors has been discussed in the literature but it has not been adequately recognised that the impact will depend upon: (i) whether or not the error (for example, under-reporting) is statistically associated with the crime rate or purely a random occurrence across jurisdiction or over time, (ii) the type of crime (serious versus non-serious, etc.) and (iii) the sanction that is measured (clearance rate, commitment rate or the severity as measured by the mean number of months served).

Blumstein et al. (1978) developed an excellent hypothetical example, which has been slightly modified for our purposes, which illustrates how under-reporting can lead to a spurious negative association between crime rate and sanction risk. They consider a number of jurisdictions, each with identical populations, the same true number of crimes and the same volume of sanctions imposed. If the true number of crimes (or the crime rate) is plotted against the true sanction risk (sanctions per crimes) all the jurisdictions will be located at the same point (1,000, 0·2). Now suppose there is variation in the rates of reporting and recording crimes among jurisdictions? . . .

The problem with their example is that it does not allow for the very real possibility that the extent of under-reporting is positively associated with the crime rate. That is, the extent of under-reporting is greater the higher the crime rate. Such systematic under-reporting may off-set an actual negative relationship between sanction risk and the number of crimes. Thus systematic under-reporting may result in estimates which obscure any deterrence that exists. . . .

(b) Confounding of Deterrent and Incapacitation Effects

Even if the association between longer sentences and lower crime rates is real and not a spurious result of measurement errors, the inference of the existence of a deterrent effect and the measurement of its magnitude is still not straightforward. The lower crime rate could result from (i) a general deterrent effect, (ii) a rehabilitation effect or (iii) the incapacitation effect. The last effect is the reduction in crime which results from the restricted ability of criminals to commit crimes while in prison.

Shinnar and Shinnar (1975), Greenberg (1977), Wolpin (1978) and others have argued that the incapacitation effect is very large for most types of crime. If this were true, the proportion of the estimated elasticities of severity which are attributable to deterrence would be small. Ehrlich (1981), however, has argued that the confounding of the deterrence and incapacitation effects have been exaggerated in the literature (Nagin, 1978) and that for most types of crime (murder is an exception) the deterrence effect probably accounts for more than 90 per cent. of the estimated elasticity with respect to longer sentences. He points out that the others have over-estimated the incapacitation effect and hence under-estimated the deterrent effect mainly because of their failure to account for "the replacement of individual offenders who are successfully removed from the market of offenses by veteran offenders or new entrants who are induced by the prevailing opportunities for illegitimate reward to fill the vacancies created by the departing offenders" (Ehrlich, 1981, p. 312).

(c) Problem of Identification

The direction of causation between crime rates and the average length of sentence (or other sanctions) may be twofold. An increase in the average length of sentence served may reduce the crime rate via the deterrent or incapacitative effects. An autonomous increase in the crime rate may also influence the average length of sentence in one of two ways. The first is through the crowding or congestion effect. An increase in crime with no expansion of the capacity of the prison system may force a reduction in the sentences served. Secondly, an increase in crime may result in a "get tough" attitude on the part of judges and parole boards which will increase the average length of sentences. "Crowding" may yield estimates of elasticity of severity which are biased upwards (indicating a stronger deterrent effect than, in fact, exists), while "get tough" policies will bias the estimates downward. It is not at all clear which of these two effects will dominate and hence to specify the direction of bias in the estimates obtained from single equation models in which the possibility of two-way causation between sentence lengths and levels of crime is not explicitly taken into account . . .

Summary

Taken as a whole the studies reviewed constitute a substantial body of evidence which is largely consistent with the existence of a deterrent effect from longer sentences. This conclusion must still be considered tentative for several reasons. None of the studies is totally devoid of the kinds of problems discussed above. There remains substantial room for improvement in the underlying theory, data sources and methods of statistical inference and design. In addition, the evidence concerning the magnitude of the deterrent effect of longer sentences for various crimes is far from uniform. Nevertheless, impartial analysis of the best available evidence suggests that criminals do respond to incentives and that longer sentences do deter crime.

References

Beyleveld, D. (1980). *A Bibliography on General Deterrence Research.* Farnborough: Saxon House.

Blumstein, A., Cohen, J. and Nagin, D. (1978). *Deterrence and Incapacitation: Estimating the Effects of Criminal Sanctions on Crime Rates.* Washington: National Academy of Sciences.

Cook, P. (1977). "Punishment and Crime: A Critique of Current Findings Concerning the Preventive Effect of Criminal Sanctions." *Law and Contemporary Problems,* **41,** 164–204.

Ehrlich, I. (1981). "On the Usefulness of Controlling Individuals: An Economic Analysis of Rehabilitation, Incapacitation and Deterrence." *American Economic Review,* **71,** 307–322.

Greenberg, D. (1977). "Crime Deterrence Research and Social Policy." In *Modelling the Criminal Justice System,* ed. by S. Nagel. Beverly Hills: Sage Publications. Pp. 281–295.

Nagin, D. (1978). "General Deterrence: A Review of the Empirical Evidence." In *Deterrence and Incapacitation: Estimating the Effects of Criminal Sanctions on Crime,* ed. by A. Blumstein, J. Cohen and D. Nagin. Washington: National Academy of Sciences. Pp. 95–139.

Shinnar, R. and Shinnar, S. (1975). "The Effects of the Criminal Justice System on the Control of Crime: A Quantitative Approach." *Law and Society Review,* **9,** 581–611.

Walker, N. (1979). "The Efficacy and Morality of Deterrents." *Criminal Law Review,* 129–144.

Wolpin, K. (1978). "An Economic Analysis of Crime and Punishment in England and Wales 1894–1967." *Journal of Political Economy,* **86,** 815–840.

 Article Review Form at end of book.

In what ways might the death penalty impact the general public? Criminals? How can the ideas of the public be changed concerning capital punishment?

College Student Attitudes about Capital Punishment:

Sources of Attitudes about the Death Penalty

Brian K. Payne and Victoria Coogle

Brian K. Payne can be contacted at the Department of Sociology and Criminal Justice, Old Dominion University, Norfolk, VA 23529. BPAYNE@odu.edu Victoria Coogle is at the Department of Criminal Justice, Louisiana State University–Eunice, Eunice, LA 70535

Three hundred seven college students were polled about their ideas of capital punishment. Their demographics such as gender, race, community size, political affiliation, former attitudes about capital punishment, and choice of college major were assessed and compared. Race and political affiliation impact lack of support or support of capital punishment more than any other variable investigated in this study. The study is important in that it adds to the growing body of literature suggesting that support for the death penalty is conditional rather than concrete. Some of the most commonly cited arguments for and against the death penalty include deterrence, cost, and racial disparity.

Capital Punishment's Deterrent Effect

Both supporters and opponents of the death penalty cite deterrence as a basis for their opinions. Supporters of the death penalty contend that the death penalty greatly deters crime in two ways. First, by executing the offender, society is assured that a particular criminal will never commit crime again. Second, by executing murderers, others who are considering committing similar crimes will be deterred from doing so.

Those opposed to the death penalty suggest that rather than deterring homicide, capital punishment embraces it, argues Dennis Stevens (1992). When the state executes a criminal, violence is re-enforced from the perspective of the violent-prone individual. It works! Such a relationship can be referred to as the brutalization argument. Those supporting this argument often cite the state of Texas as an example of how the death penalty has failed as a method of crime prevention. Since the 1972 *Furman* decision, Texas has executed more offenders than any other state. According to the theories espoused by the advocates of capital punishment, Texas should be the most crime-free state in the country since it has the highest rate of violent crime in the nation.

Cost of Implementation

A closely connected issue is whether the death penalty is cost effective. Advocates for the death penalty view it as a less expensive alternative than life imprisonment. But opponents of the death penalty suggest that the cost of trying, convicting, and sentencing someone to death, as well as the costs of incarcerating someone for the average of eight years while they await execution, can run in the millions of dollars. It is further estimated that taxpayers spend approximately $100 million annually in the state of

College Student Attitudes about Capital Punishment: Sources of Attitudes about the Death Penalty, B. K. Payne and V. Coogle. *Corrections Compendium*, 23(4), 1998, 1–5, 24–26. Reprinted with permission of the American Correctional Association, Lanham, Md.

California alone on capital punishment cases and its associated costs such as housing, food, and medical expenses. Some information suggests that executions can cost $2 million more than life imprisonment.

Supporters of capital punishment agree that the cost of executions is too high. Rather than banishing executions however, supporters often look to other means to make executions more cost effective. For example, van den Haag (1983) suggests that the cost of executions are connected to the present appeal system in the United States. Advocates who join van den Haag are calling for a revamping of the present appeal system, saying that if the system were streamlined, justice would be served quickly and at less cost to the taxpayer. Such ideas are opposed on the grounds that commutation of the sentences of those inmates on death row would lead to staggering expenses.

Racial Disparity

Although the debate over the deterrent effect of capital punishment, as well as its ensuing costs, may never be fully decided, a more tangible concern continues to engender dispute among the experts. This concern deals specifically with whether death sentences are dispensed in a racially disparative manner. Perhaps few scholars have argued their views with more passion and fervor than Aguirre and Baker (1996) and van den Haag (1996).

As abolitionists, Aguirre and Baker's (1996) crusade against the death penalty generally focuses on the racial disparity issue. They use statistics and case studies to support their assertion that the United States, and in particular those states that have re-instituted the death penalty, is still executing more minorities than whites. In fact, Aguirre and Baker (1996) conclude that as the race to execute more and more death row inmates gains speed, we may well exceed post-*Gregg* figures in the execution of minorities and in particular of African-American males. They further suggest that the issue of racial disparity should be enough of a catalyst to prod the country into abandoning this form of punishment once

and for all. Yet van den Haag (1996) asserts that the opposite conclusion should be reached by the people of the United States. While avoiding the use of statistics, he contends that if more minorities are being executed, the answer lies in executing more offenders from all races. By executing members of all races, van den Haag (1996) asserts that justice will be met, society will be safe, and the racial disparity problem will be resolved.

Measurement Issues

Regarding measurement issues, a number of researchers have questioned the overreliance on public opinion polls to gauge attitudes of the public. Among other things, these researchers contend that asking the respondents whether they are for or against the death penalty can produce misleading results. For example, Sandys and McGarrel (1995) state: "that future reports of favorability toward capital punishment, especially in the media, should be mindful of limitations associated with presenting results based solely on a general favorability-type question" (p. 211). Along a similar line, research by Jones (1996) concludes "that changes in question form would not only change the level of support for the death penalty but significantly change our interpretation and understanding of the factors that shape that opinion" (p. 49). The problem of using the standard support/oppose death penalty question format seems to lie in the fact that "most people's death penalty attitudes are based on emotion rather than information or rational argument."[1]

While a review of the literature raises several concerns, the major focus of this research was confined to an analysis of public opinion. Generally, the focus was on the attitudes students enrolled at a medium-sized Southern university held toward the death penalty. Specifically, the research questions framing this analysis were: (1) What are students' attitudes toward the death penalty? And, (2) What factors influence attitudes about the death penalty? Therefore, 307 students enrolled in various courses at the medium-sized southern university during the 1995–1996 academic year,

completed self-administered questionnaires. The courses in which the students were enrolled included criminal justice courses required of all criminal justice majors, general studies courses, and interdisciplinary social sciences courses.

Discussion

Race and political affiliation impact lack of support or support of capital punishment more than any other variable investigated in this study. Briefly, we found that blacks and Democrats were more opposed to the death penalty than their counterparts, which is consistent with prior research. In fact, we found that significant racial differences existed on each of the death penalty items, including total score, except for two items: the cost of and whether mentally retarded individuals should be sentenced to death.

Two questions seem to be important: why are blacks more likely to be against the death penalty? And, why are whites more likely to support the death penalty? Factors impacting why blacks are against the death penalty seem to stem around that consistent finding that the death penalty is applied more often to blacks than to whites. Reports of a discriminatory death penalty are found not only in the scholarly literature, but in the popular media as well. It would seem plausible that awareness of such discriminatory practices in the application of the death penalty is a primary factor impacting why blacks show little support for the death penalty. As one writer argues, "When we choose to inflict society's worst punishment on blacks at a rate of three and a half times their proportion, resentment is inevitable."

If blacks are indeed opposed to the death penalty because of the disparative manner in which it is applied, the issue that arises has to do with why whites are more likely to show support for the death penalty. We found that whites showed more support for: the death penalty as a deterrent; the idea that too many appeals are provided; viewing the death penalty as making society safe; the belief that drug dealers should be sentenced to die; the statement that only guilty people are sentenced to die. Conversely, blacks were more likely to show support for the statements generally suggesting that the death penalty is racist. As far as why whites are more likely to support capital punishment, some suggest that support is linked to prejudice against blacks. Although we could not test this assertion, an examination of the items where racial differences were not noted may help explain why significant differences were noted in the other areas.

As indicated previously, the only two areas where no racial differences were found involved statements about cost and whether mentally retarded murderers should be sentenced to die. Regarding cost, we found that nearly half of the sample (46.3%) strongly disagreed with the statement "It costs less to keep someone in prison for life than it does to execute them." In fact, nearly three-fourths of the sample disagreed with the statement at least somewhat. The question that comes up is why those generally opposed to the death penalty, in this case blacks and Democrats, nonetheless viewed the death penalty as cheaper than life imprisonment when in fact a number of studies have supported such claims.

The answer may lie in the way the death penalty is portrayed in the media. It is clear and well documented that blacks are executed at higher rates than whites. As mentioned earlier, such accounts are often provided in the media. Rarely, however, does one see media accounts describing the exorbitant fiscal costs of the death penalty that have been documented in the scholarly literature.[2] This is not to suggest that the scarcity of media accounts on the cost of executions is the sole factor contributing to why such a high percentage of our sample, or of society for that matter, views capital punishment as cheaper than life imprisonment. Showing that the death penalty is applied in a disparate manner to blacks is easier to establish than the possibility that it is cheaper to keep someone in prison than to execute them. Further, while scholars seem to agree that blacks are more likely to receive the death penalty, they do not agree on the cost issue. Thus, establishing the cost-effectiveness of life

imprisonment seems a harder sell than that it is applied unfairly.

Regarding attitudes about executing mentally retarded murderers, while no racial differences were found, we found that nearly half of our sample believed that mentally retarded individuals should be executed. Past research, however, found that "74% of the sample agreed at least somewhat with the statement that the death penalty should not be imposed on a mentally retarded person." On the surface, it may seem that our sample has more punitive attitudes towards mentally ill individuals. However, we must stress that wording was probably a significant factor.

The statement on our questionnaire was: "Mentally retarded murderers should not be executed." In our statement we used the word murderers while Sandys and McGarrel (1995) refrained from using the word. It is possible that including "murderer" in the statement biased our results some. Irregardless, differences between our study and Sandys and McGarrel's (1995) support Jones' previously mentioned claim: "changes in question form would not only change the level of support for the death penalty but significantly change our interpretation and understanding of the factors that shape that opinion" (p. 49).

We also found that political affiliation was a significant factor with significant differences found in 7 of the 11 death penalty items. Democrats have a lower death penalty score, showed more support for the statements suggesting that the death penalty is racist, and showed less support for: the belief that too many appeals are provided; the idea that the death penalty helps make society safe; the notion that drug dealers should be sentenced to die; and, the statement that only guilty people are sentenced to die. Finding that Democrats are more likely to oppose capital punishment is consistent with prior research. What it comes down to is the fact that capital punishment is a political issue which is divided on party lines with those who are more liberal more likely to be opposed to such measures and those who are conservative more likely to support these measures.

Gender differences were noted only in two areas. Females showed more support for the belief that only guilty people are sentenced to die and males showed more support for the statement suggesting that capital punishment is society's way of getting revenge. Other than these two areas, for the most part, females' attitudes were similar to males' attitudes. Finding gender differences only in two areas was surprising because previous research indicates that gender differences exist.[3] Also, finding that males were more likely to view the death penalty as revenge was unexpected, as this question was initially included as an anti-death penalty statement, which would suggest that females are more in favor of the death penalty than males. There are at least two reasons for this finding: sample characteristics and measurement error.

First, regarding sample characteristics, it is possible that the fact that the sample was derived from a Southern university impacted the findings. The conservative nature of the south is something that is well documented in the literature. As well, recent research suggests that southerners are more "cognitively primed for aggression" than northerners. If both conservatism and acceptance of violence are indeed part of the southern culture, then one might expect southerners' attitudes towards the death penalty to be different from people from other regions of the country. Although we could not test this assertion because our sample is limited to mostly southern students, it is possible that southern females are similar to southern males because of the southern cultural influences which would override potential gender differences.

Regarding measurement error, wording of the statement assessing attitudes about the death penalty and revenge may have been problematic. Specifically, we found that males were more likely to show support for the statement "The death penalty is society's way of getting revenge" than females. However, Victoria Coogle (1996) originally included this question as an anti-death penalty question because opponents of the death penalty often point to the "revenge nature" of capital punishment as one of its inherent flaws. Based on our findings, it is possible that males (who generally are more likely to be in favor of the death penalty) did not view revenge as a negative factor. Instead, if they viewed revenge as appropriate or in a positive vein, this would explain why males showed more support for the statement. Whatever the case, wording of similar questions in the future should be selected tentatively.

References

Aguirre, A. and D. V. Baker. 1996. Empirical research on racial discrimination in the penalty. *Taking Sides: Clashing views on controversial issues in crime and criminology.* New York: Dushkin.

Coogle, Victoria. 1996. Measuring death penalty attitudes. A paper presented at the annual meeting of the Alabama Academy of Science. March 11–13. Tuskegee, Ala.

Jones, Peter R. 1994. It's not what you ask, it's the way you ask it: Question form and public opinion on the death penalty. *The Prison Journal.*

Sandys, Marla and Edmund F. McGarrell. 1995. Attitudes toward capital punishment. *Journal of Research in Crime and Delinquency.*

Stevens, Dennis J. 1992. Research note: The death sentence and inmate attitudes. *Crime and Delinquency.*

van den Haag, E. 1983. The constitutional question. *The Death Penalty: A Debate:* New York: Plenum Press.

van den Haag, E. 1996. Empirical research on racial discrimination in the imposition of the death penalty. *Taking Sides: Clashing Views on Controversial Issues in Crime and Criminology.* New York: Dushkin.

Endnotes

1. Ellsworth, 1994, p. 19.
2. A. Aguirre and D. V. Baker, "Empirical Research on Racial Discrimination in the Imposition of the Death Penalty." *Taking Sides: Clashing Views on Controversial Issues in Crime and Criminology* (New York: Dushkin, 1996); Richard C. Dieter. "Secondary Smoke Surrounds the Capital Punishment Debate." *Criminal Justice Ethics* 13(1) (1994): 2–6; Jeremy Epstein. "Death Penalty Adds to Our Tax Burdens." *National Law Journal* 17(20) (1995):A23; Michael Ross. "A Voice From Death Row," *America* 172(4) (1995):6–8.
3. Bohm et al., 1993; Bohm et al., 1990; Sandys and McGarrel, 1995.

 Article Review Form at end of book.

Are certain states relying more on capital punishment than they have in the past?

Executions in 1996 Second Highest Since 1976

Richard C. Dieter

The overall pace of executions in the United States remained high in 1996 and the prospects for the future are for even greater numbers of people put to death each year. As of December 17, there were 45 executions, mostly by lethal injection. This represents a slight drop from last year when 56 executions represented the highest number since capital punishment was reinstated in 1976. The 20% decrease in executions this year was probably due to the passage of numerous federal and state laws designed to speed up executions. Some of these new laws created a legal logjam as courts considered the constitutionality of the curtailed appeal process.

Texas, the nation's leader in executions for many years, virtually stopped executions this year pending resolution of a challenge to the state's new appeal laws. Once that matter is resolved, Texas will likely renew and even accelerate its frequent executions. On the federal level, Congress passed the Antiterrorism and Effective Death Penalty Act of 1996 which will make it increasingly difficult for even innocent defendants on death row to secure federal review. Congress also eliminated all money for the death penalty resource centers which had been overseeing a major portion of death penalty appeals. Both of these pieces of legislation will result in less thorough representation for those on death row.

This year, the five states with the largest death rows (California, Texas, Florida, Pennsylvania and Illinois) together were responsible for only 8 executions. But these same states have over 1,500 people on death row, indicating that the likelihood for increased executions in the near future is great.

Racial Disparities Even More Prominent

Although the number of people executed varies from year to year, the typical death row inmate remains the same. He is likely to be a poor man who never graduated from high school. He is likely to be a member of a minority. And with only rare exceptions, he has been convicted of murdering a white person. Almost all of the executions this year involved a case with a white victim in the underlying murder. Of the 45 executions carried out this year, only 4 involved the murder of a black victim, even though blacks are murdered as often as whites in the U.S. (one additional case involved black and white victims). No white person was executed this year for the murder of a black person, while ten black men were executed for crimes involving white victims. This sends a message that black lives are worth less than white lives. Since the death penalty was reinstated, 90 black men have been executed for the murder of a white victim, while only 4 white

men have been executed for the murder of a black victim.

In Kentucky, a recent study found that none of the people on that state's death row were there for the murder of a black person, despite the fact that there have been over 1,000 blacks murdered in Kentucky since the death penalty was reinstated. Legislation to prevent further racial injustice failed by one vote in the state legislature.

The federal death penalty continues to be targeted mainly at minorities. Almost 80% of those for whom the federal government sought the death penalty under either the "drug kingpin law" of 1988 or the 1994 Crime Bill have been black or Hispanic.

Death Penalty Reality Often Differs from Expectations

Many of those executed in 1996 did not fit the stereotype of death row inmates as repeat killers who stalk strangers. In fact, many of the cases this year involved murders by close acquaintances of the victim:

- **William Flamer** was executed in Delaware for killing his aunt and uncle.

- **Jeffrey Paul Sloan** was executed in Missouri for murdering his brother and was suspected of killing other family members.

States with Most Executions Since 1976		States with Highest Per Capita Execution Rate (per 100,000 pop. since 1976)		States with Most Executions in 1996	
Texas	107	Delaware	1.20	Virginia	8
Florida	38	Texas	0.63	South Carolina	6
Virginia	37	Virginia	0.60	Missouri	6
Missouri	23	Louisiana	0.55	Delaware	3
Louisiana	23	Arkansas	0.51	Texas	3

- **James Clark** was executed in Delaware for killing his adoptive parents.

- **Joseph Savino** was executed in Virginia for the murder of his male lover when the relationship went sour.

- **Fred Kornahrens** was executed in South Carolina for killing his ex-wife, her father and her 10-year-old stepson. Kornahrens said he went out of control when his marriage broke up.

- **Emmett Nave** was executed in Missouri for murdering his landlady after confrontations about his apartment.

- **Thomas Battle** was put to death in Missouri for the murder of an 82-year-old neighbor who had befriended him.

- **William Frank Parker** was executed in Arkansas for murdering the parents of his former wife. He also shot his wife, but she survived.

- **Joe Gonzales** was executed in Texas only ten months after his conviction for murdering his former boss. Gonzales acted as his own attorney and waived his appeals.

- **Richard Zeitvogel** was executed in Missouri for the murder of a fellow prisoner. The prosecution said he murdered because he *wanted to be placed on death row*.

The most prominent capital case involving family members has been evolving this year in Delaware, the nation's per capita leader in executions. When 18-year-olds Amy Grossberg and Brian Peterson were accused of murdering their newborn infant, Delaware immediately announced that it would seek the death penalty against both of them, without full knowledge of their mental state or other crucial information.

Election Year Politics

This year was an election year, and the death penalty was the focus of both highly publicized punitive legislation and campaigns demanding swifter executions. Bob Dole campaigned in front of California's death row and criticized President Clinton's appointment of judges as soft on crime. Clinton responded by emphasizing his commitment to less federal review for death row inmates. Congress cut back the opportunity for federal habeas corpus and completely defended the death penalty resource centers. States, too, pushed for more executions. Virginia, Pennsylvania and Ohio, for example, set multiple execution dates for defendants who had not yet completed their normal appeal. This manipulation of execution dates puts additional burdens on the justice system, since every death warrant results in litigation over a stay of execution, independent of the appeal arising from errors in the case.

Electoral races in which the death penalty played a prominent role produced mixed results, with some candidates surviving attacks based on their reservations about capital punishment. Sen. John Kerry of Massachusetts was re-elected in the face of Gov. William Weld's attack on his opposition to the death penalty. In California, Representatives Vic Fazio and Walter Capps were elected to the U.S. House of Representatives, even after extreme accusations that attempted to align them with the murderer of young Polly Klass.

Politicization of judicial selection intensified. One of the latest victims was Tennessee Supreme Court Justice Penny White. White lost her position on the court after a single death penalty decision in which she *upheld* the conviction of a death row inmate, but joined a decision by other justices overturning the death sentence. A conservative anti-tax group mounted a successful campaign against White, erroneously charging her of being weak on crime because of this single decision.

Twenty Years of Capital Punishment

This year marked the 20th anniversary of the Supreme Court's decision in *Gregg* v. *Georgia* upholding the constitutionality of the death penalty under newly passed statutes. However, many of the problems which the Court had identified in the application of earlier capital punishment laws, such as its arbitrariness, racial discrimination and the potential for fatal mistakes, still remain.

Innocence: Four more inmates were released from death row in 1996 after charges against them were dropped: Verneal Jimerson (Illinois), Dennis Williams (Illinois), Roberto Miranda (Nev.) and Troy Lee Jones (Calif.). This brings the total number of death row inmates released since 1973 because of evidence of their innocence to 66. In addition, two other death row inmates had their sentences commuted to life because of strong doubts about their guilt: Donald Paradis (Idaho) and Joseph Payne (Virginia). At least four other death row inmates (Joseph Spaziano (Fla.), Donald Gunsby (Fla.), Kerry Max Cook (Tex.) and Lloyd Schlup (Mo.) had their convictions overturned in 1996 and will either be retried or permanently freed from death row.

Prosecutors Indicted: In Illinois, three former prosecutors (one of whom is now a state circuit judge) were indicted for obstructing justice in the mistaken death penalty prosecution of Rolando Cruz and Alejandro Hernandez. Cruz and Hernandez were released in late 1995 after spending years on death row for a crime they did not commit. The indictments allege that the prosecutors and police officers knowingly presented false information and proceeded with the case against individuals whom they should have known were innocent.

Volunteers: An unusually high number of inmates gave up their appeals this year, thereby "volunteering" for execution. Ten of the 45 people executed this year waived their remaining appeals, including three in South Carolina. (Forty-seven of the 358 persons executed since 1976 have waived their appeals.) The isolated and demeaning conditions on death row, coupled with discouragement over an ever narrower appeal process and the lack of representation, seems to be leading more inmates to take part in state-assisted suicide.

Methods of Execution: One man was executed by a firing squad (John Taylor in Utah) and one man was hanged (Billy Bailey in Delaware). Seven people were executed in the electric chair, and the remainder were executed by lethal injection. This latter method has been promoted as more humane, but the lethal injection of Tommie Smith in Indiana this year took one hour and seventeen minutes. The executioner could not find a vein in which to inject the poison chemicals. A doctor was summoned, and eventually the lethal injection was made through Smith's leg.

International Trends: The International Commission of Jurists released a report highly critical of the death penalty in the United States, based on its visit here. The report, entitled *Administration of the Death Penalty in the United States,* states: "By ratifying the Political Covenant and the Race Convention, the United States has accepted to submit its system of punishment for criminal offenses to the judgment of international opinion; and opinion in the Western democracies is unanimous that the death penalty offends civilised standards of decency." The Commission particularly singled out the racial disparities and due process violations evident in the use of the death penalty in the U.S.: "The Mission is of the opinion that . . . the administration of capital punishment

in the United States continues to be discriminatory and unjust—and hence 'arbitrary'—and thus not in consonance with Articles 6 and 14 of the Political Covenant and Article 2(c) of the Race Convention."

Other international rights groups, including Human Rights Watch and Amnesty International, issued reports before this year's Olympics in Atlanta criticizing the death penalty in the U.S.

Who Were Executed?

As usual, the death penalty in practice looks different from the death penalty in theory. Here are descriptions of a few who were executed in 1996:

Walter Correll—The first man executed this year was an inmate in Virginia with mental retardation. Correll had an IQ of 68. His two co-defendants blamed the murder on him and received lighter sentences.

Richard Townes, Jr.—The second man executed this year was also from Virginia. Mr. Townes represented himself at trial, questioned no witnesses, and presented no mitigating evidence regarding sentencing. The jury did not know that, had he been sentenced to life, he would never have been eligible for parole. The executioners searched 22 minutes for a suitable vein before injecting the poisonous chemicals into his foot.

Billy Bailey—Bailey was hanged in the state of Delaware in January, the first hanging there in 50 years. Bailey's legs were tied with rope, and he wore a black hood which reached to his waist. When the trap door below Bailey was sprung, he dropped and twisted before being pronounced dead by a doctor.

John Taylor—was executed by firing squad in Utah in January. Five state law enforcement officers were paid $300 each to fire their rifles at Taylor's heart, which was marked by a white circle on his blue jumper. One of the five marksmen fired a blank. Taylor waived his appeals and asked to

be executed by firing squad, just as the first person executed after the death penalty's reinstatement, Gary Gilmore, was also shot in Utah at his own request.

Stephen Hatch—was executed in Oklahoma for two murders in conjunction with a robbery. Hatch's co-defendant, the actual killer in this case, was sentenced to life in prison. Members of the victims' family watched the execution, thanks to a new law sponsored by one of the family who is now a state senator in Oklahoma. Allowing the victim's family members to view executions became a trend this year.

Ellis Wayne Felker—was electrocuted in Georgia this year. Felker's case attracted attention when the U.S. Supreme Court agreed to hear, on an expedited basis, his challenge to the new law curtailing federal review. Felker won his request to be able to file for review with the Supreme Court, despite apparent restrictions in the new law to such an approach. However, the Supreme Court did not accept his claim that new evidence of his innocence should stop his execution.

Commentary: Some Signs of Change

Although there were many executions in 1996, the long-predicted "flood" of executions has not occurred, and there was some movement away from the death penalty. The movie *Dead Man Walking* received wide acclaim and an Academy Award, generating much discussion about the wisdom of capital punishment. Sister Helen Prejean, the principal figure portrayed in the movie, traveled the country, engaging audiences with her stories and message of reconciliation. Rev. Jesse Jackson's first book, written with his son, Congressman Jesse Jackson, Jr., focused on the myriad of inequities presented by the death penalty in the United States. And shortly before his own death, Cardinal Joseph Bernardin, a strong opponent of capital punishment, demonstrated an act of compassion by visiting death row inmate Raymond Stewart in Illinois before Stewart was executed.

Virginia, which led the country in executions this year, saw its juries start to turn away from the death penalty once the alternative of life without parole became available to them. Only one person has been sent to death row in Virginia since the new sentence was instituted, whereas six people had been sentenced to death the year before, and ten the year before that. Indiana and Georgia, two other states which have recently instituted life-without-parole statues, have also experienced a decline in death sentences. In Indiana, only 2 of 19 completed capital cases have resulted in a death sentence since its new law took effect in 1993. This positive movement away from the death penalty is in line with support in opinion polls for life-without-parole as an alternative to the death penalty.

 Article Review Form at end of book.

WiseGuide Wrap-Up

- Understanding that investigative methods can be used inappropriately is important in searching for solutions.

- Controlling crime means more than passing laws and rendering prison sentences.

- Protecting innocent people should be the first priority of society and appropriately punishing guilty people should be the first priority of government.

R.E.A.L. Sites

This list provides a print preview of typical **Coursewise** R.E.A.L. sites. There are over 100 such sites at the **Courselinks**™ site. The danger in printing URLs is that web sites can change overnight. As we went to press, these sites were functional using the URLs provided. If you come across one that isn't, please let us know via email to: webmaster@coursewise.com. Use your Passport to access the most current list of R.E.A.L. sites at the **Courselinks** site.

Site name: Bureau of Justice Statistics (BJS)

URL: http://www.ojp.usdoj.gov/bjs/

Why is it R.E.A.L.? This site includes databases of arrest, clearance rates, and incarceration in the United States.

Key topics: female prisoners, male prisoners, sentencing

Try this: See if you can find the number of individuals imprisoned in your state, and the leading categories of crime that led to their convictions.

Site name: International Trends in Crime Prevention

URL: http://www.crime-prevention-intl.org/english/index.htm

Why is it R.E.A.L.? This site includes an annotated bibliography about strategies that work to prevent crime in the United Kingdom, North America, South America, and European Union. One concern is to break the cycle of violence in families, communities, and schools.

Key topics: effects on family, victimization

Try this: At this site see if you can find a few new ways to help prevent crime against young persons.

Site name: Talk Justice on the World Wide Web

URL: http://talkjustice.com/

Why is it R.E.A.L.? This is an online forum dedicated to the discussion of crime and justice issues. Included at this site are publications, chat rooms, and a world of online addresses.

Key topics: alternatives to corrections, student attitudes

Try this: Get on this site to chat with other students, read some great computer jokes, and find a huge list of criminal justice sites that can help you in your studies and on your job.

section 2

Key Points

- While the majority of offenders commit few crimes over a short period of time, the majority of crime is committed by a relatively small number of persistent "career" criminals. It is important, then, to understand the differences between these types of offenders and target intervention strategies toward the persistent, career criminals.

- Historically, the criminal justice system has been inadequate in dealing with the specific needs of minority groups. With the numbers in these groups rising dramatically, these issues must be addressed.

The Correctional Client

Sarah Brown, Ph.D.
Division of Psychology, Nene-University College Northampton, Park Campus, Boughton Green Road; Northampton. NN2 7AL.   Sarah.Brown@Nene.ac.uk

WiseGuide Intro

A key criminological finding that remains consistent throughout North America and Europe is that criminals are most likely to be young males between the ages of 15 and 25. Furthermore, most individuals who commit crimes do so in their mid to late teens for a short duration of time. Indeed, most criminal careers last for less than one year. However, as with all generalizations, there are exceptions; in this case, the small proportion of offenders who commit many offenses over long periods of time.

Despite their relatively small numbers, these individuals are responsible for a large proportion of crime. It has been estimated that the 7 percent of the male population (UK) who are persistent offenders account for 60 percent of all court appearances. Similarly, in the United States, 8 percent of the population are responsible for 61 percent of most criminal court appearances. It would therefore be an advantage if we could identify delinquent juveniles likely to continue onto a career of crime, so that we could effectively target intervention strategies. In the first article, Anderson and Walsh investigate the extent to which psychological assessment of juveniles could aid us in this endeavor.

Intuitively, it would seem logical that persistent offenders can be identified. In particular, there exists a strong assumption in western societies that dangerous offenders (most often used to refer to persistent violent criminals who are likely to cause harm to others) can be distinguished from their peers. Cohen discusses this issue, which in reality is difficult and complex, in the second reading of the section.

Persistent offenders, such as these involved in acquisitive crime, are often referred to as "career criminals." These offenders often refer to their offenses as "jobs" which may or may not be "good earners." Stolen goods are dealt with by "dealers" who know their "markets." Furthermore, individuals who have given up a life of crime may be referred to as "retired." Schmalleger, in the third reading in this section, describes the lives of these career criminals.

Incapacitation is often cited as one of the aims of incarceration: prisoners are unable to commit crime while they are detained. In addition, many believe that incarceration should also provide a rehabilitative function. In the fourth reading, Stevens illustrates that, in particular circumstances in North Carolina, both these principles have been flouted. Juveniles in prison gangs maintain a life of crime while incarcerated in detention centers and continue when they are released.

As most crime is committed by young males, it follows that it is these men who can be found in prisons. In fact, the jails and prisons of Europe, Canada and the United States predominately house young males of low socioeconomic status. It is understandable, then, that the prison services of these countries are geared toward dealing with this population. However, there are minority groups of prisoners whose needs are often overlooked.

In what ways and how effectively can we predict which juveniles will progress to an adult life of crime?

To what extent is it possible to identify dangerous offenders?

In what ways do career criminals differ from other criminals and to what extent is it fair to describe crime as their occupation?

To what extent should prison authorities take the needs of minority offenders into account?

What changes should be made for these minority groups?

Women make up a tiny proportion of the prison population, less than 4 percent in the UK and in the United States there are 20 male prisoners for every one woman. However, the number of women being imprisoned has risen considerably in recent years. In the United States in the 1980s, women prisoners more than tripled in number, while in the UK the number doubled between 1992 and 1997. Feminists have long argued that the needs of women prisoners have long been overlooked, an issue which becomes increasingly important as their numbers increase. It is this issue which is addressed by the next two readings in this section.

Elderly prisoners, too, form a minority population. This subject is addressed by King and Bass in the final reading of this section. While a small number of offenders are convicted in their later years, the majority of elderly prisoners are those who are serving long sentences. With penal policy increasingly adopting a harsher approach, exemplified by the "three strikes" policies, the population of elderly inmates is certain to increase.

? Questions ?

Reading 8. To what extent can we predict adult criminality from juvenile psychological assessment? What should we do with the juveniles we assess as being likely to commit crime as adults?

Reading 9. To what extent can we predict "dangerousness"? Is it acceptable to detain people for something they *may* do in the future?

Reading 10. How do "career" criminals differ from other criminals? To what extent can crime be regarded as a "career" or "occupation"?

Reading 11. Should delinquent juveniles be detained in detention centers? Why? What should be done to eliminate prison gangs?

Reading 12. To what extent do women prisoners' experiences differ from those of male prisoners? What, if any, special provisions should be made for women inmates?

Reading 13. Why is the number of women prisoners increasing? What, if any, special provisions should be made for women prisoners?

Reading 14. How do elderly prisoners' experiences of prison differ from those of their younger peers? What, if any, special provisions should be made for elderly inmates?

To what extent can we predict adult criminality from juvenile psychological assessment? What should we do with the juveniles we assess as being likely to commit crime as adults?

Prediction of Adult Criminal Status from Juvenile Psychological Assessment

Laurence E. Anderson and James A. Walsh

Laurence E. Anderson, Trinity Western University and James A. Walsh, University of Montana, Missoula

A total of 121 juvenile offenders assigned to a regional assessment center in Medicine Hat, Alberta, Canada, for comprehensive psychological assessment between 1979 and 1984 were administered a test battery that included the WISC-R, the MMPI, and the Rorschach test. The offenders included 84 males and 37 females ages 12 to 15; among them were 48 Native Americans. In 1992, after a mean elapsed time of 9.9 years, all 121 were followed up and classified as either guilty (n = 61) or not guilty (n = 60) of a serious offense as an adult. Stepwise discriminant function analysis was used to find the best subset of variables with which to distinguish between the adults with a serious criminal record and those without. In order of importance, the four significant predictors selected from among 20 candidate variables were (a) the WISC-R comprehension subtest, (b) gender, (c) North American Native status, and (d) DQ+ from the Rorschach. A correct classification rate of 77.8% (as opposed to a base rate of 50.5%) was achieved, Chi^2 (1) = 35.01, p .001.

One of the more important problems confronting students of criminal behavior is predicting which members of a group of adolescent offenders will go on to engage in serious criminal behavior as adults, and which ones will seek a more normal lifestyle. Such studies are notoriously difficult because after the initial effort expended in obtaining and measuring a sample of young offenders, the investigator must track these more elusive individuals over appreciable distances in time and space to observe them as adults.

The need for and utility of longitudinal research has been reinforced, however, by recent studies by Moffitt (1993) and Moffitt, Caspi, Dickson, Silva, and Stanton (1996). By following a large cohort of young males from age 3 to age 18, Moffitt and colleagues (Moffitt et al., 1996; Moffitt & Lynam, 1994) were able to identify two important groups of conduct-disorder offenders: an adolescence-limited (AL) type for which adult prognosis appeared to be relatively favorable and a life-course-persistent (LCP) type for which adult prognosis appeared unfavorable.

As adolescents, these AL and LCP types were similar with respect to most indexes of antisocial behavior, but LCP boys had more difficult temperaments, were more violent, and had more psychopathic traits (Moffitt et al., 1996). In a similar vein, Krueger et al. (1994) found in a large and representative cohort of young males and females that personality measures of negative emotionality and behavioral constraint were consistent predictors of conduct disorder and problem behaviors.

Beginning in 1979, the first author administered a comprehensive battery of standardized measures of personality, psychopathology, and intellectual functioning to 121 juvenile offenders who appeared to represent the LCP type and to be at risk for adult antisocial behavior. Thus, when the opportunity arose to do a 10-year follow-up that traced these individuals into early adulthood, he was pleased to work with the federal justice system of Canada to determine their adult status and to see which of the earlier measured variables might be related to that status.

It may be worth noting that although many studies have dealt with the problem of predicting delinquent behavior in adolescents and recidivism among juvenile legal offenders (e.g., Benda, 1989; Burdsal, Force, & Klingsporn, 1989; Dembo, La Voie, & Schmeidler, 1990; Gruenewald & West, 1989; Linster, Lattimore, & Visher, 1990; Moffitt, 1990; National Council on Crime and Delinquency, 1990; Rowley, 1990; Shelden, 1989; Smith & Paternoster, 1990; Smith, Visher, & Jarjoura, 1991), relatively few have attempted to predict adult involvement with the criminal justice system (e.g., Ashford & LeCroy, 1990; Brown, Miller, & Jenkins, 1989; Lewis, 1989; Lewis, Yeager, & Cobham-Portoreal, 1991) and, to our knowledge, only a single recent study (Lie, 1988) has based predictions of adult criminal behavior solely or principally on data derived from standardized psychological assessment devices.

Methods
Setting
The locale for this study was a mixed urban-rural area of southeastern Alberta, Canada, centered around the city of Medicine Hat. Economic activity in this region of approximately 65,000 individuals includes oil and gas production, both irrigation-based and dry land farming, cattle ranching, and employment at a large military research facility. This mix was, and remains, similar to many areas in the plains and mountain states and provinces of the United States and Canada.

Participants
The participants were 121 juvenile legal offenders assigned, because of the severity of the offense (had they been adults, all would have been charged under the criminal code with offenses endangering life or property), to the provincial government's regional Youth Assessment Center in Medicine Hat. There were 84 males and 37 females whose age at assessment ranged from 12 to 15 years (M = 14.6; SD = 1.2). Forty percent were of North American Native background, including Metis. Although 70% of the participants were from southeastern Alberta, it is noteworthy that none came from farm or ranch backgrounds or from towns or villages of fewer than 2,000 people. Because all of the juvenile offenders could be considered an at-risk grouping, the generalizability of the results to be reported below must, of course, be limited to similar populations.

Assessments
All assessments were done by the first author, a clinical psychologist of some 30 years' experience at the time the assessment process began in 1979. He functioned as part of an assessment team composed of him, other psychologists, child care workers, social workers, and teachers. The team produced three reports: (a) the first author's psychological assessment; (b) a case synthesis prepared by a child care worker; and (c) a case report prepared by a teacher. . . .

Results
Stepwise discriminant function analysis (DFA) was used to find a best subset of variables from among 20 possible predictors (reduced on logical and empirical grounds from the 48 originally scored by eliminating variables with little or no variability in this sample and, for sets of variables that correlated .90 or above, by retaining only the single variable with the largest point-biserial correlation with the criterion) with which to discriminate between the 60 adults (28 males and 32 females) with no criminal record or no offense serious enough to result in imprisonment and the 61 adults (56 males and 5 females) guilty of a serious enough offense to warrant imprisonment.

The 48 original predictors were reduced to 20 to reduce the likelihood of capitalizing on chance in variable selection in the DFA. The 20 included from the WISC-R are as follows: Factor I, Factor II, Factor III, Comprehension, Similarities, Object Assembly, and Coding; from the MMPI: the Neurotic Triad, the Psychotic Tetrad, Hypochon-driasis, Depression, Hysteria, Psycho-pathic Deviate, Paranoia, and Schizophrenia; from the Rorschach: Zf-Organizing Activity, DQ+—Developmental Quality, and Hypervigilance; and from the demographic variables: gender and ethnicity. These 20 candidate predictors generally included the most reliable variables, such as the WISC-R factor scores and the Comprehension subtest; the Neurotic Triad, Psychotic Tetrad, and Schizophrenia scores from the MMPI; and the Hypervigilance Index from the Rorschach.

In order of importance, the four predictors selected in the stepwise DFA solution were (a) the WISC-R comprehension subtest, a test designed to measure a child's evaluative skills, understanding (or comprehension) of different social situations, and verbal reasoning abilities; (b) gender of participant; (c) ethnicity (i.e., North American Native or not); and (d) score on DQ+ from the Rorschach, a measure of quality of information processing. Mean scores (or proportions), standard deviations, and DFA weights of the four variables for the two groups are given in Table 1.* As an indication of the relative contributions of these four variables to the discriminant function, the squared semipartial correlations with the function are: comprehensive = .12; gender = .10; ethnicity = .06; and DQ+ = .03.

It should be noted that, because of missing data (the psychological assessment was not totally complete for all participants), four participants could not be classified under the DFA procedure; of these, two were serious offenders and two were not. All available data were used to compute the discriminant function, but only the 117 participants with complete data on the four selected variables were classified by means of the DFA procedure. Ninety-three participants (79.5%) were correctly classified and 24 (21.5%) were misclassified.

*Not included in this publication.

Because of the relatively small number of participants, splitting the sample into analysis and cross-validation subsamples was not attempted. Instead, a jackknife procedure was used to assess the robustness of the results. Because classification can be biased if the coefficients used to classify a case are based on data from the case itself, in jackknifing, the data from the case are excluded when the coefficients used to assign it to a classification are computed. Thus, each case is classified based on coefficients that are computed from all other cases. As Tabachnik and Fidell (1992) have pointed out, jackknifed classifications reduce bias and provide a more realistic idea of how well a set of predictors can separate groups.

With jackknifing, the correct classification rate dropped to 77.8% (91 and 26, respectively). The frequencies of correct and incorrect classifications for serious and nonserious offenders are given in Table 2.* Given a base rate of 50.5% expected correct classifications (because there were 59 serious offenders and 58 others), the 27.3% increase in accuracy was highly significant with Chi^2 (1) = 35.1, p < .001.

It is noteworthy that the misclassification rate was substantially higher for the nonserious offenders than for the serious offenders (19 vs. 7). Based on bootstrap statistics (Dalgleish, 1994), the relatively large differences in proportions of males and Native American participants in the two groups appear to be responsible for this discrepancy.

Discussion

These results show that it is possible to use test data and basic demographic information obtained in the course of comprehensive psychological assessments of presumably at-risk legal offenders ages 12 to 15 to make predictions of adult criminal status 10 years later, at a level of accuracy substantially better than chance (as determined by the base rate). It should be reemphasized that this conclusion pertains to at-risk youth rather than a more normal sample.

The variable that contributed most to distinguishing between the

*Not included in this publication.

serious and nonserious adult offenders was the adolescent WISC-R comprehension subtest: Adolescents with lower comprehension scores were more likely to become serious offenders as adults. As Kaufman (1979) has noted, some of the abilities shared with verbal comprehension are evaluation, common sense in cause-and-effect relationships, verbal reasoning, and social and verbal relationships, all important factors in adult social adaptation.

Kaufman (1979) has also pointed out that comprehension is affected by cultural opportunities at home, which are related to race and social class. In this study, North American Native status was found to be a significant predictor of serious offender classification. And minority group status (if their results may be generalized to minority groups other than Blacks) has been shown by Lynam, Moffitt, and Stouthamer-Loeber (1993) to be associated with lower full-scale and verbal IQ scores in juvenile delinquents. The circular cycle of causation among these variables is widely recognized.

Although the relationship between gender and offender status is complex and females are generally incarcerated at much lower rates than males (Horwitz & White, 1987; Wolfgang, Figlio, & Sellin, 1972), it was the first author's experience that lower incarceration rates for females in Western Canada during the 1980s were in part caused by a shortage of prison space for women. Thus, the interpretation of this variable should not be limited to gender considerations.

The fact that serious offenders were more likely to have lower scores on the Rorschach variable DQ+ represents a more interesting finding. Exner (1991) treats DQ+ under information processing and states that "The coding for development quality (DQ+) appears to be related to the willingness and capacity to analyze and synthesize the stimulus field in a meaningful way" (p. 355). He also reports that it correlates substantially with Z variables, sums of which are highly correlated with measures of intelligence.

In summarizing these relationships (with the exclusion of gender, which may have an artifactual component), the thread that runs through-

out appears to be intellectual skills, especially verbal ones. Juveniles with lower and less efficient verbal functioning, especially those from minority homes in which less opportunity existed to improve their verbal capacity, were more likely to commit serious offenses—those that entail imprisonment—as adults.

Although there is some tendency to view this lack of intellectual skills, especially among minority youth, as part of an intractable larger social problem, some Canadian educators (e.g., Anderson, 1987) have begun to directly address the problem by creating curricula designed to strengthen language skills as a primary means of generating greater success in school and, hopefully, of alleviating concomitant social problems such as delinquency. The effectiveness of such approaches remains to be demonstrated.

A noteworthy finding is that no measure of psychopathology was a predictor of adult criminal status, although more than 14 candidate variables were included in the analysis. This would seem to reinforce the conclusion that intellectual functioning rather than pathological processes is the prime determinant of adult offender status. However, because an at-risk sample has been employed, it may be more likely that psychopathology distinguishes both adolescent and adult offenders from nonoffenders. Thus, at-risk adolescent offenders who are incarcerated as adults may differ from at-risk adolescent offenders who are not incarcerated as adults by a lower level of verbally mediated intellectual functioning more so than by psychopathology per se.[3]

There are several more specifically methodological issues that deserve comment. The locale of the study, a relatively sparsely populated area in the West, is in many ways unrepresentative of much of Canada and the United States. But it was, and remains, similar to a great many rural and semirural places in the plains and mountain states and provinces of the United States and Canada, and deserves consideration on this account alone. Similarly, if the way in which the criminal justice system operates has changed greatly in metropolitan areas in the last 15 years, perhaps weakening the generalizability of the conclusions stated here, it is also true that both law enforcement and the administration of the judicial systems have probably remained more stable in rural and mixed urban-rural locales. But, finally, it is an unavoidable concomitant of longitudinal research that social and cultural change is an ongoing process that necessarily weakens any attempt to apply past results to future situations.

The fact that North American Native status was a significant predictor of incarceration in this study may reflect only the simple statistical fact that greater proportions of North American Native populations than of members of the majority culture are incarcerated at any one time. Given the usual concomitants of being raised in a minority culture, this seems unlikely.

One of the instruments employed in this study, the Rorschach test, has not been commonly employed in the assessment of youth offenders and, indeed, its use in psychological assessment was on the decline for years. The utility of the Rorschach seems to have been reconsidered in more recent times, however, as in a recent book, Walsh and Betz (1995) cited it as the 10th most frequently used psychodiagnostic instrument. Many psychologists use it to tap unconscious processes, and, given the fact that juvenile offenders are noteworthy for their lack of an aware and rational approach to problem solving, it was felt that its inclusion in the test battery might shed light on otherwise unavailable cognitive functions. Moreover, the effort required to use the Rorschach is concentrated primarily in the scoring rather than in the administration. Given a response record, scoring a single index such as DQ+ is not a time-consuming task, and the first author, in working with Exner, was able to obtain (with a similarly trained colleague) interrater reliabilities generally in the .80s and .90s (.91 specifically for DQ+).

The statistical technique employed, discriminant function analysis, although a powerful tool in investigating group differences, is sometimes subject to the ambiguities of interpretation problems (Tabachnick & Fidell, 1992). However, jackknife versions, such as the one used here, are relatively robust with relatively small samples and may ameliorate some interpretational problems (Dalgleish, 1994), such as the effects of gender and ethnicity mentioned in the Results section.

Finally, the time from assessment to follow-up varied from 8 to nearly 13 years, a considerable span that could be seen as resulting in the follow-up of individuals at rather different developmental stages of their lives (Rowe & Tittle, 1977). However, all of the participants were in their 20s at follow-up, and both time to follow-up and calendar age at follow-up failed to correlate significantly with any of the other variables in the study (except, of course, the correlation between age at assessment and age at follow-up).

These methodological considerations do not substantially undermine our conclusion that lack of intellectual skills, especially verbal ones and specifically those of young people in minority homes, are a key predictor of which youth offenders are likely to commit serious offenses—those that entail imprisonment—as adults.

Notes

Notes 1 and 2 are not included in this publication.

3. We thank an anonymous reviewer for helping us clarify our thinking about this matter.

References

Anderson, S. H. (1987). The oral and written discourse performance of Native American secondary students with implications concerning cross-cultural methods of academic instruction. Unpublished doctoral dissertation, University of British Columbia, Vancouver.

Ashford, J. B., & LeCroy, C. W. (1990). Juvenile recidivism: A comparison of three prediction instruments. *Adolescence, 25*, 441–450.

Benda, B. B. (1989). Predicting return to prison among adolescent males: A comparison of three statistics. *Journal of Criminal Justice, 17*, 487–500.

Brown, W. K., Miller, T. P., & Jenkins, R. L. (1989). The fallacy of radical nonintervention. *Annals of Clinical Psychiatry, 1*, 55–57.

Burdsal, C., Force, R. C., & Klingsporn, M. J. (1989). Treatment effectiveness in young male offenders. *Residential Treatment for Children and Youth, 7*, 75–88.

Dalgleish, L. I. (1994). Discriminant analysis: Statistical inferences using the jackknife and bootstrap procedures. *Psychological Bulletin, 116*, 498–508.

Dembo, R., LaVoie, L., & Schmeidler, J. (1990). A longitudinal study of the relationships among alcohol use, marijuana/hashish use, cocaine use, and emotional/psychological functioning problems in a cohort of high-risk youths. *International Journal of Addictions, 25*, 1341–1382.

deMendonca, M., Elliott, L., Goldstein, M., McNeill, J., Rodriguez, R., & Zelkind, I. (1984). An MMPI-based behavior descriptor/personality checklist. *Journal of Personality Assessment, 48*, 483–485.

Exner, J. (1976). *The Rorschach: A comprehensive system, current research and advanced interpretation* (Vol. 2). New York: John Wiley.

Exner, J. (1991). *The Rorschach: A comprehensive system, current research and advanced interpretation* (2nd ed., Vol. 2). New York: John Wiley.

Gruenewald, P. J., & West, B. R. (1989). Survival models of recidivism among juvenile delinquents. *Journal of Quantitative Criminology, 5*, 215–229.

Hathaway, S. R., & McKinley, J. C. (1951). *Manual for the Minnesota Multiphasic Personality Inventory* (Rev. ed.). New York: Psychological Corporation.

Haynes, J. P., & Bensch, M. (1981). The P > V sign on the WISC-R and recidivism in delinquents. *Journal of Consulting and Clinical Psychology, 49*, 480–481.

Horwitz, A. V., & White, H. R. (1987). Gender role expectations and styles of pathology among adolescents. *Journal of Health and Social Behavior, 28*, 158–170.

Kaufman, A. S. (1979). *Intelligent testing with the WISC-R*, New York: John Wiley.

Krueger, R. F., Schmulte, P. S., Caspi, A., Moffitt, T. E., Campbell, K., & Silva, P. A. (1994). Personality traits are linked to crime among men and women: Evidence from a birth cohort. *Journal of Abnormal Psychology, 103*, 328–338.

Lewis, D. O. (1989). Toward a theory of the genesis of violence: A follow-up study of delinquents. *Journal of the American Academy of Child and Adolescent Psychiatry, 28*, 431–436.

Lewis, D. O., Yeager, C. A., & Cobham-Portorreal, C. S. (1991). A follow-up of female delinquents: Maternal contributions to the perpetuation of deviance. *Journal of the American Academy of Child and Adolescent Psychiatry, 30*, 197–201.

Lie, N. (1988). Boys who became offenders: A follow-up study of 2203 boys tested with projective methods. *Acta Psychiatrica Scandinavia, 15*, 7–122.

Linster, R. L., Lattimore, P. K., & Visher, C. A. (1990). *Predicting the recidivism of serious juvenile offenders*. Washington, DC: National Institute of Justice.

Lynam, D., Moffitt, T., & Stouthamer-Loeber, M. (1993). Explaining the relation between IQ and delinquency: Class, race, test motivation, school failure, or self-control? *Journal of Abnormal Psychology, 102,* 187–196.

Moffitt, T. E. (1990). Juvenile delinquency and attention deficit disorder: Boys' developmental trajectories from age 3 to age 15. *Child Development, 61,* 893–910.

Moffitt, T. E. (1993). Adolescence-limited and life-course persistent antisocial behavior: A developmental taxonomy. *Psychological Review, 100,* 674–701.

Moffitt, T. E., Caspi, A., Dickson, N., Silva, P., & Stanton, W. (1996). Childhood-onset versus adolescent-onset antisocial conduct problems in males: Natural history from ages 3 to 18. *Development and Psychopathology, 8,* 399–424.

Moffitt T. E, & Lynam, D. R. (1994). The neuropsychology of conduct disorder and delinquency: Implications for understanding antisocial behavior. In D. Fowles, P. Sutker, & W. S. Goodman (Eds.), Psychopathology and antisocial personality: A developmental perspective: Vol. 18. *Progress in Experimental Personality and Psychopathology Research* (pp. 233–262). New York: Springer.

National Council on Crime and Delinquency. (1990). *Development of risk prediction scales for the California Youthful Offender Parole Board based on the assessment of 1981–82 releases.* San Francisco, CA: Author

Rowe, A. R., & Tittle, C. R. (1977). Life-cycle changes and criminal propensity. *Sociological Quarterly, 18,* 223–236.

Rowley, M. S. (1990). Recidivism of juvenile offenders in a diversion restitution program (compared to a matched group of offenders processed through court). In B. Galway & J. Hudson (Eds.), *Criminal Justice, Restitution, and Reconciliation* (pp. 151–179). Monsey, NY: Criminal Justice Press.

Shelden, R. G. (1989). The chronic delinquent: Some clarifications of a vague concept. *Juvenile and Family Court Journal, 40,* 37–44.

Smith, D. A., & Paternoster, R. (1990). Formal processing and future delinquency: Deviance amplification as selection artifact. *Law and Society Review, 24,* 1109–1132.

Smith, D. A., Visher, C. A., & Jarjoura, G. R. (1991). Dimensions of delinquency: Exploring correlates of participation, frequency, and persistence of delinquent behavior. *Journal of Research in Crime and Delinquency, 28,* 6–32.

Tabachnick, B. G., & Fidell, L. S. (1992). *Using multivariate statistics* (2nd ed.). New York: HarperCollins.

Walsh, A. (1992). The P > V sign in corrections: Is it a useful diagnostic tool? *Criminal Justice and Behavior, 19,* 372–383.

Walsh, W. B., & Betz, N. E. (1995). *Tests and assessment* (3rd ed.). Englewood Cliffs, NJ: Prentice Hall.

Wechsler, D. (1974). *Manual for the Wechsler Intelligence Scale for Children—Revised.* San Antonio, TX Psychological Corporation.

Wolfgang, M., Figlio, R. M., & Sellin, T. (1972). *Delinquency in a birth cohort.* Chicago: University of Chicago Press.

Article Review Form at end of book.

To what extent can we predict "dangerousness"? Is it acceptable to detain people for something they *may* do in the future?

A Theoretical Model for the Clinical Assessment of Dangerousness in Offender Populations

David A. Cohen, MA

Division of Forensic Psychiatry, Be'er Ya'akov Center for Mental Health P.O.B. 16, Ayalon, Prison, Ramlah, Israel. e-mail: dazc@netvision.net.il

Introduction

Mental health professionals are being called upon with increasing frequency to provide courts with dispositions regarding the dangerousness of violent and sex offenders. In certain cases, professionals are required to spontaneously report their impression that a given patient (whether inpatient or outpatient) is dangerous, and may be held liable for damages if they do not (Gage, 1990; Simon, 1990; Tarasoff v. Regents). The Judiciary demands, and expects to be provided with such assessments in parole hearings, sentencing and sexual psychopath hearings (Halleck, 1986; Pollock, 1990). Despite protests made by mental health professionals throughout the 1980's and early 1990's that dangerous behavior could not be predicted, recent literature suggests that if certain basic rules are followed clinicians can indeed accurately predict dangerousness in certain situations (Apperson, Mulvey & Lidz, 1993; Otto, 1994; Quinsey, 1995; Serin & Amos, 1995). This article reviews these rules, and suggests a method for the clinical evaluation of dangerousness using a semi-structured clinical interview. Several brief case histories will be provided to demonstrate the method's utility.

Through the 1970's and early 1980's mental health professionals were interested primarily in the "prediction" of dangerousness in violent mental patients. These predictions were based on subjective clinical interviews which concentrated on one or two variables—usually type of offense and psychiatric diagnosis. Some authors were of the opinion that these predictions were valid some of the time and in the short term—maybe—(e.g. Monhan, 1981), while others were even less optimistic and stated flat out that psychiatrists could not predict dangerousness at all (e.g. Steadman & Cocozza, 1980), and referred to psychiatrists' predictions of dangerousness as "flipping coins in the court room" (Ennis & Litwack, 1974). Research during this period (later called the "first generation") consisted almost exclusively of natural history experiments, in which recidivism of individuals released against experts' advice were assessed. Monhan (1984) suggested that "second generation thinking" should concentrate on the development of actuarial techniques, including the incorporation of clinical material into actuarial tables, studies that vary the factors used in making predictive decisions, to include situational items, and studies that vary the populations upon which predictive "technology" is brought to bear, including short term community studies (Monhan, 1984, p. 13). However, much of the "second generation" literature consisted of academic arguments over whether or not schizophrenia was related to violent behavior (e.g. Monhan, 1992, Rice & Harris, 1992)—arguments aimed at fueling another batch of one-dimensional clinically basedprediction tools. Other second generation studies concentrated on the development of actuarial tables based on "static" variables such as type of crime, age and sex of victim, school records, age of onset of criminal behavior, etc. Such attempts did not fare much better than the first generation clinical trials (Hanson & Bussiere, 1996). Hanson & Bussiere, like Monhan before them, called for the inclusion of clinical "dynamic" factors in actuarial tables—and recent research has shown that inclusion of clinical constructs such as psychopathy in actuarial assessment tools can produce instruments which are valid, reliable and easy to implement (Webster et al., 1994; Rice & Harris, 1997).

Although actuarial assessment is generally recognized as more accurate than clinical assessment (Milner & Campbell, 1995; Webster et al., 1994), and has the advantage of being objective, universal, and easy to apply, the method does have several disadvantages: A large data base must be accumulated and validated before an assessment tool is put to practical use (Quinsey et al., 1995) and the correlations on which these tools are based are relatively low (Hanson & Bussiere, 1996). Hanson and Bussiere (1996) reviewed the literature on actuarial prediction of dangerousness, and found that the correlations of the strongest predictors were r = 0.19—low even by social science standards. In a recent study Prolux et al. (1997) found that psychometric data (static or dynamic predictors) could not predict recidivism in either rapists or child molesters.

Another disadvantage of this method is that generalizations concerning a given population cannot predict the behavior of a specific member of that population (Glasser, 1996). As Nigel Walker (1991) has written: "An individual's actual risk is not something that can be readily quantified, but it is more real—and sometimes greater—than any actuarial statistic, which probably lies in no man's land" (p. 752). Another problem is that while actuarial models can give a general estimate of if recidivism will occur, they provide little information about when recidivism will occur or how it can be reduced (Mulvey & Lidz, 1995), and therefore are not easily adaptable as tools for planning risk reduction.

Clinical assessment has been criticized as highly subjective, tending to over-estimate dangerousness, relying on highly salient information which has little predictive value, and ignoring base rates (Quinsey, 1995). There is no known set of personality characteristics that can differentiate the sexual abuser from the non-abuser (ATSA, 1997), so it is hard to say how a clinical assessment of dangerousness is made.

Despite these criticisms, there is a growing awareness that clinical assessments can be used to provide accurate and useful information if they are based on a standardized, universal methodology (Litwack, Kirschner & Wack, 1993; Mulvey & Lidz, 1995; Monhan & Steadman, 1996; Serin et al., 1997). Several years ago Litwack (Litwack, Kirschner & Wack, 1993) revised his criticism and concluded that clinically based risk assessments can be useful in aiding courts' decisions about certain offenders. He suggested that future research focus on *how* clinical evaluations are made in actual *practice*. Since then several authors have written on their methods of clinical decision making (e.g. Mulvey & Lidz, 1995, Quinsey, 1995, Serin et al., 1997; Webster et al., 1994).

This paper proposes a theoretical model for the clinical assessment of dangerousness. The model is not based on the similarity of a given person to a group of others nor on subjectively diagnosed clinical constructs which may or may not be related to dangerousness. Rather the model rests on the comparison of the biopsychosocial "situation" under which a person manifested dangerous behavior to his biopsychosocial "situation" at the time of evaluation. This model rests on four theoretical foundations:

Theoretical Basis for Proposed Model

Relative vs. Absolute Assessment

Dangerousness may be defined as "the potential to do serious physical and/or psychological harm to others and the probability of this potential being put into practice (Glasser, 1996). Assessing dangerousness may be defined as the systematic analysis of information, and the subsequent drawing of conclusions regarding a person's dangerousness. These definitions agree with Monhan & Steadman's (1996) assertion that assessments of dangerousness should be phrased in terms of low, moderate, high and very high risk, in order to facilitate clinical and legal decision making. The accuracy of 'black and white' dichotomous predictions of "dangerous" or "not dangerous" is hard to prove, and such predictions lump together patients who may need different therapeutic or legal approaches for the management or reduction of their dangerous behavior. Phrasing assessments in terms of relative risk emphasize possible treatment courses by forcing clinicians to consider situational variables which enhance or mitigate risk (Monhan, 1988; McNiel & Binder, 1991).

Multi-Variable Assessment

Dangerous behavior, like other human behavior, is a complex concept and cannot be "predicted" based on any single predictor variable. Megargee (1976) warned that both personality and situational factors must be taken into account in the assessment of dangerousness, and even provided detailed instructions for decision making based on this idea. Monhan and others (Hepworth, 1985; Monhan, 1988; Monhan & Klassen, 1982, Nachshon, 1982; Steadman & Ribner, 1982) have also stressed the importance of situational factors. Today, it is accepted that violent behavior, and therefore dangerousness, is a complex behavior which, like other behaviors is determined by biological, psychological and sociological factors (Bender, 1991, Eron, 1994; Litwack, 1994; Pollock, 1990; Quinsey, 1995; Saddler & Huglus,

1992), and it goes without saying that all such factors must be assessed in order to produce an accountable assessment of dangerousness.

Projective Nature of Assessment

Ecclesiastes (I:9) taught that "Only that shall happen which has happened, only that occur which has occurred". In clinical terms, this means that "dangerousness cannot be predicted in the absence of an established pattern of violence" (Litwack, 1994; Hall, 1987; Kozol, 1982; Pollock, 1990). For this reason, a thorough understanding of past criminal behavior is critical to any assessment of future dangerousness. Clinicians must be able to review not only the criminal records of the person being assessed, but also be able to understand the personality and situational factors which led to past violent behaviors, and be able to understand how these factors may influence future violent behaviors. In this case "pattern" entails at least two previous behaviors similar to the one being assessed. A one time offense does not necessarily constitute a pattern of behavior or a criminal lifestyle. Therefore it is important to obtain information from legal or social services, or even from family members regarding previous behaviors which may not have been reported, or which may have been reported but did not result in conviction or incarceration. When looking for a "pattern" of violence, one must elicit information on biological, psychological, and situational factors which may have served to either facilitate or inhibit violence in the past. The expert must be able to describe, with at least some accuracy and conviction, both to himself and to the Court, not only why the offender did what he did, but why he did it when he did, why he didn't do something else (e.g., if a rapist suffers from no identifiable paraphilia, why did he rape and not just beat his victim) and under what conditions he would be likely to do it again.

Situational Assessment

Assessments of dangerousness are situational. For example, Israeli psychiatrists are often called upon to assess dangerousness in various familial or hospital settings. Clinical criminologists working in prisons are called upon to assess dangerousness of prisoners before furlough or before parole. Each assessment is made in accordance with a specific request from the court or the prison service. For example, when asked to assess dangerousness of a sex offender, the assessment will refer only to sexual dangerousness, not to other types of dangerous behavior. The conclusions of assessments made for behavior in a given situation may not be the same as those given in another. A prisoner may be assessed as not dangerous for a 24-hour furlough from prison, during which he must sign in twice daily at the local police station, but he may indeed be found to be to dangerous to be granted parole—a situation in which he is free for long periods of time with varying degrees of supervision. Inherent in this principle is the assumption that dangerousness is dynamic and not static, and that a persons' level of dangerousness may change and must therefore be reassessed from time to time (Policy in Israeli prisons is to assess offenders at least once monthly for prisoners eligible for monthly furloughs and quarterly for offenders who have been judged to dangerous for such furloughs).

Suggested Formula for the Assessment of Dangerousness

The four principles mentioned above, relative probability, multi-dimensional assessment, the need to establish prior patterns of dangerous behavior, and the situational specificity of the assessment, form a basis for valid, reliable assessments of dangerousness, and the basic rules from which all others follow. Based on the above, we may propose dangerous behavior is a reaction which becomes manifest when certain biological, psychological, and environmental factors converge. It is most likely to become manifest in the future under the same circumstances in which it has been manifest in the past. Therefore, the probability of future dangerous behavior is based on the similarity of the situation for which the patient is being evaluated now to situations in which he was violent in the past. "Situation" is used as a generic term referring to biological, psychological and environmental conditions. This rule can be expressed in the simple formula

$$P(D_2) = [(B_2 \times P_2 \times E_2) - (B_1 \times P_1 \times E_1)]$$

Where $P(D_2)$ is the probability of future dangerous behavior (which specific behavior varies from situation to situation and from offender to offender). B_2, P_2 & E_2 are biological psychological and environmental factors valid at the time of the examination, and B_1, P_1 & E_1 are these same factors at times in the past when dangerous behavior was observed. The greater the similarity between the past and the present, the closer $P(D_2)$ is to 0 and the greater the probability that the dangerous behavior will repeat itself.

Theoretically, the factors B, P & E may be divided into facilitating and inhibiting factors. Facilitating factors for various types of violent behavior include mental illness (Monhan, 1992), organic disorders, (Doerr & Carlin, 1991; Hales & Yudofsky, 1987, Nachshon, 1990), object relations (Kernberg, 1992), especially borderline pathology (Hart, Dutton & Newlove, 1993; Dutton, 1994), psychopathy or antisocial personality disorder (Serin & Amos, 1995; Tiihonen & Hakola, 1994), alcohol addiction (Rice & Harris, 1995), cognitive deficits or deficits in empathic ability (Roys, 1997), familial discord or family situation (Barnett, Fagan & Booker, 1991; Freund, Watson & Dickey, 1992). Inhibiting factors include controls such as familial support, probation, past or continuing medication or psychotherapy, victim empathy and insight. (Hepworth, 1985; Reckless, 1967). These factors must be assessed as they were at the time of the offense as opposed to as they are at the time of evaluation for future dangerousness. Changes are facilitated through medication or through therapy, which must include an offense and (where relevant) an addiction-specific component. Assessors should be wary of offenders assertions that they have changed without any help, that their offense was a one time event for which they bear limited responsibility and which will never reoccur.

As much of as possible of the necessary information should be substantiated by collateral information from an objective source. Court records are readily available to forensic clinicians and community-based social workers, as well as psychiatric intakes and previous assessments of dangerousness which can provide information on past behavior and mental criminogenic and familial status. A structural clinical interview (Kernberg, 1981, 1984) designed to assess borderline pathology and object relations is an excellent framework for assessing such dangerousness. The traditional structural interview starts by asking the patient how he feels, what his complaints are and why he has come for treatment. The forensic interview should start by explaining the purpose of the examination, the patient's rights regarding the examination and possible outcome. This brief encounter usually elicits useful information not only regarding the patient's ability to give informed consent to the examination, but also regarding his basic level of object relations. For example, in certain patients my explanation that the patient has the right to appeal if he does not like my opinion may elicit a blatant paranoid reaction and panic, such as "What—have you been talking to my wife? What (expletive) has she tried to tell you about me?" or it may elicit a more manipulative, psychopathic reaction such as "but you're such a nice person—and I can tell that your religious—why would you write anything bad about me?" Such opening statement also elicits information about the patient's attitude towards his crime. For example, when I inform sex offenders that they are being examined because parole boards require mental health assessment of all sex offenders, replies range anywhere from the prognostically grave "well you can forget it, because I didn't do anything" to the more hopeful "yes it was a terrible crime which I have discussed many times with my social worker". These responses indicate the direction of the interview, in that together with objective information obtained from outside sources they provide bases for clarification and confrontation which are integral parts of the structural interview. The assessment must include a thorough discussion of the offense and the offenders attitude toward that offense, including clarification and confrontation of the offender's vs. the victim's

and the court's version of his crimes (ATSA, 1997).

Information elicited from the clinical interview and collateral information should be integrated with static predictors of dangerousness connected with the specific crime committed by the offender they are assessing (e.g., gender of victim, relationship to victim, age at offense and previous sex crimes in the case of sex offenders [Hanson, 1997]). The final recommendation should be phrased in terms of relative levels of dangerousness (high, moderate, low) and enumerate conditions necessary to mitigate dangerousness. For example offenders who present a threat to a specific person or persons (son or daughter, spouse, young boys or girls) may be assessed as low risk in situations where they have no contact with potential victims, but high risk if they are not limited to such situations or if they are incapable of complying with set limitations.

This method of assessment has the advantage of identifying high or low risk situations in which crimes are more or less likely to be committed and provides a basis for risk assessment and risk management (Serin et al., 1997; Heliburn, 1997). By identifying different factors which contribute to offending, informed decisions can be made regarding the choosing of an environment into which an offender may be safely released, the optimal level of supervision, and the type of relapse prevention best suited to the offender.

Clinical Example
Benny, 40 years old, married + 3. No previous criminal record, normal childhood, grows flowers for a living, no special problems—not in any high risk category. One day on the way home from work he picked up a hitchhiker and raped her. He was released on bail. A few months later—still out on bail—he again raped a hitchhiker on the way home from work. He is sentenced to 12 years in prison and classified as highly dangerous as a recidivist sex offender who has committed a second rape while out on bail. During assessment for dangerousness during prison leave it was ascertained that at the time he committed these crimes his

wife was either in the midst of a dangerous pregnancy or recuperating from a hard birth. He reported high levels of stress and sexual frustration—an unusual circumstance in a quiet easy-going person. He reported that in the first case he did not see himself as having committed a rape, and saw his release on bail as a sign that he was not guilty and that the sexual contact with the victim was consensual. His wife also saw the rape as infidelity, and forgave him. He also reported that during the second rape he did not use force, but knew the whole time that he was going to get into trouble for cheating on his wife again. So from the point of the "situation" at the time of the crimes there was unusual stress and sexual frustration, total misunderstanding of what he was doing, and a relatively open and forgiving environment. At the assessments in the beginning of his incarceration he totally denied his offenses, a reaction seen as a defense against stress trauma and shame of incarceration of being labeled a sex offender. After repeated confrontation with victims' statements and court records he admitted to consensual sex, and then to rape. After several months he realized that he had committed rape, but could not understand how or why, or fully understand the magnitude of his crimes. At this point—after several assessments in which he was judged to be still dangerous—the psychiatrist in charge changed her recommendation and recommended limited home leaves. His stress had gone down and he was functioning well. There were no discernible problems with formal thought or impulse control. He was terrified of having his leave revoked, and knew that the slightest deviation from the given restrictions would result in immediate revocation of privileges. He was allowed out for short periods, allowed outside only during the day and with his wife and had to sign twice daily in the police station. After several successful leaves he was moved to an open prison and enrolled in a sex offender treatment group, had regular sessions with a criminologist and enrolled in a sex offender therapy group. As time progressed he was able to explore the processes leading to the rapes, to understand the victims' reactions, and even to feel guilt and express empathy. As he progressed and I felt his internal controls were stronger, the external controls were relaxed. Sessions with his wife increased her awareness of his crimes. Towards the end of his incarceration he had only one session per month with me and bi-weekly with a social worker. He successfully completed a work release program, and after a further assessment I classified him as low risk. Based on the changes in his wife's position and the changes in empathy and cognition he was granted parole.

References

Apperson L. I., Mulvey, E. P., & Lidz, C. W. (1993). "Short-term clinical prediction of assaultive behavior: Artifacts of research methods." *American Journal of Psychiatry, 150,* 1374–1379.

ATSA (1997). *Ethical Standards and Principles for the Management of Sexual Abusers.* Beaverton, OR: ATSA.

Barefoot v. Estelle, 463 U.S. 880. (1983).

Barnett, O. W., Fagan, R. W., & Booker, J. M. (1992). "Hostility and stress as mediators of aggression in violent men." *Journal of Family Violence, 6,* 217–241.

Bender, E. P. (1991). "Looking ahead: New psychiatry, old values." *American Journal of Psychiatry, 148,* 1123–1129.

Doerr, H. O., & Carlin, A. S. (1991). *Forensic Neuropsychology: Legal and Scientific Bases.* NY: Guilford.

Dutton, D. G. (1994). "Behavioral and affective correlates of borderline personality organization in wife assaulters." *International Journal of Law & psychiatry, 17,* 265–277.

Ennis, B. J., & Litwack, T. R. (1974). "Psychiatry and the presumption of expertise: Flipping coins in the courtroom." *California Law Review, 62,* 693–752.

Eron, L. D. (1994). "Theories of aggression: From drives to cognitions." In: L. R. Huesmann (ed.) *Aggressive Behavior: Current Perspectives.* NY: Plenum. pp. 3–11.

Freund, K., Watson, R., & Dickey, R. (1992). "Sex offenses against female children perpetrated by men who are not pedophiles." *Journal of Sex Research, 29,* 409–423.

Gage, B. C. (1990). "The duty to protect in inpatient psychiatry." In: J. C. Beck, ed. *Confidentiality Versus the Duty to Protect.* Washington, D.C.: APA Press. pp. 55–76.

Glasser, M. (1996). "The assessment and management of dangerousness: The psychoanalytical contribution." *Journal of Forensic Psychiatry, 7,* 271–283.

Hales, R. E., & Yudofsky, S. C. (1987). *American Psychiatric Press Textbook of Neuropsychiatry.* Washington, D.C.: APA Press.

Hall, H. V. (1987). *Violence Prediction. Guidelines for the Forensic Practioner.* Springfield, IL: Thomas.

Halleck, S. L. (1986). *The Mentally Disordered Offender.* Rockville, MD: NIMH.

Hanson, R. K. (1997). *The Development of a Brief Actuarial Risk Scale for Sexual Offense Recidivism.* Canada: CSC.

Hanson, R. K., & Bussiere, M. T. (May, 1996) http://198.103.98.38/crd/forum/e082/e 082c.htm "sex offender risk predictions" Forum on Corrections Research.

Hart, S. D., Dutton, D. G., & Newlove, T. (1993). "The prevalence of personality disorder among wife assaulters." *Journal of Personality Disorders, 7,* 329–341.

Hepworth, D. (1985). "Dangerousness and the mental health tribune." In: D. P. Farrington & J. Gunn (eds.) *Aggression and Dangerousness.* NY: Wiley. pp. 155–183.

Kernberg, O. F. (1981). "Structural interviewing." *Psychiatric Clinics of North America, 4,* 169–195.

Kernberg, O. F. (1984). *Severe Personality Disorders.* New Haven, CT: Yale University Press.

Kernberg, O. F. (1992). *Aggression in Personality Disorders and Perversions.* New Haven, CT: Yale University Press.

Kozol, H. L. (1982). "Dangerousness in society and law." *University of Toronto Law Review, 13,* 241–267.

Litwack, T. R. (1994). "Assessments of dangerousness: Legal, research, and clinical development." *Administration and Policy in Mental Health, 21,* 361–377.

Litwack, T. R., Kirschner, S. M. & Wack, R. C. (1993). "The assessment of dangerousness and predictions of violence: Recent research and future prospects." *Psychiatric Quarterly, 64,* 245–273.

McNiel, D. E., & Binder, R. E. (1991). "Clinical assessment of the risk of violence among psychiatric inpatients." *American Journal of Psychiatry, 148,* 1317–1321.

Megargee, E. I. (1976). "The prediction of dangerous behavior." *Criminal Justice & Behavior, 3,* 3–21.

Milner, J. S., & Campbell J. C. (1995). "Prediction issues for practitioners." In J. C. Campbell (Ed.), *Assessing Dangerousness: Violence by Sexual Offenders, Batterers and Child Abusers* (pp. 20–40). Thousand Oaks, CA: Sage.

Monhan J. (1981). *The Clinical Prediction of Violent Behavior.* Washington, D.C.: GPO.

Monhan, J. (1984). "The prediction of violent behavior: Toward a second generation of theory and policy." *American Journal of Psychiatry, 141,* 10–15.

Monhan, J. (1988). "Risk assessment of violence among the mentally disordered: Generating useful knowledge." *International Journal of Law & Psychiatry, 11,* 249–257.

Monhan, J. (1992). "Mental disorders & violent behavior: Perceptions & evidence." *American Psychologist, 47,* 511–521.

Monhan, J., & Klassen, D. (1982). "Situational approaches to understanding and predicting individual violent behavior." In: M. Wolfgang & N. Weiner (eds.), *Criminal Violence.* Beverly Hills: Sage. pp. 292–319.

Monhan, J., & Steadman, H. J. (1996). "Violent storms and violent people: How meteorology can inform risk communication in mental health law." *American Psychologist, 51,* 931–938.

Mulvey, E. P., & Lidz, C. W. (1995). "Conditional prediction: A model for dangerousness to others in a new era." *International Journal of Psychiatry & Law, 18,* 129–143.

Nachshon, I. (1982). "Toward biosocial approaches in criminology." *Journal of Social Biological Structures, 5,* 1–9.

Nachshon, I. (1990). "Neurological bases of crime, psychopathy, and aggression." In: L. Ellis & R. E. Hoffman (eds.) *Crime in Biological Social and Moral Contexts.* NY: Basic Books.

Otto, R. K. (1994). "On the ability of mental health professionals to 'predict dangerousness': A commentary on interpretations of the 'dangerousness literature'. " *Law & Psychology Review, 18,* 43–68.

Perris, C. (1989). *Cognitive Therapy with Schizophrenic Patients.* NY: Guilford Press.

Pollock, N. L. (1990). "Accounting for predictions of dangerousness." *International Journal of Psychiatry and Law, 13,* 207–215.

Prolux, J., Pellerin, B., Paradis, Y., McKibben, A., Aubot, J. & Ouimet, M. (1997). "Static and dynamic predictors of recidivism in sexual aggressors." *Sexual Abuse: A Journal of Research and Treatment, 9,* 7–27.

Quinsey, V. L. (1995). "The prediction and explanation of criminal violence." *International Journal of Psychiatry & Law, 18,* 117–127.

Quinsey, V. L., Lalumiere, M. L., Rice, M. E., & Harris, G. T. (1995). "Predicting sexual offenses." In: J. C. Campbell (Ed.), *Assessing Dangerousness: Violence by Sexual Offenders, Batterers and Child Abusers.* Thousand Oaks, CA: Sage.

Reckless, W. C. (1967). *The Crime Problem.* NY: Appelton, Century, Crofts.

Rice, M. E., & Harris, G. T. (1992). "A comparison of criminal recidivism among schizophrenic and non-schizophrenic offenders." *International Journal of Law & Psychiatry, 15,* 397–408.

Rice, M. E., & Harris, G. T. (1995). "Psychopathy, schizophrenia, alcohol abuse and violent recidivism." *International Journal of Law and Psychiatry, 18,* 333–342.

Rice, M. E., & Harris, G. T. (1997). "Cross-validation and extension of the violence risk appraisal guide for child molesters and rapists." *Law and Human Behavior, 21,* 231–241.

Roys, D. T. (1997). "Empirical and theoretical considerations of empathy in sex offenders." *International Journal of Offender Therapy and Comparative Criminology 41,* 53–64.

Saddler, J. Z., & Huglus, Y. F. (1992). "Clinical problem solving and the biopsychosocial model." *American Journal of Psychiatry, 149,* 1315–1323.

Serin, R., Barbaree, H., Seto, M., Malcom, B., & Peacock, E. (May, 1997). "A Model for a Clinically-Informed Risk Assessment Tool." CSC Research Reports [Online], Available: http://www.csc-scc.gc.ca/crd/reports/r56e/r56e.htm.

Serin, R. C., & Amos, N. L. (1995). "The role of psychopathy in the assessment of dangerousness." *International Journal of Psychiatry & Law, 18,* 231–238.

Simon, R. I. (1990). "The duty to protect in private practice." In: J. C. Beck, ed. *Confidentiality Versus the Duty to Protect.* Washington, D. C.: APA Press. pp. 23–42.

Steadman, H. J., & Cocozza, J. J. (1980). "The prediction of dangerousness—Baxtrom: A case study." In: G. Cooke, ed. *The Role of the Forensic Psychologist.* Springfield, IL: Thomas. pp. 204–215.

Steadman, H. J., & Ribner, S. (1982). "Life stress and violence among ex-mental patients." *Social Science in Medicine, 16,* 1641–1647.

Tarasoff v. Regents of U. of California, 551 P2d 344, 17 Cal3d 425 (Cal Sup Ct 1976).

Tiihonen, J., & Hakola, P. (1994). "Psychiatric disorders and homicide recidivism." *American Journal of Psychiatry, 151,* 436–438.

Walker, N. (1991) "Dangerous Mistakes." *British Journal of Psychiatry, 158,* 752–757.

Webster, C. D., Harris, G. T., Rice, M. E., Cormier, C. & Quinsey, V. L. (1994). *The Violence Prediction Scheme: Assessing Dangerousness in High Risk Men.* Toronto: Centre of Criminology, University of Toronto.

Article Review Form at end of book.

How do "career" criminals differ from other criminals? To what extent can crime be regarded as a "career" or "occupation"?

World of the Career Criminal

Frank Schmalleger

During one of my first visits to a prison, as an admittedly naïve student of criminal justice, I asked an unrepentant inmate how he could be satisfied with his life as a burglar. Why, I inquired, didn't he look for an honest, steady job? We argued this point until he became so frustrated that he threw up his hands in disgust and said, "Look, you and me, we live in different worlds."

I did not realize how true that remark was until years later. Of course the burglar was right. Most of us believe that the majority of convicts are simply people who fell on hard times and turned to crime. But over the past decade I have talked to prisoners throughout the United States—first as a student and later as a professor of criminal justice—and I have learned that most of us are wrong. Although my conclusion is bound to be controversial, I am convinced that the habitual offender lives in a world apart from what may be called conformist society. Most convicts are professional criminals. They have been socialized into lives of crime just as the rest of us have been socialized into lives of conformity.

In our society people have a tendency to lump all criminals together, whether rapists, robbers, or murderers—except perhaps for making a sharp distinction between "white-collar" criminals and violent street thugs. A more relevant distinction, and one that criminals themselves recognize, is that crime is a *way of life* for some and the result of unfortunate circumstances and personal pathology for others.

It is important for us to take this distinction seriously because it challenges many widely held ideas about crime and criminals. If poverty and unemployment are principal sources of crime, as many sociologists suggest, then all we have to do is provide jobs and decent incomes. And yet most hardened criminals spurn conventional employment and mock those who work for a living. If people become criminals because of emotional disturbances or psychological impairment, then we should be able to set them straight through various forms of psychotherapy. But present therapeutic programs in prisons fail more often than they succeed— for reasons I shall discuss—and the vast majority of convicted felons go back to lives of crime whenever they get out of jail.

Prison is not necessarily an unpleasant experience for the career criminal. He may even regard an occasional prison sentence as a kind of vacation and as an opportunity to cultivate new criminal associations. Once when I was visiting a Southern penitentiary, an inmate spotted a former prisoner, who had recently been convicted for another crime, being processed in the compound, and said: "Look at all those men at the fence hollering. It's like old home week. He's gonna get some good meals and he's back with his friends. He don't have to worry."

Because most of us don't know the criminal world, we often accept the notion that better prison facilities, more humane treatment, and stronger rehabilitation programs—all valid in their own right—will cure convicted felons of their criminal habits. But the career criminal sees himself as a legitimate professional, a view reinforced by his peculiar subculture. He is indeed a member of an "underworld." Perhaps it is time we recognized that there may be validity in the claim by policemen and district attorneys that most repeat offenders are criminals out of choice and not out of necessity or unhappy circumstance.

Professional criminals not only hold square society in contempt, they also have little respect for the amateur or chance criminal whose incarceration results from a twist of fate rather than from criminal dedication. At the North Carolina Correctional Center for Women, I met an inmate serving a life sentence for the murder of her lover. Until the time of the murder she had led a conventional life and had never been involved in crime. With a nervousness that betrayed her desperation she told me: "I'm not like these other women. I can't talk to them. They're the kind of people I was always afraid of. Don't you see, I'm not really a criminal."

Of course, murder is a serious crime, but it is not an activity that even habitual offenders often choose as an occupation. Personal identities are built on careers, and radical changes in self-image rarely result from isolated acts of violence. Put simply, it is one thing to be labeled "criminal" by society, but quite another to think of oneself as criminal. Just how many individuals labeled "criminal" by society have built careers on lawbreaking is difficult to determine, but recidivism statistics can shed some light on the question. Criminologists generally agree that around 70 percent of all convicted felons will be arrested again within five years of their original conviction or prison release date. Some states have habitual-offender statutes under which repeaters receive long prison terms. Yet naïve offenders who have committed a single serious crime typically receive harsher penalties than the career criminal who makes a living by preying on society. Such sentencing procedures serve the ends of punishment much better than they protect society.

Criminality is an attitude toward life that, more often than not, begins in youth, generally in the preteen or early teen years. Many of the inmates I have met have been in trouble nearly all of their lives. When interviewed, they recall that as children they craved excitement. Constantly seeking thrills, they saw most other children as weak, and they now see conforming adults in the same light. Their first real crimes, most often vandalism, stealing, and drug abuse, usually involved a small group of like-minded thrill seekers.

These early crimes tend to be committed under peer pressure and are seen as fun. Eventually the young troublemaker recognizes how profitable crime can be and begins to commit crimes more for gain than for excitement. As he becomes adult, childhood theft is replaced by armed robbery and burglary. Some offenses, such as drug use, assault, and certain sex crimes, may be committed in order to maintain an impressive reputation within criminal society rather than for profit.

Not only does crime pay financially, but the odds against being caught and punished also favor the criminal. Estimates (based on FBI statistics and independent victimization surveys) are that out of every 100 people who commit serious crimes, only one receives a prison sentence, and many of those punished are probably inexperienced first offenders. (By serious crimes I mean those classified as Part One offenses by the FBI: murder and non-negligent manslaughter, forcible rape, robbery, aggravated assault, burglary, larceny-theft, and motor vehicle theft.) The chance of being imprisoned for lesser crimes, even if the person is a habitual offender, is about one in 300. Furthermore, plea bargaining—pleading guilty to a lesser offense—results in reduced sentences in roughly 80 percent of both state and federal criminal cases.

Accompanying the need for excitement is the development of manipulative skills. Career criminals pride themselves on their ability to talk their way out of trouble and to control others. At an early age they learn how to exploit weaknesses in the criminal justice system, playing one part of the system against another. Like bargain hunters in a department store, they shop around, offering the police or prosecutor information in exchange for leniency. As their contacts with the system multiply, so do their skills. Sometimes they are successful enough to con their way out of prosecution. In a recent case in North Carolina, a female hitch-hiker and two male companions kidnapped the occupants of a car that had stopped to pick them up. All the occupants were robbed and one was murdered. After agreeing to testify against her companions, the woman was tried on a lesser charge. Criminologist Jerome Skolnick reports a case involving two burglars caught in the act who helped the police "clear the books" by confessing to 500 additional (previously unsolved) burglaries. One of the burglars served a four-month prison sentence; the other was allowed to complete a sentence he was already serving and was released after 30 days.

No matter what the situation, career criminals see their environment in terms of chances that may or may not be worth taking. Let me cite a case in point. Not long ago a convicted thief and drug user with a history of offenses beginning in his preteens came to visit me while he was on probation. After he left I noticed that a pocket watch, which had great sentimental value, was missing. I called his probation officer, who recovered the watch. When asked why he had taken it, the probationer said simply: "I didn't think they'd miss it. They might of thought it was lost."

The special consciousness of the career criminal comes through clearly in the remarks of a 30-year-old convicted burglar. "You have to look at things in a special way to be a burglar," he told me. "You learn things. You think of how much noise you make. If you're gonna cut through a roof, you don't take a power saw. You do it by hand, and on a quiet night you saw only when traffic goes by. You look for things most people don't see—can't see. Shadows are important. So is anything you can hide behind. People can look straight at you and not see you if you're in the right place."

The criminal world attracts its members from among habitual offenders by providing a ready-made system of meaning. Criminal reality—criminals' perception of the world—is the mechanism through which life becomes comprehensible. It tells criminals who they are, who others are, which actions are significant and what they mean. In short, it endows criminal life with purpose. The concepts of criminal reality characterize criminal thought *itself*, while those of conformist reality provide a framework for theories *about* crime.

And yet it is not enough to draw a simple line between career criminals and conformists. Criminals, like the rest of us, vary greatly. Consider differences in status. Criminal careers that require exposure to personal danger and refined technical skills are the most highly regarded. The armed robber receives deference from the thief. Even conformist society glorifies the bold, skillful criminal, especially when the crime is of some magnitude. The widespread appeal of films like *The Sting* attests to this.

But all professional criminals share one characteristic: They live outside the law. Although the pimp, the drug dealer, the robber, and the burglar are involved in vastly different careers, which may or may not overlap, the energies of all are channeled into illegal pursuits and their livelihood usually depends on crime. They continue to enjoy the thrill of breaking the law and generally have as much trouble going straight as conformists would have stepping into lives of crime. Correctional programs that provide occupational skills and job placement for habitual offenders are more likely to produce job-holding criminals than conformists.

Living in a world of illegitimacy creates a time frame for the criminal in which the primary locus of reality is the here and now and the not-too-distant future. Long-range goals are rarely given much thought. As one inmate told me when I asked him about his attitude toward the future: "The present is what counts. Tomorrow is not a promise. I could get shot down with bullets the next minute." He was, of course, referring to his life on the streets.

This stunted time frame helps explain criminal behavior. All human action is significant only in relation to the end result. For example, a university education is meaningful to the conformist who plans to become a doctor or engineer. But because the temporal structure of the criminal world does not relate present behavior to distant goals, the significance of actions depends on immediate experience. The criminal does not postpone gratification; if he wants a car, or a color television set, instead of borrowing or saving the necessary money, he steals it. During a philosophical discussion, a felon serving time in a Midwestern prison told me, "If you don't live in the now, you don't live anywhere."

The fact that many criminals leave numerous clues or break the law where they are sure to be recognized has been explained by some psychologists as an indication that many criminals want to be caught. But I think this theory is a bit of conformist thinking. As I interpret criminal thought, imperfect crimes result from the criminal's emphasis on immediate goals.

Individuals called "criminal" by the criminal justice system are not necessarily judged that way by criminals themselves. The career offender experiences little personal guilt, because criminal subcultures provide sanctions for his or her behavior. Called "rationalizations" by conformists, these sanctions structure reality in a way that favors criminal enterprise and provides the knowledge necessary for individual self-understanding. Once, while on a field trip with students to a local prison, I used the word "rationalization" in questioning the reasons a prisoner gave for his habitual, crimes. "O.K.," he said. "You call that rationalizations. I know what the word means. But what you folks is doing . . . that's rationalizations. We appreciate you coming here . . . but you come because you can't stand the guilt of putting us in here."

For the conformist who has committed a crime, the consequences—discovery, formal conviction, and imprisonment—can, and usually do, have a shattering effect. But the career criminal considers these legal mechanisms irrelevant. "I don't give a damn what society says about me," an inmate in an Ohio prison told me; "I know who my friends are and I go by what they say. I don't let society tell me how to think." Asked who his friends were, he continued, "They're people just like me. Some in here, some out there. They don't buy all that propaganda society is putting out. They know what's really important."

A convicted drug dealer rationalized his activity this way: "I turn people on to the truth. That's why society is afraid of drugs . . . because they're afraid of the truth." He was certain that if enough people learned the "truth" the present social order would be replaced by enlightened leadership. Belief in his Messianic role and in the significance of drugs was strongly supported by his fellow criminals, both on the streets and in prison. His imprisonment and the vehement denial of his "truth" by conformists only made him more certain that his interpretation was right.

As in conformist culture, generational differences flavor the ways criminals legitimate illegal activities. Property crimes probably have a longer history of sanction than do other crimes. An older criminal, socialized into criminal reality before the 1960s, defended his activities by observing: "Robbing banks, stealing cars, burglary, all that doesn't hurt anybody. Everybody's got insurance. And most of them wouldn't miss it anyway."

The radical rhetoric of the 1960s has not been lost on younger offenders, whose language reflects the reality they perceive. They never had a chance to make it in the straight world, they say, because of early deprivations, discrimination, and so on. A corollary theme among them is that most people who are victimized by crime deserve what they get, since they are the oppressors of the lower classes. Some young criminals see themselves as revolutionaries, waging war against an unjust society. Robbery, burglary, theft, and even violent crime are, in their view, simply guerrilla tactics that are made necessary by a power structure that imprisons the poor.

A prisoner in Marion, Ohio, who wore a Che Guevara outfit, explained his involvement in burglary to me as follows: "What whitey has is mine. But he won't share. So I takes it from him." Later he said, "The distribution of wealth is unequal in society. Why should we have nothing? I'm trying to fix that." When I asked him if he thought of himself as a revolutionary, he said "I *am* a revolutionary."

It has been said that prison is a sort of graduate school of crime. In American prisons inmates learn more than new criminal techniques. They acquire, through association with diverse criminal types, additional socialization into criminal reality. It is in prison that careerists from different criminal subcultures come into close contact, and it is in prison that the wellsprings of a national criminal culture are nourished. Drug dealers, robbers, con men, pimps, who might never meet on the outside, can communicate face-to-face in prison. The result is a bond of common interests and attitudes. The occasional criminal who says he is sorry, who expresses guilt and admits "I didn't mean to do it," is despised and ridiculed by inmate society.

When the first offender steps through the prison gates, he finds support for almost any form of criminal activity. Those inmates who have had the most successful careers, generally the meanest and most ruthless, receive deference, privileges, and respect. One inmate I met had been a big-time narcotics dealer on the outside. He was reputed to have had people killed by professional hit men, and inmates feared him and would do anything for him. This man, I believe, had more influence than the warden over the lives of his fellow inmates.

Prison society, of necessity, is closeknit. The therapist who tries to inculcate inmates with the values of conformist society during the one or two hours he meets with his prison clients each week has little chance of success. The attitudes and beliefs of the career criminal, reinforced by prison society are too ingrained to be rooted out by conventional therapeutic methods. Similarly, correctional programs that require the inmate to develop long-range job plans and to acquire the skills necessary for a steady job are generally unrealistic, for they fail to consider the career criminal's view of time.

The 30 percent or so of the inmates who do reform probably would have done so without therapy. It is likely they were occasional criminals to begin with and basically conformists at heart. The apparent, albeit limited, success of rehabilitation programs in some prisons may be nothing more than a measure of the number of occasional criminals in the inmate population. The question that needs to be asked is how many one-time offenders become irrevocably submerged in criminal reality through their prison experience?

Based on my own work in prisons, I estimate that roughly 10 percent of all inmates in the United States are conformists at heart. They are generally people who have committed serious crimes, like the murder of a spouse or lover, and who have received long prison sentences. The longer they remain in prison the more likely they are to become immersed in criminal reality. Nearly all of this group may eventually accept some aspects of the criminal's world view.

To be effective, therapeutic programs must proceed from a recognition that there are sharp differences between one-time offenders and career criminals. Individual behavior

resulting from adaptation to criminal reality cannot be changed by therapies that challenge only selected aspects of criminal thought. The career criminal must simultaneously be made to abandon criminal reality and to construct a new reality that is consistent with conformist principles. In short, he must be converted.

Conversion is most likely to occur when certain basic conditions are met. First, the offender must be made consciously aware of the shortcomings of his former world view. These shortcomings may be demonstrated by pointing out internal inconsistencies or, when the person's identity is firmly anchored in criminal reality, by stimulating self-doubt. The goal of conversion therapy is to create a period of questioning and inner reflection. If therapeutic efforts at this stage are successful, the criminal will be set adrift between conflicting realities. He will be living in a limbo of doubt. Sometimes relentless questioning is necessary. An interview using conversion therapy would go like this:

Therapist: You're not a bad person? I mean you're not evil or anything like that?

Client: No.

Therapist: You know, your mother tells her friends that she's sorry you were born. She says you'd be better off dead.

Client: Yeah.

Therapist: Your wife left you.

Client: (Shrugs)

Therapist: Your children hope you never get out of prison. They say that if you do they never want to see you. They say all you've done is cause them misery.

Client: I know.

Therapist: And you still say there's nothing wrong with you?

Client: You just don't understand.

If this approach works the client will eventually realize that he doesn't understand why he behaves as he does. If he did, he could communicate it to the therapist. Conversion therapy brings the inmate's entire way of being under attack and, if successful, engenders a crisis of identity.

Next, conformist reality is presented to the client in such a way that doubt is resolved in conformist terms. Since people tend to maintain a consistent world view, the adoption of even a few conformist premises can lead to an increasing acceptance of conformist thought. Each time a crisis is answered in conformist terms, a new world view takes shape.

Finally, the client should be made to identify with conformist reality. In one of the most successful programs I have observed, inmates work with delinquent children. They often come to realize their own unhappiness and try desperately to save the children from a similar fate. The program may in fact do more good for the inmates than for the children.

Recognizing the existence of a special criminal reality provides a basis not only for treating individual criminals but also for understanding why career criminals behave as they do. With this understanding, we can begin to develop effective social programs designed to modify the causes of that behavior. The way to reduce crime, I believe, is to reduce the number of these professionals, and that can be accomplished only when we decide to confront the habitual offender on his own mental turf.

 Article Review Form at end of book.

Should delinquent juveniles be detained in detention centers? Why?
What should be done to eliminate prison gangs?

Origins and Effects of Prison Drug Gangs in North Carolina

Dennis J. Stevens

Dennis J. Stevens Ph.D., is an associate professor of criminal justice at the University of Massachusetts at Boston. In addition to developing a criminal justice program and teaching traditional university students, he has taught law enforcement officers at police academies such as the North Carolina Justice Academy and felons at maximum custody penitentiaries such as Attica in New York, Stateville and Joliet near Chicago, Eastern and NC Women's Institute near Raleigh in North Carolina, and CCI in Columbia, South Carolina. He is also a group facilitator for court-ordered sexually abusive parents.

Streets gangs receive immense attention by the media and in the scholarly literature, while only some attention is given to organized prison gangs (i.e., Aryan Brotherhood (AB), Black Guerrilla Family (BGF), and the Mexican Mafia [EME]) in well researched prisons (i.e., Attica in New York, Stateville and Joliet near Chicago, and Soledad in California). However, some writers argue that prison gangs originally developed in prison, and others argue that prison gangs are street gangs that moved into prison as street gang members were incarcerated.[1] On the other hand, some writers suggest that both street gangs and prison gangs are intertwined (Welling, 1994). Yet, most of

the evidence within this controversy comes from organized gangs in nationally recognized prisons. However, prison gangs in low profile prisons lacking national attention do not appear to be recognized (Camp & Camp, 1985; Early, 1991; Hadedorn, 1990; Huff, 1990). Clearly, a controversy continues about the origins of prison gangs. Does questionable official conduct depend on the perspective held about prison gang origins and effects?

Robert Dart (1993), commander of the Gang Crime Section at the Chicago Police Department, argues that one of the best ways of controlling crime and prison gangs is to crack down on street gangs. Dart finds support among the advocates who argue that prison gang members were originally incarcerated street gang members. These advocates imply that street gang members carry their street values and street norms into prison when they are incarcerated, and their current attitudes and behavior match their former lifestyle expectations (Huff, 1990; Irwin & Cressey, 1962; Wilson & Howell, 1994). For example, Jacobs (1977) argues that street values and street gangs are imported into prison environments. Prison culture, Jacobs says, is made up of the social expectations, social roles, and values of those confined. That is, prison gangs such as Disciples, Vice Lords, Stones, and

Latin Kings at Illinois' Stateville penitentiary were the same gangs with the same values as the ones on the streets of Chicago. More specifically, the 400 members of the Black P Stone Nation were governed at Stateville, "as on the streets, by the gang's president and vice president—Eugen Hairston and Jeff Fort—and by a council of the Main 21" (Jacobs, 1977, pp. 146). Furthermore, many criminal justice professionals claim that measurements of an importation model are strong predictors of inmate behavior since their vestiges of traditional sex role orientation, age, social class, previous lifestyle, and criminal history largely impact their present behavior (Alpert, Noblit, & Wiorkowski, 1977; Hartnagel & Gillan, 1980; Jacobs, 1977; Irwin & Cressey, 1962; Zingraff, 1980). Therefore, it might be easy to support official conduct that might lend itself to controversial results.

Clearly, one result in a crackdown of street gangs is that more and younger briefly incarcerated teenagers and children, some of whom, argues Mayer (1993), may be guilty only of associating with violent criminals. Imprisonment alone does not rehabilitate, and therefore an implication of Robert Dart's (1993) crackdown might increase the number of gang members in prison (Mayer, 1993; Stevens, 1995a, 1994b). Thus, this paper will argue that violent prison gangs which dominate

Origins and Effects of Prison Drug Gangs in North Carolina, D. J. Stevens. *Journal of Gang Research,* 4(4), 1997, 23–35. Reprinted by permission of National Gang Crime Research Center, publisher of the *Journal of Gang Research,* Post Office Box 990, Peotone, Illinois 60468–0990.

the prison drug trade in low profile state prison populations like North Carolina are not necessarily controlled or even connected to street gangs or nationwide organizations.[2] The importance of this study is that should the data support this perspective, curbing prison gang development in North Carolina might be aided.

Moreover, any definition of a gang should include group organization, leadership, territory, symbols, recurrent interaction, and violence (Needle & Stapleton, 1983). Specifically Miller (1975, pp. 9) defines a gang as a:

. . . group of recurrently associating individuals with identifiable leadership and internal organization, identifying with or claiming control over territory in the community, and engaging either individually or collectively in violent or other forms of illegal behavior.

Prison gangs share in this social construct.

Joining a gang or doing "gang-time" helps some prisoners since many rely on others for protection, aid, sex, drugs, and power (Early, 1992; Jacobs, 1977). Additionally, banding together in a prison gang as explained through Abraham Maslow's "Hierarchy of Needs" is one explanation for the development and growth of prison gangs (Jackson & McBride, 1992). That is, various individual needs must be met before individuals can attain a level of happiness with themselves and their environment especially if incarcerated. Gangs are tools used by individuals to fulfill their social needs including self respect and belongingness (Jackson & McBride, 1992; Maginnis, 1996, Sampson, 1995).

Of further interest, 1,206 respondents were surveyed in eight county jails from the rural farmland in the Midwest to the urban central area of Chicago (NGCRC, 1994). The data show that prison drug gang membership can be predicted within an 81% accuracy. Also, the researchers argue that the prison gangs in their study distributed drugs through violence even in the rural jails as a form of control over the inmates and the correctional officers (NGCRC, 1994). Moreover, prison gang violence can grow from the perceptions that one gang has been challenged, insulted, offended, or injured by another gang or group of individuals, argues Cohen (Huff, 1990, p. 14). Additionally, there is a social phenomenon that applies to gang violence referred to as the Law of Opposition Group Formation (Knox, 1993). That is, in any social system where one group threat arises, its natural counter-part (Mexican Mafia, then Nuestra Familia) arises too.[3] Overall, prison drug gangs largely take part in antisocial and criminal behavior and therefore it comes as no surprise that a strong link between prison gangs, drug trafficking, and inmate violence exists (Allen & Simonsen, 1994; Fagan, 1989; NGCRC, 1994). Thus, the central theme of this paper is that local prison gangs control drug trafficking through violence and intimidation in the North Carolina prison system and that the North Carolina juvenile training or detention centers are origins of North Carolina prison drug gangs through what I will call a juvenilization process.

Juvenile Justice System

In personal interviews with juvenile custody officials, most indicate that more than 75% of the young men confined in their centers will eventually be incarcerated in state penitentiaries. Government statistics seem to support their position (Bureau of Justice Statistics, 1996). Furthermore, in a recent study of U.S. juvenile detention facilities, thousands of offenders were found to be confined in facilities that violated basic living standards (Allen-Hagen, 1996). It was concluded that serious and widespread problems existed in the living space, health care, institutional security and safety, and control of suicidal behavior for juveniles in those facilities. Furthermore, John Irwin (1980) argues that extended social networks that are loosely held together by shared subcultural orientations or preprison acquaintances could form "tips and cliques" in closed institutions such as prison or perhaps a juvenile training center. That is:

There were tips of persons who had experienced the youth prisons together; lived in same town or neighborhood (homeboys), and engaged in the same criminal activities. A sense of affinity and loyalty existed between members of a tip (Irwin, 1980, pp. 58–59).

Most of these "tips," Irwin explains, were interracial and can be overlapping and connected. Silberman (1995) adds that in the 1980s, association in Irwin's concept of "tips" became a contributing factor towards group affiliation in American prisons. Goldstein (1991) suggests further that juvenile training centers can represent an "intense place attachment" that may be a stronger bond than "blood" for some juveniles especially as they grow older and learn to trust only the individuals whom they shared commonalties with. Therefore, there is some compelling evidence in the literature which suggests that juveniles confined to closed institutions might share place-intensity experiences and gang affiliation agents through tip encounters when they are subjected to standard environments and poor living conditions.

Thus, the question: Do juvenile detention centers further criminality through subsequent gang formation? Should the data lend support to this question, I can argue with confidence that a "juvenilization process" (organizational experiences of juvenile centers) can lead to gang formation, once an individual is incarcerated as an adult through a prisonization process. Subsequent incarceration promotes the social agents of gang participation through a prisonization process.

Prisonization

The researcher is asking once again: in what ways does organizational membership, impact attitudes and eventual behavioral patterns of law abiding individuals (Stevens, 1997c)?[4] One answer lies with Donald Clemmer (1940, 1958) who coined the term prisonization to refer to the longer inmates were incarcerated, the stronger their identification with inmate norms and values, and the more difficulty they would have adjusting, once released from prison. Clemmer suggests that inmate environments possess social components, too, and therefore, like other social groups, have a culture which he defines as mode of life or thought that is not peculiarly individual but which can be characterized as a shared set of attitudes that eventually impact behavioral patterns and lifestyles. Acceptance of the perspectives of a culture is more or a less an unconscious process experienced by individuals who remain in a unique social environment (Clemmer; 1940, 1958). Part of this process includes learning enough of the culture to make an individual a typical part of that environment. Part of an inmate's environment, Sykes (1966) adds, relates to the pains of imprisonment especially since inmates are stripped of worldly possessions, denied access to heterosexual relationships, divested of autonomy, and compelled to associate with other deviants. Therefore, inmates are products of their social interactions which they enter into day after day, year after year. Continuing along this thought, Stevens (1997b, 1994b) adds that the unique environment of prison, affects inmate violence levels regardless of the prior decisions made by individuals before confinement through a prisonization process. Thus, it can be argued that prisonization or an indigenous set of impersonal prison values includes the 'degree of assimilation into the inmate normative system' (Thomas, Petersen, & Cage, 1981).

The above deprivation model suggests that prisons have a unique culture of their own moving individuals through a prisonization process that influences their immediate and future conduct (Bottom, Hayes, & Sparks, 1990; Grapendaal, 1990; Stevens, 1995b, 1994b; Sykes, 1966). Therefore, this paper will suggest that juvenile detention centers are unique unto themselves, too, and that many individuals are impacted by their individual experiences through a juvenilization process. For instance, once a juvenile is released from custody, and later incarcerated at an adult prison, through a prisonization process, the juvenilization model culminates with gang affiliation. That is, adult inmates who had been at juvenile training centers are also exposed to a prisonization process that allows juvenilization to stretch into violent gang alliances.

Another perspective held by the researcher is that while there is more than one cause for every effect, each cause relates to the social environment or experience (Kruttschnitt, Ward, & Sheble 1987). That is, social facts have antecedent social explanations, as Emile Durkheim once postulated. Therefore, this paper will acknowledge that the rise of powerful prison gangs might have to do with the "hands off" doctrine concerning inmate behavior. For instance, "An abandonment" of control exposes prison regimes to outside accountability, limits an institution's recourse to coercive sanctions, and provides an inmate with the legitimate means of expression with which to challenge the system of social control (Jacobs, 1977, p. 138). Inmates have constitutional rights guaranteed them including the right of due process through *Wolff v. McDonnell* (Allen & Simonsen, 1995; Johnson, 1996)[5] Thus, I will also argue that due in part to reduced custodial control, prison drug gang behavior goes virtually unchecked. Nonetheless, the literature suggests that where prison gangs exist, prison operations are not controlled by its custodians, drugs of every sort are available but expensive, and both inmate and correctional officer safety is excessively compromised.[6] Therefore, a better understanding of prison gang origin, growth, and effect can lend itself to prison gang control thereby aiding custodial control and contributing to the safety of custodians and inmates alike.

Methodology

To test the hypothesis that gangs are trafficking drugs through violence and intimidation in North Carolina prisons and that these gangs were fathered by juvenile detention centers through a juvenilization process, 792 inmates were surveyed and 14 were interviewed in 4 different prisons during the spring of 1996. Questionnaires were utilized to test the hypothesis as one means of getting confidential data from a large number of participants at the same time especially due to the sensitivity of the issue of gangs. The interviews were used to clarify any of the implications arising from the data and was sparingly offered where the researcher thought it appropriate in the finding.

Questionnaire

There was only one version of the questionnaire used for this study. It was developed after in-depth discussions with 42 law enforcement officers from various jurisdictions throughout North Carolina. The questionnaire contains 14 demographic questions and 36 questions consisting of close-end and open-end answers. There were numerous blank spaces with notes to the respondents encouraging their thoughts, which proved to be a rich resource. . . .

Sample

The average respondent was 35 years of age, and 52% (415) were white, 42% (334) were black, 2% (17) were of other races, and 4% (26) were unknown. The average education of the respondents was 11.7 years of school, 23% (183) were married, 25% (200) divorced, 43% (344) single, and 8% (65) reported "other" as their marital status prior to confinement. Additionally, 17% (134) of the respondents spent their youth in the geographical areas from Raleigh to Greensboro, North Carolina, 22% (170) in eastern North Carolina, 9% (67) Fayetteville to Monroe to Whiteville, 8% (63) Wilmington and the coast, 15% (115) Charlotte to Asheville, 88% (63) in New York, New Jersey, Pennsylvania, or Maryland, and 21% (177) of the data show other areas or missing data. The average participant was arrested 2.7 times as an adult, and 37% of the sample were arrested an average of 2.5 times as a juvenile. Twenty-four percent (194) of the respondents spent an average of 29 weeks with a range of 1 to 150 weeks at a North Carolina juvenile training or detention center, and 74 months in North Carolina prisons with a range from 7 to 360 months.

According to the self-reported data, 27% (213) respondents were convicted of the crime of murder, 12% (95) of rape, 23% (182) of armed robbery or kidnapping, 10% (78) of aggravated assault, 12% (96) of drug trafficking, 14% (107) of property crimes, and 3% (21) of the data were missing. When the above data is compared to admission data in 1995 of inmates to North Carolina prisons, it appears the sample has more whites than blacks (52% & 42% Vs 32% & 65%), and more physically violent offenders as compared to the state's 23% who were convicted of narcotics and drugs, 14% breaking and entering, and 12% larceny (NCDOC, 1996). Otherwise, there is a strong resemblance between the demographics of the respondents in this sample and the demographics of the state's general inmate population. Furthermore, when the demographics of the sample is compared to state prison populations across the United States, there appears to be a significant similarity (BJS, 1996).

Interviews

In total, 17 inmates agreed to an interview, but only 14 kept their appointment and participated in the interview process. The interviews were conducted in the educational centers of the four prisons. One purpose of these interviews was to better understand prisoner experiences in the prisons surveyed and to clarify some of the survey responses.

Findings

The responses of the participants offer a window of prison experience that help better understand prison gang formation, activities, and effects. For example, when the participants were asked about the best methods of safety in prison, 28% (221) reported that they mind their own business. This finding is supported by Silberman (1995, p. 29) who also asked inmates about survival techniques. Most of his sample indicated a similar answer to the one above. But, had Silberman asked about gangs, he might have found that 23% (185) of his sample, like the sample in my study reported that safety in prison translates to gang membership. Additionally, 8% (64) reported that being alone was best, while 12% (95) reported giving-in is one way of surviving. Four percent (34) revealed that getting to know the correctional officers is another approach to safety, while 12% (97) reported that taking a lover is good advice concerning prison survival.[7] And, 12% (96) of the sample had not answered the question. The above data suggest that there is more than

one way to survive in prison, and that one of the most important methods is through gang membership.

Additionally, when the participants were asked about drugs, they reported that drugs were easily obtained at their institution. That is, 35% (279) of the participants strongly agreed and 37% (293) of the participants said they agreed that drugs were easily available to them. When the participants were asked how strongly they agreed that the quality of drugs was excellent in their institution, 23% (184) strongly agreed and 29% (226) agreed. When the respondents were asked if drugs were more expense in their prison versus other prisons, 19% (151) strongly agreed and 9% (71) agreed, 27% (212) disagreed, and 46% (361) were not sure. Also, when the participants were asked how strongly they agreed if drug prices were higher in their institution than on the streets, 35% (279) strongly agreed and 24% (186) agreed. It could be argued from the above evidence that drug trafficking was pervasive at the institutions of the participants.

When the participants were asked about gang-indicators at their institution, the data suggest that gangs were present and that these gangs exercised a great deal of control through the use of violence and intimidation. For instance, some social indicators of gangs relate to extreme political thought such as black or white militants or Marxist thought, the practice of satanism, gangs "hanging" together, assaults, sexual attacks, theft, and extortion (Decker, 1996; Huff, 1990; Knox, 1994; Rush, Stone, & Wycoff, 1996). Thirty-eight percent (301) of the participants reported that they agreed that extreme political thought existed among the inmates at their institution. Forty percent (318) of the respondents agreed that satanism is practiced at their institution. Also, 52% (414) of the participants reported that cliques or groups of inmates "hang" together. Additionally, 48% (382) of the respondents strongly agreed or agreed that gangs verbally and physically assault inmates. While 87% (664) of the respondents strongly agreed or agreed that gangs frequently sexually assault inmates, 82% (650) of the participants strongly

agreed or agreed that their personal property was subject to theft much of the time. Also, when the respondents were asked how strongly they agreed that family members extort inmates, 12% (97) reported that they strongly agreed, 38% (301) reported that they agreed, but 26% (204) reported said that they're not sure.[8]

Drug Distribution

When the participants were asked about drug distribution 15% (116) of them reported that correctional officers without rank distributed drugs in their prison. Nine percent (74) of the respondents reported that social service personnel such as teachers and psychologists distributed drugs. Eight percent (64) of the sample suggested that official visitors such as ministers and lawyers, and 10% (80) of them indicated that correctional officers with rank distributed contraband. Although 20% (158) of the participants neglected an answer to the drug distribution question, 38% (300) of them reported that drugs were usually distributed by a gang in their institution. Of interest, 21% (63) of the respondents who reported that drugs were distributed by prison gangs, wrote the names of the prison gangs on the questionnaire. All but three of these names appear to be local state prison gangs. These three exceptions were gangs allegedly connected to a religious organization; however, one of the two of them was not connected to drug trafficking or violence. But, the other two groups connected to religious organizations were linked to violence, hate crimes, and limited drug trafficking. Most of the drug trafficking through violence and intimidation, however, was linked to specific local gangs that cooperated with other prison gangs including the above religious gang.[9] Ethics and common sense guide confidentiality of these names.[10]

One implication of the above data is that the presence of organized gangs in North Carolina prisons exist, but they lack the organizational structure and networks of nationally known prison gangs with the possible exception of the religious group. Part of this thought is supported by the many writers who imply that the ease of drug distribution, high drug costs, and drug quality suggest the presence of organized gangs within a prison (Irwin, 1980; Jacobs, 1977; Johnson, 1996). It should be noted that many of the participants wrote on their questionnaire that whenever correctional officials questioned or detained members of the religious organization that religious and/or racial lawsuits were filed against those officials and therefore, officials "now think twice about stopping them," Finestein, a former law enforcement officer convicted of killing his partner, revealed when interviewed.

Methods Used by Gangs to Control Officers and Inmates

When the respondents were asked what methods prison gangs used to control correctional officers, 42% (336) reported that conning or lying was the most frequent method used. Also, 4% (32) reported that gangs told the correctional officers the truth, 4% (31) said that they kissed their butts, 16% (128) reported that gangs threatened custodian officers, 8% (64) reported that they reasoned with them, 4% (30) intimidated them, 8% (67) assaulted correctional officers, 4% (31) told them what they wanted to hear, and 9% (73) gave them money or stuff.

One of the most likely methods of control utilized by gangs to control inmates, the participants reported, was the threat or use of force. That is, 4% (32) of the respondents suggested that gangs con or lie to inmates to control them. Two percent (14) of the participants reported that prison gangs told inmates the truth, 1% (6) kissed their butts, 40% (316) advised that gangs threatened inmates, 47% (372) reported that prison gangs assaulted other inmates, 5% (39) intimidated inmates, 1% (7) reported that gangs told inmates what the inmates wanted to hear, and 1% (6) of the participants decided not to answer this question. Incidentally, none of the participants thought that gangs reasoned with inmates in order to control them. It is curious that prison gangs can be implicated in an enormous amount of criminal activity including violence against inmates and their custodians. Perhaps, as Jacobs (1977) and

Johnson (1996) also found, there is, indeed, a "hands off" doctrine in effect concerning inmate behavior. These writers see an abandonment of custodian control exposing a regime to outside accountability through court actions which in effect, limit an institution's recourse to coercive sanctions. One net result of such action provides an inmate, especially an inmate connected to a base of power such as a prison gang, with the legitimate means of expression to challenge the system.

Largely, as a result of the violence experienced by the respondents, 73% (577) of them want transfers to other prisons, and 87% (690) would accept protective custody if they could get it without losing some of the rights they currently enjoyed. The above is congruent with Rush, Stone, and Wycoff (1996) who also find that the existence of prison gangs can be determined by large quantities of expensive but easily obtained drugs and a large number of requests for transfer and protective custody.

North Carolina Prison Gangs

When the participants were asked how often gangs recruited inmates, 29% (233) reported always, 9% (67) reported very often, and 58% (458) said seldom. It would be expected that if gangs were present, they would recruit more often. But, during the interview process, Howard, a convicted double murderer, suggested that recruiting is a low priority for drug distribution gangs since the origin of the gang affiliation is based on hometowns and/or juvenile training centers. "If ya didn't come from a certain place or a certain ju'vy camp, ya ain't part of th' klan." That is, when the respondents were asked how prison gangs were "hooked," 23% (183) reported that gang affiliation was based on age, 46% (362) reported it was based on hometowns, 4% (32) on race, 12% (96) on religion, 4% (32) on prison time elsewhere, 10% (82) on juvenile detention centers, and 1% (5) had not answered the question.

When the data of self-reported gang members were compared with self-reported juvenile training center adjudication, the results were telling. That is, the more often a respondent reported that he was a member of a

prison gang or clique, the more likely he had spent "time" at a North Carolina juvenile center. More specifically, the centers in the Raleigh to Greensboro to Butner triangle and Charlotte to Ashville areas produced a high rate of prison gang affiliation.

Conclusion

Local prison gangs control the drug trade in North Carolina prisons through violence and intimidation, and the origin of these gangs are linked to the influences of juvenile detention centers throughout the state. Thus, organizational membership even for juveniles, affects the attitudes and ultimately, the behavior of individuals. Largely, North Carolina prison drug gang members were involuntary members of two closed institution organizations prior to becoming a gang drug member: as a child the drug gang member experienced juvenile detention center confinement, and as an adult the gang member experienced the penitentiary. It was the juvenile detention center which nurtured the social agents of gang formation through a juvenilization process, while the penitentiary advanced those agents to gang participation through a prisonization process. That is, the culmination (drug gang membership) of the juvenilization effect is influenced through a process of prisonization. Therefore, an inference of this study furthers the prisonization model of Donald Clemmer (1940, 1958). Yet, this paper describes an additional process that more fully characterizes the future criminality of juveniles, once they are released from juvenile centers and after they are incarcerated at an adult correctional facility.

Clearly, the hometowns of many inmates in the North Carolina system further gang participation, but it is the juvenile training center link that furthers drug trafficking gangs in North Carolina prisons. It is not necessary that juveniles interact at these centers or that they meet face to face since place-intensity as a component of the juvenilization process occurs between two individuals despite their ever meeting. The juvenilization process can begin during a juvenile's adjudication hearing and continues during the socialization process of detention, the living experiences, and the eventual release from the training center. It culminates after an individual's confinement at an adult prison. This experience transcends race, religion, family and friendship ties, and hometown values and norms.

A guide here might relate to adult recidivism rates. One study argues that while prisons in a specific state fall under specific directives, codes, and regulations that similar custody level penitentiaries produce different recidivism rates among similar at-risk offenders (Stevens, 1997b). Thus, one predictor of recidivism lays with regime, independent of the decisions made by an offender about violent crime prior to incarceration due in part to a prisonization process (Stevens, 1995a, 1994b). If regime impacts recidivism levels through prisonization, then is it possible that a juvenile training center regime impacts attitudes and future behavior of its residents, too, through some kind of a process? That is, it could be argued that regime is a stronger predictor of future criminality for juvenile center inhabitants than other variables including the orientations of the juveniles about violent crime, through a juvenilization process.

Thus, this juvenilization process may be stronger for youths than "blood" or religion as some juveniles elect to trust only the individuals they shared a place-intensity relationship with. "That is, at an extreme, belonging to an organization can by its very nature turn nonviolent offenders into killers and violent men into passive beings" (Stevens, 1997d, 1996a). As one inmate puts it about his juvenile training center partners, "It's hard to turn on family." One component of this family concept relates to both official and informal values and norms supported and rewarded by regime of a juvenile center. Thus, depending on the scope and the nature of these social indicators, will depend the eventual outcome of many juveniles. Furthermore, litigation and custodial decay play a major role in the loss of custodial control giving rise to the power of prison drug gangs.

Despite the street gang an offender belongs to or equally important, what experiences the street gang members holds from the streets of Chicago, New York, or Raleigh, once

he has experienced a juvenile center and subsequent incarceration at Stateville, Attica, or Central Prison, the offender assimilates the culture and the values of the prison as he had the culture and the values of juvenile center. Each closed institution has its own society, its own values, and its own priorities that are rewarded and reinforced by a particular regime of that institution. Thus, a prison gang might look like Latin Kings or Five Percenters inside prison, but a closer truth is that they are now Stateville Latin Kings or Central Prison Five Percenters. Then, too, in North Carolina prisons, offenders who have been previously confined at a state juvenile center are more likely to band together with others who have shared similar juvenile center experiences and rely on each other for protection, aid, sex, drugs, and power. They see former North Carolina juvenile confined offenders as family members and without too much vacillation, trust each other more than they trust the system that has confined them, the family that has deserted them, and/or the gangs they ran with while on the streets. These former juvenile center inhabitants now use the prison drug trade as a form of control and power, and due to the nature of their enterprise and the nature of their environment, they are both required and obligated to utilize as much violence as possible to further their objectives. This thought is supported by many writers who argue that prison violence, crime, and drug trafficking is a way of life for most inmates in high custody prisons (Decker, 1996; Early, 1992; Fagan, 1989; Irwin, 1980; Jacobs, 1977; Stevens, 1997b). More research is called for on the relationship between juvenile center regime and agents of gang formation.

References

Allen, H. E. & Simonsen, C. E. (1995). *Corrections in America.* Englewood Cliffs, NJ: Prentice Hall.

Allen-Hagen, B. (1996). Conditions of confinement in juvenile detention and correctional facilities. (On Line). Availability: http://www.mcjrs.org/txtfiles/ccdet.txt

Alpert, G. P., Noblit, G., & Wiorkowski, J. (1977). Comparative look at prisonization: Sex and prison culture. *Quarterly Journal of Corrections 1,* 29–34.

Bottoms, A. E., Hay, W, & Sparks, J. R. (1990). Situational and social approaches to the prevention of disorder in long term prisons. *The Prison Journal, LXXX* 1, 83–95.

Bureau of Justice Statistics. (1996). *Sourcebook of criminal justice statistics—1995.* (NCJ-154591). Washington DC: U.S. Government Printing Office.

Camp, G. & Camp, C. G. (1985). *Prison gangs. Their extent, nature, and impact on prisons.* Washington DC: U.S. Department of Justice.

Clemmer, D. (1940, 1958). *The prison community.* NY. Holt, Rinehart & Winston.

Curry, G. D. (1994). Extended national assessment survey of anti-gang law enforcement information resources: Preliminary results. Paper presented at the annual meeting of the American Society of Criminology, Miami, Florida.

Curry, G. D., & Spergel, I. A. (1992). Gang involvement and delinquency among Hispanic and African-American adolescent males. *Journal of Research in Crime and Delinquency,* 29 (3), 273–291.

Curry, G. D., Ball, R. A., & Fox, R. J. (1994). *Gang crime and law enforcement recordkeeping.* National Institute of Justice (NCJ Publication No. 148345). Washington DC: Office of Justice Programs.

Decker, S. H. (1996). Collective and normative features of gang violence. *Justice Quarterly,* 13 (2), 243–264.

Early, P. (1991). *The hot house.* New York: Basic Books.

Esbensen, F., & Huizinga, D. (1993). Gangs, drugs, and delinquency in a survey of urban young. *Criminology,* 31 (4) 565–589.

Fagan, J. (1989). The social organization of drug use and drug dealing among urban gangs. *Criminology,* 27 (4), 633–669.

Ford, M. C. (1994). The impact of policy shifts on correctional populations. Paper presented at the annual meeting of the American Society of Criminology, Miami, Florida.

Goldstein, A. P. (1991). *Delinquent gangs: A psychological perspective.* Champaign, Illinois: Research Press.

Grapendaal, M. (1990). The inmate subculture in Dutch prisons. *British Journal of Criminology,* 30 (3), 341–356.

Hartnagel, J., & Gillan, M. E. (1980). Female prisoners and the inmate code. *Pacific Sociological Review,* 23, 1: 85–104.

Hadedorn, J. M. (1990). Back in the field again: Gang research in the nineties. In C. R. Huff (ED.) *Gangs in America.* (pp. 240–262). Newbury Park, CA: Sage.

Hagedorn, J. M. (1994). Homeboys, dope fiends, legits, and new jacks. *Criminology,* 32 (2), 197–219.

Howell, J. C. (1994). Recent gang research: Program and policy implication. *Crime & Delinquency,* 40 (4), 495–515.

Huff, C. R. (1990). *Gangs in America.* Newbury Park, CA: Sage.

Huff, C. R. (1989). Young gangs and public policy. *Crime & Delinquency,* 35 (4), 524–537.

Hunt, G., Riegel, S., Morales, T, & Waldorf, D. (1993). Changes in prison gangs and the case of the Pepsi generation. *Social Problems*, 40, 398–409.

Irwin, J. (1980). *Prisons in turmoil.* Boston: Little Brown and Company.

Irwin, J., & Cressey, D. (1962). Thieves, convicts, and the inmate culture. *Social Problems*, 10, 142–155.

Jackson, R. K., & McBride, W. D. (1992). *Understanding street gangs.* Placerville, CA: Copperhouse Publishing.

Jacobs, J. B. (1977). *Stateville: The penitentiary in mass society.* Chicago: The University of Chicago Press.

Johnson, R. (1996). *Hard times.* Belmont, CA: Wadsworth Publishing.

Kalinisch, D. B. (1980). *The inmate economy.* Lexington, MA: Lexington.

Kennedy, L. W., & Baron, S. W. (1993). Routine activities and a subculture of violence. A study of violence on the street. *Journal of Research in Crime and Delinquency*, 30 (1), 88–112.

Klein, M. W., Maxson, C. L., Cunningham, L. C. (1991). "Crack," street gangs, and violence. *Criminology*, 29 (4), 623–650.

Knox, G. (1995). *An introduction to gangs*, 3rd Edition. Bristol, IN: Wyndham Hall Press.

Kruttschnitt, C., Ward, D., & Sheble, M. A. (1987). Abuse-resistant youth: Some factors that may inhibit violent criminal behavior. *Social Forces*, 66 2, 501–519.

Lopez, A. (1995). Gang warfare, dadz in the hood. *The Economist*, 19.

Marginnis, R. L. (1996). Youth gangs: Out of control and getting worse. Family Research Center (On Line). Available: om/townhall/FRC/insight/is95j3cr.html

Maxon, C. L., & Klien, M. W. (1993). *The scope of street gang migration in the U.S.: An interim report to survey participants.* Los Angeles: The University of Southern California.

Mayer, J. J. (1993). Individual moral responsibility and the criminalization of youth gangs. *Wake Forest Law Review*, 28 4, 943–986.

Miller, W. B. (1975). *Violence by young gangs and groups as a crime problem in major American cities.* Washington, CD: U.S. Government Printing Office.

National Gang Crime Research Center (NGCRC). (1994). Gangs and guns: A task force report. Paper presented at the annual meeting of the American Society of Criminology, Miami, Florida.

Needle, J., & Stapleton, W. V. (1983). *Police handling of youth gangs.* Office of Juvenile Justice and Delinquency Prevention. National Juvenile Justice Assessment Centers. Washington DC: U.S. Department of Justice.

Pryor, D. W., & McGarrell, E. F. (1993). Public perceptions of young crime. *Youth and Society*, 24 (4), 399–418.

Rush, J., Stone, S., & Wycoff, J. (1996). A preliminary report of gang activity in state run juvenile facilities. Paper presented at the Academy of Criminal Justice Sciences annual conference Las Vegas, NE.

Silberman, M. (1995). *A world of violence.* Belmont, CA: Wadsworth.

Skalitzky, W. G. (1990). Aider and abettor, the continuing criminal enterprise, and street gangs. A new twist in an old war on drugs. *The Journal of Criminal Law and Criminology*, 81 (2), 348–397.

Stevens, D. J. (1997a). Influences of early childhood experiences on subsequent criminally violent behavior. *Studies on Crime and Crime Prevention*, 6 (1), 34–50.

Stevens, D. J. (1997b). Prison regime and drugs. *The Howard Journal of Criminal Justice*, 36 (1), 14–27.

Stevens, D. J. (1997c). Lengths of imprisonment and female prisoners' anticipation of future violence: Female prisonization effects. *The Howard Journal of Criminal Justice.* In Press.

Stevens, D. J. (1997d). Research Note: Urban communities and homicide: Why blacks resort to murder. *Policing and Society.* In Press.

Stevens, D. J. (1997e). Attitudes of police officers about their jobs: A study of trust, discretion, and training. *International Criminal Police Review.* In press.

Stevens, D. J. (1996a). Explanations of homicide: Interviews with female killers. Paper presented at the annual meeting of the American Society of Criminology in Chicago, November.

Stevens, D. J. (1996b). Correctional officer decay. Paper presented at the Southern Criminal Justice meeting, Savannah, GA.

Stevens, D. J. (1995a). The impact of time served and custody level on offender attitudes. *Forum on Corrections Research*, 9, 12–24.

Stevens, D. J. (1995b). American criminals and attitudes. *International Review of Modem Sociology*, 25 (2), 27–42.

Stevens, D. J. (1994a). Predatory rape and victim targeting techniques. *The Social Science Journal*, 31 (4), 421–433.

Stevens, D. J. (1994b). The depth of imprisonment and prisonisation: Levels of security and prisoners' anticipation of future violence. *The Howard Journal of Criminal Justice*, 33 (2), 137–157.

Stevens, D. J. (1992a). Research Note: The death sentence and inmate attitudes. *Crime & Delinquency*, 38, 272–279.

Stevens, D. J. (1992b). Examining inmate attitudes: Do prisons deter crime? *The State of Corrections—American Correctional Association: 1991.* 272–279.

Stevens, D. J. (1988). Education: The Assembly. *Urban Education*, 23 (1), 107–114.

Sykes, G. M. (1966). *The society of captives.* New York: Atheneum.

Welling, A. D. (1994, August). Experts unite to combat street and prison gang activities. *Corrections Today*, pp. 148–149.

Williamson, H. E. (1990). *The corrections profession.* Newbury Park, CA: Sage.

Wilson, J. Q., & Howell, J. C. (1994). Serious and violent juvenile crime: A comprehensive strategy. *Juvenile and Family Court Journal*, 45 (2).

Zingraff, M. (1980). Inmate assimilation: A comparison of male and female delinquents. *Criminal Justice and Behavior*, 7 (3), 275–292.

Endnotes

1. For more details see Johnson (1996, pp. 141–143) and especially the work of Peter Early, 1992; Irwin, 1980; Jacobs, 1977; Silberman, 1995.

2. It is believed that the more sophisticated prison gangs including Aryan Brotherhood, Mexican Mafia, Nuestra Familia, the Black Guerrilla Family are schooling and nationally recruiting members into their more established and structured organizations (Welling, 1994). As a result, it is feared by some writers that many prison gangs could evolve into multi-jurisdictional drug organizations throughout the nation (NGCRC, 1994; Welling, 1994).

3. Furthermore, there are some compelling arguments suggesting that many inmates perceive their custodians as a gang and feel threatened by the regime, its correctional officers, and the pains that come from imprisonment and, therefore, band together to counter and/or neutralize these perceived threats (Johnson, 1996; Stevens, 1997a, 1997c; Sykes, 1966).

4. For an in-depth look at how organizational membership through the contradictions of social institutions give rise to corrupt official behavior of law enforcement officers and correctional officers see Stevens (1997e, 1996b). Also, some nonviolent battered women and some nonviolent ghetto blacks may see homicide as an appropriate response in what they perceive as at-risk environments (Stevens, 1997d, 1996a).

5. This "hands off" doctrine is also witness to the 39,000 federal cases filed by prisoners in 1994 at a cost of $81.3 million to defend against producing a yielding correctional policy directed by the courts rather than correctional professionals (Cannon, 1996; Johnson, 1996).

6. Allen & Simonsen, 1995, Early, 1991; Huff, 1990; Irwin, 1980, Jackson & McBride, 1992; Jacobs, 1977; Rush, Stone, & Wycoff, 1996; Silberman, 1995; Stevens, 1997a, 1997c, 1994b; Williamson, 1990.

7. "It came as a surprise when 12% (97) of the participants reported that taking a lover is one method of safety in prison. Largely, a common perspective about high custody prison life is that many inmates are raped. While this perspective is supported by a vast body of evidence, one of the implications emerging from this current finding is that many inmates actually seek out powerful inmates for protection. Perhaps, I might speculate that a sexual relationship could emerge for some inmates after in-depth exchanges of interactions as a matter of circumstance and/or as a matter of just being human. When the participants of this study were asked about sexual relationships in this study, 67% of them reported that

those relationships would end once an inmate was released.

8. In interviews with inmates, it was learned that inmate extortion relates to drug trafficking activities through prison gang activity. For example, when an inmate is in a position to further drug distribution due to his job or relationship with an officer, a family member on the outside can be intimated or threatened to ask the inmate to comply with the wishes of the gang. In my own experience, an inmate's four-year-old daughter was threatened with rape if he refused the prison gang. He did, she was!

Sometimes, inmates while going through a legal appeal process are told that if they do not comply with prison drug gang demands that their appeal will be lost or that a particular lawyer will not handle their case. Sometimes family members are in prison themselves and subject to prison drug gang attack. "Other times," Jimmy, a convicted armed robber said during the interview process, "it's the family member who's in the gang pushing the dope and pretends to be pushed by someone else."

9. Names such as Aryan Brotherhood (AB) appeared with some frequency.

Names such as Black Guerrilla Family (BGF), Mexican Mafia [EME], and other known prison gangs from heavily populated states were not mentioned in any of the questionnaires with the exception of the Disciples, largely, an Illinois prison gang, and names that seem to describe Nuestra Familia, largely, a California prison gang.

10. The pages of the questionnaire where gang names were written have been discarded.

 Article Review Form at end of book.

To what extent do women prisoners' experiences differ from those of male prisoners? What, if any, special provisions should be made for women inmates?

Women in Prison

Women have become the hidden victims of the state's zeal for incarceration, as the number of California prisoners surged past the 100,000 mark in April of 1991.

California now has the uncertain distinction of having the most women prisoners in the nation, as well as the world's largest women's prison.

Since 1980, the number of women imprisoned in the U.S. has tripled. Now, on any given day, over 90,000 women are incarcerated in U.S. jails and prisons.

In 1992, there were 50,493 women incarcerated in federal and state prisons. Amazingly, the rate of women's imprisonment grew from 6 per 100,000 in 1925 to *37 per 100,000* in 1992. The rate of imprisonment in California is approximately 45 per 100,000.

It is important to add that the above data includes only time served for women who have been released; therefore, the numbers mentioned above may give the false impression that overall, women are serving shorter sentences. In reality, that is not the case.

When it comes down to it, this policy direction will not be beneficial to families, nor will it keep families intact.

According to the May 1994 issue report of Women's Economic Agenda Project

Eleven things you should know about women in prison in the U.S.:

1. There are over 90,000 women in prison in the U.S. today. The majority are in prison for economic crimes. The most typical convictions resulting in imprisonment for women are property crimes, such as check forgery and illegal credit card use. 80% of women in prison report incomes of less than $2,000 per year in the year before their arrest, and 92% report incomes under $10,000.

2. Of the women convicted of violent crimes, the vast majority were convicted for defending themselves or their children from abuse. In California alone there are 600 women in prison for killing their abusers in self-defense. Average prison terms are twice as long for killing husbands as for killing wives.

3. 54% of women in prison are women of color.

4. Ninety percent of women in prison are single mothers. They lose contact with their children,

sometimes forever. There are 167,000 children in the U.S. whose mothers are incarcerated.

5. The average age of women in prison is 29, and 58% have not finished high school.

6. Racism and economic discrimination are inextricably linked to sexism in our culture, creating severe inequalities in the court system and the prison system. For example, Black women are twice as likely to be convicted of killing their abusive husbands than are white women. Black women, on average, receive longer jail time and higher fines than do white women for the same crimes.

7. 25% of political prisoners in the U.S. are women.

8. The number of women in prison has increased 138% in the last ten years. This is partly due to the worsening of economic conditions for women, and also due to the increase in arrest rates due to the "war on crime" and "war on drugs".

9. Women prisoners spend, on average, 17 hours a day in their cells, with one hour outside for

exercise. Compare to men prisoners, who spend, on average, 15 hours a day in their cells, with 1.5 hours outside.

10. The Women's High Security Unit at Lexington, KY, was closed in 1988 because of a national and international human rights campaign. The prison kept the women in years of isolation in subterranean cells, conducted daily strip searches, allowed extreme sleep deprivation practices, and as policy, condoned a compete denial of privacy, including male guards watching the showers, and an intense campaign of sexual abuse.

11. The late Senator Hart estimated that the annual cost of corporate crime was between $174–231 billion dollars, while the economic cost of "street crimes" (e.g., burglary and robbery) was $3–4 billion. We must look at why the state focuses on enforcing laws which penalize the types of actions taken by poor and working class men and women while systematically ignoring the more destructive white-collar crimes.

 Article Review Form at end of book.

Why is the number of women prisoners increasing? What, if any, special provisions should be made for women prisoners?

Critical Statistics:

Women in California Prisons, May 1998

Compiled by Women for Leadership Development (WILD) for Human Rights and Legal Services for Prisoners with Children

Since mandatory sentencing laws went into effect in the mid-1980s, the California female prison population has skyrocketed. At the end of 1986, women in California's prisons totaled 3,564. Today the population now numbers 10,987, an increase of 305% in twelve years. (California Department of Correction [CDC] data)

As of June 30, 1996, 77.6% of women in California prisons were imprisoned for nonviolent offenses, the majority of which were drug-related. (Criminal Justice Consortium; CDC)

Every prison for women in California is 160% or more above its designed capacity. The federal women's prison in Dublin is more than 128% over capacity. (as of March 31, 1998, CDC Population Report; May 7, 1998 BOP Population Report)

Although African American women make up roughly 13% of California's female population, they constitute 33.6% of the California female prison population. And although white females are around 48% of the female population of California, they make up only 37% of the states female prison population. Hispanic females constitute 22.3% of the female prison population. (Dept. of Finance, CA Statistical Abstract & CDC Monthly Ethnicity Report)

Although African American women are 33% of the population of Valley State Penitentiary for Women, they represent 45% (the highest number) of the women in the Security Housing Unit (SHU) at Valley State. (as of April 30,1998, CDC Monthly Ethnicity Report)

According to a Department of Justice Statistics report released in April 1998, 48% of women in United States jails reported being sexually or physically abused prior to their detention; 27% reported being raped. Given the general underreporting by women in the area of sexual assault, the actual percentages are likely to be much higher.

A 1995 study of women in the California prison system found that 71% of incarcerated women had experienced ongoing physical abuse prior to the age of 18 and that 62% experienced ongoing physical abuse after 18 years of age. The report also found that 41% of women incarcerated in California had experienced sexual abuse prior to the age of 18 and 41% experienced sexual abuse after 18 years of age. Such a background further inhibits the ability of female inmates to report or seek recourse in cases of abuse within the

prison system. (Barbara Bloom, Barbara Owen, *Profiling the Needs of California's Female Prisoners,* 1995)

Access to prisons by social service agencies and organizations is entirely dependent upon the prerogative and power of prison wardens. In many cases, attorneys and local organizations spend months waiting for prison officials to respond to their requests for access.

Harsh media restrictions instituted by the CDC and presently in effect for all California state prisons severely limit the ability of the press to document abuses within the system. The media rules prohibit reporters from scheduling news interviews with specific prisoners in California prisons. Previous news interviews conducted before the institution of these rules led to the publicizing of violations of prisoners' human rights by California prison officials. Under the new rules, reporters may only appear at the prison and interview at random individuals the prison determines are available. The new constraints make it far more difficult for the media to obtain the testimonies of inmates who may claim similar abuses.

All potential visitors to California prisons must submit a visiting questionnaire that requires the individual to state personal information such as one's full arrest record and criminal history. Verification time for questionnaires can be

---

Critical Statistics: Women in California Prisons, May 1998, is reprinted by permission of Legal Services for Prisoners with Children, Women's Institute for Leadership Development and California Coalition for Women Prisoners.

lengthy, and if any piece of information proves to be incorrect, access can be denied for up to six months.

Despite the fact that drug addiction is a reality for many women entering California's prisons, there is no comprehensive support structure for detoxification when a female addict enters the prison system. While California does operate some drug treatment programs/facilities for inmates, space is limited and detoxification drugs such as methadone are not permitted.

 Article Review Form at end of book.

How do elderly prisoners' experiences of prison differ from those of their younger peers? What, if any, special provisions should be made for elderly inmates?

Southern Prisons and Elderly Inmates:

Taking a Look Inside

Kate King

State Texas A & M University

Patricia Bass

State University of West Georigia

Introduction

Inmates, fifty-five years and older, have traditionally constituted only three to four percent of the total prison population in this country (Walsh, 1992). The current "get tough" attitude, with stiffer penalties, mandatory sentencing laws, restrictive parole policies, and the abolition of parole in some jurisdictions, is not only increasing prison populations, but keeping people incarcerated well into old age. Walsh (1992) estimates that by the year 2000 there will be over 100,000 inmates in America over the age of 55. The Federal Bureau of Prisons predicts that by the year 2005, 16 percent of their population will be over 50 (Morton & Jacobs, 1991). George Washington University National Law Center's Project for Older Prisoners (1991) estimates there will be more than 125,000 elderly inmates by the year 2,000.

It costs prisons more to keep an older inmate: roughly $69,000 per year, or about three times the cost of the average inmate (Holman, 1997). Most of that increase is due to necessary medical care. Prisoners tend to suffer from ailments typical of old age much younger than the general public. Prison is a stressful environment (Vega & Silverman, 1988; Aday, 1994). Extortion and physical assaults are common. Predatory inmates prey on the weak, stealing their food, cigarettes, and soap (Irwin, 1980; Kelsey, 1986). Many inmates have a history of drug or alcohol abuse, poor nutrition, or lack of lifetime medical care (Holman, 1997). Older prisoners have been found to have combinations of debilitating physical, emotional, and social problems (Chaiklin & Fultz, 1983).

Mobility is also a problem as one ages. Aging inmates may need extra assistance in getting around or specialized equipment like wheelchairs, walkers, or canes. Older inmates may need ground floor accommodations, lower bunks, special meals, and more sleep. Elderly inmates may also be more sensitive to harsh physical conditions in the prison and have trouble adapting to damp or drafty cellblocks (Vito & Wilson, 1985; Dugger, 1988).

Debilitating diseases like cancer, heart disease, and stroke may require constant monitoring and/or special medication. Most prison infirmaries were not designed to administer long-term, labor-intensive medical care. Since the constitution requires that prisons provide medical care for inmates (*Estelle* v. *Gamble*; *Newman* v. *Alabama*) and prisoners are staying in longer, America's prison administrators are grappling with how to meet their obligations to this particular segment of the population.

This paper examines preliminary data gathered from thirteen prisons in five southern states on healthcare issues and the elderly inmate. Questionnaires were mailed to prison administrators in Alabama, Florida, Georgia, North Carolina, and South Carolina. Information requested included the population of the facility, sex of the inmates, age and race distribution, health problems typically dealt with, location of treatment facilities, number of times inmates were treated annually, approximate cost of treatment, and any special program information on older inmates.

Age presented the most difficult aspect of this project. Various disciplines define elderly in different ways. Depending on the discipline, "older" may bedefined from thirty for criminologists to sixty-five for gerontologists (Anno, 1991). Morton and Jacobs (1991) report that within

Southern Prisons and Elderly Inmates: Taking a Look Inside, K. King and P. Bass. Paper presented at the annual meeting of the American Society of Criminology, San Diego, Calif., November 1997. Reprinted by permission of the author.

prisons themselves, the age definition for "elderly" inmate ranges from 50 to 65. For the purpose of this study, forty-five is the operational definition of elderly and it is then broken into ten year segments (i.e., 45–54, 55–64, 65–74, 75–84, 85+).

Special Needs of the Elderly

Generally, the elderly acquire special needs as they age. Their physical bodies and mental states deteriorate with the aging process. Therefore, physical as well as mental health care is required. In a stressful prison environment, deterioration of the entire being may be accelerated (Gillespie & Galliher, 1972).

According to Anno (1991), three basic rights have emerged from court litigation concerning health care for inmates. First, is the right to access to care. "Access to care must be provided for any condition, be it medical, dental or psychological, if the denial of care might result in pain, suffering, deterioration or degeneration" (Anno 1991, p. 36). Second, is the right to care that is ordered. ". . . [A] constitutional violation is presented when needed prescribed care is denied to an inmate" (Anno 1991, p. 36). The third right is the right to a professional medical judgment. This assures that "decisions concerning the nature and timing of medical care are made by medical personnel, using equipment designed for medical use, in locations conducive to medical functions, and for reasons that are purely medical" (Anno 1991, p. 36).

In reviewing the data from this project, Florida exhibited the most comprehensive evaluation of elderly inmates. From their research, they assessed special needs and problems to be addressed related to the following:

1. chronic health problems—physical, dental, psychological

2. substance abuse

3. vulnerability to victimization by younger, more aggressive inmates

4. lack of interest in prison programs, such as educational and vocational programs

5. inability to participate in many recreation programs

6. if sex offenders, ineligibility for work release or community-based drug programs

7. lack of financial resources

8. ineligibility for employment with PRIDE

9. lack of family or family members who are financially able to contribute

10. the continuation of the aging process in prison

11. the need for transition release programs, such as health, family, housing, and financial support.

Although Georgia does not maintain chronological statistics, they reported multiple health care problems with related needs for treatment, including special meals and medications, more physical disabilities, less ability to work, and victimization as special problems facing the elderly inmates.

Alabama, North Carolina, and South Carolina all reported chronic health problems, lack of mobility, and inability to work as the biggest problems facing their elderly prisoners.

Prison-Based Programs and/or Facilities for Elderly Inmates

Florida has two specialized housing institutions and one specialized dormitory specifically for older inmates. The two institutions house males and the dormitory houses females. Within the two male institutions, infirmaries provide basic medical care, while serious medical problems are sent to nearby local hospitals. Access to educational or vocational training is provided. Recreational programs include shuffleboard, parlor games, bocci, and watching television. Inmates with physical limitations are assigned easier jobs. Within the female dorm, most older inmates have lighter job assignments. Pre-release orientation is offered for both males and females. Needs assessment committees have been established to further develop strategies to meet the special needs of the elderly inmate.

Georgia does not segregate by age, however, those with medical and/or physical needs are housed in a "nursing home like" facility in Men's Correctional Institution. Special needs are remedied by prison infirmaries, unless more extensive care requires community resources. Even though age is not a determinant for special housing, more than half of the population of this facility is over the age of 50. In addition, it is estimated that over half of the inmates are chronic care cases. Six hundred of these inmates suffer from more than one disability, primarily cardiac conditions.

Two facilities in North Carolina house elderly inmates. McCain Correctional Hospital provides an acute care hospital and a geriatric unit for minimum custody inmates. Aged and infirm inmates with higher custody levels are housed in Central Prison in Raleigh. Age, and not solely medical condition, is a determinant for housing assignments as some inmates are transferred to these facilities based on their age alone. Treatment for medical ailments is provided in the housing unit.

South Carolina's State Park Correctional Center has one minimum security geriatric and handicapped unit for older men and women. To be assigned here, the inmate must be 55 or older with some health limitation. Residents are required to care for their rooms, attend meals, get out of bed and stay dressed throughout the day. Primary staff concerns are medical care, death and loss counseling, and individualized programming. This facility is not a nursing home, but rather, a geriatric/handicapped unit. The majority of older inmates with higher custody levels are housed at the Broad River Correctional Institution.

Issues Facing Prison Officials

A 1993 status report on elderly inmates prepared by the Youth and Special Needs Program Office of the Florida Department of Corrections provides information concerning the national profile of the elderly inmate. According to this report, "the number of inmates 55 and older more than doubled from 1981 to 1990"

(p. 5). The following facts in the report provide a profile of the older inmate nationwide.

- Over 95% are males.

- A majority are white; however, minorities (black, Latino, Native American) are disproportionately represented.

- Their health is fair to poor, with a history of substance abuse and depression.

- Most are single, widowed, separated, or divorced.

- Most have less than a high school education.

- Most are unskilled or semiskilled, often with lower-level clerical or sales abilities.

- Offenses include the following:

  Type 1—long-term offenders; committed major felonies (homicide)

  Type 2—chronic recidivists; committed property crimes and sexual offenses (including rape and child molestation)

  Type 3—late-life, first time offenders; committed crimes against the person (homicide, aggravated assault, and vehicular homicide)

- The recidivism rate is less than 5% and goes down as age goes up.

- Research indicates that older inmates are better behaved in prison than younger inmates.

- They have much lower recidivism rates following release. Many states and the federal prison system take this lower recidivism rate into account when making parole decisions involving older inmates.

- Research indicates that older inmates prefer living in units separated from younger inmates, primarily for safety reasons.

- Several states are providing special housing and programs for older inmates. Most of these policies, however, are based primarily on the inmates' health rather than age.

- Many studies indicate that most existing programs are not designed structurally or programmatically for older inmates and do not meet their needs.

- Many are serving long sentences and are not eligible for early release or parole.

- A large number of elderly male inmates are not eligible for community-based programs due to the nature of their sentences. Many are sex offenders, which means they are automatically excluded from work-release or community-based drug programs.

- Elderly inmates are the most expensive to incarcerate.

A general description of the elderly inmate then, is one who is a white male, in poor health, often with a history of substance abuse and depression, uneducated, unskilled, with no close family, and serving a long sentence for a major offense. Even though older inmates are better behaved than younger ones (Wiegand & Burger, 1979; Wilson & Gennaro, 1986; Holman, 1997; but see McShane & Williams, 1990) this criteria may seem insignificant to a parole board when the type of offense and the inmate's chance of establishing residence and procuring and maintaining employment is considered. Because of the general characteristics of the elder inmate then, he remains a poor parole risk (Goetting, 1983; Wiegand & Burger, 1979).

The most crucial issue facing prison officials concerns healthcare. According to the research that has been conducted and the data from this project, chronic and/or terminally ill conditions must be addressed. Anno (1991) recommends that "[p]risons housing elderly offenders should have immediate access to properly equipped and staffed emergency services, and the availability of round-the-clock nursing care" (p. 146). Not only should inmates have regular healthcare staff available, but also "specialists to address their chronic and age-related illnesses and conditions" (Anno 1991, p. 146). As more inmates gray in prisons, prisons are facing escalating healthcare costs.

From the survey data that was recorded chronologically, the following trends emerge. Keep in mind that these numbers are conservative because not all of the thirteen prisons surveyed keep chronological records. In the 45–54 age group, the inmate population was 4,881, or about 67% of the total elderly population, with hypertension being the most prevalent health problem and diabetes second. Forty percent suffered from hypertension, 24% from diabetes, 8% suffered prostate trouble, arthritis, and chronic obstructive pulmonary disease (COPD), and 4% suffered headaches, seizures, and poor vision.

A dramatic drop in population occurs between the 55–64 and the 45–54 age range. From the 4,881 inmates in the 45–54 age group, the count decreased to 1,762 in the 55–64 age range, making the 55–64 age group comprise approximately 24% of the total elder population sampled in this study. When examining the health problems of this group, headaches and poor vision were not recorded, but, heart disease was added. A lower percentage of inmates suffered from hypertension and diabetes, but an increase in arthritis, COPD, and prostate were recorded.

The age group 65–74 comprises approximately 7% of the total elder population. This group demonstrated yet another increase in arthritis and heart disease. In addition, psychological and respiratory problems began to surface. Other diseases and/or problems remained fairly constant.

Even though the 75–84 age group accounts for only 1% of the total aged population, other serious problems emerged. Mental health problems such as disorientation and dementia as well as nutritional problems contribute 11% each of the total health problems with still another increase in both heart disease and arthritis at 22% each and a slight decrease in hypertension from 25% to approximately 22%.

For immediate treatment of health problems, the prison infirmary and local hospital share the same percentage of 42.9, while the unit nurse, prison doctor or local doctor treat the remaining patients. As problems become persistent, the prison infirmary handles 52.6% of the cases while the local hospital drops to 10.5%. The unit nurse and prison doctor share in the remaining treatment. From persistent to chronic care, the prison infirmary caseload increases to 57.9%. Rather than the local hospital being utilized, special clinics treat 15.8% of the problems with the unit doctor and nurse participating. For constant medical care, the prison infirmary treats 76.5% of the caseload, with the correction center helping with 5.9%. The local hospital handles only 17.6% of these cases.

As age increases, so do health problems. Georgia reported that as an inmate ages, he is more likely to suffer from multiple problems. Even though the total population of inmates decreases in age category, the number of health problems increases. As illustrated above, prison infirmaries assume more responsibility for care as an inmate's medical condition progresses from acute medical care to chronic medical care. Little or no outside funding is available. Thus, the cost of healthcare falls upon the prison system.

Florida, whose elder inmate population ranks third in the nation, is taking the initiative to study these issues they find most critical: 1) mainstreaming versus specialized units, 2) physical facility, 3) programming and services, 4) staff selection and training, and 5) community involvement.

Conclusion

Relatively little research has been conducted on elderly healthcare in prison. Because most prisons do not keep chronological medical records, the scope of elderly inmates' healthcare needs and treatment costs is difficult to assess. Indeed, none of the prisons surveyed kept total records regarding the number of times aged inmates were treated or knew the cost of treating elderly prisoners. As the prison population ages, health problems increase both in numbers and severity. With the current trends in prison healthcare, prisons will bear the brunt of the cost. Unless preventative measures are promptly utilized, both prison systems and elderly inmates are likely to suffer the consequences. Other states would be wise to follow Florida's proactive approach in addressing and dealing with the predictable increase in elderly inmates and their problems.

References

Aday, R. H. (1994). "Aging in Prison: A Case Study of New Elderly Offenders." *International Journal of Offender Therapy and Comparative Criminology*, 38(1):79–91.

Anno, B. J. (1991). *Prison Health Care: Guidelines for the Management of an Adequate Delivery System*. National Institute of Corrections, U.S. Department of Justice.

Chaiklin, H. and L. Fultz. (1983). "Service Needs of Older Offenders." Paper presented 1983 NASW Professional Symposium, Washington, D.C.

Dugger, R. L. (1988). "Graying in America's Prisons: Special Care Considerations." *Corrections Today*, 50(3):26–30.

Florida Department of Corrections. (1993). *Status Report on Elderly Inmates*.

George Washington University National Law Center. (1991). *Project for Older Prisoners (POPS)*. Washington, D.C.

Gillespie, M. W. and J. F. Galliher. (1972). "Age, Anomie, and the Inmates' Definition of Aging in Prison: An Exploratory Study." In Donald P. Kent, Robert Kastenbaum and Sylvia Sherwood, eds. *Research Planning and Action for the Elderly*. Behavioral Publications, Inc. New York, pp. 465–483.

Goetting, A. (1983). "The Elderly in Prison: Issues and Perspectives." *Journal of Research in Crime and Delinquency*, 20:291–309.

Holman, J. R. (1997). "Prison Care" *Modern Maturity*, 40(2):30–36.

Irwin, J. (1980). *Prisons in Turmoil*. Glenview, IL: Scott, Foresman and Company.

Kelsey, O. W. (1986). "Elderly Inmates: Providing Safe and Humane Care." *Corrections Today*, 48(3):56, 58.

Morton, J. B. and N. C. Jacobs. (1991). *Older Inmates in State and Federal Prison: State of the Art*.

Vega, M. and M. Silverman. (1988). "Stress and the Elderly Convict." *International Journal of Offender Therapy and Comparative Criminology*, 32(2):153–162.

Vito, G. and D. G. Wilson. (1985). "Forgotten People: Elderly Inmates." *Federal Probation*, 49(1):18–24.

Walsh, C. E. (1992). "Aging Inmate Offenders: Another Perspective" in *Correctional Theory and Practice*, Clayton A. Hartjen and Edward E. Rhine, eds. Nelson Hall, Chicago. pp. 197–212.

Wilson, D. G. and G. Vito. (1986). "Imprisoned Elders: The Experience of an Institution." *Criminal Justice Policy Review*, 1(4):399–421.

Cases

Estelle v. *Gamble* (1976) 429 U.S. 97
Newman v. *Alabama* (1981) 349 F. Supp. 282

 Article Review Form at end of book.

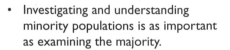
WiseGuide Wrap-Up

- Investigating and understanding minority populations is as important as examining the majority.

- Efficiently and accurately identifying offenders who will re-offend is particularly difficult and complex.

- Those incarcerated within prisons, jails, and detention centers may continue to engage in criminal behaviors.

R.E.A.L. Sites

This list provides a print preview of typical **Coursewise** R.E.A.L. sites. There are over 100 such sites at the **Courselinks**™ site. The danger in printing URLs is that web sites can change overnight. As we went to press, these sites were functional using the URLs provided. If you come across one that isn't, please let us know via email to: webmaster@coursewise. Com. Use your Passport to access the most current list of R.E.A.L. sites at the **Courselinks** site.

Site name: Forum of Correctional Services of Canada

URL: http://198.103.98.138/crd/forum/

Why is it R.E.A.L.? This site provides a large number of articles on corrections research. Topics include investigating methods of predicting those who will re-offend and examining minority prison populations.

Key topics: female prisoners, male prisoners, overcrowding, prisoner rights

Try this: See if you can find the article in this book: *Women and Fraud: Results of a Program at the Prison for Women.*

Site name: The Other Side of the Wall

URL: http://www.wco.com/~aerick/

Why is it R.E.A.L.? This site has articles written by inmates. A regularly updated newsletter is published here and contains articles covering the different corrections perspectives of inmates, prisons officers, and other criminal justice personnel.

Key topics: capital punishment, female prisoners, male prisoners, miscarriages of justice, sentencing

Try this: See if you could live the life of a convicted killer on California's death row.

Site name: United Nations Crime and Justice Network

URL: http://www.ifs.univie.ac.at/~uncjin/uncjin.html

Why is it R.E.A.L.? This site provides a global perspective to crime and justice. In particular, it contains information exploring UN standards and minimum requirements for prisoners.

Key topics: gangs, juveniles, public attitudes, victimization

Try this: At this site, see if you can pick a country like Mexico and review the data about organized juvenile crime.

Site name: RAND

URL: http://www.rand.org/

Why is it R.E.A.L.? Rand analyzes choices and developments in many areas, including national defense, education and training, health care, criminal and civil justice, labor and population, science and technology, community development, international relations, and regional studies.

Key topics: criminal life styles, gangs, reintegration, treatment

Try this: Most of the studies conducted by Rand are applied research. Click on this site and look over the applied research suggesting that drug treatment among offenders works. In what way might you disagree with their findings?

section 3

Key Points

- Prisons punish by depriving liberty and autonomy.

- The intent of sentencing and the reality of incarceration may by far removed from one another.

- Prisons can be violent and dangerous places where both staff and prisoners are at risk.

- Prisons indirectly punish more people than those sentenced and may well cost society more than just the resources necessary to run prisons.

Prison Life

Joanna R. Adler Ph.D.
Department of Psychology; Keynes College, The University of Kent at Canterbury; Canterbury, UK CT2 7NP   J.R.Adler@ukc.ac.uk

WiseGuide Intro

Prisons around the world hold an assortment of people from the dispossessed to the dangerous. There are those who are currently awaiting trial and are therefore normally considered innocent; there are those who have defaulted on fines; there are those who have committed heinous acts and those who have committed minor offenses. And, what of the different characteristics of men, women, and children in prison? There are the young and old, those serving their first custodial sentence, and people who have grown up and grown old in and around institutions including prisons; there are those who have a learning difficulty and there are those with university degrees. In short, no matter what the jurisdiction, a prison or jail holds so many different types of people from so many different racial, ethnic, and socioeconomic backgrounds that you could be forgiven for thinking that life inside would be a microcosm of life outside, but it isn't.

Prisons vary in the levels of security around and within them from places where prisoners may go outside to work to those where they spend 23 our of 24 hours a day (or even all 24 hours) in the cell assigned to them. Yet, something that seems to mark out a prison is the loss of autonomy that a prisoner feels. A few prisoners may find it preferable to be denied freedom of choice and responsibility within an institution but for the vast majority, the function of punishment is fulfilled by the deprivation of liberty. But, this is not where punishment stops. According to Gresham M. Sykes in *Society of Captives*, prisons punish in five ways: they produce a sense of rejection in prisoners; prisoners suffer from extreme material deprivation; deprivation of heterosexual relationships; deprivation of autonomy, and they are forced to associate with other criminals. These five, so-called pains of imprisonment have provided a focus for literature produced by academics, practitioners, and ex-prisoners who have recorded life within jails and it is to examples of such literature that we now turn.

This section begins with two readings that reflect some current themes about "doing time." It opens with an assessment of prisoners' perceptions about punishment. From there we move on to a report about prisoners' evaluations of the effectiveness of imprisonment—in this case, how likely they are to be violent in the future. The section then moves on to look at victimization and fear in prisons. We then change perspective again and give you the view of women held in prisons who are mothers and conclude with a reading examining the vicarious effects of imprisonment on families.

Can prisons fulfill the aims of sentencing?

Do they fulfill the aims of sentencing?

Based on their experiences inside prisons, how would you expect people to behave after release?

How would you evaluate the effects of imprisonment on the families of offenders?

? Questions ?

Reading 15. Do people who impose sentences and those they imprison agree about the effects and purposes of prison? Is prison likely to deter people from crime?

Reading 16. How does the organization of a prison affect prisoners' predictions about their future behavior? What are the other factors that influence prisoners' predictions about future violence?

Reading 17. Has previous research trivialized the impact of seemingly routine aggression in prisons? What are the implications of "normalized" aggression for life after prison?

Reading 18. Are staff aware of the fears of prisoners? Is fear in prison something about which we should be concerned?

Reading 19. Does imprisoning mothers increase the chances that they will re-offend?

Reading 20. How might stigmatization of an offender's family affect their quality of life? What might be the effects upon visitors of the ways in which both adults and children are searched?

Do people who impose sentences and those they imprison agree about the effects and purposes of prison? Is prison likely to deter people from crime?

The Meaning of Punishment:

Inmates' Orientation to the Prison Experience

Patricia Van Voorhis
Sandra Lee Browning
Marilyn Simon
University of Cincinnati
Jill Gordon
Virginia Commonwealth University

As the federal and state governments implement the latest series of crime control bills, policy makers confidently claim to have achieved punishment strategies that will capture the attention of criminals. Embedded in such legislation is new-found confidence that additional boot camps, "three-strikes-you're-out" laws, "truth in sentencing," intermediate sanctions, and the elimination of Pell Grants, good time, and weight rooms will go far toward solving the crime problem. And, for the time being, these new ideas seem to have achieved unprecedented media attention and vote-getting appeal.

News accounts and political speeches underscore the reasoning behind the new laws: (a) some criminals must be put away for a long time, (b) incapacitation is the only sure way to stop a criminal, and (c) if our current sentences are not solving the crime problem, we must not be administering enough punishment. Thus tougher sentences will incapaci-

tate and deter future criminals better than current sanctions, particularly anything supportive of offender rehabilitation. This line of reasoning seems largely speculative. In the United States Congress, for example, neither the legislation nor the rationales were presented to the scrutiny of correctional practitioners or scholars (Corrections 2000, 1994), and numerous provisions of the new bills, in fact, are not supported by correctional experts *or* extant research (American Correctional Association, 1994).

Although the assumption that the new bills will have an impact on offender perceptions is a weak one, such reasoning illustrates a long tradition of speculating about what offenders will think about their sanction, and history tells us that such assumptions carry a good deal of weight in generating crime control policies. In truth, however, we know very little about how offenders make sense of the punishment experience. We know even less about whether or not offender perceptions have any impact on prison adjustment or future crimes. Simply put, the purpose of corrections is typically the design of lawmakers and less frequently jurisprudential scholars; a current theory or philosophy is almost never supported by evidence that offenders make sense of their punishments in the same way.

This article explores the orientations of two different prison populations, a minimum security federal prison camp and a maximum security federal penitentiary. We examine the extent to which inmates experience traditional correctional purposes (e.g., deterrence, rehabilitation, incapacitation, and retribution). After serving at least 4 months of their prison terms, the subjects of this study were surveyed and asked questions pertaining to how they were making sense of their sentence. Did they see it as deserved? Was it a punishment? What is a deterrent? Could it be rehabilitative? Was it teaching them a lesson? Alternatively, was no purpose being served? We examine (a) the extent to which inmates perceive traditional sentencing intents, (b) whether or not these perceptions differ across different correctional environments, (c) interrelationships between orientations, and (d) psychological, demographic, and criminal record correlates of correctional perceptions.[1]

Review of the Literature

An overview of the literature on the purpose of punishment shows us that inquiry is limited mostly to theoretical and philosophical analysis, public surveys, and policy analyses of the impact of sentencing changes on aggregate crime rates. Scholarly analysis and debate of the most optimal purpose of punishment dates back to the work of Classical scholars Jeremy Bentham and Cesaria Beccaria, proceeds through the time of the positivist criminologists and on to the formation of the Justice Model (American Friends Service Committee, 1971; Fogel, 1979; Morris, 1974) and its critics (Cullen & Gilbert, 1982; Currie, 1985; Palmer, 1983). More recently, the discussion focuses on a renewed interest in punishment as a deterrent (Paternoster, 1987) or as an effective means of incapacitation (Blumstein & Cohen, 1978; Newman, 1978; Sherman & Hawkins, 1982; Zimring & Hawkins, 1995). Public surveys are numerous. But although these data appear to support the notion that prisons should be punitive (Zimring & Hawkins, 1991), they also support prison rehabilitation programming (Cullen, Skovron, Scott, & Burton, 1990; McCorkle, 1993; Public Agenda Foundation, 1987). Surprisingly, offender viewpoints are seldom sought.

In the absence of the criminals' views, the assertions of scholars, policy makers, activists, and the public are surprisingly presumptuous. Yet such assumptions are well-embedded in American correctional history. They include the Quakers' vision of the penitent inmate who wold think about his transgressions while in solitary confinement. From time to time scholars have also maintained that many prisoners are not interested in rehabilitation but rather profess rehabilitative intents in order to impress parole boards (Mitford, 1973; Morris, 1974). Additional assumptions include (a) retributive sentences are overly punitive to inmates (Menninger, 1966), and (b) rehabilitative, indeterminant sentences are overly punitive (American Friends Service Committee, 1971; Fogel, 1979; von Hirsch, 1976). More recently, Hawkins and Alpert (1989) note that given the current overcrowded conditions of most prisons, most correctional goals are severely compromised, if not totally unattainable, and inmates can spot the resulting hypocrisy. Finally, some hold that we can give up on notions of rehabilitation, retribution, and deterrence; a modest level of selective incapacitation is our most realistic

hope (Sherman & Hawkins, 1982; Zimring & Hawkins, 1995). In this last instance, it doesn't really matter *what* inmates think.

In sum, most discussions of the purpose of prison, or of any sanction, embody modest to strong suppositions regarding how offenders will perceive (or not perceive) the sanction and how these perceptions might then affect future criminal behavior. Ironically, most of these same discussions omit any empirical evidence of offender viewpoints.

Deterrence Research

One exception to this trend emerges from a body of research pertaining to perceptions of deterrence. Although this research offers very little (Paternoster, 1987) to equivocal (Klepper & Nagin, 1989) evidence of a sanction's severity serving as a deterrent, most studies sample the general population, focusing on the notion of general deterrence. In contrast, empirical studies of prison inmates cast serious doubt on any hopes that prison might be considered by inmates to be a deterrent (Sherman & Hawkins, 1981; Zimring & Hawkins, 1995). Furthermore, studies of the effectiveness of deterrent punishments (e.g., scared straight, shock probation) find these "get tough" strategies to be less effective than alternatives (Gendreau & Ross, 1987).

On a more complex note, the effects of specific deterrent and punitive options are highly idiosyncratic (Bonta & Gendreau, 1990; Gibbs, 1975; McClelland & Alpert, 1985). Even Wilson and Herrnstein (1985), while speaking to the importance of offenders' assessments of the costs and benefits of crime, inform that such calculations are likely to vary from individual to individual. Of course, these observations come as no surprise to the behavioral psychologists who assert that the impact of punishment on future behavior is affected by such individual perceptions as the legitimacy of the punishing agent and one's personal repertoire of instigators and inhibitors (Bandura, 1973). Others tell us that biological and cognitive factors may predispose "unconditionable" individuals to dismiss the severity of a specific sanction (Eysenck, 1977; Quay, 1965).

Rehabilitation Research

Limiting our inquiry to whether or not offenders perceive their sanctions as punitive or deterrentignores another, albeit less popular, correctional purpose—rehabilitation. Clearly, offender orientations to rehabilitation would appear to be an extremely important notion to examine. Readers will perhaps recall claims of inmates "using" treatment participation not for the intended purposes of self-improvement, but rather to impress parole boards into granting an early release (Mitford, 1973; Morris, 1974). Although the notion of "the parole game" lent powerful support to the "Nothing Works" movement and to shifts in correctional policy that favored punishment over rehabilitation (Cullen & Gilbert, 1982), empirical support for inmates using rehabilitation to manipulate parole boards is difficult to find. Mitford (1973) cites a National Council on Crime and Delinquency (NCCD) survey of inmates conducted 40 years ago, where inmates' lack of enthusiasm was attributable to poor programming as much, if not more, than to their insincerity or lack of interest in self-improvement. Certainly, superficial attempts at programming can breed some level of cynicism among inmates (Hawkins & Alpert, 1989), and research may have difficulty separating inmates' insincerity from the quality of the programming.

In contrast, surveys that tap inmates' opinions about correctional priorities, asking what *should* happen rather than what is happening, offer rather strong support for rehabilitation (Cullen & Gilbert, 1982; Hawkins, 1976; Toch, 1977; Wright, 1989). The most convincing evidence in this regard appears in responses to Toch's Prison Preference Inventory where inmates are asked to rank their main concerns of prison life. Respondents consistently rank "support" (in the form of programming leading to self-improvement or development) as their highest priority, above even safety, privacy, and freedom (Toch, 1977; Wright, 1989). . . .

This article will address most of the issues raised in the preceding discussion: (a) Do inmates consider their immediate prison term to be a deterrent? (b) Do they see it as punitive? (c) Is the sentence teaching them a lesson? (d) Do inmates take rehabilitation seriously? (e) Are they conning the parole board? (f) How do the orientations of a maximum security population differ from those among minimum security inmates? (g) What is the relationship among orientations? (h) What are the demographic, psychological, and criminal record correlates of traditional correctional orientations? In contrast to other studies (e.g., Crouch, 1993; Petersilia & Piper-Deschenes, 1994), however, we are not asking inmates to compare their sanction to an alternative option. Neither do we examine the effects of the inmates' orientations on future behaviors.

Methodology

Data for this study were part of a larger classification study conducted at the United States Federal Penitentiary and the Federal Prison Camp at Terre Haute, Indiana, between 1986 and 1988. On the Federal Bureau of Prison's security system, the penitentiary is considered low maximum security and the prison camp is designated minimum security. We use data collected in a follow-up survey of the prison inmates administered at a minimum of 4 months following their admission to prison.

Sample Characteristics

A total of 179 penitentiary and 190 prison camp inmates participated in the larger classification study. . . .

This article does not focus on the entire sample, but rather 111 (64%) penitentiary inmates and 114 (69%) prison camp inmates who completed a follow-up survey. As might be expected, the penitentiary inmates differed from the prison camp inmates in substantial ways. The prison camp inmates can be portrayed as slightly older than the penitentiary inmates. . . .

Results

Perhaps one of the most surprising findings from this portion of the analysis concerns the similarity of responses between the two groups. Notwithstanding substantial differences in criminal histories, prison experience, and current offenses,

difference of proportion tests revealed no significant differences between groups. Slight differences were noted on two items: (a) *deterrent*, where 10% more prison camp inmates than penitentiary inmates indicated that their sentence was a specific deterrent, and (b) *deserts*, where 10% more of the prison camp inmates than the penitentiary inmates disagreed with the assertion that they deserved to be punished. In the first instance, these differences may reflect the minimum security inmates' lack of experience or familiarity with prison or the criminal justice system—so that relative to the familiar, life in even a minimum-security institution was a deterrent. The second difference also makes sense. Given the less serious nature of the criminal careers and offenses of minimum-security inmates, more may feel that prison is undeserved. Just the same, similarities between the two populations far outweighed any differences.

The notions adhered to by the majority of inmates (in both settings) were rehabilitation, deterrence, the need to impress the parole board, and the idea that the prison experience was serving no purpose. In contrast, far fewer inmates believed that they were "paying back" society, deserved to be incarcerated, or needed to be incarcerated for the safety of society. Similarly, relatively few inmates adhered to a belief that they could scam the staff. Thee orientations agreed to by the highest proportion of inmates were that their experience was a deterrent (67% penitentiary and 77% prison camp) and that, at some point, they would have to impress the parole board.

For an appropriate interpretation of these responses, one must examine the meaning of the index items carefully. We have made an attempt to differentiate inmates' beliefs and priorities (i.e., what prison should be) from their actual experiences (what prison is). With respect to rehabilitation, for example, subjects were asked not whether they wanted to participate in rehabilitation programs, but whether they were actually finding programs that would help them grow. We don't know whether a negative response to the items means that the inmate was not interested in rehabilitation or that he

was not able to find meaningful programs. However, during an intake interview, discussions of the ideal purpose for prison revealed different findings. In the interview, the majority of both the penitentiary inmates (60%) and the camp inmates (58%) indicated that rehabilitation *should* be the priority for corrections. In contrast, none of the remaining options, such as deterrence, incapacitation, retribution, punishment, or "no purpose," received more than 15% of the interview responses.[5]

Interrelationships Between Inmate Perceptions of Correctional Intents

An examination of the interrelationships between these notions adds more perspective to the findings discussed in the previous section. The matrix shows considerable agreement among some of the items. In fact, attitudes, in a general sense, were either favorable or unfavorable. For example, inmates scoring high on the rehabilitation items *also* indicated that they deserved to do time, were being taught a lesson by the sentence, adhered to the notion of reparation, and believed that some purpose was being served by their sentence. More modest relationships are found between *rehabilitation* and *show board* and between rehabilitation and *scam staff*. Additional strong interrelationships are noted between *deterrence* and *retribution* and *deserts* and between *incapacitation* and deserts. It is also noteworthy that inmates who believed that no purpose was being served were generally not the same inmates who agreed with the more traditional purposes of prison. Finally, a moderate negative relationship between scam staff and retribution finds those inmates who agreed that they were "paying back" for their offense to be less likely to believe that they could scam staff.

Was rehabilitation chosen solely in order to please the parole board? Pearson's r for the relationship between show board and rehabilitation, although significant, was modest, indicating that many inmates were not equating rehabilitation with "playing the parole game"—but some were.

The results appear to suggest that inmates either agreed with a package of traditional correctional intentions or they did not. In other words, they either perceived the societal purposes of prison or they did not. In order to fully support this interpretation, however, one must first dismiss the very real possibility that these data instead indicate response biases or the subjects' desire to offer socially desirable responses to researchers. In response, it is not the case that agreement is only between those responses that cast a favorable light on the inmate and those that do not. First, it is apparent that it was not true that these inmates simply examined a list of items and agreed with those that "looked good." For example, they did not agree with an assertion that society was safer with them in prison. In addition, some inmates who agreed with the notion of rehabilitation also thought it possible to scam staff or to look good to the parole board. One would assume that a subject would not choose such options if he wanted to look good on the survey. Moreover, some of the similarities cease as we observe distinct patterns of correlates in the next analyses. At this point, then, we would limit our caution to the observation that surveys are more susceptible to higher intercorrelations than some other type of measure might be, but that response bias is refuted in several instances.

One sees similar interrelationships between favorable attitudes and generally unfavorable ones as was noted for the survey results of the penitentiary inmates. There are noteworthy exceptions, however. In this environment, specific deterrence is not as consistent with rehabilitation and retribution as it is among penitentiary inmates. Recalling that the prison camp inmates were more likely to perceive the deterrent effects of their sanction, it appears that they viewed deterrence as conceptually distinct from rehabilitation. For these inmates, only the notion of deserts appeared consistent with deterrence. Otherwise, the deterrence item is somewhat conspicuously a response from a distinct group of inmates.

The *no purpose* variable was negatively related to all but one orientation, scam staff and deterrence, where there were no relationships. As with the penitentiary surveys, the inmates responding to the no pur-

pose item were quite consistent in their attitudes and quite distinct from other inmates.

The *show board* item was positively related to *rehabilitation, retribution,* and *deserts items* and negatively related to the *no purpose* and *scam staff* items. In both samples, findings for the *show board items* cast some doubt upon the image of inmates as insincere consumers of rehabilitative programs. Indeed, while the show *board item* is modestly related to *rehabilitation,* inmates responding favorably to this item generally were not manipulators of staff or possessive of cynical orientations to prison (no purpose).

Demographic, Psychological, and Criminal Record Correlates of Correctional Orientations

We turn now to a bivariate examination of the psychological, demographic, and criminal record factors associated with the various correctional intents. Understandably, perhaps, one of the orientations, show board, was found to have no correlates. In the case of the rehabilitation measure, however, age, IQ, race, employment, and prison experience were found to be significantly related, indicating that inmates who found the prison experience helpful were younger, non-White inmates, who were unemployed at the time of their arrest and had evidenced no prior prison experience and relatively low IQ scores.

In terms of the other orientations, we note somewhat fewer differentiating factors. But inmates *not* diagnosed as aggressive were more likely to agree that their sentence was deserved (deserts) or could serve as a way to pay back society (reparation), whereas aggressive inmates were more likely to believe that staff could be scammed. All three of these relationships were weak. At the same time, dependent inmates were significantly more likely to feel that their sanction was reparative. As in other studies (e.g., McClelland & Alpert, 1985) experienced inmates (those who had served prior prison terms) were less likely to agree that prison was serving as a deterrent.

There were a few more demographic correlates of the correctional orientations than sychological ones. Most notable, inmates who felt that prison was teaching them a lesson were young and had no previous incarcerations. On the other hand, older, White inmates, and those whose incarceration had interrupted full-time employment, tended to see no purpose to the sanction. Younger inmates were more likely to believe that staff could be scammed. Finally, those who were not married prior to arrest were slightly more likely to orient to the notion of incapacitation—that society was safer with them in prison.

An examination of the same issues among minimum-security inmates reveals four main correlates: (a) IQ, (b) age, (c) race, and (d) prison experience. Inmates with low IQ scores were more likely to believe that prison was incapacitating them and allowing them to repay society; inmates with higher IQs were slightly more likely to believe that no purpose was being served. Younger inmates were significantly more likely to believe that prison was rehabilitating them, offering an opportunity to repay society, deserved, and serving purposes of incapacitation. At the same time, younger inmates were more likely to believe that staff could be scammed. Older inmates and those with prior prison experience were more likely to believe that no purpose could be served by their sentence. Non-White inmates were more likely to agree with the purpose of retribution and incapacitation. Prior prison had an impact on a need to present oneself favorably to the parole board; those without prior terms were more likely to see this as a priority. At the same time, less prison experience also was correlated with the belief that one could achieve something constructive in prison (rehabilitation).

Personality was not a strong factor, except that inmates classified as aggressive on the Jesness Inventory were significantly more likely to believe that one could scam staff.

A clearer examination of these profiles is facilitated by the following multivariate analysis. We move to that also in order to explore similarities and differences between the two types of prison populations.

Conclusion

Prior to discussing the implications of these findings, let us first review what it was we measured. We measured actual inmate experiences of the prison environment, rather than prescriptive impressions of what they thought prison should be. There are both limitations and benefits to this approach. One clear limitation occurs as we attempt to differentiate inmates' values and priorities from the effects of the prison environment. The rehabilitation scale, for example, shows us whether inmates felt they could achieve personal growth in the current prison setting. But was a positive response attributable to the inmate's motivation or to his experience in specific treatment programs? Probably both. On the other hand, the advantage of this approach is that these measures have somewhat clearer policy relevance and a greater potential for testing the impact of the prison experience. What, for example, is one to do with a prescriptive measure (e.g., that prison *should be* rehabilitative) when we don't know what experiences would in fact be rehabilitative? At the same time the cognitive psychologists and more recently medical scholars inform us that one's perceptions of experiences can often be more important determinants of outcome than actual experience (Ellis, 1973; Meichenbaum, 1977).

With this context in mind, we highlight what we consider to be the most important observations of this research. First, although the maximum and the minimum security prison settings offered dramatically different living environments and terms of imprisonment, the meaning of the punishment experience was remarkably similar in both settings. A reasonable explanation, of course, is that the similar perceptions may actually be attributable to the differences among samples. A minimum-security setting, for example, may be as much of a deterrent to an inexperienced inmate as the maximum-security facility is to the experienced. Although the differences were not significant, fewer minimum security inmates felt that prison was deserved, and proportionately more prison camp inmates than penitentiary inmates felt that the experience

was a deterrent. Future studies may find it beneficial to examine these findings in terms of Andrews and Bonta's (1994) observation that intensive interventions for relatively low-risk inmates are counterproductive. We are also reminded of the often repeated responses of a group of University of Chicago scholars that prisons should be reserved for the most serious offenders (Morris, 1974; Zimring & Hawkins, 1991). More conclusive findings, of course, await research on the impact of offender perceptions on future crimes.

Our analysis of the interrelationships between orientations would typically be performed as a methodological prelude to multivariate analysis. In this case, however, the importance of the findings of the correlation matrix extend beyond measurement issues. We did not anticipate the clustering of orientations that we found. Instead of finding a focus on one purpose, we noted subjects who simultaneously experienced several correctional intentions at once, that is, the prisons' rehabilitative, incapacitative, retributive, *and* deterrent effects. It appeared that one group of inmates accepted several rationales simultaneously, whereas another group was more cynical, believing that no purpose could be served and that staff could be manipulated. We caution, however, that surveys can amplify the magnitude of interrelationships among items. However, in this study, the interitem correlations did not interfere with subsequent bivariate and multivariate analysis. If we take the observation that inmates either adhered to a package of traditional sentencing purposes or they did not on its face value, we can also note that these inmates do not differ substantially from their counterparts in the policy arena. Policy discussions and published agency materials routinely mention numerous goals at once. Historically, some have speculated that corrections suffers from goal confusion or a contradiction of purposes, but the inmates in these samples are not inconsistent with more recent correctional scholars whose writings assert that treatment and control (Palmer, 1992) or treatment and punishment (Andrews & Bonta, 1994; Bonta & Gendreau, 1990) can and perhaps should coexist.

In related research (Crouch, 1993; McClelland & Alpert 1985; Petersilia & Piper-Deschenes, 1994), experienced offenders, African Americans, unmarried, and older inmates tended to view prison as less punitive than certain types of community sanctions. Even though our sample is different (inmates rather than probationers or arrestees) and our questions pertain to the immediate situation rather than to the selection of a preferred sanction, our findings are somewhat consistent. In our study, age, race, prearrest employment status, and the extent of one's criminal career and prison experience were important determinants of how offenders made sense of their sentence. In exploring additional factors, IQ and personality also had an impact on prisoners' orientation to the experience. Marital status, however, had very little influence. Consistent with the earlier research, younger inmates with less prison experience were more likely to view prison as a deterrent. We go beyond the earlier research, however, in observing that not only were older inmates slightly less likely to see prison as a deterrent, in both settings, they saw *no* purpose to prison.

Perhaps the most relevant aspect of these factors is seen in the penitentiary sample in a comparison of those inmates who thought they were getting something out of prison (young, non-White, unemployed, situational, with less prior prison experience) with those who saw no purpose (White, older, and previously employed inmates). We are able to support one of the suggestions put forward by Petersilia (1990), citing Wilson (1987). The profile of the penitentiary inmate who believed that he was getting something out of prison shows a disadvantaged individual, who had no employment prior to his arrest, perhaps had limited opportunities for securing employment, and was non-White. Adding the personality measures to these analyses afforded an opportunity to separate offenders with more entrenched criminal values and experience from those who were less experienced. Interestingly, those who felt they could gain from prison programming were non-White individuals who were not experienced criminals; a significant proportion of these inmates had no prior prison experience, and were classified as Situational personality types. This adds an individual who held to basically prosocial values (rather than to criminal values) to this profile. In contrast, inmates who felt that nothing could be gained from the penitentiary experience were older, White inmates who had been employed prior to prison. We could speculate that these were inmates who had social investments that were interrupted by incarceration; however, the fact that marriage/families were not a correlate discourages us from going too far in this line of interpretation.

Our findings also point us toward a better understanding of specific correctional goals, most notably deterrence and rehabilitation. A substantial group of inmates in both settings noted that prison was not only a deterrent, but that the deterrent influences of the punishment would dissuade them from future criminal activities. Thus, although we did not offer these subjects the opportunity to compare sentencing options, as did and Petersilia & Piper-Deschenes (1994) and Crouch (1993), it would be most difficult to say that prison is not punitive or a deterrent to one who is actually serving a sanction.

It remains to be seen, however, whether or not inmates' perceptions of deterrence favorably affect criminal behavior upon release. And it is on the matter of its impact on future crimes that deterrence breaks down. Further, any tendency we might have to seize upon our deterrence findings as supportive of "get tough" movements should be viewed with caution. For one thing, these subjects told us that *these* specific environments were deterrents. These findings, in other words, would not generalize to the "get tough" approaches that place a qualitatively different emphasis on deterrence. Furthermore, extant research has shown us, rather consistently, that deterrence, for its own sake, is not effective (Gendreau & Ross, 1987).

In addition, we are interested in the correlations between deterrence and other rationales noted for the penitentiary sample, and the lack of a similar finding among the prison camp inmates. It would have been enlightening to explore further the minimum security inmates' perspectives on deterrence. They did not hold the deterrent aspects of their experience to be consistent with its rehabilitative aspects (as the penitentiary inmates did). We did, however, find a bivariate correlation between deterrence and deserts, suggesting that many of those who were deterred also felt that they deserved their sanction.

With respect to rehabilitation, we have learned that a substantial portion of the inmates express a desire to participate in rehabilitative programming. This is consistent with the research of Toch (1977), Wright (1989), and others. In our study, a somewhat lower proportion of inmates indicated that they are actually experiencing meaningful rehabilitative programming in prison. Were they simply using treatment to "play the parole game"? Probably not. We observed a moderate correlation between the rehabilitation item and the parole board item in the prison camp setting and a weaker but nonsignificant one among penitentiary inmates. Generally, inmates in the prison camp, especially, did not use the prospect of parole as the overriding motive. Those who indicated positive responses on the show board item also scored high on a belief that they were repaying society and deserved to be punished. Further, they stood apart from those inmates who saw no purpose in prison. Our reasons for not questioning the sincerity of the penitentiary inmates are somewhat different. Here the *show board* item was unrelated to any other orientation, suggesting that perhaps these inmates may have been a separate group from those who responded positively to other items. But the most important evidence questioning the validity of the parole game concerns the absence of any positive relationships between show board and the two other measurements of inmate cynicism (*no purpose* and *scam* staff). Perhaps this finding suggests not so much that inmates are exploiting rehabilitation, but that they realistically realize that success will have its payoffs. The findings might be likened to the student who achieves good grades, the employee who secures a stellar work evaluation, the person who faithfully saves money, and the colleague who is trusted by his or her coworkers. These individuals could hardly be expected to ignore the impact of their performances on their futures.

Some might be tempted to conclude on the basis of these observations that rehabilitation's strong relationship with other correctional goals, particularly deterrence, might suggest that the prison experience in itself may be rehabilitative—we don't need specific rehabilitation programs. We would caution against such a conclusion and remind readers of the findings for bootcamps and intermediate sanctions (Cullen, Wright, & Applegate, 1993) or perhaps for correctional programming in general (Gendreau & Ross, 1987). There is no evidence to suggest that sanctions with no treatments are indirectly serving as treatments. In fact, even with the advent of intermediate sanctions, we did not have positive effects on recidivism until the treatment components were added. Our results suggest, instead, that rehabilitation need not be inconsistent from other correctional intentions such as deterrence, retribution deserts, and incapacitation.

Finally, there are some unsettling, but important aspects to the profile of the inmate who thinks he can get something out of a maximum security prison experience. He was young, unemployed, non-White, was not evidencing procriminal values or an extensive prison experience, and the somewhat limited programming that this and other institutions are prepared to offer him was seen as a way he could grow. One is reminded of William Julius Wilson's "truly disadvantaged" or perhaps of the earlier words of John Irwin with regard to those who held out hope for the prison experience:

They were led to believe that they would be able to raise their education level, to learn a trade, to have physical defects corrected, and would receive help in various individual or group therapy programs in solving psychological problems. In effect, they were led to believe that if they participated in prison programs with sincerity and resolve, they would leave prison in better condition than when they entered and would generally be much better equipped to cope with the outside world. (1970, p. 52)

If indeed the prison experience and the participation in prison programs has the potential to foster growth and development on the part of the individual inmate, minority males because of their greater numbers in the system as well as their lack of opportunities elsewhere stand to benefit the most.

Based on data obtained from the Department of Justice Statistics, the 1990 Sentencing Project Report found that 1 in 4 (23%) Black males between the ages of 20 and 29 were under some form of correctional supervision—jail, prison, probation, or parole (Mauer, 1990). In their follow-up study, "Young, Black Americans and the Criminal Justice System: Five Years Later," Mauer and Hurling (1995) found that the Black male incarceration rates rose to 1 in 3 (32%), resulting in approximately 827,440 young Black males being involved in the criminal justice system.

Thus, with the growing number of young, non-White, previously unemployed males in the system, the rehabilitative services provided in prison have the potential to serve as an educational and employment training program. Thurston (1993) makes this point with respect to Adult Basic Education Programs. In this light, the prison experience for certain groups of inmates could serve as a resource—an opportunity to improve their lives.

However, as cautioned by Michael Tonry (1995), we should not look to the criminal justice system to solve problems of poverty, unemployment, and an inadequate educational system. At best, the system can "resolve not to exacerbate fundamental social problems and to do as little harm as possible" (Tonry, 1995, p. 163). From a policy standpoint, however, it seems tragic to continually ignore this group of inmates—justifying our neglect perhaps through specious reference to growing crime, decline in values, and assumptions about what may or may not be going on in the minds of offenders.

How these perceptions ultimately determine prison outcomes and future behavior, of course, remains to be seen. We found a number of inmates indicating such favorable responses as "I have learned my lesson," "I deserve to be here," or "I can experience personal growth in here." But we do not know what these orientations mean in terms of either prison adjustment or future criminal behavior. An emerging body of research, however, is beginning to recognize criminogenic attitudes as one of the major predictors of future crimes (see Andrews & Bonta, 1994).

The future directions for this research seem clear. First, the impact of correctional orientations on prison adjustment will be conducted using the same sample. In addition, an assessment of the impact of these orientations on the recidivism of these offenders would be extremely valuable. Finally, we would like to see a similar study conducted among state prison inmates, preferably a maximum security sample.

Notes

1. Analysis of the impact of correctional orientations on prison adjustment and recidivism will be the subject of a future article. It is beyond the scope of the present article.

Note: Footnotes 2–4 are not referenced in this edited version.

5. We should note, however, that this item was difficult to rate; the percentage interrater agreement for the item was 59%.

References

American Correctional Association. (1994). ACA issues positions on crime bill. *ACA On the Line, 17*(2), 1.

American Friends Service Committee. (1971). *Struggle for justice.* New York: Hill and Wang.

Andrews, D., & Bonta, J. (1994). *The psychology of criminal conduct.* Cincinnati, OH: Anderson.

Bandura, A. (1973). *Aggression: A social learning analysis.* New York: Prentice Hall.

Blumstein, A., Cohen, J., & Nagin, D. (1978). *Deterrence and incapacitation: Estimating the effects of criminal sanctions on crime rates.* Washington, DC: National Academy of Sciences.

Bonta, J., & Gendreau, P. (1990). Re-examining the cruel and unusual punishment of prison life. *Law and Human Behavior, 14,* 347–372.

Bukstel, L., & Kilmann, P. (1980). Psychological effects of imprisonment on confined individuals. *Psychological Bulletin, 88* (3): 469–493.

Caspi, A., Moffit, T., Silva, P., Stouthamer-Loeber, M., Krueger, R., & Schmutte, P. (1994). Are some people crime prone? Replications of the personality-crime relationship across countries, genders, races, and methods. *Criminology, 32*(2), 163–195.

Corrections 2000. (1994). Federal crime bill in final stages. *Corrections Alert, 1*(1), 1–2.

Crouch, B. (1993). Is incarceration really worse? Analysis of offenders' preferences for prison over probation. *Justice Quarterly, 10*(1), 67–88.

Cullen, F., & Gilbert, K. (1982). *Reaffirming rehabilitation.* Cincinnati, OH: Anderson.

Cullen, F., Skovron, S., Scott, J., & Burton, V. (1990). Public support for correctional treatment: The tenacity of rehabilitative ideology. *Criminal Justice and Behavior, 17*(1), 6–18.

Cullen, F., Wright, J., & Applegate, B. (1993, November). *Control in the community.* Paper presented at a conference of the International Association of Residential and Community Alternatives, Philadelphia, PA.

Currie, E. 1985). *Confronting crime: An American challenge.* New York: Pantheon.

Ellis, A. (1973). *Humanistic psychotherapy.* New York: Pantheon.

Eysenck, H. (1977). *Crime and personality.* London: Granada.

Flanagan, T. (1983). Correlates of institutional misconduct among state prisoners. *Criminology, 21,* 29–39.

Fogel, D. (1979). *"We are the living proof:" The justice model for corrections* (Vol. 2). Cincinnati, OH: Anderson.

Gendreau, P., & Ross, R. (1987). Revivification of rehabilitation: Evidence from the 1980s. *Justice Quarterly, 4*(3), 349–407.

Gibbs, J. (1975). *Crime, punishment, and deterrence.* New York: Elsevier.

Hart, H.L.A. (1961). *The concept of law.* Oxford: Oxford University Press.

Hawkins, G. (1976). *The prison: Policy and practice.* Chicago: University of Chicago Press.

Hawkins, R., & Alpert, G. (1989). *American prison systems: Punishment and justice.* Englewood Cliffs, NJ: Prentice Hall.

Irwin, J. (1970). *The felon.* Englewood Cliffs, NJ: Prentice Hall.

Jesness, C., & Wedge, R. (1983). *Classifying offenders: The Jesness Inventory Classification System.* Sacramento, CA: California Youth Authority.

Klepper, S., & Nagin, D. (1989). The deterrent effect of perceived certainty and severity of punishment revisited. *Criminology, 27*(4), 721–746.

Mauer, M. (1990). *Young, Black men and the criminal justice system: A growing national problem.* Washington, DC: The Sentencing Project.

Mauer, M., & Hurling, T. (1995). *Young, Black Americans and the criminal justice system: Five years later.* Washington, DC: The Sentencing Project.

McClelland, K., & Alpert, G. (1985). Factor analysis applied to magnitude estimates of punishment seriousness: Patterns of individual differences. *Journal of Quantitative Criminology, 1*(3), 307–318.

McCorkle, R. (1993). Research note: Punishment or rehabilitate. *Crime and Delinquency, 39*(2), 240–252.

Megargee, E., & Bohn, M. (1979). *Classifying criminal offenders: A new system based on the MMPI.* Beverly Hills, CA: Sage.

Menninger, K. (1966). *The crime of punishment.* New York: Vintage.

Meichenbaum, D. (1977). *Cognitive-behavioral modification: An integrative approach.* New York: Plenum.

Mitford, J. (1973). *Kind and unusual punishment: The prison business.* New York: Alfred A. Knopf.

Morris, N. (1974). *The future of imprisonment.* Chicago: University of Chicago Press.

Myers, L., & Levy, G. (1978). Description and prediction of the intractable inmate. *Journal of Research in Crime and Delinquency, 15,* 214–228.

Newman, G. (1978). *The punishment response.* New York: Lippincott.

Palmer, T. (1983). The "effectiveness" issue today: An overview. *Federal Probation, 46,* 3–10.

Palmer, T. (1992). *The re-emergence of correctional intervention: Developments through the 1980s and prospects for the future.* Beverly Hills, CA: Sage.

Paternoster, R. (1987). The deterrent effect of perceived certainty and severity of punishment: A review of the evidence and issues. *Justice Quarterly, 4*(2), 173–217.

Petersilia, J. (1990). When probation becomes more dreaded than prison. *Federal Probation, 54*(1), 23–27.

Petersilia, J., & Piper-Deschenes, E. (1994). What punishes? Inmates rank the severity of prison vs. intermediate sanctions. *Federal Probation, 58*(1), 3–8.

Public Agenda Foundation. (1987). *Crime and punishment: The public's view.* New York: Edna McConnell Clark Foundation.

Quay, H. (1965). Psychopathic personality: Pathological stimulation-seeking. *American Journal of Psychiatry, 122,* 180–183.

Quay, H. (1983). *Technical manual for the behavioral classifications system for adult offenders.* Washington, DC: U.S. Department of Justice.

Sherman, M., & Hawkins, G. (1982). *Imprisonment in America: Choosing the future.* Chicago: University of Chicago Press.

Shipley, W. (1940). A self-administering scale for measuring intellectual impairment and deterioration. *Journal of Psychology, 9*(2), 371–377.

Thurston, L. (1993). *A call to action: An analysis and overview of the United States criminal justice system, with recommendations.* Chicago, IL: Third World Press.

Toch, H. (1977). *Living in prison.* New York: Free Press.

Toch, H., & Adams, K. (1989). *Coping: Maladaptation in prisons.* New Brunswick, NJ: Transaction.

Tonry, M. (1995). *Malign neglect: Race, crime and punishment in America.* Oxford: Oxford University Press.

Van Voorhis, P. (1983). Theoretical perspectives on moral development and restitution. In W. Lauffer & J. Day (Eds.), *Personality theory, moral development, and criminal behavior.* Lexington: D.C. Health.

Van Voorhis, P. (1985). Restitution outcome and probationers' assessments of restitution: The effects of moral development. *Criminal Justice and Behavior, 12*(3), 259–287.

Van Voorhis, P. (1994). *Psychological classification of the adult, male, prison inmate.* Albany, NY: State University of New York Press.

Van Voorhis, P. (1995, November). *Personality and the crime paradigm: Directions from the classification research.* Paper presented at the Annual Meeting of the American Society of Criminology, Boston, MA.

von Hirsch, A. (1976). *Doing justice.* New York: Hill and Wang.

Warren, M. (1983). Applications of interpersonal maturity to offender populations. In W. Lauffer & J. Day (Eds.), *Personality theory, moral development, and criminal behavior.* Lexington: D.C. Heath.

Wilson, J. (1987). *The truly disadvantaged: The inner city, the underclass, and public policy.* Chicago: University of Chicago Press.

Wilson, J., & Herrnstein, R. (1985). *Crime and human nature.* New York: Simon and Schuster.

Wright, K. (1989). Race and economic marginality in explaining prison adjustment. *Journal of Research in Crime and Justice, 26*(1), 67–89.

Zachary, R., Crumpton, E., & Spiegel, D. (1985). Estimating WAIS IQ from the Shipley Institute of Living Scale. *Journal of Clinical Psychology, 41*(4), 532–540.

Zimring, F., & Hawkins, G. (1991). *The scale of imprisonment.* Chicago: University of Chicago Press.

Zimring, F., & Hawkins, G. (1995). *Incapacitation: Penal confinement and the restraint of crime.* New York: Oxford University Press.

 Article Review Form at end of book.

How does the organization of a prison affect prisoners' predictions about their future behavior? What are the other factors that influence prisoners' predictions about future violence?

The Depth of Imprisonment and Prisonization:

Levels of Security and Prisoners' Anticipation of Future Violence

Dennis J. Stevens

America uses confinement as a form of punishment in an attempt to create order from disorder. That is, since Americans see social disorder arising from accelerating violent crime trends making its members at risk more often than members of any other nation in modern times (Rand 1990; U.S. Department of Justice 1992c), they believe that the courts should impose harsher measures against offenders;[1] furthermore, experts like James Q. Wilson (1975) postulate that imprisoning anyone convicted of a serious offence for several years referred to as incapacitation reduces violent crime. This is a policy that works, he argues, since potential offenders weigh the pains of swifter and severe punishment and refrain from criminally violent behaviour. Consequently, the American criminal justice system locks-up more of its population per 100,000 than any other country on earth; yet, escalating violent crime rates seem unaffected (U.S. Department of Justice 1992c; Weiner 1991). But, prison population demo-

graphics suggest that incarceration is an out-of-control dumping ground for the lower class (Bartollas 1990; Irwin 1980; Reiman 1990). However, to what extent, we might ask, is the very practice of confinement helping the cause of violence? Donald Clemmer (1958) held one answer when he coined the term prisonization to refer to the longer inmates are incarcerated, the stronger their identification with inmate norms and values, and the more difficulty they would have adjusting to life once released. Clemmer suggests that prison, like other social groups, has a culture which he defines as a mode of life or thought that is not peculiarly individual but which can be characterised as a shared set of attitudes that can eventually impact behavioural patterns and lifestyles. As individual's acceptance of the perspectives of a social group is a 'more or a less unconscious' process experienced by most individuals who remain in different or unique social environments; part of this process includes learning enough of the culture to make an individual characteristic of the environment. Part of this envi-

ronment, others add, has to do with the deprivations of liberty, 'stripped of worldly possessions, denied access to heterosexual relationships, divested of autonomy, and compelled to associate with other deviants' or what Sykes (1966) refers to as the 'pains of imprisonment' (p. 131). Furthermore, since all inmates share in these deprivations, not only do they see imprisonment as punishment but they are also bound together to reduce their individual pain. Thus, Sykes argues that inmates are a product of their patterns of social interaction which the prisoner enters into day after day, year after year. Thus, prisonization or an indigenous set of impersonal prison values includes the 'degree of assimilation into the inmate normative system' (Thomas, Petersen, and Cage 1981). However, prisonization is thought to be U-shaped as opposed to a linear process; that is, inmates enter prison with a relatively prosocial orientation, become progressively prisonised in the middle phase and undergo a shift back to conventional values toward the end of their sentences (Wheeler 1961).

The Depth of Imprisonment and Prisonization: Levels of Security and Prisoners' Anticipation of Future Violence, D. J. Stevens, *The Howard Journal of Criminal Justice*, 33(2), 1994, 137–157. Reprinted by permission of Blackwell Publishers.

Other writers, however, suggest that values and norms observed in prison populations are similar to their lower class perspectives which exist outside of prison environments; that is, they argue that the lower class imports its cultural norms into prison or importation perspective (Jacobs 1977; Irwin and Cressey 1962). For example, an important lower class perspective occasionally linked with criminally violent behaviour is 'machismo' or 'manhood,' reports John Irwin (1977). He explains that in the lower class, manhood is proven through physical violence when threatened. Jacobs (1977) notes further that when vast numbers of gang members from chicago were imprisoned at Stateville, its prison society changed too. Thus, one conclusion that can be inferred from those explanations is that lower class males similarly respond in prison as they had on the streets.

However, prison environments have changed enormously, and due to those changes, prison society has changed too, 'interactives' argue. Irwin's (1988) perspective typifies those changes:

Violence rose and eventually many prisons became settings in which warring cliques or gangs of prisoners, often organized on racial lines, dominated and threatened the prison world . . . prisons are excessively violent, crowded, cruel, and ineffective.

Thus, these advocates suggest that indigenous and imported theories inadequately explain the social systems found in prisons (Irwin 1988). Irwin argues that Clemmer's cultural assimilation perspective suggested that an inmate society was an accommodative system that emerged, in part, to 'solve the pains of imprisonment and the administration's need to maintain control with limited direct or formal means.' Irwin suggests that the system's primary components were a convict code and group leaders seemed hostile to control methods but made the job easier. Therefore, prison social order and convict self respect were maintained. But he argues these perspectives were inconsistent with his own prison experiences.

Therefore, Irwin (1980) suggests that an 'interactive' perspective best

explains prison society. For example, prison power structures are shaped by both outside influences such as policies and budgets and inside influences such as a 'segmented order' of small, mutually hostile cliques, held together by a contraband economy (Irwin 1980; Stastny and Tyrnauer (1982). Thus, both inmate and staff populations are influenced by their current social setting and by formal policy of the administration.

However, despite prison changes in Clemmer's window, it might be that importation perspectives blame the victims (Ryan 1981) while interactive views apply to a few prisons with unusual circumstances. Perhaps, Grapendaal's (1990) notion that both deprivation and importation models explain prison society especially since contemporary evidence points to a prisons subculture, and both situational and idiosyncratic factors contribute to it or an 'integration' model. That is, when comparing maximum prisons like Attica whose inmate population is largely from a city 325 miles away and staff are locals to urbanised Stateville near Chicago or rural McCormick in South Carolina, how many orientations and management policy differences would we find? Certainly, their confinement mission of control may be similar, but political, cultural, and environmental influences impacting control methods produce operational and response differences from the flag pole to the last key; thus, each of these components impacts the regime of the custodians and the daily life of every inmate. Other writers add that when comparing prisons with substantially similar populations, one prison is considered safer, more secure, and more trouble-free than the other (King 1991). Bottoms, Hay, and Sparks (1990) argue that every prison has its own unique features, due in part to its history, architecture, prisoner and staff demographics, prior experiences and memories of staff and inmates, and regime.

While each perspective has merits and limitations, begging for inquiry within this debate is the ignored perspective of making obvious that which is obvious; that is, which cultural component has a universal affect upon future violent crime? Do

non-violent apprehended criminals resort to violence due to their prison experience? Perhaps the situation in most maximum-security prisons is appropriately characterised by Irwin (1980):

The reverberations from the 1960s left most [American] men's prisons fragmented, tense, and often extremely violent . . . prisons are divided by extreme differences, distrust, and [racial] hatred. (p. 181)

Prison Violence

Bartollas (1990) shares some of his insights about violence in American prisons:

Disorder was apparent in the daily existence of inmates. A misspoken word, a slight bump of another inmate, an unpaid gambling debt, a racial slur, or an invasion of the 'turf' of another often brought about a violent attack.

Violence is pervasive in prisons and includes assaults on correctional staff which increased from 6,049 to 9,220 between 1984 and 1988 (Herrick 1989). At least 21 staff members and 390 inmates were murdered in state and federal prisons between 1984 and 1989 (American Correctional Association 1991). In 1985 alone, there were 117 prison suicides (Camp and Camp 1985). Sullivan (1990) contends that arbitrariness of prison control and inmate degradation is a source of extreme frustration, bitterness, and anger. Some men who feel helpless may change their behaviour by using violence to gain what they feel they may have lost—control (Cellini 1984).

Prisoners may reflect values of their custodians as well as other inmates, argue Hepburn and Smith (1979). The implication is that force and violence are seen by prisoners as one way custodians maintain control and order, maintain status and deference, get promotions, and build solidarity (Marquart 1986). Many guards keep control by backing vulnerable inmates into corners. Thus, many inmates might mirror that behaviour to show that they are not vulnerable and search for those inmates who are (Hepburn and Smith 1979). Frequently, these predators rape and robe in the prison cells of their victims, but their violence is often overlooked by prison administrators or unreported (Bowker 1980; Eichental and Jacobs 1991). Also, if prison crime is reported, it is rarely investigated by officials and an aggressor is rarely charged, say Eichental and Jacobs (1991). Underenforcement of criminal law in prisons suggest that crimes committed in general populations are different from crimes committed in prison populations. The writers suggest that most Americans including the criminal justice community do not believe that prison victims are 'real victims,' and that prison inmates are not entitled to democratic processes or protection. David Eichental and James Jacobs (1991) argue, and a view that could be accepted by many law enforcement officers (Fielding and Fielding 1991) that when convicted criminals are sent to prison, crime is not reduced on the streets, in fact, the 'system pulls its punches'; furthermore incapacitation does not work since habitual offenders have simply changed locations from one where crime is more likely to be reported to one where reporting is less likely. Thus, John Irwin (1980) suggests that survival for most inmates depends upon how violently they behave towards others regardless of their orientation before incarceration, and for others, it depends upon how much they co-operate with predators and custodians.

Then, too, in the past 22 years, there have been major riots in many U.S. prisons resulting in torture and murder of many inmates and guards. For example, in February 1980, convicts took control of The New Mexico State Penitentiary at Santa Fe. By the time authorities took back control, 33 prisoners were murdered, many had been raped and beaten by other inmates, and eight guards had been tortured (Sullivan 1990). During a four day uprising at Attica in New York, many inmates and guards were killed and many more were wounded when the New York National Guard and state law enforcement officers took control of the prison (Adams 1992). However, most prison riots are not as violent as New Mexico or Attica, but the spirit of those riots is known by many inmates and guards. Attica became the symbol of American prison brutality and oppression.

Due in part to violence and in part to failures of resocialisation efforts throughout most English-speaking countries, custody models of operation are emphasised as opposed to rehabilitation models of operation, hence correctional communities use whatever force is necessary to maintain order (Early 1991; Grapendaal 1990; Sullivan 1990).

Furthermore, there is mounting evidence that confinement is harsh and produces psychologically damaging effects on inmates and probably the people who work there (Gibbs 1991). Reiman (1984, p. 14) adds: 'We know that our prisons undermine human dignity and the ex-con stigma closes the door to many lawful occupation.' He says that most violent crime is committed by recidivists—people who have experienced incarceration. Thus, there appears to be a cycle of violence centered on incarceration.

In sum, the entire high custody level prison practice including its social structure, norms, and objectives seem to reward and praise violence with the blessing of the American public who remain in the 'dark ages' about crime and punishment. Thus, from the perspective of inmates and their custodians, violence is routine in high custody prisons.

Perhaps high custody prisons turn out violent men because prisons are forced to receive and deal with persons with violent dispositions? It may be that prison is not a causal agent of violence at all; they may merely reflect their 'clientele.' Thus, to meet part of their mission of control, authoritarian regimes are utilised by most high custody managers; however, as Sykes (1966) points out and Roy King (1991) recently confirms, regardless of prisoner demographics, prison regimes do not have to be repressive to inmates to control their criminal populations. Nonetheless, what plays a central part to this paper is how many inmates in high custody prisons were not violent offenders before their original incarceration? Nationwide, violent offenders comprised an estimated 45% of all inmates in 1991, and 21% of them had been violent recidivists as compared with 55% of the inmates who were non-violent criminals and only 14% had been involved in prior violent

crime (Greenfield 1993). Yet, 36% of all inmates are housed in maximum facilities and 50% are housed in medium prisons (U.S. Department of Justice 1992a). Evidently, most American state prison systems incarcerate both violent and nonviolent offenders in maximum and medium custody prisons.[2] Moreover, incarceration advocates fail to recognise that prison space is a finite resource that cannot expand without expenditures of tax funds. Also, they feel that the size of the criminal population is fixed and through longer incarceration, criminals and first time offenders can be controlled. But, the reality is in American prisons regardless of the crimes an inmate committed, he most likely will be released (U.S. Department of Justice 1992a, 1992b); as Wikberg and Foster (1990) report, the average time served for criminal homicide across the U.S. ranged from a low of 39 months in Oklahoma to a high of 78 months in Ohio; furthermore, chances are, highly skilled predatory offenders are rarely apprehended let alone incarcerated (Epstein 1990). Alas, we are left with the inquiry as to whether non-violent offenders living in high custody prisons become violent offenders, once released.

Current Hypothesis

The central question to this study is: Can membership in certain types of organisations lead its members into extraordinary acts? Borrowing an inquiry from Travis, Schwartz, and Clear (1983, p. 96), can the very nature of a 'setting make individuals become fascist killers, commit suicide, or administer lethal shocks to a man begging for mercy.' That is, can a non-violent criminal be so motivated by his prison experience that once released, he commits violent crimes? It is hypothesised that inmates assimilate into the normative prison system comprised of violence promoted by both inmates and custodians. One method of determining this assimilation lies with non-violent incarcerated offenders in maximum and medium custody prisons and violent incarcerated offenders in work release centres.

Once apprehended and convicted, offenders join violent prison

Table 2 Self-Reported Fear of Future Imprisonment

Group	$100,000	Rape	Murder	Aggravated Assault	Want It Take It	Drug/ Alcohol	None
Maximum*	70*	38	21	48	32	51	24
Medium	75	43	24	51	41	54	18
Work release	37	00	00	18	14	18	98
College	04	01	00	00	01	22	99

Notes:

* Maximum N = 166, medium N = 131, work release N = 165, college N = 126.

** Rounded percentages.

Categories do not total 100 since many checked more than one category.

populations, and this study will argue, they accept the values and lifestyle of their round-the-clock environment which is centered on violent orientations. This idea is essentially consistent with Clemmer (1958) in that most high custody inmates become completely 'prisonized' while few are allowed to 'do their own time.' However, this paper argues that violence is the primary attitude accepted by high-risk inmates regardless of their previous decisions towards violence. What is unique about this study is that self-reported violent crime attitudes of inmates in maximum and medium custody level prisons are compared to attitudes of inmates in low custody level prison and college students are used as a control group as their responses are expected to be entirely different.

If the data are produced as expected, it might steer policy makers to alternatives of supervision for offenders. The idea for this study grew from earlier work where the threat of prison was not found to be a deterrent to violent crime for repeat offenders (Stevens 1992b).

Methodology

This study surveyed, as described in Appendix 1, 166 inmates in a maximum custody prison, 131 respondents in a medium facility, 165 inmates in a minimum or work release centre, and 126 university students totalling 588 participants. An inmate is assigned a custody level facility based upon the type of 'perceived' supervision required to keep an inmate controlled and confined.[3]

All of the data in this study are based upon self-reports of appre-hended criminals and university students. All of the subjects were volunteers and contributed without incentive. Furthermore, other researchers have experienced validity problems with inmate populations, thus they compared inmate responses with criminal files and learned that largely only rapists tend to under-report their crimes (Scully 1990). But, those techniques clearly affect confidentiality of participants as each participant might identify himself by signing the appropriate release forms and other required documents limiting state and department of correction liability. Thus, confidentiality is compromised as well as the safety of a researcher (Stevens 1993). Also, criminal files rarely reflect activity known only to the offender. . . .

Findings

The data suggest that some persons incarcerated in maximum and medium custody prisons for non-violent offences say they might commit violent offences, once released. On the other hand, persons in a work release centre who had committed violent crimes say that violent crimes were not options for them, once released.

The subjects were asked, what crimes they would risk if they might go to prison for them? As Table 2* shows, 70% of the maximum respondents admitted that they would steal $100,000 knowing they would return to prison for that crime. Also, 38% of the maximum and 43% of the medium participants admitted to the possibility of rape regardless of the

* Table 1 does not appear in this publication.

threat of prison. Additionally, 21% of the maximum and 24% of the medium subjects admitted that they might murder, while 48% of the maximum and 51% of the medium subjects said they might commit aggravated assault despite possible prison time. Of great concern is that only 24% of the maximum and 18% of the medium subjects as compared to 98% of the work release inmates and 99% of the college subjects reported that they would not commit crimes in the future. The data are consistent with recent findings of Stevens (1992a) at Stateville and Joliet penitentiaries, in that participants were asked a similar question producing similar results. However, since recidivism of maximum and medium inmates, in general, is drastically high, more of the sample will probably commit violent crime after release than indicated above (U.S. Department of Justice 1992a). Also, this data finds congruence in Daniel Glaser's (1969) findings when he surveyed high custody inmates who indicated that about three-quarters of the offenders in their prison would return to crime, once released. But, Glaser reveals that inmates perceive other inmates as more criminalistic than they are in fact.

Non-Violent Offenders

The data indicate that a high percentage of the participants were not violent offenders before incarceration. For example, 31% of the maximum participants, 42% of the medium participants, and 56% of the work release participants reported that they had never committed or been arrested for a violent crime as either adults or as juveniles. These percentages of non-violent offenders in high custody prisons are congruent with U.S. Department of Justice (1992a) statistics of convicted offenders. So, why were these inmates a 'confinement risk'? Perhaps they presented themselves like 'violent offenders' during the 'in-take' process. This finding is supported with Cellini's (1986) argument that individuals who suddenly feel helpless, may use or suggest violence to feel in control. That is, some individuals being processed through the criminal justice system might feel uneasy and helpless and use violence or violent non-verbal cues as a way to keep control of their environment, regardless of their class orientations. On the other hand, work release respondents were older and better educated than the two high custody groups suggesting they may have been better prepared to deal with the uncertainty of prison life process. Also, Glaser (1969) reveals that many of the inmates he interviewed said that they had permanently changed their perspectives about crime due to their unpleasant prison experiences. Recidivism rates imply something different, but the point is, criminals like other members of social groups offer culturally appropriate explanations in keeping with their immediate experience (Mills 1940).

Nonetheless, not all of the participants who admitted to future violent crime potentials were violent offenders before their experiences at either the maximum or the medium prison. Yet, 32% of the work release respondents were violent offenders, although 98% of them said they would not commit violent crime, once released. Could this finding be consistent with Straus's (1991) 'cultural spillover' concept suggesting that violence in one sphere of life tends to encourage violence in other spheres for an individual? That is, greater legitimate violence leads to greater tendencies for criminals to use force to get what they want. Perhaps, too, many non-violent participants have controlled their 'tempers' or violent behavioural patterns throughout their lives until placed into a prison environment, and once they accepted the values of prison life, they made decisions toward violence. However, those individuals who were not exposed to the violence of high custody prisons tend to reject violence as an option. That is, they might know what to say to whom, to get low custody status, which also could mean they know how to sound like non-violent offenders.

Additionally, the participants were asked to rate from 5 [the most] to 1 [the least] amount of violence they had witnessed in or by the following categories: cops, judges, prisons, friends, parents, siblings, school, and streets. When their responses were pooled, it first appeared that maximum and medium participants similarly rated their violent experiences as had the work and college participants. For instance, the participants in maximum and medium groups similarly rated the total categories producing a total average score of 2.9. Thus, a high correlation existed between the maximum and medium subjects (R = 0.93).

Also, as the pie chart for the maximum custody participants indicate, they said that almost 48% of the violence they had seen was on the streets, or by law-enforcement officers, or in prison or 17%, 15%, and 15% respectively. Also they suggested that their families including their brothers and sisters were involved with violence less often than their friends, parents, or judges. It is interesting that the participants rated violence in the streets as more pervasive than violence in prison.

When we compare the medium custody responses about prison as demonstrated in their pie chart, it appears that the medium custody inmates experienced more violence than those in a maximum facility; and in fact, their selections indicated that they had witnessed more violence in prison than elsewhere producing a numeric average of 4.6. A point of interest is that as Appendix 1 implies, there are more regulations and restrictions including inmate freedom of movement at the medium facility than at the maximum facility; perhaps, this data supports Roy King (1991) who finds that a well-managed prison where there is little room for inmates to make personal decisions, delivers little in terms of safety, services, and regime. Additionally, Bottoms, Hay, and Sparks (1990) suggest that control problems tend to be less in a facility where its staff utilise more preventive control than situational control like that in the maximum custody prison in this study. That is, a key feature of a restrictive regime is that it places more restrictions of the freedom of movement of prisoners, to reduce the total number of prisoners out of cell at any time, and hence to reduce opportunities for disorder. Additionally, the medium subjects indicated that over 50% of the violence they had witnessed, like the maximum custody inmates as on the streets, or by law enforcement officers, or in the prison or 16%, 16%, and 19% respectively.

The work respondents rated the categories with a total average score of 2.4. As their pie chart shows, the work release participants also reported witnessing more violence on the streets, by cops, and in prison than they had elsewhere; however, they reported less violence in prison than the two higher custody groups.

Surprisingly, the students' pie chart shows that they rated the streets, cops, and prisons as places and persons where they witnessed the most violence. Also, they rated their friends as more violent than their brothers, sisters, or parents. Maybe they witnessed violence in the streets, but cops and prisons as choices seem doubtful as most had never been involved with law enforcement much less in prison. One acceptable explanation for their curious responses is that this was a subjective inquiry and the students perceived violence levels as high as the work release inmates; in fact, the data show that a high correlation exists between the responses of work release and college participants (R = 0.82). But, work release and university participants are different individuals as the inmates were apprehended criminals and almost one-third of them admitted committing violent crimes including murder and rape. Part of the answer could be that witnessing violence is a subjective response left to each participant to interpret at their level of experience. This finding is consistent with the findings of C. Wright Mills (1940) who suggests that individuals live in immediate acts of experience and their attentions and motives are directed outside themselves.

Also, in a comparison of variances between and within each of the categorical groups or an 'F' Test, there is statistically little difference at the 5% level of significance or $F = 1.4078$ between or within any of the groups. Thus, any member of one group could have been a member of any other group when subjectively rating violence.

One interpretation for the similarities in responses of the inmate and student groups is that they all have been exposed to similar media like television, radio, and magazine photographs about violence. That is, many of the students and inmates watch 'Top Cops' and look at similar motion pictures displaying enormous amounts of violence and sexuality including *Penthouse* magazine and the like. Certainly, the correlations can be explained through gender; that is, males tend to be culturally trained to express aggressive and violent attitudes more often than females, regardless of their class position or environment. Therefore, violence may be a male attitudinal quality as also confirmed by Tavris and Wade (1984).

Conclusion

The self-reported responses of convicted felons suggest that the environment of prison affects inmate violence levels regardless of the personal decisions about violence prior to their confinement. That is, at an extreme, belonging to an organisation can by its very nature turn non-violent offenders into killers and violent men into passive beings. One latent result which supports this interpretation is that the inmates polled in the medium custody prison admitted that they would commit more violent crimes than the sample at the maximum penitentiary. Are those inmates responding to the restrictiveness of prison regime or their violent behaviour and/or orientations which they brought into prison? If medium custody prisoners held more violent perspectives than prisoners in maximum custody, something about the scope of this paper is happening! Thus, what this study argues about prisonization and violence is far more supported than other perspectives.

Other implications of the data suggest that non-violent offenders should reside in work release type facilities should we wish to control criminally violent behaviour. Thus, less perceived legitimate violence and/or force can lead to less criminal violence and/or force for many offenders.

Nonetheless, all four groups reported similar levels of perceived witnessed violence, yet work release and college respondents reported that they would not involve themselves in criminally violent activities as often as the other participants. Thus, a degree of assimilation into an organisational normative system and adoption of its values might seem evident despite prior cultural experiences particularly since many of the work release subjects were also from the lower class, yet their views seem different than those in other prisons. This notion finds consistency with Daniel Glaser (1975) who suggests that inmates should never be set apart from and out of communication with law-abiding persons any more than safety necessitates should the criminal justice community wish to release them with minimum risk. Furthermore, this paper and Glaser suggest that there are specific objectives which prisons can utilise to make this principle most effective including maximising visitations for inmates by outside persons, maximising participation of inmates in the management of their own affairs, and maximising outside legitimate responsibilities while inmates are incarcerated. It is clear that membership in an organisation forces its set of rules, norms, and values upon an individual demanding conformity to its appropriate level of behaviour; thus, inmates need to be as much a part of a law-abiding culture as possible. Some thinkers might say that law breakers were part of a conforming community before committing crimes; for some criminals, it may be true that they were never really assimilated and other offenders might have played a 'conforming' role to have access to perceived vulnerable prey, much like the serial rapists described in Stevens' (1994) study. But, for most offenders it's highly unlikely that they were integrated into a law-abiding community when they were committing crime.

This idea is old stuff. It is consistent with classical arguments of Emile Durkheim and contemporary writers like Travis Hirschi. Moreover, the findings of this study are consistent with Donald Clemmer's early work on prisonization. However, some attitudes and values of inmates seem to be shaped before their arrival into prison adding some support to a importation perspective, but not as much as researchers would like us to believe. Thus, falling in with bad companions—the functionalists, isn't as bad as some writers suggest!

Limitations of this study include self-reported data by apprehended criminals currently serving prison sentences and the orientation of the researcher. Thus, the findings of this study might relate specifically to the samples who reported the data. Further research needs to be done on the relationship between prison time served, seriousness of crimes committed, and future criminal activities.

Notes

1. The U.S. Department of Justice (1992a) reports that in a public opinion poll (*Table 2.55*) conducted by the National Opinion Research Center, 80% of those surveyed in the General Social Survey believed that the courts do not deal harshly enough with offenders.

2. For instance, South Carolina Department of Corrections (1991, p. 48) shows 11,095 newly admitted inmates in 1990 of which over 67% had been convicted of non-violent offences classified as property or public order such as 16% for traffic (hit and run, transporting dangerous material, and driving under the influence); 14% for larceny (purse snatching without force, shoplifting, and housebreaking); 10% for burglary (forcible and non-forcible entry); and 46% for 'other' including forgery, family offence (neglect or non-support), stolen vehicle, stolen property, drunkenness, weapon offence, public peace, accessory, commercialised sex, vagrancy, and licensing violations. Drug offences account for 15% of SC's 1990 inmate admission, yet drug possession convictions accounted for over two-thirds of drug convicts while one-third accounted for trafficking and distribution.

3. That is, a correctional in-take counsellor can determine risk assessment of an inmate based upon severity of current offence, sentence length, detainers, history of violence, escape history, prior convictions, offences in current

commitment, age, alcohol/drugs associated with current offence, mandatory time to serve before parole or release, and interview data. Inmates may also be classified into 'psychological types' denoting aggressiveness levels determining specific housing assignments. Thus, there may be two indicators for each inmate: one indicating facility and another indicating 'wing' or 'housing unit' within the prison. For instance in South Carolina, inmates assigned to CCI in Columbia, their highest custody level prison, are further separated by manipulators or alphas and dependents or gammas, and are housed in different wings within the prison. Also, re-evaluation can occur every six to twelve months in some states but can also be a permanent individual rating in other states. See Levinson (1988) for more insight into classification.

References

Adams, R. (1992) *Prison Riots in Britain and the USA*, New York: St. Martin's.

American Correctional Association (1991) 'Study reveals in-prison murder figures,' *On the Line, 14*, 2–4.

Bartollas, C. (1990) 'The prison: disorder personified,' in: J. Murphy and J. Dison (Eds.), *Are Prisons Any Better? Twenty Years of Correctional Reform*, Newbury Park, CA: Sage.

Bottoms, A., Hay, W. and Sparks, J. (1990) 'Social and situational approaches to the prevention of disorder in long-term prisons,' *Prison Journal, 70*, 83–95.

Bowker, L. (1980) *Prison Victimization*, New York: Elsevier Books.

Camp, G. and Camp, C. (1985) *The Corrections Yearbook 1985*, South Salem, NY: Criminal Justice Institute.

Cellini, H. (1986) 'The management and treatment of institutionalized violent aggressors,' *Federal Probation, 50*, 51–4.

Clemmer, D. (1958) *The Prison Community*, New York: Holt, Rinehart and Winston.

Early, P. (1991) *The Hot House*, New York: Basic Books.

Eichental, D. and Jacobs, J. (1991) 'Enforcing the criminal law in state prisons,' *Justice Quarterly, 8*, 283–303.

Epstein, A. (1990) 'Crime less likely to be solved,' *The Charlotte Observer*, April, 14.

Fielding, N. and Fielding, J. (1991) 'Police attitudes to crime and punishment,' *British Journal of Criminology, 31*, 39–53.

Gibbs, J. (1991) 'Environmental congruence and symptoms of psychopathology,' *Criminal Justice and Behaviour, 8*, 351–74.

Glaser, D. (1969) *The Effectiveness of a Prison and Parole System*, Indiana: Bobbs-Merrill.

Glaser, D. (1975) *Strategic Criminal Justice Planning*, Rockville, MA: National Institute of Mental Health.

Grapendaal, M. (1990) 'The inmate subculture in Dutch prisons,' *British Journal of Criminology, 30*, 341–55.

Greenfeld, L. (1993) 'Profiling inmates by custody level,' *Corrections Today*, July, 172–7.

Herrick, E. (1989) 'The surprising direction of violence in prison,' *National Journal for Corrections Professionals, 14*, 1–2.

Hepburn, J and Smith, C. (1979) 'Alienation in prison organization,' *Journal of Criminology, 17*, 251–54.

Irwin, J. (1977) *The Felon*, Englewood Cliffs, NJ: Prentice Hall.

Irwin, J. (1980) *Prisons in Turmoil*, Boston: Little, Brown and Company.

Irwin, J. (1988) 'Donald Cressey and the sociology of the prison,' *Crime and Delinquency, 34*, 328–38.

Irwin, J. and Cressey, D. (1962) 'Thieves, convicts, and the inmate culture,' *Social Problems, 10*, 142–55.

Jacobs, J. (1977) *Stateville: The Penitentiary in Mass Society*, Chicago: University of Chicago Press.

King, R. (1991) 'Maximum-security custody in Britain and the USA,' *British Journal of Criminology, 31*, 126–51.

Levinson, R. (1988) 'Developments in the classification process,' *Criminal Justice and Behavior, 15*, 24–38.

Marquart, J. (1986) 'Prison guards and physical coercion,' *Journal of Criminology, 24*, 357–61.

Mills, C. (1940) 'Situated actions and vocabularies of motive,' *American Sociological Review, 5*, 131–47.

Rand, M. R. (1990) 'Crime and the nation's households,' *Bureau of Justice Statistics*, Washington, DC: US Department of Justice.

Reiman, J. (1990) *The Rich Get Richer and The Poor Get Prison*, New York: Macmillan.

Ryan, W. (1981) *Equality*, New York: Pantheon.

Scully, D. (1990) *Understanding Sexual Violence*, Boston: Unwin.

South Carolina Department of Corrections (1991) *Annual Report 1989–1990*, Columbia, SC: SC Department of Corrections.

Stastny, C. and Tyrnauer, G. (1982) *Who Rules The Joint?*, Lexington, MA: Lexington.

Stevens, D. (1992a) 'Prisons as criminal deterrence and inmate attitudes,' *The State of Corrections*, Laurel, MD: American Correctional Association.

Stevens, D. (1992b) 'Research Note: The death penalty and inmate attitude,' *Crime and Delinquency, 38*, 272–9.

Stevens, D. (1993) 'Predatory rape and inmate attitudes' (paper presented at annual meeting of Academy of Criminal Justice Sciences, Kansas City, MO).

Stevens, D. (1994) 'Predatory rapists and victim selection techniques,' *Social Science Journal* (in press).

Straus, M. (1991) 'Discipline and deviance: physical punishment of children and violence and other crime in adulthood,' *Social Problems, 38*, 133–49.

Sullivan, L. (1990) *The Prison Reform Movement: Forlorn Hope*, Boston, MA: Twayne Publishers.

Sykes, G. (1966) *Society of Captives*, New York: Atheneum.

Tavris, C. and Wade, C. (1984) *The Longest War: Sex Difference in Perspective*, Itasca, IL: Peacock.

Thomas, C., Petersen, D. and Cage, R. (1981) 'A comparative organizational analysis of prisonization,' *Criminal Justice Review, 6*, 36–43.

Travis, L., Schwartz, M. and Clear, T. (1983). *Corrections: An Issues Approach*, New York: Anderson Publishing.

US Department of Justice (1992a) *Sourcebook of Criminal Justice Statistics—1991*, Washington, DC: Bureau of Justice Statistics.

US Department of Justice (1992b) *Prisons and Prisoners in the United States*, Washington DC: Bureau of Justice Statistics, NCJ 137002.

US Department of Justice (1992c) *Criminal Victimization in the United States, 1990*, Washington, CD: Bureau of Justice Statistics, NCJ 134126.

Wikberg, R. and Foster, B. (1990) 'The long-termers: Louisiana's longest serving inmates and why they have stayed so long,' *Prison Journal, 80*, 9–14.

Wilson, J. (1975) *Thinking About Crime*, New York: Basic Books.

Weiner, T. (1991) 'U.S. tops world in crime,' *Knight Rider Newspapers*.

Wheeler, S. (1961) 'Socialization in correctional communities,' *American Sociological Review, 26*, 697–703.

Appendix I
About the Prisons in This Study

The inmate population was surveyed of a maximum-security prison within walking distance from the state capital building of South Carolina. When someone first sees this penitentiary, they might stare at its wired walls which are easily dwarfed by several antediluvian buildings surrounded by two modern tinted-glass rifle towers. New inmate arrivals imply that it transcends their worst clues about prison life as it's filled with wetness, whaled cries, endless halls going nowhere, and to enter some cells and rooms even short men have to duck. The prison was built in 1871 and over the years, it hasn't changed other than a few additions built by inmate-labour. Its average daily population was 1,340 at the time of data collection for this study which is about 100 inmates over its designed capacity. All parts of the prison are connected by one outside tunnel which is locked-down when necessary, but guards and inmates idly stand in open unprotected areas. Security and daily routines change continually depending on the orientation of the guard in-charge. Overall, the day begins at 6:00 A.M. and ends at 10:00 P.M.; there are five counts a day, three meals served in a centrally located dining area, a small educational area, a church, and a library. All inmates are given a security level in addition to their maximum custody risk rating. Inmates eat in security level shifts, so there is constant movement in and out of the dining room; and they pray in similar groups, too. Inmates can move around within their security level living unit [except segregation], but they can not enter the tunnel since each unit is locked-down. Many of the units are further segregated; for example while 200 inmates are in 'A' unit consisting of five floors of cells, with 35 inmates on each of floor; each floor can be seen from the ground floor since the open hall in front of the cells is enclosed with chicken-koop wire; also the highest security level is on the 5th floor and those inmates can not leave that floor. Guards are stationed inside each unit to control inmate movement.

A few hundred inmates are in protective custody; they have freedom of movement but only within their living unit. The general prison population, however, does not have access to this unit. Other inmates are in 'segregation' which means he is locked-down 23 hours per day allowing one hour of exercise; they eat and sleep alone, and never see anyone other than an assigned guard. These individuals are the highest security level in this prison and require special attention and isolation. None of these inmates were part of this study.

Most of the time, inmates lift weights, play sports in the large field facing the city's business district several blocks away built upon a ridge, or go to technical or academic school. Few work. Most are idle. Visitation is once a week, and security routines often change. It's been rumored that inmates have sex with strangers and get anything else they want in the visitation areas. Drugs are available throughout the prison and the drug of choice is marijuana but most street drugs are also available from visitors and staff. During the time of this study, a female graduate

student was caught throwing a bag of drugs over the wall by the expressway.

Unlike Jacobs (1976) or Irwin's (1980) descriptions of prison, this maximum facility has few if any gangs, however, if someone attacks an inmate from Charleston, then other inmates from Charleston would defend him. Likewise, those from Columbia defended each other and so on. Largely, race is not an issue in prison relationships. There were many stabbings between inmates, some serious, but not many serious incidents between inmates and guards. Inmate personal relationships were numerous, and many inmates belonged to many different informal groups. Inmates do not have furloughs away from the prison or conjugal visits. Lastly, the tension and regulations of Attica and Stateville were not present, probably because the SC guards were inmate-friendly and relationships existed between custodians and inmates; most guards and inmates came from similar environments and many were black as was the inmate population; in general, the rudeness of inmates and guards of the northern states especially Attica existed less often. In a sense, I felt safer walking through the tunnel to the educational department even though it was often filled with hundreds of inmates, then when I saw ten well-guarded inmates lined up for medicine at Attica or Stateville.

The medium facility is also in Columbia, South Carolina and five miles from the above facility. It is newer and although it has 1,236 inmates [792 more than capacity] who are less risks than those above, routine is fixed, counts are often, and many inmates work, and attend technical or academic school. The day begins at 6:00 A.M. and ends at 10:00 P.M.; hallways and general areas are secured with guards and protective stations. Inmates work, go to technical or academic school, lift weights, or play sports. The choice is theirs. Many are idle. Inmates do not have furloughs away from the prison or conjugal visits. Visitation is once a week, and every guest is searched and must show identification which is verified before they enter. The custodians rarely interact with inmates,

however, there are many volunteers and other non-custody people who informally dealt with inmates. Overall, however, there was less tension than at similar northern prisons, but more than at the above maximum-security prison. There was a successful escape the month the data was collected for this paper and many fights between inmates and between inmates and staff. In some respects, life was more complicated at this facility than it was at the above location, yet the inmates were safer.

The coed work release prison of 195 inmates [80 males] is 45 miles from the Columbia and five miles from Aiken, South Carolina. It has no walls, no gates, and the newer sleeping units resemble a retreat, but the units are visible from the bedroom windows of an adjoining neighbourhood. Many of the inmates work; some in town, some on the roadways, some on construction sites, and some in the gardens throughout the area. A stream of white buses transport many of the inmates at 7:00 A.M. and return around 4:00 P.M. Many inmates work at night, too. Pay checks are sent to the prison and held until the inmate is released. Funds are deducted for room, board, and transportation to and from work. A few inmates have vehicles owned by their employers, thus, they drive to and from work. Prison officials seek employment opportunities for the inmates in the surrounding communities. Many inmates are also on accelerated pre-release which means they go home during the day and sleep in the facility at night or on weekends. Counts are in the morning and evening. Inmates have individual freedom to visit each other but can not leave the grounds of the prison or work alone unless authorised in advance; breaking rules here means being sent to a maximum or medium custody prison. Visitation with friends and family is encouraged, and many go home on weekends if they worked during the week. Many of the inmates attend church services and group-help meetings in town. Escapes are non-existent and the necessity for disciplinary action is rare.

 Article Review Form at end of book.

Has previous research trivialized the impact of seemingly routine aggression in prisons? What are the implications of "normalized" aggression for life after prison?

Routine Victimisation in Prisons

Ian O'Donnell and Kimmett Edgar

Ian O'Donnell is Director, Irish Penal Reform Trust, Dublin. Kimmett Edgar is Research Officer, Centre for Criminological Research, University of Oxford.

This paper aims to provide a snapshot of the extent and nature of victimisation and violence in prisons and young offender institutions. It is not a study of the sensational acts of violence and disorder which sometimes occur in penal institutions, although some of the incidents described are certainly shocking. Rather, it is an examination of the more mundane victimisation to which inmates are exposed and which defines the prison experience. It is an attempt to explore the consequences for inmates of exposure to a regular threat of minor harm. This risk exists in addition to the distant threat of serious harm which is so often the focus of concern.

However, the work reported here is more than just a victim survey. It is an analysis of the functions which victimisation serves, the guises in which it appears, and the meanings ascribed to it by those involved. It is an exploration of the social relationships within which victimisation flourishes.

The effects of routine victimisation in prisons have rarely been considered in the academic literature. From the classic works of prison sociology we can learn something of the nature of inmate hierarchies and the processes of socialisation and prisonisation, particularly the defining features of the inmate 'code.' Sykes (1958), for example, described how prisoners maintained an uneasy balance between solidarity and mutual exploitation. However, his analyses of inmate-on-inmate predation gave no indication of the scope of the problem.

Others saw inmates as a cohesive and stable group, united in opposition to their captors (for example, Clemmer 19140; Garabedian 1963; Irwin and Cressey 1962). Breaches of the code which governed their behaviour (for example by passing information to staff) were met with violence. The primary focus of such work was on conformity to the code rather than the social dynamics of prisoner-prisoner interactions. It is possible that interactions between inmates received little attention because of the assumption that they were determined by a sense of solidarity and shared values, which meant that their outcome was predictable and as such not worthy of study.

Some scholars have investigated the most extreme forms which inmate-inmate victimisation can take, such as homicide (Porporino *et al.* 1987), sexual assault (Davis 1968; Dumond 1992; Lockwood 1980), riots (Adams 1994), and hostage-taking (Davies 1982). We also know something about the correlates of prison violence and how it may be related to factors such as overcrowding or population density (Farrington and Nuttall 1980; Gaes and McGuire 1985), defensible space (Atlas 1983), penal reform (Engel and Rothman 1983), increased security (Bidna 1975), the activities of inmate gangs (Fong 1990), prisoner characteristics such as psychiatric impairment (Baskin *et al.* (1991) or age and time in custody (Cooley 1993), and regime factors such as staff morale and training (Cooke 1991).

More recent work has attempted to untangle the extent to which inmates' behaviour in custody is an extension of the 'criminal subculture' more generally (the 'importation hypothesis') or is a mode of adaptation to the pains of confinement (the 'deprivation hypothesis'). For examples of studies in this tradition see Grapendaal (1990), McCorkle *et al.* (1995) and Woldredge (1994). Others have examined the structures and processes which generate and maintain 'order' within the prison community (Sparks *et al.* 1996).

In addition, there is growing interest in the related subject of 'bullying,' a special form of predatory victimisation which is characterised by an enduring and exploitative dominance relationship. The nature and consequences of bullying have recently become a source of concern, particularly in schools (Besag 1989; Byrne 1994; Olweus 1993), and young offender institutions (Beck 1995; Howard League 1995; Prison Service 1993, Tattum and Herdman 1995). For an authoritative and comprehensive review of this literature see Farrington (1993).

The work reported here is novel in several ways. First, rather than examining how inmates relate to the prison code, it homes in upon interactions between inmates. Second, rather than attempting to identify the factors associated with major disorder, it focuses upon the routine victimisation which shapes prison life. Third, it is not limited to bullying, but is much more inclusive, taking as the starting point inmates' experiences of six discrete forms of victimisation: assault, robbery, threats of violence, cell theft, exclusion and hurtful verbal abuse. . . .

The Extent and Dynamics of Prison Victimisation

The results presented here are based on the questionnaires returned by inmates who had been at the institution where the fieldwork was being carried out for at least one month, the reference period for this study (n = 1,182). . . .

The rates of victimisation were broadly similar in the young offender institutions. There was a similar degree of consistency in the adult prisons. Overall however the rates for young offenders were much higher than those for adults. Five of the six types of victimisation were reported by greater proportions of young offenders than adults. For verbal abuse and exclusion the rates were over twice as high. Cell theft was the only type of victimisation which was more commonly reported by adult prisoners. Amongst young offenders verbal abuse was most common, followed by threats and assaults. Amongst adults cell theft was most common, followed by threats and verbal abuse. The lowest rates in each institution were for exclusion and robbery.

Assaults

Assault in prison serves diverse functions and arises from a variety of circumstances, just as it does in the outside world. Inmates described a wide range of physical attacks: from minor slaps to life-threatening woundings; from spontaneous aggression to chronic beatings. The interviews carried out for this study

revealed that the motivations for assaults typically followed one of several patterns. These included the wish to settle a conflict with force, the nature of an individual's offence, the desire to enhance one's status, simple retaliation, the lure of material gain, or the relief of boredom. Assaults sometimes also occurred in the context of a trading relationship.

A key function of assault was conflict-management. Crudely speaking, prison conflicts were sometimes dealt with through force. Occasionally, as in the following example, the victim believed he merited the attack. This inmate respected the attacker's motives and was confident that the assault had resolved the dispute:

I found phonecards at the telephone. There was no name on them so I took them. He found out, came to my cell. 'Have you got my cards?' I said no. He found out that I did, though, and came back and hit me a number of times. I gave him back the cards. Afterwards he apologised. We shook hands, had a cigarette and no more problems. I asked for it myself. He didn't want to do it but I lied to him.

It was sometimes the view of participants that fights which were mutually initiated relieved tension and restored the status quo. In some of these cases, far from initiating a cycle of retaliation, a fight established a bond between the two foes:

He was winding me up about my work, throwing plates at me. Been boiling up for a few days. I said: 'If you want to start something, then start something'. I got hit over the head three times with a kitchen ladle. He got worse after he done that. I went mad and busted him up. I got the ladle off him and whacked him. We get on better now 'cause he knows he can't take the piss. It's usually that way—you get on better after you've had a fight.

Some assaults were directly related to the victim's offence. One young offender's problems began following the disclosure of his case in a newspaper. Until this point he had managed to survive on normal location, but a series of increasingly vicious attacks eventually wore down his resistance and he requested a move to the Vulnerable Prisoner Unit:

No one on the wing would associate with me. Three or four guys were saying that I was in for rape. I said I wasn't. They'd read the newspaper account of the trial.

They said: 'You're in for rape you nonce. I'm going to kill you'. One went to hit me in the face which I blocked. One hit me on the face. Next thing I knew I was banged on the head and blacked out. Then another day during association 30 guys—everybody on that side of the wing—came around and beat me up, shouting, spitting etc. They left me on the floor where a few minutes later officers found me. I was cut and bruised all over. This led to my moving off the wing.

Other attacks are motivated by status. One inmate was explicit about how he used assaults to establish his position, particularly in a situation where he was unknown:

In prison, you've got to prove yourself. When I go on a wing I look, and I pick out a respected person. And not right away but if he says something to me I tell him: 'Let's go in the showers'. And we fight. And then the pressure's off me.

Another interviewee felt insecure about his status, and believed that his credibility had been compromised by the allocation to his cell of an inmate he considered inferior. In order to force the other prisoner to move out of the cell he attacked him viciously:

I was in a double cell. They brought in some geezer who said he was in for begging. I told him he was a fraggle and to get out of my cell. But he wouldn't. Plus he smelled. So I beat him up. He said: 'You could kill me but I'm not going'. I hit him with batteries in a pillow case, mostly hit his body. I took a sharpened tooth brush to him. He wasn't fighting back. He was going: 'Go on, kill me. I got nothing to live for', enticing me to do it.

Some inmates espoused the principle that if one is wronged there is a duty to retaliate. These retaliatory strikes were among the most serious of the assaults. It was widely believed that an inmate who failed to take revenge might signal vulnerability to others. Furthermore, it was accepted that personal retribution for wrong-doing was entirely legitimate. Hence, those who described assaults involving retaliation did not seem to feel that their motivation required any further explanation:

At night someone told me to suck my mother, to perform oral sex. When I came out in the morning I told one of the officers what he said and that I wanted to fight him. The officer said: 'Yeah,' because it was a fair story. So then we had a fight. He didn't want to fight but I hit him. One of the officers bent the rules. They let me hit him and stopped it when it got serious. They just took him back in his cell. They didn't nick us for fighting.

In other cases the violence was used in self-defence. Sometimes the victim played a very active role and it was an open question who victimised whom:

I was called to my window by my next-door neighbour. I was called names. He said my dad was a beast. He said my mum was a bitch and a slag. I couldn't get to him then because we were locked up. Next day at work he pushed me. I punched him in the face and he ran straight to one of the officers on his hands and knees, crying, bleeding from his nose, saying I hit him.

Assault was also used to enforce debts. It was generally understood that being beaten for failing to repay a debt did not settle the debt. The assault was considered to be a way of persuading the person to repay:

Someone owed me an ounce of burn [tobacco]. I got him in a corner on association, and told him: 'Give me burn or I'll slap you.' I hit him. He had bruises to his arms and legs. I told him if he grassed me up I would do him.

Some incidents began as games designed to pass the time. It should be noted that both of the incidents reported next took place in four-man dormitories, which seemed to provide an ideal setting for such harmful behaviour. The first episode shows that prisoners can be assaulted regularly and suffer significant emotional harm despite a lack of serious physical injuries:

They used to have pillow fights and I used to get battered. It would turn from fun into all three on me. They would turn off the light. I was getting headaches from all the pillows. Happened twice, three times a week.

The second episode shows how serous assaults could emerge with explosive speed from minor play-fighting. A small number of victimisers said that they enjoyed such violence. In the following example drug use and the dormitory setting clearly aggravated the seriousness of the offence, leading the attackers to behave in increasingly damaging ways. It is important to point out that although there was a sexual element in this case, sexual assaults were

rarely reported in the institutions studied:

There were four of us in one dorm. One come off his visit with some cannabis. He shared it out. We started pillow fighting. He showed he was the weakest. All three of us set on him. We had books stuffed in the pillows. It turned nasty and we were punching him. It started as a joke, but it got serious. My friend held him down on the bed and I put a pillow over his head and held it. And he was crying and we started hitting him. I said: 'If you don't stop crying we will do it for real.' I put the pillow back on and held it for longer. My friend got a broomstick and put it up his boxer shorts. If he had done something to resist, it would have ended right there. If he had tried to stand up for himself, then things might have been different. But he just stayed still and the other boy shoved it up his arsehole. I don't know why we did it. In the dorms, people get bored and look for entertainment and fun. Unfortunately, it is the weak who are the entertainment.

Threats of Violence

All threats aim to force someone to do something against their will. In the interviews, adults and young offenders described threats as a tool used in conjunction with some other form of victimisation, either to coerce a person into surrendering his goods, or to invite another to fight, or to secure some service, or to put an end to an escalating round of insults.

By definition, of course, attempts at robbery must involve a threat:

One or two say: 'I'm going to batter your head in the shower.' They want my canteen. They pick on me because I'm black and weak.

Sometimes threats were a means to enforce debts:

Someone owed me something. So I threatened to beat him up. He was banged up and I threatened him through the door. I said: 'Where's my stuff you owe me?' He said he hasn't got it. I said: 'Well, we'll meet in a cell and sort it out.'

Threats had two opposing functions when used in situations of conflict. First, they could be used to force the other to back down in order to win the dispute without having to resort to physical violence. Second, threats sometimes functioned to 'wind up' the other person, to provoke a fight which the perpetrator could justify:

This geezer was waiting to play pool. It was my turn and he said it was his turn next, not mine. I told him I'd hit him round the head with a pool ball if he took me for a cunt. He backed off so I invited him up to my cell and he wouldn't come up and fight.

A young offender described how threats were sometimes issued in a speculative attempt to obtain drugs:

If someone comes in with drugs everyone shouts out the window: 'Give me some or I'll get you tomorrow.'

Occasionally pressure was brought to bear on inmates in order to persuade them to bring drugs into the prison after a visit. This is an example of co-ercing services from other prisoners, a technique known as 'tasking':

They wanted me to bring in Class A drugs. They would arrange a visitor for me. They knew I had a habit in the past so they said I could have half of what I brought in. I refused point blank, said that if they wanted it, they could bring it in themselves.

In another example of 'tasking' an inmate was threatened with a beating if he did not bring in money. He tried to do so, was caught and ended up in the segregation unit for his own protection:

Someone came up to me and said that this guy was going to do me in unless I brought in some money. I got money at a visit but was strip searched after the visit and it was found. I can't risk going back onto any wing here. I don't know what would happen. Someone could slash me with a razor blade.

One of the adults described having received written threats. This was highly unusual in that it gave the victim documentary evidence which staff could use as proof if they elected to charge the perpetrator. Clearly inmates believed that they could act with impunity against this particular individual.

In a final example, a young offender who was interviewed minutes after he had been attacked described a complex web of victimisation, of which threats were an integral part, but which also included insults, 'tasking' and assault:

Today, working in the kitchens, someone said: 'Your mother's a slag.' Someone else came up and put a sharp knife against my throat. Everyday I get pushed and slapped around by some black guys. They want me to steal things from the kitchen for them. This time I went to an officer and said: 'I ain't going to say why but I've got problems and I want out.' The officer said: 'You can wait.' I went to walk out the gate and somebody head-butted me from behind. As soon as I started walking I was jumped from behind and bang I was on the floor. They were kicking my body and the back of my neck. They walked off. I just laid there for a few seconds then walked down the corridor punching a few windows. I broke my wrist in here already punching my cell wall out of frustration. They know I won't fight back. They try to push me to my limit so that I'll lose it.

Robbery

The act of taking possessions by force is robbery. 'Taxing' is the term used to describe such behaviour in English prisons. The use of such language legitimises and trivialises the behaviour by drawing a parallel with revenue collection by the State. This offence is often thought to be the essence of victimisation in prisons, although in reality it occurs relatively infrequently. By definition it involves both a threat and an attempt to steal. It is often accompanied by verbal abuse and in its more serous form can also involve an assault. It is a complex form of victimisation.

Victims and victimisers described a range of techniques. Sometimes robbery was carried out by an inmate with the support of others, sometimes inmates acted alone. The target goods varied from the trivial, for example cigarettes or biscuits, to valuable possessions such as radios or cannabis. Tobacco, drugs, radios or phonecards could be desirable objects in their own right or used as currency to purchase something else.

As a 'taxing' relationship develops between inmates it may intensify. The following example shows how trivial requests were replaced by more serious demands, coupled with an expectation that the victim would routinely surrender his goods:

Every week I would get parcels in the post. Four boys would come on to me. First they asked me for a loan. So I was giving them 1/2 oz here and there. Then they started demanding it. They threatened to slash me. I started blaming myself for giving in, in the first place.

In another case an attempt at robbery built up over several days. The prisoner being victimised was fully aware that the sole objective was to take his radio from him. Assault featured as a part of the perpetrator's method:

For three or four days he was trying to get me to lend him my radio. I wasn't having it, 'cause I knew he wasn't planning on giving it back. He started threatening: 'If you don't you will be knocked out'. It's all prison talk. Only one per cent really happens. I told him no. He whacked me on the jaw; started saying: 'You still think you're brave?' I got away. He wasn't trying to injure me, he was trying to frighten me.

This victim knew that the assault was purely a means of reinforcing the attempted robbery. The slaps on the face were unpleasant, but the victim was able to neutralise their seriousness by accurately interpreting their purpose. He knew he was engaged in a war of nerves and that he was unlikely to be seriously harmed if he continued to resist. As the perpetrator had only a few days left to serve, the victim resolved to wait it out.

It is interesting to trace the development of 'taxing' relationships over time. The following extract shows how the victim's resistance gradually increased to the extent that he threatened his victimisers:

These black boys come into my cell and say: 'Right I'm taking your radio.' I didn't want to get in a fight, so I said: 'Take it.' One said: 'If you grass me up I'm gonna do you.' This other boy said: 'I want all your canteen.' I told him: 'Go suck out your girl.' I told an officer. He went and got my radio back. Later the same three took my phonecards and matches and Rizzlas. I put a razor blade up to his throat and told him: "Give me that phonecard back before I cut your throat.' And he gave the phonecard back.

Phonecards were a popular target. They were simple to take, easily hidden, in plentiful supply, and could be kept for personal use or traded for tobacco or drugs at standard, reliable rates. Some felt they had no choice but to change their routine activities in order to mimimise the risk of further victimisation.

I was talking to my wife. When I put the phone down, he took my card from me. 'I want to use that,' he said. I said: 'Give it back.' But he wouldn't. There were 38 units left on it. Now I'm frightened to go upstairs and use the phone if they're there. I phone now in the morning before they get up.

For many prisoners illicit drugs were the ideal item to steal because victims would be unlikely to report their loss to staff. Indeed, the purpose of taking other goods was often to trade them for drugs. The remote probability of an official response encouraged robbers to act without fear of the consequences. Young offenders were particularly forthcoming about situations in which they robbed others of their drugs. There was no doubt that the most systematic and serious 'taxing' was drug related:

A little boy came back from a visit with cannabis. I pushed him into my cell and shoved a pencil against his throat. I said I would stab him if he didn't give me the cannabis. Then I punched him and he got frightened and handed it over. I target his kind because I know he will give it up without problems. I find most people prefer to take the easy way and give it up instead of fight.

Another described how successful he was at maintaining a heavy use of cannabis while in custody, at the expense of many others. Indeed he welcomed the opportunity which his forthcoming promotion to red-band (trusted prisoner) would give him to move outside his wing and find new victims so that he could increase his consumption:

No one refuses me. I wouldn't take no one's biscuits, just drugs. If I know someone has a £20 draw and they won't give it, I'm taking it man. They can't report it 'cause its drugs. When I'm made a red band next week I'll have about £40 worth every day. I can't wait!

Cell Theft

Cell theft was sometimes purely opportunistic—the perpetrator saw an open cell door and quickly took what he could:

Once in a blue moon—when there's an easy opportunity. Door ajar. Looked in. Saw the watch on the table. Thought: 'I haven't got one. I can have one for myself.' If you see something, take it. Just like a burglar.

One young offender made a sport of the behaviour:

If a cell is open I nip in, thieve things out: biscuits, edible stuff, smoking stuff—everything I could get. I do it for a laugh—see if I can get away with it. If I get caught I just laugh it off.

Sometimes cell theft did appear to be a petty type of victimisation:

I was going to work one morning. I thought my door was shut but the bolt was on. After work I came back. Some stuff was gone. Juice, stamps, burn, Just because my door was open.

In another case the loss was not trivial. The victim's interpretation of the episode, based on his suspicions about the identity of the perpetrator, suggested it was not coincidental that he had been the victim of theft:

I was cleaning. When I come back someone had been in and took everything. All my canteen, burn, bikkies, the lot. £28 worth. They also took my medicine. It is out of order. He's the same one has been trying to tax me.

However, prisoners generally felt fatalistic about cell theft because the identity of the perpetrator was usually unknown. Furthermore they were largely dependent on staff to defend their property and keep their cell doors locked. For these reasons many simply resigned themselves to the inevitability of such losses, which were seen as part of the hazards of prison life:

When I went down for meals I had stuff stolen. Very vulnerable because officers are not patrolling the landings during meal times. You can't lock your doors every minute.

Verbal Abuse

Following the usual pattern, hurtful insulting language was much more common in YOIs than in adult establishments. In the previous month, over half (56%) of all young offenders had borne the brunt of comments which they felt to be offensive and upsetting, compared with a quarter (26%) of adults.

Insults were frequently used as a tool in the first stages of building a relationship of dominance. Three types of malicious insults emerged from the victims' descriptions. These were manipulative insults, slander, and racist abuse.

Insults which were manipulative were intended to break the inmate's spirit. The person making the remarks goaded the victim, playing on any perceived weakness:

Only thing that really annoys me is when they make comments about my girlfriend. She's just lost my baby. They say she's a whore and all that. They know it winds me up.

Common terms of abuse included 'nonce' or 'beast' (sex offender), 'fraggle' (mentally disordered offender), 'muppet' (vulnerable prisoner; inadequate), and 'grass' (informer). The purpose of such labelling is to damage the prisoner's reputation. Unless the victim can demonstrate that he does not fit the label, the rest of the wing may accept its validity and ostracise him.

One type of insult which carried great force amongst adults was to be accused of being a sex offender:

Even if I just step out my door I get called a child molester, dirty nonce bastard and so on. Even when I walk down to get my dinner at night they're always shouting their mouths off. 'We know what you're in for. You had intercourse with a fifteen-year-old girl. Here comes the child-snatcher.'

Given the widespread antipathy towards sex offenders and informers, to be identified as such—even without foundation—put an inmate at risk of attack (both physical and verbal) from other prisoners:

On the wing in the evening, while we were locked up, this guy started shouting I was a rapist. He was shouting, wanting everyone to hear. He wanted to turn people against me.

The final form is racist abuse:

Outside they don't say those things to me, but here they call me Paki. It don't bother me 'cause I'm not from Pakistan. I could say: 'You white bastard, you black cunt.' But what good would it do? I ignore it and they go quiet.

Verbal abuse may also function as a tool of victimisation by isolating the victim from his support base. Prisoners who are successfully isolated are confirmed in their vulnerability. This use of insults resembles the sixth form of victimisation studied, exclusion, to which we turn next.

Exclusion

The exclusion of one inmate by another often involved threats, and sometimes physical assaults. On occasion it was no more than avoidance of a despised prisoner. Exclusion arose in conflicts over control of shared equipment such as games or television. Two equals could argue about who was next to play table tennis or pool, but exclusion was used to prevent someone considered to be of lower status from their right to take a turn. Exclusion sometimes inflicted profound wide-ranging harm as victims could face threats if they even attempted to enter the television room or use the telephone.

Like robbery, rates of exclusion were comparatively low. 18% of young offenders and 7% of adults reported that they had been excluded at least once during the preceding month.

The interviews revealed that some instances of excluding another inmate were attempts to establish dominance.

Playing table tennis, this geezer who didn't like me came in with his friend and tried to take over the table. He goes: 'It's my game now.' He tried to take my bat and I carried on playing. Then he hit me on the face with his fist. I put the bat on the table and walked out. His friend tried to stop me going out the door so they could continue hitting me but I pushed past and got out.

A pattern of exclusion over time could lead to an inmate being cut off from all possible allies. Many of those who had been excluded once or twice changed their behaviour so that they did not put themselves in situations where they could be ostracised. If someone knows that their attempts to play pool or table tennis will be rebutted, it is futile even to try to do so. As such, one experience of exclusion could have long-lasting effects on the victim, forcing him to change his lifestyle in order to avoid situations of potential conflict.

Those who have been excluded resigned themselves to their lower status. One man described how exclusion had affected many aspects of his life on the Vulnerable Prisoner Unit:

I don't get a chance to play games. Get pushed off it. At evening meal time, we were standing at the gate, first in the queue. We got pushed out of the way. I've been told not to use the phone, but I've got to keep in touch so I risk it. Now I've been told not to use the shower.

Another inmate described how he had been isolated from the potential support of his peers. This situation was engineered over a considerable period of time by one prisoner who gradually brought others around to his point of view. Once social support has been withdrawn the victim becomes progressively more vulnerable:

Another prisoner put round the rumour that I was a nonce. It took me quite a long time to know what he was doing. I became aware of the vibes from former friends. People started moving away from me. When I come on the landing they all duck behind their doors. When I was becoming isolated from others the rest of the harassment began.

Like verbal abuse, exclusion could be very damaging to the victim's self-esteem. Unlike insults, however, there was little possibility that the victim of exclusion could retaliate in kind. Like robbery, exclusion was accomplished by a show of superior strength, proving to the victim his insignificance. But exclusion was a demonstration of power and influence as distinct from robbery with its primary goal of material gain. As stated above, incidents of exclusion often arose over access to resources, just as assaults were sometimes the result of such conflicts. It could be argued that, where conflict arose over a shared resource, those who gave way rather than resisting through negotiation or force, were by definition victims of exclusion.

Conclusion

Self-reports showed victimisation to be frequent, particularly among young offenders, of whom 30% had been assaulted and 44% threatened with violence on at least one occasion in the previous month. For adults the respective figures were 19% and 26%. Although many of these incidents were undoubtedly minor, the fact that a third of young offenders and a fifth of adult male prisoners had been assaulted in one month demonstrates a level of harmful activity which is frustrating for staff, frightening for

inmates and potentially destabilizing for regimes.

The routine victimisation which we have described shapes the social ethos of prisons and young offender institutions. The potential for assault, theft and verbal abuse grinds down prisoners and shifts their attitudes about the boundaries of acceptable behaviour. Hence, custody can be damaging in gradual, subtle ways which are all the more pernicious for being intangible and difficult to quantify.

One finding of this study, which is reported in detail elsewhere (O'Donnell and Edgar 1996a) was that previous experience of custody did not reduce the risk of being victimised. Although first-time prisoners may complain more about their victimisation this could reflect not increased risk, but rather a lower threshold of tolerance for such behaviour, and perhaps a degree of naivety regarding how informing staff is viewed by other inmates. However, prior custodial experience did increase the probability that a prisoner would victimise others. The capacity to assault, threaten and rob was in this sense acquired, and was a likely consequence of having been assaulted, threatened or robbed by others. Thus, not only do prisons allow for the transmission of specific criminal techniques, but they also de-sensitise people to the effects of their actions on others.

The pervasiveness of victimisation makes clear the scale of the challenges facing the Prison Service as it strives to fulfil its statement of purpose, that is: '. . . to serve the public by keeping in custody those committed by the courts . . . to look after them with humanity and help them lead law-abiding and useful lives in custody and after release.'

In recent years the Prison Service has risen to meet these challenges. A national strategy on bullying has been formulated (Prison Service 1993) and a variety of imaginative approaches have been developed at individual establishments. These are characterised by a shift away from the traditional focus on providing shelter for victims and potential victims to the creation of a whole prison approach, which recognises the widespread impact of victimisation and calls upon everyone in

the institution to take personal responsibility for reducing the problem. For a description of the major components of any strategy to tackle victimisation see Edgar and O'Donnell (1997) and O'Donnell and Edgar (1996b, 1998).

It is clearly difficult to provide prison environments which are safe all of the time. The findings reported here demonstrate the need for the Prison Service to continue to build on the initiatives already in place for reducing the risks of victimisation. By shedding light on some of the reasons for this harmful behaviour and on the circumstances in which it occurs, this study will hopefully contribute to the process of finding an effective response to a problem which has too often been dismissed as intractable.[1]

Note

1. During the course of this research, Ian O'Donnell was a Research Officer at the Oxford Centre for Criminological Research and a Fellow of Linacre College. We are indebted to Diane Caddle and John Ditchfield of the Home Office Research and Statistics Directorate and Pam Wilson from Prison Service Security Group (Order and Control Unit). As always, Roger Hood, Director of the Oxford Centre for Criminological Research, was a constant source of support, encouragement and advice. Thanks are also due to the prisoners whose thoughts and experiences form the basis of this study.

References

Adams, R. (1994) *Prison Riots in Britain and the USA*, 2nd ed., London: Macmillan.

Atlas, R. (1983) 'Crime site selection for assaults in four Florida prisons,' *Prison Journal*, 53, 59–71.

Baskin, D.R., Sommers, I. and Steadman, H.J. (1991) 'Assessing the impact of psychiatric impairment on prison violence,' *Journal of Criminal Justice*, 19, 271–80.

Beck, G. (1995) 'Bullying among young offenders in custody,' in: N.K. Clark and G.M. Stephenson (Eds.), *Criminal Behaviour: Perceptions, Attributions and Rationality* (Issues in Criminological and Legal Psychology No. 22), Leicester: British Psychological Society.

Besag, V.E. (1989) *Bullies and Victims in Schools*, Milton Keynes: Open University Press.

Bidna, H. (1975) 'Effects of increased security on prison violence,' *Journal of Criminal Justice*, 3, 33–46.

Byrne, B. (1994) 'Bullies and victims in a school setting with reference to some Dublin schools,' *Irish Journal of Psychology, 15,* 473–86.

Clemmer, D. (1940) *The Prison Community,* New York: Rinehart.

Cooke, D.J. (1991) 'Violence in prisons: the influence of regime factors,' *Howard Journal, 30,* 95–109.

Cooley, D (1993) 'Criminal victimization in male federal prisons,' *Canadian Journal of Criminology, 35,* 479–95.

Davies, W. (1982) 'Violence in prisons,' in: P. Feldman (Ed.), *Developments in the Study of Criminal Behaviour,* vol. 2, Chichester: John Wiley and Sons.

Davis, A.J. (1968) 'Sexual assaults in the Philadelphia prison system and sheriff's vans,' *Transaction, 6,* 8–16.

Dumond, R.W. (1992) 'The sexual assault of male inmates in incarcerated settings,' *International Journal of the Sociology of Law, 20,* 135–57.

Edgar, K. and O'Donnell, I. (1997) 'Responding to victimisation,' *Prison Service Journal, 109,* 15–19.

Engel, K. and Rothman, S. (1983) 'Prison violence and the paradox of reform,' *The Public Interest, 73,* 91–105.

Farrington, D. (1993) 'Understanding and preventing bullying,' in: M. Tonry (Ed.), *Crime and Justice: A Review of Research,* vol. 17, Chicago: University of Chicago Press.

Farrington, D. and Nuttall, C. (1980) 'Prison size, overcrowding, prison violence and recidivism,' *Journal of Criminal Justice, 8,* 221–31.

Fong, R.S. (1990) 'The organizational structure of prison gangs: a Texas case study,' *Federal Probation, 54,* 36–43.

Gaes, G.G. and McGuire, W.J. (1985) 'Prison violence: the contribution of crowding versus other determinants of prison assault rates,' *Journal of Research in Crime and Delinquency, 22,* (1), 41–65.

Garabedian, P.G. (1963) 'Social roles and processes of socialisation in the prison community,' *Social Problems, 11,* 139–52.

Grapendaal, M. (1990) 'The inmate subculture in Dutch prisons,' *British Journal of Criminology, 30,* 341–57.

Howard League (1995) *Banged Up, Beaten Up, Cutting Up: Report of the Howard League Commission of Enquiry into Violence in Penal Institutions for Teenagers under 18,* London: The Howard League for Penal Reform.

Irwin, J. and Cressey, D.R. (1962) 'Thieves, convicts and the inmate culture,' *Social Problems, 10,* 142–55.

Lockwood, D. (1980) *Prison Sexual Violence,* New York: Elsevier.

McCorkle, R.C., Miethe, T.D. and Drass, K.A. (1995) 'The roots of prison violence: a test of the deprivation, management, and "not-so-total" institution models,' *Crime and Delinquency, 41,* 317–31.

O'Donnell, I. and Edgar, K. (1996a) 'The extent and dynamics of victimization in prisons' (unpublished report to the Home Office Research and Statistics Directorate).

O'Donnell, I. and Edgar, K. (1996b) *Victimisation in Prisons* (Research Findings No. 37), London: Home Office Research and Statistics Directorate.

O'Donnell, I. and Edgar, K. (1998) *Bullying in Prisons* (Occasional Paper No. 18), Oxford: Centre for Criminological Research, University of Oxford.

Olweus, D. (1993) *Bullying at School: What We Know and What We Can Do,* Oxford: Blackwell.

Porporino, F., Doherty, P. and Sawatsky, T. (1987) 'Characteristics of homicide victims and victimizations in prisons: A Canadian historical perspective,' *International Journal of Offender Therapy and Comparative Criminology, 31,* 125–35.

Prison Service (1993) *Bullying in Prison: A Strategy to Beat It,* London: Prison Service.

Sparks, R., Bottoms, A.E. and Hay, W. (1996) *Prisons and the Problem of Order,* Oxford: Clarendon Press.

Sykes, G.M. (1958) *The Society of Captives: A Study of a Maximum Security Prison,* Princeton, NJ: Princeton University Press.

Tattum, D. and Herdman, G. (1995) *Bullying: A Whole-Prison Response,* Cardiff: Institute of Higher Education.

Wooldredge, J.D. (1994) 'Inmate crime and victimization in a southwestern correctional facility,' *Journal of Criminal Justice, 22,* 3367–81.

 Article Review Form at end of book.

Are staff aware of the fears of prisoners? Is fear in prison something about which we should be concerned?

Fear in Prisons:

A Discussion Paper

Joanna R. Adler

Introduction

Prisons can be frightening places. Not only do they house many individuals with a long history of violence. The macho culture of prison also encourages the use of force by both prisoners and staff. Assaults are common, and murder is not uncommon. For many prisoners, fear is a constant companion. Some, particularly those convicted of sexual crime, spend their entire time in prison segregated for their own protection. Others may develop physical or mental illness related to the stress of living under threat of attack or injury, whether perceived or actual. Prisoners who cannot cope with the prison environment sometimes take refuge in self-harm or even suicide.

The purpose of this paper is to examine some of these issues with a view to encouraging debate within the prison system. In particular, it attempts to gain a detailed picture of the number of prisoners and staff who live in fear in gaol. It asks questions about precisely where and of what prisoners and staff are afraid. And it considers the implications for practice in the Prison Service.

Method

In order to test the relationship between prison and fear, prisoners and staff were interviewed at three prisons. These comprised the lifer assessment centre at HMP Wormwood Scrubs, two wings at HMP Wandsworth (one in the VPU and one remand wing) and two wings in HMP Littlehey (one with a population consisting almost entirely of vulnerable prisoners and one with a mixed population of vulnerable and 'non-vulnerable' prisoners). Unfortunately, it was not possible to arrange access to either of the two female establishments approached and, as a result, all of the prisoners interviewed were male.

At least 30 prisoners and five prison officers on each wing took part in semi-structured interviews, most of which lasted about 30 minutes. As far as possible, the interviewees included a range of ages and members of different ethnic groups. Participation was voluntary, with prisoners being randomly selected from the prison computer system LIDS. However, given the prison wings selected, they did not comprise a representative sample of the prison population as a whole: 41 of the 150 prisoners interviewed were serving life sentences and a further 63 were serving sentences of over three and a half years. Staff selection was also random, and in all a total of 50 staff were interviewed. Four of these were female and one was black.

Results

To put their responses in some sort of context, interviewees were first asked about their attitudes to prison life. In general, prisoners were fairly positive about the prison routine: only one was very critical of the regime in his prison. Staff exhibited greater concern about the regime: four of the 50 staff described their routine as bad.

Relationships in Prison

Prisoners' attitudes towards the staff were mixed. Some 13 per cent of prisoners rated officers as 'bad' or 'very bad,' and 26 per cent said that they had problems with the staff. A total of 20 per cent of prisoners also reported that they had problems with other prisoners, with six prisoners reporting daily problems. Liebling and Krarup (1992), however, found that 66 per cent of vulnerable prisoners and 43 per cent of other prisoners reported difficulties interacting with other prisoners.

Some 33 of the 50 members of staff said that they had problems with prisoners. In addition, nine had no confidence in their colleagues and 11 reported having problems with fellow officers.

Incidence of Fear

Overall, 51 per cent of prisoners and 67 per cent of prison officers said that they were scared at some time in prison. Some 13 per cent of the prisoners who were fearful felt at risk all the time.

The incidence of fear disclosed by this survey is considerably higher than that which emerged from the National Prison Survey, which concluded that only 18 per cent of prisoners were fearful. Of these, 33 per cent felt constantly at risk. The difference between the two sets of results is striking, although it may partly be due to the open-ended questions used in this survey. However, it is perhaps significant that the proportion of prisoners who felt constant fear was almost the same in both—seven per cent of the sample in this survey and six per cent in the National Prison Survey.

Where Are Prisoners and Staff Afraid?

Perhaps surprisingly, the place in which prisoners experience greatest fear is their cell. Cells were named as the most worrying location by no fewer than one quarter of prisoners who admitted feeling fear in prison. This level of fear was recognized by some staff: 23 per cent of officers repeated prisoners' concerns about safety in their cells.

Other parts of the prison which worried prisoners included recesses, showers and corridors; however, significantly more prisoners reported that other prisoners feared these locations (14 per cent, seven per cent, and ten per cent respectively) than were prepared to admit that they themselves were scared.

These locations were not necessarily consistent across goals; particular prisons exhibited particular problems. For example, concerns were expressed about the hospital at Wandsworth (a finding which has also emerged from a bullying survey conducted by the prison's psychology department).

The fear of corridors came almost entirely from Littlehey A wing: the interviews revealed that prisoners were called by tannoy to the hospital to collect their medication; because the tannoy could be heard throughout the prison, it was possible for prisoners to be assaulted whilst walking the long, unsupervised corridors. Staff at Littlehey expressed similar concerns about their own safety in these corridors.

The general pattern of fear was repeated for prison officers. Cells were one of the locations in which staff were most concerned for their

safety (nine per cent), along with the landings (nine per cent) and the block (seven per cent). Nine per cent of officers who experienced fear also said that they were fearful when they were away from their colleagues. However, almost half of prison officers (48 per cent) reported that their fears were primarily related to specific situations, rather than a response to a particular location.

Of What Are Prisoners and Staff Afraid?

Violence and intimidation were the most frequently cited explanations of fear. Assaults, hot water, and the threat presented by other prisoners (particularly mentally disordered prisoners) worried prisoners. Staff themselves were rarely cited as engendering fear.

However, a range of other factors also worried prisoners. The effect of prison, on themselves or on their families, was mentioned by 13 per cent of prisoners. A further five per cent were concerned about coping with prison, and three per cent were scared of themselves. Criminal justice processes were also a source of worry, with uncertainty about the outcome of their court case being a particular source of stress. In addition, prisoners were concerned about the possibility of having time added to their sentences because of disciplinary offences, about whether they would be granted parole, and about how they would cope after release.

Perhaps the most surprising omission from the prisoner list was any mention of bullying. Bullying was cited by nearly a quarter of staff as the major source of prisoner fear, but was not mentioned by any prisoner. It is possible that the sample size was insufficiently large to include anyone who was being bullied, although two prisoners said that they had been bullied in other prisons. It may also be the case that the fear of being labelled a 'grass' made prisoners reluctant to cite bullying.

Staff fears were less easy to quantify. The overwhelming majority of respondents talked of situational factors. However, as with prisoners, prison staff also cited mentally disordered or 'unpredictable' prisoners as

a source of fear. Stress, low staffing levels, and searching sex offenders were also mentioned.

What Affects the Incidence of Fear?

There was little evidence that the level of fear experienced by prisoners was related to their individual characteristics. The level of fear did not vary according to a prisoner's offence, first-timers did not seem to be any more fearful than those with previous experience of prison and younger prisoners were no more fearful than older ones. However, in some prisons race was a factor: in Wandsworth VPU and remand wing, prisoners from minority ethnic groups were significantly more likely to report fear than were white prisoners. In Wormwood Scrubs, the effect was reversed.

The level of fear expressed by prisoners did vary from prison to prison and from wing to wing. The highest incidence of fear was found in Wormwood Scrubs (73 per cent), although the accuracy of this finding has been strongly questioned by management at the prison. This compared with 54 per cent at Littlehey and 34 per cent at Wandsworth. The latter two figures concealed variations between the two wings surveyed in each gaol: Littlehey A wing produced a rate of 70 per cent, compared to 40 per cent in D wing. Conversely, Wandsworth PU (containing much the same sort of prisoners as Littlehey A wing) showed a 30 per cent rate of fear, compared to 45 per cent on the remand wing.

Some of these findings seem to contradict earlier research. Liebling and Krarup (1992) concluded that younger prisoners and those on Rule 43 experienced most difficulties in interacting with other prisoners. There was no age effect found in this survey. When compared with older prisoners, younger prisoners were no more likely to report fear. The finding that prisoners on Rule 43 in Wandsworth were less fearful than prisoners in Littlehey seems to indicate that vulnerable prisoners feel safer in VPUs than in integrated regimes. Even in the latter location, prisoners appeared to feel safer than in the lifer wing at Wormwood

Scrubs, where the relatively high security levels and the fact that prisoners were right at the start of their sentences may have had some impact.

The impact of prisoner/staff ratios on the level of fear was difficult to disentangle. Some—albeit relatively few—staff cited low staffing levels as a source of fear. However, no prisoners named this as a problem. Moreover, the different functions of the prisons and their different security levels meant that the staff on duty were occupied in very different ways on each wing surveyed. Their impact on the wing culture was therefore likely to be very different in each case.

Conclusions

Conclusions drawn from a small-scale study of three prisons, and based upon semi-structured interviews with prisoners and staff, can only be tentative. Even with representative samples, the opinions and experiences of individual interviewees, the gender of the interviewer, and the location of the interview can all crucially affect the outcome. More particularly, the fact that fear is an in-tangible construct, meaning different things to different people, makes it hard to pin down.

However, the evidence from this survey raises some important issues. First, the level of fear experienced by prisoners and staff is clearly not a simple effect of the category of prison or the type of prisoners it holds. The number of variables which can crucially affect fear—down even to the functioning of individual services such as the hospital or the design of the prison tannoy—defy any simple solutions. As with prison suicides, reducing the incidence of fear demands paying attention to all aspects of prison life, no matter how seemingly irrelevant.

Second, the Prison Service has to accept that fear can never be totally eliminated from the system. Partly, this is because prisons, by their very nature, contain a number of dangerous and difficult individuals; no matter how hard it tries, the system will never rid itself of the disturbed and unpredictable individuals whose behaviour causes concern to prisoners and staff. Partly too, however, it is because many prisoners' fears are about things outside the prison gates: the welfare of their fam-ily; the outcome of their court case; life after discharge. Staff attitudes are also affected by these domestic fears and concerns.

If this is the case, it is clearly of vital importance that the Prison Service gives priority to supporting prisoners and staff who are fearful and to asking them about the sources of their fear. In interviews with staff, governors were seen as being out of touch with the day-to-day realities of prison life and uninterested in the opinions of rank and file officers. This was particularly true of female officers, who felt unsupported by a predominantly male management. Prisoners in turn felt that staff, particularly senior staff, did not understand the source of their fears and were not prepared to listen to their suggestions for improvement.

Reference

Liebling, A. and Krarup, H. 1992. Suicide Attempts in Male Prisons: Summary of a Report Submitted to the Home Office, (July), Institute of Criminology, University of Cambridge, Cambridge.

 Article Review Form at end of book.

Does imprisoning mothers increase the chances that they will re-offend?

Incarcerated Mothers and the Foster Care System in Massachusetts:

A Literature Review

Does Department of Social Services involvement during incarceration increase the chances for family reunification and decrease the recidivism rate?

Jordan B. Bistrian

Foster Care Review Unit, Massachusetts Department of Social Services

Background of Incarcerated Women

The number of women in United States prisons and jails has been increasing for the past decade. At the end of 1993, there were more than 55,000 women incarcerated in federal and state prisons ("Women in Prison," 1995, p. 1). These women accounted for 5.8 percent of the total state and federal prison population and 9.3 percent of the county jail population ("Women in Prison," 1995, p. 1). Between 1980 and 1993, the growth rate for the female prison population increased by approximately 313 percent for women, compared to 182 percent for men ("Women in Prison," 1995, p. 1). Massachusetts has seen a growth in the number of women in their correctional facilities as well. In 1990, there were 511 incarcerated women in Massachusetts correctional facilities; by 1995, this number had grown to 596 women (Department of Correction, 1996). These women represented six percent of the total offender population in Massachusetts (Department of Correction, 1996). Because of this national increase, the United States has had to build many new correctional facilities for both men and women (Chesney-Lind and Immarigeon, 1994). To respond to the growing population of female offenders, there needs to be an understanding of the makeup of this population in order to identify their needs.

Nationally, women prisoners are ethnically diverse. African-American women make up about 46 percent of women in prison and 43 percent of women in jail ("Women in Prison," 1995, p. 1). Caucasian women comprise 36 percent of women in prison and 38 percent of women in jail whereas Hispanic women comprise 14 percent of women in prison and 16 percent of women in jail ("Women in Prison," 1995, p. 1). At the Massachusetts Correctional Institution at Framingham (MCI-Framingham), the only state facility for women, Caucasian women make up 66 percent of the offender population with African-American women comprising 19 percent and Hispanic women comprising 14 percent (Department of Correction, 1994).

Family demands on women prisoners differ greatly than that of

Incarcerated Mothers and the Foster Care System in Massachusetts: A Literature Review, Jordan B. Bistrian. Foster Care Review Unit, Massachusetts Department of Social Services, 1997. Reprinted by permission. Jordan B. Bistrian, MSW, was a graduate intern under the supervision of Katherine May, MSW, of the Massachusetts Department of Social Services when this article was written.

men prisoners. Over 75 percent of incarcerated women are mothers, most of which have two or more children (Breaking the Cycle, 1995, p. 1). It has been estimated that, on average each day, 165,000 children are affected by their mother's incarceration (Breaking the Cycle, 1995, p. 1). Most of these women are single parents (Women in Prison, 1995, p. 2). Over seventy percent of incarcerated mothers had custody of their dependent children before they were incarcerated (Bloom, 1994, p. 25). However, only 50 percent of incarcerated fathers had custody of their children prior to incarceration (Women in Prison, 1995, p. 2). Furthermore, between 8 and 10 percent of women are pregnant when they enter prison (Bloom, 1994, p. 23).

These children usually reside with their grandparents, other relatives, or friends ("Women in Prison," 1995). It has been found that 74 percent of children of incarcerated mothers are cared for by their relatives or friends, and of this number, only 25 percent of the fathers assume responsibility for them ("Women in Prison," 1995, p. 2). Similarly, in Massachusetts, 75 percent of children of incarcerated parents live with relatives and 25 percent are in the care of the state, either in foster care or group care (May, 1997). In addition, the majority of women incarcerated in Massachusetts are between the ages of 30 and 39 (Department of Correction, 1994). What is interesting is that, nationally, 89 percent of children of incarcerated fathers are cared for by the child's mother ("Women in Prison," 1995, p. 2).

What appears to be a determinant to the incarceration of women is poverty. The majority of incarcerated women are poor; prior to the mother's arrest, the family typically survived on less than $500 per month ("Breaking the Cycle," 1995, p. 1). Fifty-three percent of women prisoners and 74 percent of women in jail were unemployed prior to their incarceration ("Women in Prison," 1995, p. 1). Thus, women are more likely than men to be serving sentences for drug offenses and other nonviolent crimes with economic motives. In 1991, in comparison to one in six males, one in four women

reported committing their offense in order to acquire money to buy drugs ("Women in Prison," 1995, p. 2). In the same year, thirty-two percent of women incarcerated in state prisons were serving sentences for drug-related offenses ("Women in Prison," 1995, p. 1). An additional 29 percent of these women were serving sentences for property offenses such as larceny, theft, bribery, or fraud ("Women in Prison," 1995, p. 1).

Similarly, in federal prisons, almost 64 percent of incarcerated women were serving sentences for drug-related offenses ("Women in Prison," 1995, p. 1). Like women in state prisons, the next most common offenses were property offenses such as larceny or theft. The latter making up 6.3% and extortion, bribery, or fraud making up 6.2% ("Women in Prison," 1995, p. 2). 1994, the Department of Correction in Massachusetts reported that 24 percent of incarcerated women were serving sentences of drug-related offenses, 32 percent were serving time for property offenses, and 32 percent were serving sentences for "other offenses" (Department of Correction, 1994).

Another determinant of incarceration is a history of childhood or adult abuse. Prior to their incarceration, more than 40 percent of women in state prisons and 44 percent of women in jail had either been physically or sexually abused at some point during their lifetime ("Women in Prison," 1995, p. 2). In addition, domestic violence is a common tragedy that many incarcerated women have survived. More than 30 percent of incarcerated women serving sentences for murder were convicted of killing a husband, ex-husband, or boyfriend ("Women in Prison," 1995, p. 2). Moreover, 17.2 percent of incarcerated women lived in a foster home or group home during their childhood ("Breaking the Cycle," 1995, p. 9).

The Foster Care System in Massachusetts

This paper on incarcerated mothers and their children serves the purpose of identifying the effect visitation and overall continued contact with family

members has on incarcerated mothers. Conclusions will be drawn about the involvement of the Massachusetts Department of Social Services (DSS), or other public social service agencies, from findings in previous research on the relationship between family contact and family reunification, in addition to family contact and recidivism.

DSS was created in 1978, and began operation as a department under the Executive Office of Health and Human Services in 1980. It serves as the state department responsible for "strengthening and encouraging family life so that every family can care for and protect its children" (Reilly, 1992, p. 150). Although DSS makes every effort to keep the family unit intact, if a family is not providing the necessary amount of care for a child, DSS will intervene (Reilly, 1992). This intervention is necessary due to the department's mandate to protect the rights of a child to develop normally both physically and emotionally (Reilly, 1992). Here, DSS has the difficult task of meeting this mandate while simultaneously respecting the right of families to "be free from unwarranted state intervention" (Reilly, 1992, p. 150). In addition, the Adoption Assistance and Child Welfare Act of 1980 called for social workers to make every effort to either achieve family reunification, or provide children with alternatives which will establish permanence (Beckerman, 1994).

In Massachusetts, parental incarceration does not serve as a reason for the loss of parental rights (Reilly, 1992). In determining whether an incarcerated mother's parental rights will be terminated, courts now investigate two standards: the parental fitness of the mother and the best interest of the child (Reilly, 1992). A determination that a mother is unfit must be established at the current time (Reilly, 1992); in other words, a mother's current situation as an incarcerated person cannot deem her unfit to parent. Nonetheless, if women do not maintain contact with their children while in prison, they may lose the right to parent their children ("Breaking the cycle," 1995, p. 6). In addition, the average amount of time served in United States prisons is 16 months for females and 66 months for males; this forces most prisoners with children in foster care to face the federally mandated deadline for permanency planning of their children before, or immediately after their release (Norman, 1994, p. 132).

Although there has been a recent increase in women in jails and prisons nationwide, little attention has focused on the concerns of women in the criminal justice system ("Women in Prison," 1995, p. 1). Prior to the increase in the population of incarcerated women, these women were often ignored due to their small size and the short sentences they received in comparison to their male counterparts ("Women in Prison," 1995). Thusfar, this paper has focused on incarcerated mothers. Consequently, attention needs to be focused on the children of incarcerated mothers.

Children of Incarcerated Mothers

Children with mothers in prison are a high-risk population. The average age of children when their mother is incarcerated is between seven and 12 years old ("Breaking the Cycle," 1995, p. 3). When a parent is involved with the criminal justice system, the family is usually in crisis; for some families, incarceration of a mother triggers this crisis ("Breaking the Cycle," 1995). However, for most families, criminal deviance represents one more manifestation of the effects of substance abuse, poverty, and domestic violence ("Breaking the Cycle," 1995). When a mother is incarcerated, children usually experience a period of instability and uncertainty; without her children, a mother often loses her drive to rebuild her life ("Breaking the Cycle," 1995). As a result of their mother's incarceration, these children can experience tremendous amounts of trauma, anxiety, guilt, shame, and fear ("Breaking the Cycle," 1995).

Kampfner (1994) conducted a study on children of incarcerated mothers. In this study, it was found that children of incarcerated mothers were traumatized by their experiences of maternal crime, arrest, and incarceration. As a result, they showed several symptoms associated with acute Post-Traumatic Stress Disorder (Kampfner, 1994). Although their caregivers made efforts to protect them from trauma-related cues, their circumstances, including the social stigma attached to maternal incarceration and their lack of emotional supports, combined in ways that made it difficult for them to overcome the effects of trauma (Kampfner, 1994). The author further noted that the relationship between mother and child is important and necessary, does not disappear with maternal incarceration, and must be fostered (Kampfner, 1994). When these children enter adolescence, this suffering is often manifested in poor academic achievement, juvenile delinquency, gang involvement, and violence; in addition, adult criminal behavior is often a result ("Breaking the Cycle," 1995). This criminal behavior represents the "final link in an intergenerational cycle of criminal justice involvement" ("Breaking the Cycle," 1995, p. 3).

Foster Care Reviews/Permanency Planning

Incarcerated women who had custody of their children prior to their imprisonment must make child care arrangements with relatives or friends (Reilly, 1992). If a woman is unable to make these arrangements, a mother may voluntarily place her child with DSS, or DSS may seek custody of the child (Reilly, 1992). One of the greatest concerns of incarcerated women is being separated from their children and having to make child care arrangements (Reilly, 1992).

DSS recognizes the unique difficulties faced by incarcerated mothers of children in foster care (Reilly, 1992). When a child is placed in the custody of DSS, an ongoing caseworker is assigned to the family. Ongoing casework involves the establishment of a service plan. The service plan for families usually requires that a parent maintains contact with their child (Reilly, 1992). In addition, a parent is required to assist in establishing and implementing the service plan (Reilly, 1992). These tasks become quite difficult for an incarcerated mother.

It has been estimated that more than 80 percent of incarcerated mothers plan on living with their children when they are released ("Breaking the Cycle," 1995, p. 6). For many mothers, regaining custody of their children is a motivation to stay sober and rebuild their lives ("Breaking the Cycle," 1995, p. 6). As the nature of incarceration poses greater risks to permanent separation, regulations provide for additional efforts to be made by DSS for the encouragement and promotion of a continuing relationship between mother and child (Reilly, 1992). These efforts include regular visitation and conducting foster care reviews and other conferences at the correctional facility (Reilly, 1992).

The purpose of foster care reviews is to identify whether the family situation has changed, ensure that DSS and the parent(s) are accomplishing their tasks outlined in the service plan, determine if the goals for the family are still appropriate and necessary, and if not, set new goals, and review the reasons why the child is in the care of DSS (Reilly, 1992). The foster care review panel can recommend additions and changes in the service plan (Reilly, 1992). The panel's determinations of a goal change may be appealed by the parent(s) of the child, or the child (through his or her attorney, if necessary) (Reilly, 1992).

In a study of incarcerated mothers who had children in foster care in New York State prisons, prerequisite activities between mothers and caseworkers were identified as incidence of correspondence, telephone contact, and notification of court hearings. Out of a sample of 53 women, 68 percent did not receive telephone calls and about 49 percent received no correspondence from caseworkers (Beckerman, 1994, p. 11). In addition, less than 50 percent of the women were familiar with the procedures that would enable them to appear for court hearings (Beckerman, 1994, p. 12). Failure to become involved in such activities threatens the parental status of the incarcerated mother (Beckerman, 1994).

Visitation

Visitation between mother and child is needed in order to preserve the parent-child relationship. Hairston (1991) explained that imprisonment is detrimental to parent-child relationships, but that the impact of separation can be lessened by efforts taken to strengthen communication between parents and children. Furthermore, ongoing communication is vital in maintaining parent-child attachment and in allowing parents to maintain their role and carry out parental responsibilities (Hairston, 1991). As a result, visitation is an important aspect of casework with incarcerated mothers whose children are in the care of DSS (Reilly, 1992). Visits allow children to discuss their emotional reactions to their mother's criminal justice involvement. Due to the fact that children can feel too ashamed to confide in their friends or classmates, this is an area which they may not be able to discuss with other people ("Breaking the Cycle," 1995). Being honest with children about their mother's whereabouts and allowing frequent visits can alleviate a child's fear about their mother's well-being ("Breaking the Cycle," 1995).

It has also been found that the frequency of visits is the most important factor in determining whether the family will be reunited once the mother is released ("Breaking the Cycle," 1995, p. 6). This is due to the fact that frequent contact allows both the mother and the child to view each other realistically; seeing each other often also enables them to heal the damage to their relationship caused by the mother's criminal justice involvement ("Breaking the Cycle," 1995). In addition, Bloom (1994) explained that inconsistent contact between mother and child, as well as between the mother and the caregivers of these children, was associated with problems during reunification with their children.

Although prisons usually offer contact visits for families, most jails have visiting rooms where children must sit across a table from their parent where they are often separated by a glass partition ("Breaking the Cycle," 1995). Very few jails offer play areas for children in the waiting room or the visiting area ("Breaking

the Cycle," 1995). This is in addition to the fact that the proximity of the jail from home is usually very far (Fuller, 1993). Because there are fewer prison facilities for women, women are usually placed in facilities much farther from their homes than men ("Women in Prison," 1995) This distance can cause transportation problems for the children of prisoners; as a result, this distance can deprive incarcerated women of frequent contact, or any contact with their children (Fuller, 1993).

There are other obstacles to children visiting their mothers. These obstacles include the restrictive rules governing visitation, as well as caretaker concerns about the effect visiting a prison may have on the children ("Breaking the Cycle," 1995). These obstacles often prevent children from having regular contact with their mother. It was found that only 9 percent of women have weekly visits from their children, 18 percent have monthly visits, 21 percent have less than monthly visits, and 52 percent have no visits at all ("Breaking the Cycle," 1995, p. 7). This was further supported in a study that found that 54 percent of children of incarcerated mothers never visited their mothers (Bloom, 1994, p. 25).

Family Reunification

As the aforementioned explains the importance of visitation and how it can lead to family reunification, it is important to note that the struggle is not over for the mother or her children when she is released from jail or prison. Once a woman is released, her ability to reconnect with her children can be impaired due to being separated from her children for years; this is compounded by the difficulty of reintegrating into society ("Breaking the Cycle," 1995).

There are many pressures on women exiting the correctional system; often, these pressures become obstacles to reintegration into society. Because women receive little pre- or post-release planning, or support to help them reunite with their family, women often find themselves homeless, penniless, and struggling to remain clean and sober ("Breaking the Cycle," 1995). In Massachusetts, providers at several homeless shel-

ters reported an increase in the number of formerly incarcerated men and women who seek shelter (Dowdy, 1977). "Somewhere between 5 and 10 percent [of former inmates] now come directly out of corrections and into the shelter system . . . five years ago it might have been 1 percent," explained Philip Mangrano, Executive Director of the Massachusetts Housing and shelter Alliance (Dowdy, 1997, p. B2).

Shelter administrators explained that this increase may be due to new stringent policies of the Department of Correction which make it more difficult for inmates to get into pre-release programs; in addition, four halfway houses were closed down which eliminated at least 250 beds for inmates who would work in the community (Dowdy, 1997). Furthermore, on the national level, there are not many educational or vocational services which can be accessed while in prison, leaving newly released women at risk for alcohol and drug abuse, in addition to criminal behavior ("Women in Prison," 1995).

For those parents who gave formal custody to a caregiver, or whose children are in foster care, regaining legal custody can be a long and difficult struggle. The decisions are not easy, especially when the mother and child have not had contact for a long period of time ("Breaking the Cycle," 1995). Here, the courts must balance a child's need for permanence and stability against a parent's desire to raise her child and the benefit to the child of living with his or her biological parent ("Breaking the Cycle," 1995).

Although it has been found that prior incarcerations reduce the likelihood that mother and child will be reunited after the mother's current jail or prison term (Norman, 1994), incarcerated women in Massachusetts whose children are in the care of DSS, are more likely to experience post-release success. These women have met regularly with their social worker, established a service plan, attended foster care reviews and other necessary meetings, and have had regular visitation with their children. Therefore, it would seem that these women are more likely to reunite with their family and less likely to return to crime. . . .

Policy Issues and Recommendations

Family Law

Upon incarceration, many women face losing custody of their children. Although most women have family members who will care for their children while they are incarcerated, as this paper has pointed out, some children will be in the care and protection of the state ("Women in Prison," 1995). As mentioned earlier, approximately 75 percent of children of incarcerated parents in Massachusetts live with relatives and 25 percent are in the care of the state, whether that is foster or residential care (May, 1997). Incarcerated mothers with children in the care of the state, need continual support advocacy from DSS in order to ensure a healthy reunification with her family.

It is of utmost importance that local, state, and federal governments support the incarcerated mother's relationship with her children as family ties during imprisonment can decrease the recidivism of the offender (Hairston, 1988). This support can include family visitation, or alternative-to-incarceration programs. However, these initiatives can only be successful when the parent-child relationship is preserved. By creating more alternative facilities and by adjusting sentencing guidelines and imprisonment statutes to allow more qualified women to be placed in alternative-to-incarceration programs, incarcerated mothers would be able to both serve their sentences and continue their relationships with their children ("Women in Prison," 1995).

In response to the growing population of incarcerated women in Massachusetts, the Commissioner of the Department of Correction requested the Research Division to investigate programs in other states that allow children to remain with their mother during all or some period of their sentence (Knight, 1993). In 1992, there were twelve states that had programming for women that allowed some infants and children to stay with their mothers; seven more states had plans for initiating such programs, and three other states had previously had such programs, but had abandoned them due to financial concerns (Knight, 1993). At this time, it is unknown if the results of this study have provided any additional opportunities for incarcerated women in Massachusetts.

Drug Treatment and Education

The increase in the female correctional population has occurred simultaneously with the increase in alcohol and other drug addictions by women prisoners ("Women in Prison," 1995). It has been found that 70 percent of incarcerated women have alcohol or drug problems ("Women in Prison," 1995, p. 2). As a result, there has been an installment of mandatory minimum sentences for most drug offenses ("Women in Prison," 1995).

Drug treatment should be available to all addicted incarcerated women. Because drug use is a primary risk factor for HIV/AIDS, prison officials and administrators must collaborate with public health specialists to develop drug treatment programs which emphasize AIDS education and family planning ("Women in Prison," 1995).

Pre-Release Planning

One of the largest concerns of the correctional system, both for male and female prisoners, is the lack of discharge planning. As a result, many released prisoners either find themselves homeless, or find themselves in an environment where maintaining sobriety and abstinence, and avoiding future criminal behavior is not possible ("Women in Prison," 1995). Incarcerated women need access to family planning to prevent unplanned pregnancies, HIV-infection, or other sexually transmitted diseases ("Women in Prison," 1995). Family planning services are very poor in prison and access to pregnancy termination services is limited, or nonexistent ("Women in Prison," 1995).

The incarcerated mother, whose children are in the care of the state, needs continual support and advocacy in order to ensure a healthy family reunification and to ensure that she will not return to the criminal justice system. However, this can only occur when she has access to services and to her children, as well as ongoing pre-release planning during incarceration.

Implications for Social Work Practice and Research

Services for incarcerated women, such as family visitation, drug counseling, and pre-release planning have thus far been substandard. But, this growing number of incarcerated women greatly increases the need to respond. Social workers will continue to be called on to provide clinical services to this population. It has been hypothesized that DSS involvement may reduce recidivism and increase the chances for family reunification for incarcerated mothers, this advocacy should be recognized as a model for all incarcerated persons. If the United States spends over three million dollars a day to imprison all women inmates "Breaking the Cycle," 1995, p. 1), changes are needed to ensure success upon release from correctional facilities in order to reduce the effect of the "revolving prison door."

There must be a response to the growing population of women prisoners in the United States. This problem is not going to disappear unless there is a response by the correctional system. Incarcerated women need to be viewed from both within and outside of the prison system. There needs to be a collaboration between organizations that provide services to incarcerated mothers. During their incarceration, women must receive the educational and vocational skills necessary to obtain meaningful employment after their release. Finally, policymakers and social workers must work with community organizations to initiate the creation of more post-release programs that provide women, who have a criminal history, continued access to alcohol and drug treatment, educational and vocational training, and emotional support.

Future research should identify how many incarcerated women in Massachusetts are parents, including the ages of their children, the frequency of contact, and the community service needs of the children. It is also important to identify how many incarcerated women are involved with DSS, as well as how many are pregnant upon entering the criminal justice system. Without this knowledge, the Commonwealth of Massachusetts cannot appropriately respond to the growing needs of women in prison and the children who are left behind.

References

Aid to Incarcerated Mothers [Brochure].

Beckerman, A. (1994). Mothers in prison: Meeting the prerequisite conditions for permanency planning. *Social Work*, 39, pp. 9–14.

Bloom, B. (1994). Imprisoned mothers. In Gabel, K. & Johnson, D. (eds.). *Children of Incarcerated Parents*. Boston, MA: Lexington Books.

Breaking the cycle of despair: Children of incarcerated mothers. (1995). New York, NY: Women's Prison Association, pp. 1–12.

Chesney-Lind, M., & Immarigeon, R. (1994). Alternatives to women's incarceration. In Gabel, K. & Johnston, D. (eds.). *Children of Incarcerated Parents*. Boston, MA: Lexington Books.

Department of Correction (1996). "A statistical description of the sentenced population of Massachusetts Correctional Institutions."

Department of Correction (1994). 1994 Dowdy, Z. R. (1997, February 3). From prison cot to shelter cot.

Fuller, L. G. (1993). Visitors to women's prisons in California: An exploratory study. *Federal Probation*, 57(4): 41–47.

Hairston, C. F. (1991). Family ties during imprisonment: Important to whom and for what? *Journal of Sociology and Social Welfare*, pp. 87–102.

Hairston, C. F. (1988). Family ties during imprisonment: Do they influence future criminal activity? *Federal Probation*, pp. 48–52.

Kampfner, C. J. (1994). Post-traumatic stress reactions in children of imprisoned mothers. In Gable, K. & Johnston, D. (eds.). *Children of Incarcerated Parents*. Boston, MA: Lexington Books.

Knight, J. W. (1993). "Incarcerated women with their children: A national survey of boarding-in programs." [unpublished study by the Massachusetts Department of Correction].

Marr, M. (February 25, 1997). Interview with Maureen Marr, Unit Administrator of Hodder House.

May, K. (March 25, 1997). Interview with Katherine May, DSS Director of the Foster Care Review Unit.

MCI-Framingham treatment and program department. (1995). [unpublished document by the Massachusetts Department of Correction].

Norman, J. (1995). Children of prisoners in foster care. In Gable, K. & Johnson, D. (eds.). *Children of Incarcerated Parents*. Boston, MA: Lexington Books.

Reilly, S. A. (1992). Incarcerated mothers and the foster care system in Massachusetts: Working together to preserve parental rights. *New England Journal on Criminal and Civil Confinement*, 18, pp. 147–181.

Women in prison. (1995). Washington, DC: National Women's Law Center, pp. 1–7.

 Article Review Form at end of book.

How might stigmatization of an offender's family affect their quality of life? What might be the effects upon visitors of the ways in which both adults and children are searched?

The Effects of Incarceration on Families of Male Inmates

Judee Howard

According to the U.S. Department of Justice, in 1991 there were 627,847 male inmates in the United States (1993). Of these, 18.1% were married at the time. This translates into 121,785 wives also doing time with their husbands. The U.S. Department of Justice, also states that in 1991 there were 770,841 children under the age of 18 whose fathers were in prison.

Families of inmates have been called the "hidden victims of crime" (Carlson & Cervera, 1992, p. 5). When a crime is committed, there are victims other than the primary victim(s). These secondary victims include the families of the primary victim and another often overlooked group of victims—family members of the person who has committed the crime. The families of inmates are often overlooked in research and in designing social programs, yet many suffer devastating consequences as a result of a loved one's incarceration.

Schneller (1976) refers in his book to a quotation from Cesare Beccaria's book, *On Crime and Punishments*. Beccaria writes that while "innocent people can suffer when a criminal is punished," the "families of criminals are especially harmed by certain types of punish-

ment which are meant only for the family head" (pp. 14–15). Schneller also points out that imprisonment is the most common type of punishment used today, and the separation not only punishes the inmate, but it punishes the family also.

There are various reasons why the family of a prison inmate might be called secondary victims of the crime. Carlson and Cervera (1992) state it very well in referring to wives; "often they become an invisible minority with many unmet needs resulting from their husband's incarceration." There are many ways the families pay the price for their loved one's crime.

Many families feel stigmatized because another family member has been incarcerated (Carlson & Cervera, 1992). This feeling can be intensified due to the nature of the crime: for example, a sex offense. The "social stigmatization" is probably the most damaging effect on children whose parent is incarcerated, according to Hostetter and Jinnah (1993, p. 7). This report goes on to say that the children are often ostracized or made fun of by other children and even adults. These children often exhibit aggressive behavior or may withdraw or become very depressed.

Because of this feeling of social disrepute, the family is most often denied the "normal social outlets for

grieving the loss of a loved one from the family" (Hostetter and Jinnah, 1993, p. 4). Studies have shown that a higher percentage of wives of inmates experience more grief symptoms than do wives of prisoners of war and servicemen missing in action (Daniel & Barrett, 1981). The adjustment for a child with a parent in prison seems to be much harder for those who had a good relationship with the parent before the incarceration. The child "mourns the loss of their parent" (Hostetter and Jinnah, 1993, p. 7). Children often worry about how their parent is being treated and how they are doing (Daniel & Barrett, 1981). Children may also blame themselves or the parent that remains with them. Carlson and Cervera (1991) note that some theorists believe that losing a loved one to prison is "even more demoralizing to wives and children than losing a loved one to death" (p. 279).

Sometimes a wife may not only feel like an outcast by society, but she may also feel strong disapproval from other family members. Her parents may become unsupportive of the marriage and encourage her to divorce her husband and go on with her life (Carlson and Cervera, 1992). Carlson and Cervera also note that inlaws may even blame the wife for their son's incarceration or vice

The Effects of Incarceration on Families of Male Inmates, Judee Howard. 1994. Reprinted by permission of the author. Available (online) http://members.aol.com/nuhearts/effects.htm

versa. When there is little support from her family, additional stress is placed on the wife, children, and family unit.

There is not very much research on parents of inmates except to show that mothers tend to stay constant and stable if the relationship was that way before the incarceration. Mothers tend to remain loyal, visit, and write (Brodskey, 1975). From my experience as president of Family Awareness Project, a group formed to help meet the needs of families of inmates at the South Dakota State Penitentiary, many parents feel stigmatized as well. They may have problems in their business from their clients' newfound feelings of distrust or a general feeling of discomfort around their coworkers. Sometimes the parents are blamed by others or they blame themselves for what has happened. Also, their standing in the community may suffer.

Family members may also feel shame and embarrassment (Carlson and Cervera, 1992). Michael Locke (1992) writes in his article about the children of inmates, that many keep their parent's incarceration a secret and become quiet and reclusive. He also says the children may carry around a load of guilt because their parent is in prison or because they may not want to visit the parent. Sometimes the children are not told the truth about where their father is. This lie just compounds the problem when they later learn the truth. Sometimes, the embarrassment is too strong and wives or parents of inmates will even lie to friends and other family members, saying he is away for awhile. (Fishman, 1981). Many times, a family will move in order to get away from the feeling that they are stigmatized (Carlson and Cervera, 1992).

Often the families are labeled with "guilt by association" as stated by Pauline Watson, chair for Centerforce Board of Directors in Centerforce's 1990 Annual Report to the Legislature. Centerforce is a non-profit organization in California, founded in 1975, to service the needs of visitors to the California correctional facilities. Centerforce has dedicated the 1990's to the children of prison inmates as "The decade of the forgotten child" (Centerforce, 1990).

According to a research summary by Hostetter and Jinnah (1993), another area where the family may experience the feelings of guilt and shame is during visits to the correctional facility. Often they are subjected to humiliating searches, regarded with suspicion, and subject to rules which may change at any time.

As a regular visitor to the South Dakota penitentiary for the past year, I can state that from my own experience that these observations are true. After turning in a picture ID to the control room officer, visitors are asked to take a seat in the visitors' lobby to wait for their names to be called. When their names are called, visitors step through a metal detector and turn in any books or papers brought for the visit, to a guard for a thorough inspection. Usually, only legal paperwork, Bibles, photographs, and maybe some of the children's schoolwork are allowed to come into the visit room. Sometimes the visitors are led into a room to be "pat-searched" for contraband. They are asked to empty out their pockets, shake out clothing, and are patted down. Occasionally, visitors are asked to remove their shoes and socks which are checked for contraband. After this humiliation, they are allowed to enter the first gate on the way to the visit room.

After the gate slams shut behind them, their hands are stamped and another gate opens into the visit room. In the visit room, inmates and visitors are under the constant watch of the guards. Two-way mirrors are used, as well as large round viewing mirrors strategically placed so that the guards can observe all behavior. There are anywhere from 30–60 other people visiting in the same room. Couples are only allowed to hold hands. Any other behavior can be considered inappropriate and result in a reprimand and possibly a write up for the inmate. Last year I served as president of Family Awareness Project, and a common problem discussed at our meetings was the stress experienced due to visit room procedures. Over one-third of our group of 20 members experienced stomachaches, headaches and nausea before, during, or after visits.

Visiting can be especially hard on the children. They are confined to a small area near their parents for the duration of the visit. They cannot make a lot of noise that would disrupt other visits. Children are expected to follow the posted rules also. Leaving is another hardship on the children. In a report by Hairston, one child is quoted as saying "After the visit is over, on the way home we feel sad because we are leaving our father at the prison"(1991).

Another very real hardship for the families can be financial—especially when the breadwinner is removed from the home. If there were financial resources before the arrest, they are often drained by court and attorney costs. The wife may need to enter the job market with very few marketable skills, and many times a family ends up as part of the welfare system (Daniel & Barrett, 1981). If her husband has been moved to a facility far from home, she will have the cost of travel to see him.

In a survey done by Family Awareness Project in 1994, of 900 inmates in the South Dakota State Penitentiary, of whom 226 responded, almost half of the inmates have visitors that travel over 200 miles one way. This same survey showed about 30% of the families had incomes below $10,000 a year. The family may decide to move closer to the inmate, which would be another great expense, not to mention the additional stress of moving to a new community. She may have to seek out social agencies to help her. This can be not only confusing and draining, but also humiliating.

Another financial burden comes from phone bills. This is a common complaint among families in the Family Awareness Project group. Phone bills have been called the "second rent" by some. A local phone call from the prison in Sioux Falls, South Dakota costs the family $1.50 for 20 minutes. The inmate must call collect and the expense shows up on the receiver's bill. If the call is not local, the cost can range from $5.00 to $7.00 each. For a family going through the trauma and chaos of this forced separation, the phone calls can help maintain some sanity and stability. Even as time wears on, it is important for many to keep communication daily. Some inmates do write, but many are illiterate or do not write very well. Their calls can add up to sizable phone bills. Most inmates are only able to help with a small portion each month, if at all. Most families find a way to pay their phone bill at the expense of other necessities. Many times, they will have their long distance service cut off when they are unable to pay the bill. This adds more burden and stress to their relationship.

In talking with inmate families, many mention that loneliness is probably the hardest stress to deal with on a day-to-day basis. If the relationship was a close one, the wife misses being able to share the everyday happenings with her partner. Simple things such as sharing a meal, tucking in the kids or having coffee together become important memories. And as Carlson and Cervera mention, sexual frustration is another stress on the wives during incarceration (1992).

One of the greatest stressors for both the inmate and the rest of the family to deal with is the change in the family roles (Carlson & Cervera, 1992). The wife now becomes the head of the household. Carlson and Cervera say that the husbands do sometimes try to maintain control as the head of the family, but at the same time, they lose touch with day-to-day realities. This can be a frightening experience for some wives who were very dependent on their husbands. The wife becomes responsible for daily decisions in not only the mother-role, but in the father-role as well (Daniel & Barrett, 1981). She is now responsible for the children's involvement with their school activities, emotional well-being, and discipline. Many women experience difficulty in these areas because these areas were most often shared with her husband (Daniel & Barrett, 1981). As the wife gains confidence in her new role, she may become more independent. This can be very hard on the marriage, especially if the husband becomes jealous or feels threatened (Carlson & Cervera, 1992).

In the survey distributed by Family Awareness Project, 35% of the inmates stated that one of the greatest needs of their families is the need for information. This includes visit times and rules, what is allowed to be sent in to the inmate, and policies and procedures for the inmate. Families can feel so helpless and frustrated in the first few confusing months of a loved one's incarceration. Another major need shown in the survey was a need for temporary lodging while visiting. Inmates responded that 36% of their families had need of affordable and safe temporary shelter when they came to town to visit. Joan Husby, executive director of Friends Outside in Monterey County, says she noticed that families with already tight budgets and limited financial resources were paying a great deal for lodging. Some would sleep in cars and in bus stations. She says that as well as being costly and unsafe, these conditions limit the number of times family members are able to visit (Burton, 1988).

There are a few programs designed to help families and friends cope. The California program called Centerforce was founded by a man who saw the needs of the visitors to the penitentiary and wanted to help. Eventually, a bill was passed in the California legislature making it mandatory to have a visitor's center at each correctional facility in the state. Every center provides information pertaining to visits, coffee and snacks for visitors while they are waiting to get in and when they come out, and emergency clothing for those who come dressed "inappropriately" according to the rules. Visitors are greeted warmly and acceptingly. Many of the centers offer child care so couples can spend part of their visit "alone" together and so the children can play for a while in a less stressful environment (Centerforce, 1990).

Friends Outside in Monterey County responded to the need for affordable and safe temporary lodging by forming a hospitality house. The key element to its success is service: "the kind of relationship in which there is a commitment to the person as a human being worthy of respect" (Burton, 1988, p. 13). The services provided by Friends Outside include "(1) overnight lodging for women and children visitors, (2) local transportation, (3) shopping for family visits, (4) crisis intervention, (5) supportive counseling/group sessions, (6) information and referral to other resources, and (7) emergency food" (p. 13). Friends Outside now has many chapters in California and Nevada.

The most extensive program I read about is called Women in Crisis, located in Hartford, Connecticut. Women in Crisis provides volunteers who act as friends to those who have lost the support of their family. These volunteers will stay with the family from the beginning, before the trial, on through the sentencing and a couple of months into the incarceration (Fishman, 1981). They feel these services and the manner in which they are given are important and necessary. Fishman describes the services they provide: The volunteer first enters the scene during the pretrial state. The volunteer helps to explain the court process, putting things in easier to understand language. This is often a very confusing time for families and everyone else is too busy to explain how things work to the families. The volunteer is trained to be very objective, informative, and supportive as a good listener. This is the first crisis period for a family beginning with the arrest and separation from the loved one for the first time. The family is experiencing shock, denial, and a lot of pain. Having someone there to help explain things can take away some of the fear. Carlson and Cervera (1992) cite a study which found that almost half of the marriages ended in separation or divorce prior to the actual incarceration.

The second period of crisis Fishman (1981) describes comes on sentencing day. Many times the family is totally unprepared. When the sentence is pronounced, often the inmate is whisked away and the family is left in a state of shock. They don't know what to do next. A volunteer is nearby to explain the process and be a listener during this difficult time.

The next step is the initial period of incarceration. This is just as confusing. As Fishman notes, there are rules and questions, lots of questions. "Where will he be? When can she visit? How can she get there? Can she write to him now? Will he be okay? Will she be okay? Can the children visit?" (p. 373). A volunteer helps the family answer these questions and even accompanies the family to their first visit at the correctional facility. The volunteer waits in the lobby until the end of the visit to see how things went and to answer more questions.

Women in Crisis also carries this process one step further. Fishman (1981) reports that they have a pre-/post-release program to help families prepare for the reentry of the husband/father into the family. This is also a time filled with anxiety. Many times the inmate is intending to pick up where he left off, but many changes have taken place since he left. The Return to Community project provides professional assistance to reorganize and prepare for the inmate's reentry into the family with realistic expectations.

A report by Family and Corrections Network (FCN) states that while there are efforts in most states to strengthen family ties of prisoners, most of these are small and non-profit. They are only reaching a very small portion of those who are in need. More research needs to be done to evaluate the effectiveness of the programs that are already up and running. According to the FCN report, recent information regarding demographic data of prisoners shows that the experience of incarceration weakens the prisoner's family structure which may lead to "increased criminality in the next generation" (Families of Offenders, 1994, p. 1).

The FCN report says even though children of inmates are at higher risk "for behavior problems and delinquency," (p. 1) current educational and social organizations are not meeting the needs of these children. According to this report prisoners are likely to have relatives who have done time, yet there are very few programs designed to help prevent these problems from continuing.

In a day when we are so concerned with how our tax dollars are spent, we must not overlook the needs of these hidden victims and recognize the natural resource they are for our corrections programs. "Family ties are instrumental in reducing the stress felt by individuals separated from their loved ones, in assuring families that their imprisoned relative is all right, in promoting the prisoner's mental health, in maintaining family bonds, in decreasing recidivism and increasing public safety" (Hairston, 1991). By not recognizing and meeting the needs of these families now, we are costing our society much more down the road. More research needs to be done on the long-term effects on wives and children of prison inmates.

References

Brodskey, S. L. (1975). *Families and friends of men in prison: The uncertain relationship.* Lexington, Mass.: Lexington Books.

Burton, B. (1988). Is there hospitality in the house? Overnight housing for prison visitors. *Nurturing Today,* 10, 13, 33.

Carlson, B. E., and Cervera, N. (1991). Incarceration, coping, and support. *Social Work,* 36, 279–85.

Carlson, B. E., and Cervera, N. (1992). *Inmates and their wives: Incarceration and family life.* Westport, Conn.: Greenwood Press.

Centerforce. (1990). *1990 Annual Report to the legislature.* San Quintan, CA.

Daniel, S. W. and Barrett, C. (1981). The needs of prisoner's wives: A challenge for the mental health professionals. *Community Mental Health Journal,* 17, 310–22.

Families of Offenders: A key to crime prevention. (1994, July). Family and Corrections Network Report, 1.

Fishman, S. H. (1981). Losing a loved one to incarceration: The effect of imprisonment on family members. *The Personal and Guidance Journal,* 59, 372–75.

Hairston, C. F. (1991). Family ties during imprisonment: Important to when and for what? *Journal of Sociology and Social Welfare,* 18, 87–104.

Hostetter, E. and Jinnah, D. (1993, December). Research summary: Families of adult prisoners. Prison Fellowship.

Locke, M. (1992, June 28). Children sentenced to suffer: Parents behind prison walls. *The Press Democrat.*

Schneller, D. P. (1976). *A prisoner's family: A study of the effects of imprisonment on the families of prisoners.* San Francisco: R & E Research Associates.

U.S. Department of Justice Statistics. (1993). *Sourcebook of criminal justice statistics 1993.* Washington D.C.: U.S. Government Printing Office.

 Article Review Form at end of book.

WiseGuide Wrap-Up

- Prison punishes, reforms, rehabilitates, or deters in a number of ways, some more successful than others. However, one side effect is that it creates an abnormal environment that may be difficult for prisoners to cope with while incarcerated and may have detrimental effects on their behavior after release.

- Prisoners and staff live with the ever-present expectation of disruption and violence. The effects of such environments are not limited to those who live and work within them but impinge upon the lives of the families of offenders and staff.

- Prisons are not good at providing support for staff or for prisoners for the problems that they may encounter "inside" or "outside." Such problems include the effects of victimization and harassment but are by no means limited to them.

R.E.A.L. Sites

This list provides a print preview of typical **Coursewise** R.E.A.L. sites. There are over 100 such sites at the **Courselinks**™ site. The danger in printing URLs is that web sites can change overnight. As we went to press, these sites were functional using the URLs provided. If you come across one that isn't, please let us know via email to: webmaster@coursewise.com. Use your Passport to access the most current list of R.E.A.L. sites at the **Courselinks** site.

Site name: The Redwood Highway

URL: http://www.sonoma.edu/cja/info/infop4.html#correct

Why is it R.E.A.L.? As university sites with link pages go, you get few better than this. It is an excellent place to begin a search for information on the effects of imprisonment and punishment in practice.

Key topics: education, gangs, probation, student attitudes

Try this: See if you can find information on this site about California's highest custody level prison, Pelican Bay State Prison, which is the "maxi-maxi" warehouse of the "worst of the worst," including prison gang members.

Site name: School of Criminal Justice (CJ) at the University of Albany

URL: http://www.albany.edu/scj/links.html#prison

Why is it R.E.A.L.? This is another superb example of a university web site. It has links on many criminal justice themes and is also an excellent place to start for research on criminal-justice based issues, including the courts, corrections, and law enforcement.

Key topics: law, overcrowding, student attitudes

Try this: See if you can find information on the Constitution of the United States, adopted by the convention of states, September 17, 1787.

Site name: Journal of Prisoners on Prisons

URL: http://www.jpp.org/

Why is it R.E.A.L.? The Journal of Prisoners on Prisons attempts to make the accounts, experiences, and analyses of the criminalized heard and allows them to be discussed by providing an educational forum in which women and men can participate directly in the development of research that concerns them directly.

Key topics: male prisoners, miscarriages of justice, prisoner rights

Try this: See if you can find information on the state of Ohio attempting to extradite an inmate (Little Rock Reed) on fabricated charges in order to silence his outspoken writings and activities surrounding Native American prisoners' rights.

section

4

Rights of the Sentenced Offender

Jim Thomas, Ph.D., Department of Sociology
Northern Illinois University, DeKalb, IL
jthomas@sun.soci.niu.edu

Key Points

- Because of their problems with the law and removal from society, prisoners tend to have more legal problems than other people. Therefore, they are in special need of access to legal resources.

- Prisoners are not denied all constitutional protections simply because they are in prison; they lose only those that bear on the goal of punishment and the need to maintain institutional security.

- Rather than hinder prison administration in running a smooth prison, jailhouse lawyers may actually help keep prisons running more smoothly.

- Contrary to common belief, the rate of prisoner civil rights suits has been declining, not increasing, in the past two decades.

WiseGuide Intro

Because prisoners' legal problems often begin, rather than end, when they enter prison, the United States Supreme Court has made it clear that "There is no iron curtain drawn between the Constitution and the prisons of this country." The fact of being in prison does not relieve prisoners of obligations from debts, contracts, mortgages, or other legal obligations. In fact, incarceration may make legal problems worse for prisoners because of the problems that arise when they are removed from society.

Since the 1960s, prisoners have used a piece of legislation passed shortly after the Civil War, the so-called "Ku Klux Klan Act," which we know today as U.S.C. 42, Section 1983. This legislation allows people to sue government officials or employees who, acting "under color of law" in their jobs, are perceived to violate the complainants' civil rights. Because prison administrators and correctional officers are government employees, they may be sued under Section 1983 for violating prisoners' constitutional rights. Examples of these rights include protection from inhumane or brutal treatment, lack of access to legal resources, and deprivation of adequate housing, food, and medical care.

The readings in this section address legal issues of both male and female prisoners. In the first reading, McArthur, McKee and Thomas describe recent trends in prisoner litigation following the federal Prisoner Litigation Reform Act, which was intended to reduce prisoner's rights. The second reading summarizes the results of *Shumate* v. *Wilson,* which successfully challenged the medical prisons of Chowchilla women's prison in California. Next, Van Ochten identifies specific needs of incarcerated women that tend to be ignored.

In examining jailhouse lawyers and prisoners' rights in male institutions, Milovanovic and Thomas argue that prisoner litigation represents a type of rebellion against the oppressiveness of control and punishment while also serving to make prisons more humane. In the final selection, Thomas, Keeler and Harris identify many of the myths and misconceptions of prisoner litigation to argue for expanding prisoners' legal rights. Because of these misconceptions, politicians have argued that prisoners have too many rights and that prisons are too soft.

Should prisoners have rights?

What are some of the legal needs you might have if you were a prisoner?

Has the pendulum swung too far back in attempts to make prisons harsher and more punitive?

What are the advantages and disadvantages of curtailing prisoner litigation?

What are some of the myths of prisoner litigation, and how do these readings dispel them?

? ? ? Questions ? ? ?

Reading 21. Explain how the "tough-on-crime" ethos characterizing the close of the twentieth century has shaped prisoner discipline and correctional officer response. In what way has correctional intervention changed due in part to prisoners' rights issues?

Reading 22. To what extent should the state be responsible for the medical care of incarcerated women? Should it provide preventive medical care, such as pelvic and breast exams, pap smears, and mammograms, for incarcerated women?

Reading 23. How do the legal needs of women prisoners differ from those of men?

Reading 24. Are those who use law in attempts to change the conditions of social existence revolutionaries, or merely ineffective idealists?

Reading 25. Are those who use law in an attempt to change the conditions of social existence rebels, revolutionaries, or merely ineffective idealists?

Explain how the "tough-on-crime" ethos characterizing the close of the twentieth century has shaped prisoner discipline and correctional officer response. In what way has correctional intervention changed due in part to prisoners' rights issues?

Update:

Reversing the Pendulum of Prisoners' Rights

**Andrew McArthur,
Teresa Andrew McGee,
and Jim Thomas**

Northern Illinois University

The so-called "explosion" of prisoner litigation in the mid-1960s and 1970s resulted in increased prisoners' rights and dramatic prison reforms in virtually all federal and state prisons. However, these reforms may have been short-lived. Ironically, the successes in expanding prisoners' rights have led to a political and judicial backlash in the 1980s, culminating with the federal Prisoner Litigation Reform Act in 1995. The result of this backlash has led to decreased prisoner filings as well as to an increasing reluctance of judges to intervene in prison matters. Here, we examine several consequences of the backlash against prisoners' rights in the 1990s. We suggest that the "tough on crime" ethos characterizing the close of the twentieth century may have the ironic effect of making prisons and prisoners more, rather than less, difficult to manage.

Background of Prisoner Litigation

Historically, state and federal courts adhered to the "hands-off" doctrine, which held that the judiciary had no business meddling in prison affairs. The hands-off doctrine began eroding with the prisoners' rights move-

ment. "Prisoners' rights" are those Constitutionally protected rights that prisoners retain as members of our society and dates from the early 1960s, when state prisoners began using federal courts to redress grievances against prison officials. Prisoner litigation, which spawned and fed the growth of prisoners' rights, derives primarily from post–Civil War civil rights legislation, especially Title 42 U.S.C. Section 1983 and the Fourteenth Amend-ment, which allow federal legal challenges against government officials who, while acting in their official capacity, violate a person's civil rights. The relevant language of the 14th Amendment holds that:

No state shall make or enforce any law which shall abridge the privileges or immunities of citizens of the United States; nor shall any state deprive any person of life, liberty, or property, without due process of law; nor deny to any person within its jurisdiction the equal protection of the laws [emphasis added].

At the same time, Congress passed a civil rights act (Title 42 U.S.C. [Section] 1983), which provides the basis for contemporary civil rights litigation, including that by prisoners. Although modified and renewed several times between 1866–1877, the relevant language of the original civil rights legislation today remains essentially unchanged:

Every person who, under color of any statute, ordinance, regulation, custom, or usage, of any State or Territory, subjects, or causes to be subjected, any citizen of

the United States or other person within the jurisdiction thereof to the deprivation of any rights, privileges, or immunities secured by the Constitution and laws, shall be liable to the party injured in an action at law, suit in equity, or other proper proceeding for redress.

Since the federal government began maintaining statistics on prisoner civil rights filings in 1966, prisoners have filed a low of 288 civil rights petitions (1966) to a high of 40,569 (1995). This apparently dramatic increase has prompted legislative and judicial attempts to restrict prisoner access to the courts in the belief that the pendulum driving prisoners' rights has swung too far. This belief is based on the perception that a majority of prisoners file repetitive and frivolous law suits that subvert administrative control over prisoners (Doumar, 1994). The mounting hostility toward prisoner rights followed litigation successes that challenged prison policies and conditions through the 1970s, but gradually declined in the 1980s (Eisenberg, 1993; Palmer, 1996). Although criticisms of prisoner litigation began from the inception in the 1960s (Thomas, 1988), a successful concerted assault was not mounted until the early 1990s.

Retrenchment: The Assault of the Nineties

Many factors contributed to the roll-back of prisoner litigation in the 1990s, but two are most visible. First,

Update: Reversing the Pendulum of Prisoners' Rights, Andrew McArthur, Teresa Andrew McGee and Jim Thomas, Northern Illinois University. Reprinted by permission of the authors.

U.S. Supreme Court decisions reflected increased unwillingness to intervene in addressing alleged abuses of power or review complaints of harsh conditions. Second, state and federal statutes reduced prisoners' rights and privileges in order to make prisons more punitive.

Court Decisions

Recent U.S. Supreme Court decisions make it clear that the federal judiciary has become unsympathetic toward prisoners' rights. Typical of these are *Farmer* v. *Brennan* (510 U.S. 941, 1994), in which the Court—faced with an Eighth Amendment cruel and unusual prison issue among others—argued that The Eighth Amendment does not outlaw cruel and unusual "conditions"; it outlaws cruel and unusual "punishments." In *Lewis* v. *Casey* (518 U.S. 343, 1996) the court restricted inmate access to legal resources by ruling that prisoners' "access to law" does not require availability of a law library or legal assistance; it requires only access to courts in order to challenge a conviction or prison conditions. Reduced access to law, a higher threshold of tolerance for harsh conditions, and an increased willingness to grant prison staff latitude in dealing with prisoners suggest that federal courts are no longer an effective venue for protecting prisoner rights.

Legislation

Between 1994 and 1997, several bills that were introduced into or passed by Congress could turn back many of the rights that prisoners have gained in the past three decades. A few examples typify the language of legislation proposed or enacted that would subvert prison conditions.

One "get tough" bill, the "No Frills Prison Act" (H.R. 169) introduced into the House of Representatives in early 1997, amended the Violent Crime Control and Law Enforcement Act of 1994 to withhold federal funds from states unless they demonstrated that the state prison system:

1. provides living conditions and opportunities within its prisons that are not more luxurious than those that the average prisoner would have experienced if not incarcerated;

2. does not provide to any such prisoner specified benefits or privileges, including earned good time credits, less than 40 hours a week of work that either offsets or reduces the expenses of keeping the prisoner or provides resources toward restitution of victims, unmonitored phone calls (with exceptions), in-cell television viewing, possession of pornographic materials, instruction or training equipment for any martial art or bodybuilding or weightlifting equipment, or dress or hygiene other than is uniform or standard in the prison; and

3. in the case of a prisoner serving a sentence for a crime of violence which resulted in serious bodily injury to another, does not provide housing other than in separate cell blocks intended for violent prisoners, less than nine hours a day of physical labor (with exceptions) . . . (H.R. 169, 1997).

Although Finn (1996) argues that "no frills" legislation may make it more difficult to manage prisons and may be self-defeating, he notes that it has served as a model for states to implement their own "no-frills" legislation.

Other federal legislation includes the "100 Percent Truth-in-Sentencing Act" (1997), which reduces all good time credits for prisoners convicted of a violent crime; an amendment to the "Religious Freedom Restoration Act of 1993," which restricts the religious freedoms of incarcerated persons; the "Prison Security Enhancement Act" (1997), which would prohibit prisoners from engaging in activities designed to increase their physical strength or fighting ability, as well as prohibit related equipment. Other legislation would require prisoners to pay for health care, eliminate grants and other resources for higher education, restrict filings of habeas corpus petitions, and limit the number of appeals and range of issues in capital convictions.

The Prisoner Litigation Reform Act (PLRA)

The most severe attack on prisoners' rights was the Federal Prisoner Litigation Reform Act of 1995 (Public Law No. 104-134), a bill that contained a series of provisions intended to restrict state and federal prisoners' civil rights litigation in federal courts.

Supporters of the PLRA argued that prisons were becoming too soft because of repetitive filings of frivolous civil rights complaints. Senator Robert Dole stood before his colleagues to defend the Senate version of the Act and presented an argument that summarized the key concerns of critics of prisoners' rights:

Unfortunately, the litigation explosion now plaguing our country does not stop at the prison gate. According to Enterprise Institute scholar Walter Berns, the number of "due-process and cruel and unusual punishment" complaints filed by prisoners has grown astronomically—from 6,600 in 1975 to more than 39,000 in 1994. These suits can involve such grievances as insufficient storage locker space, a defective haircut by a prison barber, the failure of prison officials to invite a prisoner to a pizza party for a departing prison employee, and yes, being served chunky peanut butter instead of the creamy variety. The list goes on and on.

These legal claims may sound far-fetched, almost funny, but unfortunately, prisoner litigation does not operate in a vacuum. Frivolous lawsuits filed by prisoners tie up the courts, waste valuable legal resources, and affect the quality of justice enjoyed by law-abiding citizens. The time and money spent defending these cases are clearly time and money better spent prosecuting violent criminals, fighting illegal drugs, or cracking down on consumer fraud.

The National Association of Attorneys General estimates that inmate civil rights litigation costs the States more than $81 million each year. Of course, most of these costs are incurred defending lawsuits that possess no merit whatsoever.

Let me be more specific. According the Arizona Attorney General Grant Woods, a staggering 45 percent of the civil cases filed in Arizona's Federal courts last year were filed by State prisoners. That means that 20,000 prisoners in Arizona filed almost as many cases as Arizona's 3.5 million law-abiding citizens. And most of these prisoner lawsuits were filed free of charge. No court costs. No filing fees. This is outrageous and it must stop (Dole, 1995).

Other supporters portrayed litigation as undermining punishment and litigators as bored victimizers of society:

Many people think of prison inmates as spending their free time in the weight room or the television lounge. But the most crowded place in today's prisons may be the law library.

Today's system seems to encourage prisoners to file with impunity. After all, it's free. And a courtroom is certainly a more hospitable place to spend an afternoon than a prison cell. Prisoners file free lawsuits in response to almost any perceived slight or inconvenience—being served chunky instead of creamy peanut butter, for instance, or being denied the use of a Gameboy video game—a case which prompted a lawsuit in my home state of Arizona.

These prisoners are victimizing society twice—first when they commit the crime that put them in prison, and second when they waste our hard-earned tax dollars while cases based on serious grievances languish on the court calendar (Kyl, 1995).

Although there is strong evidence discrediting these extreme anecdotes (Burnett, 1998), the Senate was swayed by the rhetoric and the Act passed overwhelmingly. Five particular provisions of the Act impose significant burdens on prisoners. First, prisoners filing in forma pauperis (as poor persons, for whom normal filing fees are waived) are now required to pay the full filing fee of $150 on installments (codified in 28 USC 1915). Second, prisoners whose petitions fail to state a meritorious claim or are judged malicious in three filings are permanently barred from filing further in forma pauperis filings. Third, prisoners risk losing good time if a suit is judged malicious or fails to state an actionable claim. Fourth, with the exception of life-threatening circumstances, prisoners must exhaust all administrative remedies before filing a civil rights complaint in Federal court. Finally, the Act limits judicial intervention into directing or monitoring changes in prison conditions or policies.

The PLRA contains several ironies. First, it may actually cost more money to implement than it saves. The administrative costs of collecting fees and tracking prisoners' prior litigation activity may not offset the savings in reduced litigation. More importantly, most prisoners return to the streets within three years of their incarceration. The psychological and social costs of readjustment are not reduced by increasing the punitive burdens of prison, especially if the legal means of challenging excessive burdens are restricted.

Second, the PLRA may increase prison violence, thereby reducing the safety of staff and prisoners, by curtailing a mechanism for peaceful dispute resolution. This possibility is based on the view that prisoner litigation has a "safety valve" function (Thomas, 1988) or possesses "therapeutic value" (Eisenberg, 1993: 440–441).

Rather than "reform" litigation, the PLRA may be just another means to appease a fearful public with a "tough on crime" ideology, while doing little to increase prisoners, respect for law, reduce court costs, or reduce the stress of litigation on prison administrators, which are a few problems resulting from prisoner filings. Hence, the PLRA and similar legislation may possess the ultimate ironic effect of not only subverting "rehabilitation," but of nurturing debilitation.

The Premises of the PLRA

Two claims are made by supporters of the PLRA and similar legislation that would restrict prisoner litigation (Abraham, 1995; Dauber, 1994; Hatch, 1995). First, the "explosion" in prisoner litigation reflects an increase in prisoners' legal aggressiveness. Second, prisoners file repeatedly, and curtailing repeat filers will dramatically reduce the burden on the courts. Although there is some merit in both claims, neither can be accepted uncritically.

The Explosion Myth

When Senator Bob Dole raised the specter of a "plague of litigation" contributed to by prisoners, he was partially correct. The number of prisoner civil rights petitions filed in federal court have increased each year for the past 32 years, as Table 1 shows.

However, Table 1 also shows that states' prison populations have also grown. The growth in prisoner litigation corresponds closely to the increase in prison population. In fact, the rate of state prisoner civil rights filings peaked in 1981 at 4.69 filings per 100 prisoners and gradually declined and then remained relatively stable into the mid 1990s. The data do not support the "increased aggression" thesis, and suggest that, even prior to the PLRA, prisoners were becoming less aggressive. Further, although the filing rate exceeded 4 filings per 100 prisoners in 1994 and 1995, there is some evidence that this increase is attributable to prisoners attempting to litigate prior to the PLRA taking effect in April, 1996 (Thomas and McArthur, 1999). The decline in both the number and rate of filings from 1995 to 1997 suggests, however, that the PLRA has been initially effective in reducing both the number and rates of prisoner civil rights suits.

One-Shot Players or Repeat-Filers?

The "three strikes" provision in the PLRA is based on the premise that prisoners repeatedly file petitions. Eliminate the repeat players, so the logic goes, and prisoner litigation will drop. While Table 2 provides some support for the view that multiple filers constitute a significant share of the litigation, it also shows that the vast majority of prisoners file three suits or less. About half (49) percent of prison suits are filed by prisoners who file only one suit during their full prison careers, and about 32 percent of all suits are filed by prisoners filing more than three.

However, as Table 3 shows, almost 94 percent of litigating prisoners file three or less complaints, and the heavy filers (four or more) constitute only about 6.6 percent of all filers. More simply, while repeat players do, in fact, contribute a disproportionate share of filings, they constitute a relatively small share of filers. Hence, it appears that the three-strikes provision of the PLRA will hurt relatively few prisoners and may, in fact, deter the relatively small percentage of prisoners who abuse the filing process. However, if this is true, then it would appear that the burden of a full filing fee on all prisoners is not necessary, because it discourages those prisoners who file only a few petitions and who are not burdening the courts with unnecessarily repetitive filings.

Conclusion

The significant prison reforms resulting from prisoner litigation in the past 30 years have improved both the conditions and administration of prisons. However, the 1990s mark the decade of retrenchment, as the pendulum of

| Table I | State Prisoner Populations, Civil Rights Filings, and Filing Rates in U.S. Federal District Courts, 1966–1997 |

Year	Civil Rights Suits By State Prisoners	State Prisoner Population	Civil Rights Filings Per 100 State Prisoners
1966	218	180,409	.12
1967	878	175,317	.50
1968	1,072	168,211	.64
1969	1,269	176,384	.72
1970	2,030	176,391	1.15
1971	2,915	177,113	1.65
1972	3,348	174,379	1.92
1973	4,174	181,396	2.30
1974	5,236	196,105	2.67
1975	6,128	216,462	2.83
1976	6,958	235,853	2.95
1977	7,752	267,936	2.89
1978	9,730	277,473	3.51
1979	11,195	287,635	3.89
1980	12,397	295,819	4.19
1981	15,639	333,251	4.69
1982	16,741	375,603	4.46
1983	17,687	394,953	4.48
1984	18,034	417,389	4.32
1985	18,491	451,812	4.09
1986	20,072	486,655	4.12
1987	22,972	520,336	4.41
1988	24,025	562,605	4.27
1989	24,809	629,995	3.94
1990	25,008	684,544	3.65
1991	25,364	728,605	3.48
1992	29,646	778,495	3.81
1993	33,018	828,566	3.98
1994	37,925	904,647	4.19
1995	40,569	989,007	4.10
1996	39,996	1,033,186	3.87
1997	27,661	1,059,588	2.61

rights continues to swing back toward the judicial "hands-off" doctrine and increased judicial and legislative tolerance for "cruel conditions" and harsh punishment. The Prisoner Litigation Reform Act appears to have been successful in reducing the volume of litigation in the first two years after taking effect. However, it is too early to determine whether reducing the quantity of litigation will have a corresponding reduction on reducing judicial workload or the costs of litigation to taxpayers.

If the data from Illinois' Northern Federal District typify other jurisdictions, it may well be that the PLRA, while deterring frivolous suits from overly litigious prisoners with the three-strikes provision, will also deter meritorious suits from prisoners who cannot afford the full filing fee. Because the "three strikes" are cumulative over possibly successive and prolonged prison stays, the PLRA also penalizes successful and responsible litigants by prohibiting pro se litigation from a prisoner who may file 20 suits and have three rejected as unmeritorious. This aspect of the PLRA hampers jailhouse lawyers who have been most active in generating responsible litigation (Thomas, 1988b).

In one final irony, it may be that prisoner litigation in fact serves the same interests as its critics (Milovanovic and Thomas, 1998). Both prisoners and staff have an interest in maintaining effective, efficient, flexible, and stable prison communities (Belbot and Marquart, 1998), and prisoner litigation has been a significant factor in pursuing these communal goals. As a consequence, it might be that prisoner litigation should be encouraged rather than restricted.

Bibliography

Abraham, Spencer. 1995. Hearings on "Prisoner Litigation Reform Act." *Congressional Record,* September 27.

Belbot, Barbara A. and James W. Marquart. 1998. "The Political Community Model and Prisoner Litigation: Can We Afford Not to Try a Better Way?" *The Prison Journal,* 78(September): 299–329.

Burnett, Kathleen. 1998. "Frivolous" Claims by the Attorney General." *Social Justice,* 25(2): 184–204.

Dole, Robert. 1995. Hearings on "Prisoner Litigation Reform Act." *Congressional Record,* September 27.

Doumar, Robert G. 1994. "Prisoner Cases: Feeding the Monster in the Judicial Closet." *St. Louis University Public Law Review,* 14(1): 21–40.

Eisenberg, Howard B. 1993. "Rethinking Prisoner Civil Rights Cases and the Provision of Counsel." *Southern Illinois University Law Journal,* 17(Spring): 417–490.

Finn, Peter. 1996. "No-Frills Prisons and Jails: A Movement in Flux." *Federal Probation,* 60(September): 35–44.

Hatch, Orrin. 1995. Hearings on "Prisoner Litigation Reform Act." *Congressional Record,* September 27.

Kyl, Jon. 1995. Hearings on "Prisoner Litigation Reform Act." *Congressional Record,* September 27.

Milovanovic, Dragan and Jim Thomas. 1998 (forthcoming). "(Re)Visiting the Jailhouse Lawyer: An Excursion into Constitutive

Table 2 Number of Suits Filed by One-Shot and Repeat Section 1983 Litigants in Illinois' Northern District, 1977–1997

Suits	Number of Litigants Filing	Number of Suits Filed (and Percent of Total Filings)	
1	4,853	4,853	(49.1)
2	606	1,212	(12.3)
3	229	687	(7.0)
4 (or more)	405	3,141	(31.7)
Total 9,893	6,093	9,893	
All multi-filers	1,240	5,040	

Table 3 Number of Single-Shot and Repeat Section 1983 Litigants in Illinois' Northern District, 1977–1997

Number of Litigants Who File	Number of Litigants Filing (and Percent of Total Litigants)	
1 suit	4,853	(79.6)
2 suits	606	(9.9)
3 suits	229	(3.8)
3 or more suits	405	(6.6)
Total litigants	6,093	

Criminology." S. Henry and D. Milovanovic (eds). New York: SUNY-Albany Press.

Palmer, John W. 1996. *Constitutional Rights of Prisoners* (Fifth Edition). Cincinnati: Anderson.

Scalia, John. 1997. *Prisoner Petitions in the Federal Courts, 1980–96.* Washington, D.C.: Bureau of Justice Statistics, U.S. Department of Justice.

Thomas, Jim. 1988a. "Inmate Litigation: Using the Courts or Abusing Them?" *Corrections Today*, 50(July): 124–127.

———. 1988b. *Prisoner Litigation: The Paradox of the Jailhouse Lawyer.* Totowa, N.J.: Rowman and Littlefield.

Thomas, Jim and Andrew McArthur. 1998. "The Ironies of the Prisoner Litigation Reform Act: Malice in Wonderland?" Graduate Colloquium Series, Northern Illinois University. August 27.

Article Review Form at end of book.

To what extent should the state be responsible for the medical care of incarcerated women? Should it provide preventive medical care, such as pelvic and breast exams, pap smears, and mammograms, for incarcerated women?

California Women Prisoners Win Improvements to Deficient Medical Care

Sacramento—A federal district judge has been asked to approve a settlement agreement intended to improve the medical care given women prisoners at two California facilities.

Prisoners at the Central California Women's Facility and the California Institution for Women filed a federal class action lawsuit, *Shumate v. Wilson,* against the state and the California Department of Corrections in April 1995 charging that prisoners with serious illnesses are being denied crucial medical care and are suffering needlessly.

The plaintiffs have argued that they are systematically deprived of essential medical care, in violation of their constitutional right to be free from cruel and unusual punishment. Prisoners with HIV and AIDS further argued that the policies and practices at the prisons resulted in routine disclosure of their HIV positive status.

If the settlement is approved by the Court, an assessor will monitor health care in the two prisons with the assistance of four medical experts over a 16-month period to determine if the state is in compliance with requirements, including:

- Making timely referrals to physicians for patients needing urgent care.

- Prohibiting untrained employees from making judgments about prisoners' medical care.

- Ensuring that prisoners receive necessary medications without undue—and potentially life-threatening—lapses and delays.

- Providing necessary physical therapy.

- Offering preventive care, including periodic physicals, pelvic and breast exams, pap smears, and mammograms.

- Protecting patient privacy by restricting access to medical records and ending practices that publicly and unnecessarily identify women with HIV and AIDS and other infectious diseases.

If, after the first eight months, the assessor reports that the state has not complied with the terms of the settlement agreement, he will continue to monitor health care at the prisons for an additional eight months. If the assessor determines that the state has met its obligations under the agreement, the case will be dismissed. If health care remains inadequate at the end of the assessment period, the case will proceed to trial.

"We are very pleased with the settlement," said lead counsel Elizabeth Alexander, Director of the ACLU's National Prison Project.

"California's prisons have a responsibility to provide decent, humane health care for the women in their custody," Alexander added. "I congratulate the women who brought this suit for their courage and perseverance.

"I also want to thank Michael Keating, the mediator and assessor, because, after some very long-fought litigation, the parties have cooperated in crafting a responsible settlement that promises to serve the public and the prisoners well."

Ellen Barry, director of Legal Services for Prisoners with Children, agreed. "The women who brought this suit aren't asking for 'Cadillac Care' and they aren't out for money or fame," she said. "They've stuck

California Women Prisoners Win Improvements to Deficient Medical Care. American Civil Liberties Union Freedom Network, August 15, 1997. Reprinted by permission.

their necks out and stood up to the state for one simple reason: to hold the state of California responsible for meeting their basic medical needs.

"We will continue to monitor the situations at CCWF and CIW during and after the assessment period," Barry added. "We are hopeful that the settlement agreement will result in significant improvements in the provision of adequate health care for women prisoners."

If plaintiffs had brought this case to trial, they would have presented evidence like the following:

- A woman prisoner had painful lumps in her breasts for a long period. When a large lump developed on her right breast, she tried to convince a prison doctor to perform a biopsy. He refused. The lump grew so large that it protruded through the skin. A biopsy was finally performed in August 1995—more than 10 years after she first complained of her symptoms to correctional officials—and her cancerous right breast was removed. In late 1996 she was diagnosed with cancer in her left breast and underwent a second mastectomy.

- A woman who arrived at prison with severe burns over 54 percent of her body was denied standard bandages and medical supplies. As a result of her injuries, she was unable to walk, but did not receive physical therapy. She has since been released from prison and taught herself how to walk again.

- After experiencing chest pains for two days, a woman was taken to the prison infirmary, but not evaluated by a physician. She was returned to her cell, continuing to complain about chest pain. Only after the patient collapsed and two staff members were unable to revive her was a doctor called—

four and a half hours after she went to the infirmary. An ambulance finally arrived in time to pronounce her dead.

- A woman eventually diagnosed with cancer complained for months about pain, weight loss, and the passage of blood clots before she was allowed to see a doctor. Despite severe pain and debilitating swelling in her legs, she did not receive adequate pain medication and was forced to walk to the dining hall if she wanted to eat. She died approximately nine months after her diagnosis.

"These are not isolated cases, and these are not complaints about stubbed toes and hangnails," said Fresno attorney Jack Daniel. "The settlement gives hope to women suffering from chronic diseases and other serious illnesses."

Stephen Hibbard, a partner with McCutchen, Doyle, Brown & Enersen, which represented the group of plaintiffs with HIV and AIDS, said that "prisoners with HIV and AIDS are entitled to have personal medical information kept private by doctors and medical staff, and to expect correctional officers and staff to obey state laws requiring that information about a prisoner's HIV status be kept confidential."

The failure to adequately protect medical confidentiality can have serious consequences, Hibbard said. "Prisoners with HIV and AIDS face many forms of discrimination and are subject to violent attacks," he explained.

"Also, when women cannot believe personal medical information will be kept private, they do not get tested and do not receive desperately needed medical treatment," Hibbard added. "The settlement agreement requires the CDC to take a number of steps to protect patient confiden-

tiality. We hope these steps will help protect the health and safety of the growing HIV-positive population in California's women's prisons."

Now that attorneys for both the plaintiffs and the state have signed the settlement agreement, it will be the subject of a fairness hearing conducted by U.S. District Judge William Shubb. Judge Shubb will determine whether the plaintiffs' interests have been addressed properly in the settlement and whether the settlement will take effect.

"We are happy with the agreement we've forged with the state," said Dale Rice, a partner with Heller, Ehrman, White & McAuliffe who is representing the plaintiffs.

"But," she continued, "Charisse Shumate and the other plaintiffs have endured too much suffering and taken too many risks by coming forward for us to consider that this case is over.

"We hope that the Department of Corrections will implement the settlement in good faith, but in case they do not, we are prepared to return to court to protect the women's constitutional rights," Rice said.

The plaintiffs are represented by attorneys from the National Prison Project of the ACLU; Legal Services for Prisoners with Children; Catherine Campbell and Jack Daniel, private attorneys; the University of Southern California Post Conviction Justice Project; the ACLU of Northern California; Heller, Ehrman, White, & McAuliffe, which is providing its services pro bono; and McCutchen, Doyle, Brown & Enersen, which is representing the plaintiff sub-class and is also providing pro bono services.

 Article Review Form at end of book.

How do the legal needs of women prisoners differ from those of men?

Legal Issues and the Female Offender

Marjorie Van Ochten, J.D.

Marjorie Van Ochten, J.D., is the administrator of the Office of Policy and Hearings for the Michigan Department of Corrections.

The Issue of Parity

In prisons, the doctrine of "separate but equal" is permissible. Male and female inmates can be, and often are, housed in separate institutions. The problem for most states has been there are so few female inmates relative to the number of male inmates that equality in programming and other areas has been difficult to achieve. In addition to cost concerns and other problems, the day-to-day crises of the 95 percent or more of the population that is male are often so overwhelming that the 5 percent or less of the population that is female gets neglected. This can be a very costly mistake.

Michigan has struggled with this issue since a federal judge ruled in 1979 that the state was not providing equal programming for its female inmates. The case in which this ruling was made, which has been referred to as the "leading case" in this area, is *Glover v. Johnson* (478 F. Supp. 1075 [1979]). In this class-action lawsuit, it was claimed that the Department of Corrections had denied its female inmates their constitutional right to due process and equal protection by offering educational and vocational rehabilitation oppor-

tunities substantially inferior to those provided to male inmates.

The department argued that its women's prison (at the time there was only one) offered programming that was at least comparable, if not better, than what was offered at a similarly sized male facility. The judge, however, cited the fact that while male inmates could be sent to a variety of prisons and thus had access to programming at all of these facilities, female inmates had only one place to go and thus were limited to the programming offered at that single facility. The judge decided that equal protection required parity of treatment, as contrasted with identical treatment, to provide female inmates with the same access to rehabilitation opportunities that were being provided to male inmates.

The final order in *Glover* was not issued until 1981, after more than a year of negotiations between the parties as to its terms, and covered a wide range of issues (*Glover v. Johnson*, 510 F. Supp. 1019 (1981]). The department was ordered to provide two-year college programming, enhanced vocational offerings, apprenticeship opportunities, and prison industries, which had previously existed only at men's institutions. The court also ordered paralegal training and access to attorneys to remedy past inadequacies in law library facilities. It required the department to redo its inmate wage policy to ensure that female inmates were provided equal wages and ordered that a minimum secu-

rity camp for females be provided to permit female inmates to have access to the unique programming that was provided at camps that had previously been available only for men.

In the area of vocational programming, the court was particularly concerned about what it found to be the inferior quality and types of programs offered to the women, as well as the fact that fewer programs were offered. For example, the judge cited the food service program at the women's facility, which was geared to noncommercial short order cooking skills, while the programs at a men's prison focused on commercial cooking. The judge was clearly troubled by sexual stereotyping in the types and quality of programming offered, as has been reinforced several times in subsequent years as the deparment has struggled to comply with the court's directives. There has been a continual emphasis on "nontraditional" programming for women, such as providing vocational courses in automotive maintenance and carpentry.

The *Glover* case is an ongoing concern of the Michigan Department of Corrections. The state has been involved in two lengthy contempt proceedings and two appeals to the U.S. Court of Appeals for the Sixth Circuit. In 1991, the department hired a special administrator, at the order of the court, to design and implement a plan to bring the department into compliance with the orders in *Glover*.

The lesson to be learned from Michigan's experience is to provide

Legal Issues and the Female Offender, M. Van Ochten. Excerpt from *American Correctional Association, Female Offenders: Meeting Needs of a Neglected Population*, pp. 31–36. Lanham, MD: ACA Press, 1993. Reprinted by permission of the author.

programming and other opportunities to female inmates at a level that will withstand court scrutiny to avoid having to develop and implement these programs under a court's watchful eyes.

Several other states have been faced with litigation regarding the issue of parity of female programming, although such cases are often settled by consent judgments. According to Nicole Hahn Rafter (1990), a professor of criminal justice at Northeastern University:

The majority of these cases do not go to trial. Sometimes the mere threat of litigation forces states to take action. On other occasions, state and inmates reach an agreement that avoids trial.

She cites cases in Connecticut, California, Wisconsin, and Idaho, all of which have been settled without trial. Other states have litigated such claims with limited success. (See *McCoy* v. *Nevada Department of Prisons*, 776 F. Supp. 521 [1991].) In *McCoy* the court again emphasized the heightened standard of review for claims of unequal treatment based on sex and clearly stated that only important government objectives could justify unequal treatment.

If a state believes that it has achieved parity and equal treatment for female inmates based on the above standard but is still faced with litigation, it can take heart from a decision of the Sixth Circuit Court of Appeals involving claims by female inmates in Kentucky that their rights had been violated. In 1989, in the case of *Canterino* v. *Wilson* (869 F. 2d 948), the court of appeals reversed the lower court and ruled that the inmates had failed to prove their allegations of discrimination. Thus, claims of unequal treatment are not always successful.

The Right to Privacy

While parity and equal treatment in programming and conditions of incarceration are clearly the major legal issues that should concern correctional administrators when dealing with female inmates, it is not the only issue that has been litigated. An emphasis on equal employment opportunity, as well as other factors, has increased the use of male correctional

officers in women's prisons. This has, in turn, created litigation involving the alleged violation of female inmates' right to privacy by the assigning of male officers to housing units and subjecting female inmates to searches done by male officers.

In an early case in this area, a federal court in New York ruled that male officers could not be assigned to the night shift in a housing unit where they might see a female inmate unclothed or using the toilet during their rounds. However, the court upheld the assignment of male officers to daytime duties where adequate accommodations could be made to achieve a balance between the inmates' right to privacy and the state's need to maintain order and security in the prison. For example, by the use of modesty panels in shower areas. However, the Court of Appeals for the Second Circuit overturned the lower court on the issue of night assignments and ruled that male correctional officers could perform such duty as long as proper sleepwear was provided to the female inmates. (See *Forts* v. *Ward*, 621 F. 2d 1210 [1980].)

Most of the court cases in which inmates have argued that their right to privacy has been violated have involved complaints by male inmates about female officers. Almost all of these cases have also been unsuccessful in establishing a violation of inmates' rights. This makes all the more surprising a 1988 decision by the Court of Appeals for the Seventh Circuit in the case of *Torres* v. *Wisconsin Department of Health and Social Services* (854 F. 2d 1523) where the court upheld a ban on male officers being assigned to the housing units in a female facility. However, privacy interests were not the basis for this decision, and in fact, the court rejected that claim. The winning argument for the State of Wisconsin was that the assignment of male officers to women's housing units would impede rehabilitation efforts of female offenders due to the large percentage of them who had been physically and sexually abused by males. Although the U.S. Supreme Court declined to hear an appeal of this decision, it is questionable how much weight the decision would be given in other circuits in light of the overwhelming number of decisions

that have been found in favor of equal employment opportunity for both male and female officers rather than inmates' rights.

The other area where the rights of female inmates and male officers clash is in the performance of pat-down and strip searches. As with challenges to housing assignments, most search cases have been brought by male inmates objecting to searches done by female staff. In one case brought by female inmates was *Jordan* v. *Gardner* (953 F. 2d 1137 [1992]). The case involved routine pat searches of female inmates by male correctional officers. The U.S. Court of Appeals for the 9th Circuit reversed a lower court decision and held that such searches did not violate the inmates' rights. The lower court had found persuasive the argument that differing treatment of women in free society caused greater concern for female inmates who were pat searched by males than was the case for male inmates being searched by female officers. While this argument may well have some basis in fact, the court of appeals was not convinced that the impact was significant enough to justify a different result than had been their holding in earlier decisions where they had upheld searches of male inmates by female officers. The results in this case reinforce the belief that the *Torres* case may be an aberration.

The issue of male officers conducting routine strip searches of female inmates has not been litigated, probably because few correctional administrators would permit such a practice both for practical reasons and due to the court decisions involving male inmates and female staff, which clearly seem to limit such searches to nonroutine or emergency situations. In one reported case involving a female inmate, *Lee* v. *Downs* (641 F. 2d 1117 [1981]), the Court of Appeals for the Fourth Circuit upheld the use of male officers during the strip search of a female inmate due to the emergency nature of the situation. Judging from this case, the same standards of emergency would seem to apply in strip searches of female inmates with male staff involved as has been the case for male inmates with female staff involved.

In many of these search cases, the issue of the professionalism of staff is a central concern. If male officers are being allowed to pat search female inmates it is clearly advisable to ensure that proper training is provided and that professional standards are carefully enforced.

Sexual Contact

The issues raised by the question of searches also surface in another area where courts have become involved in the subject of the interactions between female inmates and male staff. That area is sexual contact between staff and inmates, including claims of sexual assault. Michigan is not unique in having had such litigation brought by female inmates. These issues surface wherever there is cross-gender supervision, and even where there is same-sex supervision. But clearly the undercurrent of the cases involving searching and housing assignments, if not the clear arguments of plaintiffs in such cases, involves an acknowledgment that sexual harassment and assault of women by men is much more prevalent than the reverse. Correctional administrators attempting to integrate male staff into a female facility may find themselves faced with increasing legal activity in the form of prosecutions of staff for sexual assault as well as lawsuits by female inmates claiming a violation of their Eighth Amendment rights by failure to protect them from sexual assaults.

Clearly, care in the selection, training, and supervision of staff is essential in dealing with such claims and avoiding potential liability. Besides considerations of professionalism, an additional incentive for staff in the State of Michigan to avoid such sexual contact has been the enactment of a statute in 1988 that makes even consensual sexual contact with a inmate by an employee of the Department of Corrections a misdemeanor punishable by up to two years of imprisonment. Such a law makes arguments of "enticement" a moot issue.

Health Care Concerns

A final area where legal issues may be raised is that of health care services to female inmates. The same legal theories may be used as are used in parity cases, but they surface in a unique manner. Where there are medical concerns that affect only female inmates, such as pregnancy and childbirth, correctional administrators must be careful to ensure that they do not enact policies that treat these medical conditions differently than other conditions, both in terms of access to necessary treatment and eligibility for programming and work assignments.

The provision of mental health services is another area where states may be vulnerable. As with other programming, the small number of female inmates in proportion to the number of male inmates may raise problems of equal access to services. Many prison systems have a sufficient number of mentally ill male inmates to devote an entire hospital facility to their care. However, unless the facility is constructed to also permit the safe housing of mentally ill female inmates, they may not receive comparable care. Some states provide for such services through their state department of mental health or private contractors, but whatever is done, care must be taken to ensure that mentally ill female inmates receive the same services provided to mentally ill male inmates, even if the per capita cost of providing such services is greater for females.

Female Inmates and Litigation

If you are a correctional administrator, at this point you may be wondering why you have never been sued on any of these issues if they are indeed of such concern. The answer may lie in the fact that female inmates simply do not file lawsuits as often as male inmates. The experi-

ence in Michigan has certainly shown that to be the case.

Michigan officials recently took a look at the number of lawsuits filed by female inmates in 1988 and 1989. (These years were chosen because the subsequent years of 1990 and 1991 were complicated by the closure of women's prisons and movement of inmates to formerly male institutions.) Although women comprised approximately 5 percent of the prison population in 1988, they initiated only 1.5 percent of the lawsuits filed by inmates against the department that year. In 1989, when inmates filed a total of over 1,200 lawsuits against the department, less than 1 percent of those cases were filed by female inmates.

The reasons for this are not clear in that female inmates in Michigan have access to the same lawbooks as male inmates and have had that access for several years. They also have a comparable, if not higher, rate of literacy. In addition, due to the *Glover* case, they have been provided with paralegal training. Several theories have been put forth to explain this lesser inclination to litigate on the part of female inmates, such as their greater focus on other concerns like the well-being of their children, as well as the social conditioning of women, which makes them less likely to assert their rights.

Whatever the reasons may be, it is clear that the lack of litigation by female inmates is not due to a lack of issues to be litigated. Correctional administrators who have not yet been faced with these issues may do well to take the opportunity to remedy any problems they may have in the areas discussed to avoid costly and troublesome litigation.

Reference

Rafter, Nicole Hahn. 1990. Equal protection forcing changes in women's prisons. *Correctional Law* (September).

 Article Review Form at end of book.

Are those who use law in attempts to change the conditions of social existence rebels, revolutionaries, or merely ineffective idealists?

Overcoming the Absurd:

Prisoner Litigation as Primitive Rebellion

Dragan Milovanovic and Jim Thomas

A theme central to the literature of existentialism is that when the conditions of life seem to preclude meaningful and efficacious action, one must find meaning and humanity in resistance, in effect, in saying "no" (Camus, 1956:13). To acquiesce to the deadening contradictions and meaninglessness of an absurd existence is to mirror the tragedy of Joseph K. in Kafka's (1972) *The Trial:* a victim unable to act yet unable to say "no." In this paper, we draw on these existentialist themes to examine the circumstances and actions of one category of prisoners who use the law as a weapon against the absurdity of their lives in prison. Based on our past research on these "jailhouse lawyers" (JHLs; see Milovanovic, 1987; Thomas, 1988, 1989), we argue that although not revolutionaries who bring fundamental social change, these prisoners are like Hobsbawn's (1969) primitive rebels who, through their resistance, confront and help to hold at bay their own and other prisoners' complete oppression. Our discussion proceeds from the premise that social existence can be read like any other text and that the concept of "the absurd" provides one useful exegetic tool for interpretation.

Our data and observations come from our experiences in prison research and from work with pris-

oner litigants since 1980. These data include several thousand pages of interviews with prisoners, jailhouse lawyers, and other litigants; data from court records and case summaries; and documents from prisoners, corrections institutions, and courts. For a detailed summary of our perspective, methods of data collection, and background, see Milovanovic (1987) and Thomas (1988). All quotes of prisoners are verbatim, taken from transcribed interviews in Illinois maximum security prisons between 1982 and 1987.

Absurdity, Existence, and Prisons

The characterization of modern life as "absurd" is found throughout a body of literature produced and/or influenced by existentialist philosophy. Among the most well-known and often cited works are Brecht's *Galy Gay* (*A Man's a Man*, 1964), and Kafka's *The Trial* (1972), Sartre's *No Exit* (1955), and the general corpus of works of Albee, Adamov, Beckett, Ionesco, Jarry, and others who have written in what is broadly called the "theater of the absurd" (see Esslin, 1961). Borrowing from Esslin (1961:xix), by absurd we mean a condition of existence out of harmony with reason, a set of circumstances devoid of ostensible purpose that makes behavioral choices futile. An absurd existence is one in which we

are unable to discover the meaning and significance of our social world. Activity rooted in reflexivity, self-affirmation, collective development, and social praxis (or world transformative activity), are, as a consequence, impossible.

Existentialist literature depicts the individual as faced with the dilemma of choosing between acquiescence and constraint, on the one hand, and resistance and freedom, on the other. By acquiescing, however, one embraces and promotes one's own further domination. Resistance, choosing to act while offering an avenue of escape from absurdity, comes at the price of embracing the understanding that, in Goodwin's (1971:832) words, such *"action will resolve nothing"* (emphasis in original). The unhappy irony, of course, is that only through such action can one live with more rather than less freedom. Yet, when individuals confront absurdity through resistance, they may give meaning both to their existence and their actions by creating dissonance (Goodwin, 1971:843), regardless of whether they are successful in ultimately altering their conditions.

Following Goodwin (1971), we suggest that confronting absurd institutional conditions also may be a way of rejecting the status quo and altering existing definitions of power and authority. Our research has made us deeply familiar with one such absurd institutional setting, the prison. As Fairchild (1977:313) has observed:

The inmate is faced with certain dilemmas in his relation with those in positions of authority over him. He continues to exist in an atmosphere of subjection, at best paternalistic, at worst repressive and arbitrary. The best way for him to achieve his goal of getting out as soon as possible remains conformity and passiveness on his part toward the prison system. He is expected, however, to stress self-determination and individual responsibility as a rehabilitative goal.

Prison life may be seen as an allegorical analogue to other forms of social existence in which the potential to act is obstructed and social actors remain powerless relative to their potential to engage and transcend their circumstances. Choices suppressed or pacified lead only to organizationally determined identities; one becomes what the environment dictates. The debilitating conditions that reduce autonomy and personal freedom, coupled with a hostile and often violent ambience, do not provide significant opportunity for self-expressions that deviate from the desired norms of staff or other prisoners. Prisons illustrate an absurd environment that smothers the psyche and the will to act meaningfully, by conventional standards.

Resistance, Prisoner Litigation, and the Jailhouse Lawyer

Within the prison environment, however, there exist some ways to mediate absurdity with reason. Using threats and/or violence is one way, but such a strategy seems, inevitably, to bring punishment and greater oppression and dehumanization. Another way, litigation, seems to offer an occasionally effective way of acting meaningfully and rationally in what is experienced as a chaotic environment. One prisoner who had pursued litigation expressed the appreciation of not using violence due to its consequences:

We don't want to be locked up [placed in lockdown status]. We don't want everybody locked up. We don't want them shutting down the schools. We don't want them stopin' us from going out getting a couple hours of fresh air, we don't want to be left in our cells when it's 90 or 100 degrees in our cells. We don't

want that. So guys will come and sit and talk about those types of problems (interview, JHL).

When the problems cannot be readily resolved through interpersonal means or institutional channels, and if it appears that a Constitutional issue is at stake, then the law or threat of its use may be invoked. From our observations of and interviews with prisoners who have turned to JHLs with their problems, law is viewed as a resource to act against various conditions of their and other prisoners' lives. This provides one way prisoners can attempt to overcome the powerlessness of their position to challenge behaviors and policies that make little sense to them and seem capricious and unjust.

In the past two decades, state prisoners have increasingly turned to federal courts in attempts to resolve private troubles in public forums. This is called prisoner litigation. Critics of prisoner litigation contend that prisoners sue primarily because they are either unwilling to accept their conviction or because they wish only to hassle their keepers by "abusing the law" (Thomas et al., 1987). However, prisoners who challenge policies or conditions to which they object do so for a variety of reasons, many of them certainly as honorable as those of their litigious civilian counterparts.

There seem to be two types of prisoner litigants (see Milovanovic, 1988a). First are those who file a single suit during their entire incarceration and who generally require the assistance of others to do it. Between 1980 and 1986, Thomas (1989) found in his study of 3,350 prisoner petitions filed in Illinois that nearly three quarters (71%) of all litigants filed only one suit but accounted for only half (49%) of all litigation. Second are those who make a prison career out of law. We call these specialists jailhouse lawyers.

We here are concerned with the more common kind of prisoner litigants who use the law not only on their own behalf but, more commonly, also to help others decide whether a complaint is adjudicable, identify the relevant legal and substantive issues, and shape the case narratives into what are judged to be the most persuasive stories. The most

talented JHLs attempt to link a particular issue that affects only a single inmate to one that may ultimately affect broader prison policies. These JHLs also serve as gatekeepers between prisoners and the federal courts by weeding out suits that do not possess legal merit from those that do.

The jailhouse lawyer of interest here, then, is a prisoner knowledgeable in law who helps other prisoners shape or translate the personal troubles and problems of prison life into legal issues and claims. These legal claims are diverse and can include preincarceration problems with landlords or employers, family problems involving divorce and child custody, or postconviction complaints. However, JHLs most often assist inmates with grievances against the keepers.

Models of Understanding Litigation in the Prison

Explanations of behavior within a prison culture typically proceed from one of three general models. Conventional researchers have tended to examine prisoner behavior as the consequence of either a set of norms or values imported into the prison from the streets (the "importation" model) or as a reaction to the deprivation of prison conditions (the "functional" or "deprivation" model). Irwin (1970), for example, has argued that prisoners' roles are largely a recreation of roles brought in from the streets. Still others theorize that prisoners possess a Marxian "revolutionary consciousness" that guides their conduct in prison. . . .

An Existential View

In many ways, prisoner litigants resemble the protagonists in existential literature—both the winners and losers—in that they are surrounded by mysterious forces that threaten to overwhelm them, yet they do not readily acquiesce. In this light, prisoner litigation may be seen as a form of overcoming, of actively dealing with irrationality, of attempting to make sense of senselessness, and of yearning to be human in an inhumane environment. One JHL described the typical frustration that led him to the law as a means of resisting. After describing and documenting a series of perceived no-win situations created by staff, he concluded:

This leads to total madness. It's like being put into a cage and having them poke at you constantly. You don't have to do nothing, just because you're in that position, in that cage, they throw your water at you and throw your meat at you, and sit back and laugh at you, and constantly watch you, and poke sticks at you. And you have no recourse. You can't run nowhere, you can't hide nowhere, you can't even beg [the guards] . . . (interview, JHL).

It seems, then, that it is not so much the function of prisons as "houses of punishment" that impels resistance, but the way staff, through interaction with prisoners, generate animosity:

And [staff behaviors are] wrong. Because you can't do this to human beings and expect them to accept it and lay down and play dead, because 80 percent of the people in this institution are here because they're violent. The other 20 percent shouldn't be here (interview, JHL).

One universally perceived method of harassing prisoners is through disciplinary proceedings in which privileges may be lost and the length of time incarcerated increased by loss of "good time":

An officer can make it virtually impossible for you not to go to G-house, to segregation. An officer, male or female, can come in here and make it so difficult for you to vent your hostility, because they treat you as though you are the lowest form of life on earth (interview, JHL).

In fact, disciplinary proceedings against prisoners reveal many of the absurd characteristics of prison life, and disciplinary hearings constitute about 11 percent of prisoners' civil rights suits in the federal courts (Thomas et al., 1988). For example, a guard may command an inmate to obey an order that seems to have no legitimate basis in existing rules, such as standing in a given spot waiting for the officer to return. The inmate asks, "Why?" The guard replies, "Because I said so!" After an hour, the inmate leaves to perform assigned tasks and is later disciplined for not remaining. "Why was I

disciplined?" asks the inmate. The guard replies, "Because you violated the rules." Or the inmate may wait, and when the guard returns after nearly an hour, he disciplines the inmate for not reporting to a work assignment. The guard reasons that, considering the delay, the inmate should have realized that the guard would not return as planned.

These examples, drawn from prison disciplinary documents and from our disciplinary hearings observations, illustrate the catch-22 situation of rule-following. To obey the rule and remain risks punishment for not being on, for example, a work assignment. To leave and avoid possible punishment for other rule violations risks punishment for "disobeying a direct order," which is a rule violation. Thomas et al. (1988) provide other examples of the double-binding dilemmas that prison rules often present.

This escalating merry-go-round of absurdity has one clear end: The inmate is given a disciplinary ticket and later unsuccessfully attempts to explain this absurdity to a disciplinary committee. The explanation ("I was told to stay, but the guard never came back") ultimately indicates guilt, and punishment for "rule infraction" follows. The absurdity of both the situation and the consequences remains. For the JHL, however, the matter does not end here.

Using the Law to Mediate Absurdity

Despite arguments to the contrary (Landau, 1984), the evidence suggests that law is quite effective in challenging the prisons' absurdities (Mika and Thomas, 1988). This, however, must be tempered with several caveats. First, one must be chary of romanticizing the legal practitioner lest litigation behavior be falsely elevated to the status of political activism. Law, despite its utility, does not engender dramatic structural changes. Hence, changes in prison conditions brought about by litigation are, at best, modest. Second, some critics correctly suggest that even reform occurring through litigation may increase coercive control by strengthening legitimate prior practices or by masking existing illicit ones under the "color of law"

(Brakel, 1987; Mandel, 1986). Examples include legal reforms of sentencing that have shifted discretionary power of release from the judicial to the correctional realm (Bigman, 1979; Jacobs, 1983a) and the irony of legal reform of disciplinary proceedings that seem to have enhanced, rather than curtailed, staff's coercive power (Thomas et al., 1988). Finally, the dual character of law as both emancipatory and repressive means that, even if changes occur, the authority of prison administrators is preserved, albeit in a different form or by a new discourse.

However, one set of truths does not obviate others. Recognizing litigation as an act of existential rebellion allows us to understand litigation as a dialectical process that creates and mediates the contradictions of prison power, culture, existence, and transcendence. Litigation may mediate absurdity in several ways.

Litigation as Self-Help

There is some evidence that prisoner litigation may be a form of what Irwin (1980:16) has called gleaning, or using the prison experience and resources for self-improvement. In a related context, Black (1983) has suggested that crime may be conceptualized as grievance-expression. In an ironic twist, those who formerly expressed a grievance in ways defined as socially unacceptable now have learned new and acceptable means by which to express dissatisfaction. One JHL attempted to withdraw from a street gang as a way of avoiding problems, but was soon faced with other problems that drove him to law:

I knew I couldn't be in this gang, because it was hurting me [physically] and I'm not into pain under any circumstances whatsoever. So, I started going over to the library a lot, playing around with the typewriters that was for the public population usage; also, I started having small conflicts with the correctional officer. I didn't like the way they treated me, so I started writing complaints on them concerning their action towards me (interview, JHL).

The transition from a passive recipient to whom things "just happen" to a more conscious actor attempting to take control over the immediate life-world can take many forms, and entry into the world of law is just one. In this way, litigation can become a newly-learned skill for exerting a growing "personhood." Moreover, these skills and ways of thinking increase the probability and the facility of saying no. Once the utility of law is recognized as a force in solving personal disputes, its role in helping others is also soon perceived. For example, JHLs seem to pass through a "save the world" phase in which they begin to feel that law is a means of changing prison conditions (Thomas, 1988:210–11).

In sum, JHLs identify the primal emotions of desperation, anger, and the will to resist as the reasons to explain their attraction to law (Thomas, 1988:201). For them, law becomes a form of self-help to overcome the problems they face in prison when there is no alternative means to secure relief. For some, these emotions may have emerged during their trials, where they perceived themselves to be judicial victims—not in the determination of guilt, but in the pre-trial or sentencing process. For others, treatment by staff prompted a desire for retaliation. For all, the acquisition of literacy and analytic skills, coupled with functional knowledge of judicial processes and practices, became a path to personal salvation.

Litigation as Efficacious

There is a view among critics of litigation that it is frivolous, and only the exceptional suit entails any grievance of substance (Anderson, 1986; Burt, 1985; Federal Judicial Center, 1980; Reed, 1980). Hence, litigation is seen not as rebellion, but as abuse of the courts by those already "proven" to be antisocial. "Frivolousness," however, is embedded in a variety of social meanings and is not value-neutral. As a legal term, it means lacking in judicial merit. But, the legal use is often translated into the lay meaning of "worthless," and a suit that is not adjudicable then becomes, in the lay view, one that totally lacks substance. There is considerable evidence that prisoners, in the main, file neither excessively nor frivolously (Thomas, 1989). Even if there is no adjudicable remedy or relief, there is usually a substantive problem over which the plaintiff sues. The problem

may seem trivial (deprivation of toilet paper) or severe (held a year past formal release date) but, to the prisoner, it is not frivolous.

DiIulio (1987) has provided a powerful argument that there is no "prison crisis," but rather an "administration crisis." In DiIulio's view, problems impelling litigation, violence, fiscal crisis, recidivism, and other factors commonly associated with a "failing system" can be traced directly back to incompetent administrators, which he sees as the norm, not the exception. Although we believe that prison problems can not be fully understood without analysis of broader social relations, we find much of merit in DiIulio's argument. Prisoners sue to redress a wrong, and these wrongs tend to exist because of the actions of staff or administrators. The act of challenging a decision, policy, or condition defined as unacceptable thus becomes an act of rebellion in that it resists the "what is" and attempts, through action, to change it into something more to the prisoner's liking. Examples of such changes can include reducing staff harassment, increasing security of vulnerable inmates from predatory attacks by other inmates, increased access to showers, health care, or prison programs, reducing overcrowding, changing "catch-22" rules, or making minor, but more humane, changes in facilities (for example, improved lighting, sanitation, or general ambience).

Litigation as Negation

Litigation, or even its threat, can often curtail perceived staff abuse of power. A suit signifies that a monologic or asymmetrical power relation is momentarily replaced by a dialogic and more symmetrical state of affairs, albeit a formal one (see Blum, 1974; Bakhtin, 1981).

Whether a suit is substantively won or lost, the act of filing the suit *requires* a formal response from prison officials. Presumably, even abusive staff and insensitive administrators would prefer to avoid additional paper work, visibility, and hassle, especially at the behest of prisoners. By challenging the expression of power, the conditions it engenders, and its extreme uses by power holders, such litigation can

negate at least some of the deleterious conditions of the prison conditions (see Palmer, 1985).

Litigation as the Subversion of Hierarchy

Critics correctly claim that prisoner litigation does little to change the structure of hierarchical power arrangements (Mandel, 1986). However, it does not follow that there has been no impact of litigation on the exercise of power in prisons (Jacobs, 1983a:54–60). An act of no rebellion begins with a refusal to accept the existing structure of power. Prisoners' suits challenge the prison staff's power. When, for example, the administration of Cook County jail refused to allow inmates to possess hardcover books because they were potential weapons, a suit overturned the policy (*Jackson* v.. *Elrod et al.*, 86-C-1817, N.D. Ill. 1986). When the isolation, lack of health care, and living conditions in Menard's condemned unit became unbearable, a federal decision alleviated at least some of the problems (*Lightfoot et al.* v. *Walker et al.*, 486 F. Supp. 504, 1980). When staff refused to properly deliver an inmate's legitimate mail, a law suit corrected the problem for that inmate (*Woods* v. *Aldworth*, 84-C-7745, N.D. Ill. 1984).

These examples seem relatively trivial, but they typify inmate civil rights complaints. They also symbolize acts of resistance and refusal to cooperate with and reaffirm the power of officials to control existence. In such cases, law mediates domination by staff power, and although it does little to rearrange or redistribute power, litigation imposes constraints on the ability of staff to exercise it. Resistance, then, may not necessarily change the power hierarchy, but it can rearrange the use of power within it (although, see *Holt* v. *Sarver*, 300 F.Supp 825 [E.D. Ark. 1969]; *Ruiz* v. *Estelle*, 650 f.2d 555 [fth Cir. 1981] in Arkansas and Texas).

Litigation as "Victory"

If the popular view that prisoners rarely win their cases is true, it would seem to follow that prisoners are not effective rebels. But we do not accept the argument that to be a legitimate rebel one must "win." Nor do we find convincing evidence that prisoners rarely win. Of course, what counts as a victory for one person may be perceived as a defeat by another. The conventional method of scorekeeping simply calculates the number of cases won and lost by prisoners, a method that, for several reasons, we find unsatisfactory.

First, the measure of success must be determined, at least in part, by whether the suit curtailed or corrected the objectionable behavior. A prisoner who sues staff for $1 million for an improper conviction in a disciplinary hearing may have the case dismissed without any formal judicial action taken, but may nonetheless have the improper conviction expunged from the record and any lost goodtime restored. A prisoner who is injured because of staff's recklessness may opt to settle for remedial action or token damage awards out of court. Official records record these as "victories" for state defendants (Thomas, 1989), even though the prisoner's challenge has resulted in a consequential form of resistance.

Second, although prisoners are rarely awarded all that they request in a suit, we reject the general conclusion that they lose in the legal forum. In a study of 2,900 cases in Illinois's Northern federal district, Mika and Thomas (1988) found that while about 38 percent of prisoners' complaints are dismissed on pleading, about 62 percent of those surviving result in a "victory" of some kind. The outcomes, usually settled out of court, may result in token damage awards, but more often they are in the form of rectification of the original problem, modification of prison policies, or discouragement of objectionable staff behavior toward the plaintiff. We must caution that, unless a complaint challenges a policy or specific conditions that affect others, the impact of most suits is limited to a single individual.

Third, as one experienced JHL argued, "Just the doin' of it, we win!" In this view, litigation can provide a symbolic victory to the extent that, even if the case is lost, it makes staff aware that they may be accountable for future actions. Milovanovic (1988a) suggests that one objective indicator of the effectiveness of JHLs might be how much legal "action" has been mobilized (see also Black,

1976). In this view, an inmate returning to court for redress, appeal, suppression hearings, or other action, can be seen as attaining some symbolic gain to the extent that they continue to keep their issue before the courts. Similarly, in civil rights cases, litigants usually gain at least temporary respite from the objectionable action even prior to case termination.

The Political Value of Jailhouse Law

What then is the political value of jailhouse law and the action of the JHLs? The answer to this question lies in how one views the role of law in social change (Milovanovic, 1988a). While conceding the lack of a consistent collective political consciousness, we see prisoners' litigation as social praxis, specifically, in affirming the act of saying no. Even while reinforcing the ideology of the rule of law, prisoners simultaneously subvert the expression, if not the structure, of certain existing power arrangements in the prison. The problem is not that law is ineffective, but that the effectiveness of law is misdirected. As Klare (1979:132) has written in defending "law-making as praxis,"

My argument is that we can conceive law-making as, *in theory,* a form of expressive social practice in which the community participates in shaping the moral, allocative, and adjudicatory texture of social life, but that in class society, this process is alienated. In history, law-making becomes a mode of domination, not freedom, because of its *repressive* function (emphasis in the original).

The utility of jailhouse law as social praxis, then, is not unqualified. Both its content and its form of expression recreate and sustain the broader class and other power arrangements that lead to unnecessary social domination. As Klare (1979:135) has suggested, the exercise tends to promote the instrumental pursuit of client or self-interest at the expense of "political lawyering."

But objections to viewing the JHL as a rebel, although sometimes cogent, tend to neglect the subtleties of the meaning of litigation as both a means of change and as a form of existential negation. Rebellion defines the relationship of an act to its con-

text, not its consequence nor its motive. Rebellion begins when one moves from passive acquiescence to active resistance against forces that threaten to dominate or overwhelm. Sometimes resistance is carefully planned and implemented, as occurs in social movements or in such individual acts of defiance as refusal to pay taxes or terrorism. Other times, rebellion is more subtle, as occurs when people reject the authority of the state by exceeding the speed limit or refusing to wear seat belts. A prison rebel is not a revolutionary:

"Revolutionary" action is defiant action that seeks to change the prison structure or its relation to the external environment in a fundamental way. The most important factor associated with revolutionary action is identification with defiant counter communities (Useem and Kimball, 1987:106).

A primitive rebel, then, is one who has learned to say "no" and intentionally resists authority, but has not yet developed a consciousness capable of translating action into a consistent critical theory or systematic ideologically informed assault. While there are, of course, exceptions, those few JHLs who possess exceptional skills in political analysis and attempt to link their legal actions to broader issues are not the norm.

The litigation of the JHL may be viewed as an existential response to repression. Where most conventional social theory tends to look for "laws" or "processes," and too often ignores the meanings by which the concepts underlying research are shaped and defined, existential literature evokes a theoretical imagery of action-taking in which individuals confront their environment, even if the confrontation appears futile.

We do not impute to JHLs an explicit existential consciousness, and do not suggest that they are necessarily striving toward authenticity as a coherent philosophical or political act. We are concerned with the more general issue of understanding resistance as a way of creating meaning through social action. In the case of litigation, self-awareness is connected to social formation to the extent that "saying no" symbolizes a rejection of the status quo. When negation is coupled with social action (in this case, legal struggle), there occurs the potential for an accommodation between the resisters and those resisted. It is this dialectical tension between those who impose meanings and those who challenge them that imbues prisoner litigation with its capacity for existential rebellion.

Discussion

By conceptualizing litigation as more an existential than a political act, one that may be viewed as a continuum ranging from extreme individualism to sophisticated political action, we have attempted to reframe the meaning of activist law and applied our analysis to one category of litigant. At one end are those who acquiesce. At the other stand those who resist. In prisons, these are jailhouse lawyers. But, the JHL is a "doer," not an ideologist; a reformer, not an articulator of system-generated repression. He is a person who has come to understand how to respond to absurdity with existing tools, but has not developed the broader political or social understanding to use those tools to address the meaning and embeddedness of existence. The efforts of the JHL lie somewhere between conscious and reflective behavior and what Kosik (1976:39) has called procuring, or mundane social activity:

The individual moves about in a *ready made system of devices and implements,* procures them as they in turn procure him, and has long ago "lost" any awareness of this world being a product of man. . . . Procuring is praxis in its *phenomenally alienated form* which does not point to *the genesis* of the human world (the world of people and of human culture, of a culture that humanizes nature) but rather expresses the praxis of everyday manipulation, with man employed in a system of *ready made* "things," i.e., implements. In this system of implements, man himself becomes an object of manipulation (emphasis in original).

The JHL has gone beyond simple procuring but does not yet act in a way consistent with a fully-aware political consciousness. The action remains at the intermediate level of resisting institutional absurdity, but does not yet, and perhaps cannot, transcend it.

If Lukacs (1971:199) was correct in his assertion that "Whether an action is functionally right or wrong is decided ultimately by the evolution of proletarian class consciousness," then prisoner litigation may be "politically incorrect." But this seems too uncharitable because social change, as a historical process, occurs in many cases with successive acts of saying no. Precisely when an act becomes transformed from mundane practice to rebellious praxis is an empirical question, and the effects of an act may not be visible until some future date.

Of itself, this may not lead to fundamental social change but, in the dialectic of social struggle, neither do fundamental changes occur through the efforts of any single social group. Social change arises from social action, and a group "in itself" can contribute to the creation of circumstances that can help it congeal in a group "for itself," as has occurred with such groups as feminists, blacks, and gays. Obviously, reforms are only a partial victory, but they function to exacerbate other conditions, and the dialectic of struggle continues.

Our argument suggests several questions for research. First, it suggests the need to reconceptualize the, meaning of JHL activity in particular and the role of legal activists in general. Rather than view legal struggle by examining its consequences, we should also examine the meanings of the use of law in the context of "saying no." Second, existentially oriented research gives attention to institutional and other social arrangements that constrain both behavior and consciousness. Especially in total institutions, the often contradictory structure promotes double-bind, no-win situations, and inconsistent practices that must be continually negotiated and managed. Third, consistent with Marxian and conflict theory, this research reminds us, as Goodwin (1971) has cogently argued, that people may seek dissonance as much as consonance. Dissonance offers not only an instrumental means of potential resistance, but provides as well a source of meaning to an otherwise meaningless existence. Fourth, given our contention that JHLs are primitive rebels, one crucial research task requires, as Fairchild (1977) suggests, identifying the relationship between the correctional experience and social and political empowerment. More simply, what factors impel some prisoners to resist while others acquiesce? Under what conditions does simple rebellion become transformed into explicit political action? Finally, this research shifts attention from the alleged "pathological" or abusive motives of litigants to the meanings litigation has for those who pursue it for themselves and others who share their situation. This suggests that litigation should be interpreted diagnostically as reflecting the pathology of the deeper institutional structures that impel resistance while simultaneously offering the means for challenge.

These symbolic meanings of this prison litigation lead us to view the JHL as a primitive rebel. By refocusing attention on the existential conditions of resistance, we cautiously temper the contentions of some, such as Foucault (1979), who impute excessive unilateral power to those in charge of discipline. A position informed by the existentialist tradition recognizes the mediating, yet often ironic and futile, capacity of human beings:

It is essentially a struggle against great odds to allow the individual to realize his *existential freedom* and to feel his capacity to influence his future and to participate in the decisions which affect him (Fairchild, 1977:316; emphasis in original).

References

Anderson, Debra J. 1986. *Curbing the Abuses of Inmate Litigation.* College Park, MD: American Correctional Association.

Bakhtin, Mikhail. 1981. The *Dialogical Imagination.* Austin TX: University of Texas Press.

Bigman, Paul. 1979. *Discretion. Determinate Sentencing and the Illinois Prisoner Review Board: A Shotgun Wedding.* Chicago: Law Enforcement Study Group Report/John Howard Association.

Black, Donald. 1976. *The Behavior of Law.* New York: Academic Press.

———. 1983. "Crime as social control." *American Sociological Review* 48:34–45.

Blum, Alan. 1974. *Theorizing.* London: Heinemann, Ltd.

Brakel, Samuel Jan. 1987. "Prison reform litigation: has the revolution gone too far?" *Corrections Today* 49:160–68.

Brecht, Bertolt. 1964. *Baal, A Man's a Man, and the Elephant Calf.* New York: Grove Press.

Burt, Christine. 1985. "Rule 9(a) and its impact on habeas corpus litigation." *New England Journal of Criminal and Civil Confinement* 11:363–94.

Camus, Albert. 1955. *The Myth of Sisyphus.* New York: Vintage Books.

———. 1956. *The Rebel: An Essay on Man in Revolt.* New York: Vintage Books.

———. 1958. *Caligula and Three Other Plays.* New York: Vintage Books.

DiIulio, John J., Jr. 1987. *Governing Prisons: A Comparative Study of Correctional Management.* New York: The Free Press.

Esslin, Martin. 1961. *The Theatre of the Absurd.* New York: Anchor Books.

Fairchild, Erika S. 1977. "Politicization of the criminal offender." *Criminology* 15:287–318.

Federal Judicial Center. 1980. *Recommended Procedures for Handling Prisoner Civil Rights Cases in the Federal Courts.* Washington, DC: The Federal Judicial Center.

Fitzgerald, Mike. 1977. *Prisoners in Revolt.* Harmondsworth, England: Pelican Books.

Foucault, Michel. 1979. *Discipline and Punish: The Birth of the Prison.* New York: Vintage Books.

Goodwin, Glenn A. 1971. "On transcending the absurd." *American Journal of Sociology* 76:831–46.

Hobsbawm, Eric J. 1969. *Bandits.* London: George Weidenfeld and Nicolson, Ltd.

Irwin, John. 1970. *The Felon.* Englewood Cliffs, NJ: Prentice Hall.

———. 1980. *Prisons in Turmoil.* Boston, MA: Little, Brown.

Jackson, George. 1970. *Soledad Brother: The Prison Letters of George Jackson.* New York: Coward-McCann.

Jacobs, James B. 1983a. "Sentencing by prison personnel." *UCLA Law Review* 30:217–70.

———. 1983b. *New Perspectives on Prisons and Imprisonment.* Ithaca, NY. Cornell University Press.

Kafka, Franz. 1972. *The Trial.* Harmondsworth, England: Penguin Books.

Klare, Karl. 1978. "Judicial deradicalization of the Wagner Act and the origins of modem legal consciousness, 1937–1941." *Minnesota Law Review* 62:265–339.

———. 1979. "Law-making as praxis." *Telos,* 40:123–35.

Kosik, Karel. 1976. *Dialectics of the Concrete: A Study on Problems of Man and World.* Boston, MA: D. Reidel.

Lukacs, George. 1971. *History and Class Consciousness.* London: Merlin Press.

Mika, Harry and Jim Thomas. 1988. "The dialectics of prisoner litigation: reformist idealism or social praxis?" *Social Justice* 15:48–71.

Milovanovic, Dragan. 1987. "Jailhouse lawyers and jailhouse lawyering." Unpublished manuscript.

———. 1988a. "Jailhouse lawyers and jailhouse lawyering." *International Journal of the Sociology of Law* 16:455–75.

———. 1988b. *A Primer in the Sociology of Law.* New York: Harrow and Heston.

Milovanovic, Dragan and Jim Thomas. 1988. "The ironies of jailhouse law." Unpublished manuscript.

Pallas, John and Bob Barber. 1980. "From riot to revolution." Pp. 146–54 in T. Platt and P. Takagi (eds.), *Punishment and Penal Discipline: Essays on the Prison and the Prisoners' Movement.* Berkeley, CA: Crime and Social Justice Associates.

Palmer, John W. 1985. *Constitutional Rights of Prisoners.* Cincinnati, OH: Anderson.

Reed, Anne Willis. 1980. "Guilt, innocence, and federalism in habeas corpus." *Cornell Law Review* 65:1123–47.

Sartre, Jean-Paul. 1955. *No Exit and Three Other Plays.* New York: Vintage Books.

Thomas, Jim. 1988. *Prisoner Litigation: The Paradox of the Jailhouse Lawyer.* Totowa, NJ: Rowman and Littlefield.

———. 1989. "Repackaging the data: the 'reality' of prisoner litigation." *New England Journal of Criminal and Civil Confinement* 15.

Thomas, Jim, Kathy Harris, and Devin Keeler. 1987. "Issues and misconceptions in prisoner litigation." *Criminology* 24:901–19.

Thomas, Jim, Anmarie Aylward, Harry Mika, and Jerome Blakemore. 1988. "Prison disciplinary proceedings: the social enactment of power." Paper presented to the Midwest Criminal Justice Association, Chicago.

Useem, Bert and Peter A. Kimbal. 1987. "A theory of prison riots." *Theory and Society,* 16:87–122.

Wald, Karen. 1980. "The San Quentin six case: perspective and analysis." Pp. 165–75 in T. Platt and P. Takagi (eds.), *Punishment and Penal Discipline: Essays on the Prison and the Prisoners' Movement.* Berkeley, CA: Crime and Social Justice Associates.

 Article Review Form at end of book.

Are those who use law in an attempt to change the conditions of social existence rebels, revolutionaries, or merely ineffective idealists?

Issues and Misconceptions in Prisoner Litigation:

A Critical View

Jim Thomas, Devin Keeler, and Kathy Harris

Northern Illinois University

All inmates are looking for the key to the front door. Law suits are the current vogue. Many serve to justify the existence of the new "camp followers," now that the Civil War is over and the civil rights battles have subsided. Inmates are the cannon fodder.
—Anonymous grant reviewer, National Institute of Justice, 1983.

It is unequivocally obvious that for the past 25 years, state and federal prisoners have appealed to federal courts to resolve a variety of disputes, as have their civilian counterparts. In 1960, combined state and federal prisoner filings in federal district courts totaled 2,177; by 1984, the total was 31,107, an increase of 1,329%. Since 1960, a combined total of nearly 400,000 suits have been filed by state and federal prisoners. Over 142,000 have been filed between 1980 and 1984, representing approximately 36% of all filed since 1960. Prisoner litigation in 1984 alone accounted for 12% of all federal litigation filed in that year. In citing these figures, critics of prisoner litigation have variously called it an "explosion," an "avalanche," a "del-

uge," "legal pollution," and an "epidemic." One observer called the tendency to turn to the courts "America's national disease" (Manning, 1977: 767) and compared the phenomenon to a "heartworm that has a literally fatal potential for the body politic of this country" (Manning, 1977: 770). This has led Chief Justice William Burger to advocate federal legislation to limit prisoner access to courts. Such *hyperlexis* or excessive litigation (Galanter, 1983; Manning, 1977) assumes abnormal filing rates, and locates this abnormality in the characteristics of plaintiffs (those filing) or of judicial permissiveness that has allowed even the most frivolous of claims the right to judicial review. In challenging the hyperlexis view, Galanter (1983: 69) has argued for a contextual reading of the litigation landscape, one that looks beneath the terrain of raw numbers and critically examines the detailed contour in which it exists.

There is, as Bedau (1981) has suggested with irony, no simple way to argue about prisoner litigation. One not-so-simple way is to critically examine interpretations and beliefs that have broader theoretical or policy relevance. The conceptions and misconceptions surrounding such litigation provide a useful window into

the world of prisoners and their litigation. In this paper, conceptions and misconceptions of alleged prisoner "hyperlexis" are examined and an alternative interpretation is suggested.

Types of Prisoner Filings

Prisoner litigation refers to suits filed in federal courts by incarcerated persons who are attempting to resolve problems for which there is rarely a viable alternative remedy. There are two broad classifications of federal litigation. U.S. suits are those in which the federal government is the defendant. Private suits are all others, including those in which state prison officials are defendants. These filing categories properly refer to the status of the defendant rather than the plaintiff. In practice, however, federal prisoners sue federal officials, and state prisoners sue state officials, thus allowing for identification of the petitioner by the nature of the filing category.

There are also two basic categories of prisoner litigation. The first are those suits which challenge the fact of an inmate's detention. These are typically filed under federal *habeas corpus* legislation. The second category of suits is based on civil rights statutes, particularly 42 U.S.C.

Issues and Misconceptions in Prisoner Litigation: A Critical View, J. Thomas, D. Keeler, and K. Harris, *Criminology*, 24(4), 1986, 775–797. Reprinted by permission of the American Society of Criminology.

Section 1983 was enacted after the Civil War to protect freed slaves from potential civil rights abuses, and became known as the Ku Klux Klan act. Although modified and renewed several times between 1866 and 1877, the relevant language of the Act today remains essentially unchanged and precludes any state official from depriving persons of their Constitutionally protected rights under color of law.

Prior to the civil rights movement of the 1960s, federal and state courts followed a hands-off policy in which convicted felons were not legal subjects and thus not subject to constitutional protection. Prisons and jails were, therefore, held to be beyond judicial review. Despite the existence of federal civil rights legislation, few suits were filed before 1906, and rarely was one reviewed favorably to the prisoner. Since the early 1960s, however, federal courts have become more willing to intervene on behalf of prisoners seeking relief from alleged Constitutional violations of prison policies and practices, and of perceived misconduct in conviction proceedings.

The availability of federal *habeas corpus* relief to state prisoners was dramatically expanded by four cases. In 1953, *Brown* v. *Allen* (344 U.S. 443, 1951) established the use of federal *habeas corpus* in redetermining Constitutional questions in state criminal proceedings. A decade later, *Sanders* v. *U.S.* (372 U.S. 1, 1963), *Townsend* v. *Sain* (372 U.S. 293, 1963) and *Fay* v. *Noia* (372 U.S. 391, 1963) expanded federal review of constitutional questions arising in conviction in state courts. There were fears that especially the 1963 trilogy would precipitate a deluge of prisoner suits in their wake.

Prisoner civil rights litigation was stimulated by *Monroe* v. *Pape* (365 U.S. 167, 1961), which resurrected the use of post-Civil War civil rights legislation. This decision provided the fundamental theory on which most subsequent prisoner civil rights litigation has been based, but among other decisions, *Cooper* v. *Pate* (378 U.S. 546, 1964) and *Johnson* v. *Avery* (393 U.S. 483, 1969), were particularly important. The Cooper decision was significant for two reasons. First, it allowed state prisoners to bring suit against their keepers

under the Civil Rights Act. Prisoners now had an explicit and direct avenue to federal courts. Second, in recognizing Black Muslims as a legitimate religion, the court explicitly provided prisoners with expanded religious freedoms and implicitly extended Bill of Rights protections to inmates. The Johnson decision protected prisoner access to law by forbidding prison officials to interfere with jailhouse lawyers working on behalf of other inmates. This provided unskilled or illiterate inmates with the means to petition courts when they would not otherwise be able. These decisions, combined with lesser prisoner victories in the 1960s, established the courts as the ultimate protector of prisoners' rights.

Issues and Misconceptions

There are a number of issues, some legitimate, others not, that currently guide discussions of prisoner litigation. Some of the most salient include the following.

First is the use of the metaphor of an "explosion" in prisoner filings since 1960. When observers speak of the "explosion," they usually mean that the number of suits in recent years is proportionately much higher than the number of suits filed two decades ago, and continues to expand disproportionate to other forms of litigation. The number of all prisoner suits filed in 1984, for example, is over 14 times greater than the number filed in 1960. This single statistic creates an image of prisoners flooding the courts with their claims, and seems to strongly corroborate the hyperlexis thesis. But this figure is misleading. When the average annual increase of suits by litigating prisoners is compared with civilian litigation, a rather different image emerges. A different view of litigation is also obtained when one distinguishes between federal and state prisoner filings. By illustrating broad national trends in prisoner litigation, and by comparing these with civilian litigation rates, it becomes easier to understand the utility of these distinctions and to begin exploring the underlying issues.

A second conception suggests that prisoners tend to file frivolous suits, and that most cases "ought be dismissed, even under the most lib-

eral definition of frivolity" (Federal Judicial Center, 1980: 9). Chief Justice Warren Burger has written (1976: 189):

Federal judges should not be dealing with prisoner complaints which, although important to a prisoner, are so minor that any well-run institution should be able to resolve them fairly without resorting to federal judges.

For lawyers, "frivolity" is a term used to describe suits lacking legal merit. For prisoners and civil rights advocates, the term refers to suits lacking substantive merit. Thus, whether a suit is frivolous seems to depend as much upon one's perspective as upon the content of a specific suit. The legal meaning of frivolousness connotes a value implying "worthlessness," even if there is a substantial grievance to be remedied. Further, media dramatizations of substantive frivolity tend to emphasize extreme cases, such as a female prisoner seeking a sex change operation, complaints of prison commissary deodorant (Possley, 1980: 20), cold toilet seats, failure to provide outside television antennas (Locin, 1981: 6), or the Illinois case of a prisoner who filed an injunction to stay prison officials from reading his thoughts. Other suits may be dramatized to make them seem trivial, even though there is a legitimate underlying grievance. For example, a suit over a protracted kiss between a prisoner and his wife, while portrayed by the media as trivial, in fact may represent grievances of harassment of a prisoner's family by guards during visits. Some prisoner suits, then, may be frivolous, but these are substantively, if not legally, few (Thomas, in press), and as Possley (1984: 1) has indicated, "frivolity" plagues civilian litigation as well.

Third, many observers argue that prisoner litigation, especially *habeas corpus* suits, reflects attempts by prisoners to retry their cases once they have been lost (Bator, 1963; Friendly, 1970; Reed, 1980). Although *habeas corpus* cases usually challenge either procedures or sentencing related to the original case, in Illinois about one third of *habeas corpus* petitions are unrelated to the original case. Unrelated petitions typically challenge revocation of good time, parole revocation, and record keeping or calculation (rather than imposition) of sentence. Despite research to the contrary (Allen, Schactman, and Wilson, 1982: 677n; Thomas, Aylward, Oldham, Casey, Moton, and Wheetley, 1985; Turner, 1979: 612), the view persists that "turn-me-loose" suits continue to represent the overwhelming bulk of prisoner litigation.

Fourth, prisoner litigation is perceived to undermine the criminal justice system by reducing respect for the law through delaying finality of punishment and making "certain punishment" for crimes uncertain (Bator, 1963). Some argue that this leads to the Supreme Court's "progressive trivialization of the writ" (Jackson, 1952: 536). According to this argument, litigation may in fact promote crime by conveying to prisoners that even if they are convicted and sentenced, they may soon be released by finding a technicality in the original criminal proceedings. This, it is argued, reduces the principle of celerity and certainty of punishment by opening the possibility that even the most heinous acts may go unpunished. But overwhelming evidence indicates that few prisoners obtain release by overturning the original conviction (Allen et al., 1982; Justice, 1973; Shapiro, 1973).

Fifth, the proliferation of "frivolous" habeas corpus suits may result in the worthy cases being overlooked. One Supreme Court justice (Jackson, 1952: 537) has argued that

It must prejudice the occasional meritorious application to be buried in a flood of worthless ones. He who must search a haystack for a needle is likely to end up with the attitude that the needle is not worth the search.

This view is shared by both liberal and conservative observers and even by most jailhouse lawyers (Aylward and Thomas, 1984; Thomas, in press). This is based on a "Gresham's law" theory of litigation in which groundless cases are seen as debasing the value of meritorious ones, both increasing the work and decreasing the credibility of those active in prisoner rights. Even advocates of prisoners' rights are sensitive to the need to assure that legitimate complaints not be jeopardized because of possibly less-meritorious complaints (Friendly, 1970). Yet, no evidence has been offered to support this contention, and

it remains open to considerable doubt. Judges do seem patient in reviewing the merits of prisoner petitions (Suchner, Aylward, and Thomas, 1986), suggesting that the wheat in fact remains when the chaff is separated. Judges also quickly dismiss "garbage" suits, and, as one judge indicated, prisoner suits are on the whole conceptually simple and rarely require more than a few minutes to ascertain whether an adjudicable issue exists (Federal judge, personal interview, January, 1985).

Sixth is the conception that federal intervention in state correctional affairs exacerbates tensions between state and federal governments (Bator, 1963), thus raising the federalism versus states' rights debates. This, as Attorney General Edmund Meese has consistently argued, goes beyond the "original intents" of judicial review (Meese, 1985a, 1985b, 1985c). Much of the current controversy over civil rights litigation has its roots in post-Fourteenth amendment decisions in which the federal government effectively expanded its power over state judicial decisions, thus giving this conflict view some credence. This argument has been rekindled, especially since 1980, due to the interpretation of the "Reagan mandate," which some have perceived as grounds for limiting the scope of federal intervention in both civilian and prisoner review (Meese, 1986). There may be some merit in this position. In such states as Texas, Arkansas, Michigan, and Illinois, federal court orders have required changes in jail or prison conditions and policies, many of which have rankled both administrators and legislators. Further, as of January 1985, 29 states were under court order regarding conditions of confinement, and 23 had population ceilings set by the court (Camp and Camp, 1985: 28). On the other hand, there is some evidence that state politicians and prison administrators on occasion welcome certain types of law suits as politically expedient, or as a means of increasing resources by court order (Harriman and Straussman, 1983). They appear to be "forced" to comply with decisions that result in prison reforms that would have otherwise been politically unpalatable (Thomas, 1984). This is a complex issue, and prisoner litigation cannot

so easily be criticized by claiming states' rights prerogatives.

Finally, there is a variety of conceptions about why prisoners sue. Various explanations have been suggested, and these can be grouped into several broad categories.

First are the psychological explanations, which interpret litigation as reflecting the contentiousness of prisoners or as a product of their generally anti-social tendencies. One variant interprets litigation as a form of transference in which hostile impulses are merely transferred from targets outside the walls to the courts or prison personnel. This view provides an image of hordes of jailhouse lawyers who have nothing better to do with their time than "hassle" administrators (Anonymous, 1982). A second variant is the "front door" (or "freedom") thesis, in which prisoners are seen as litigating primarily to secure their release (Bator, 1963; Reed, 1980). If this view is correct, then most suits would be expected to be petitions for writs of habeas corpus, which are challenges to confinement. Because both psychological views posit the increase in filings as directly related to the nature of offenders, one would expect filings to rise directly proportional to the number of prisoners. As one conference pundit argued, "When you get more 'loonies,' you get more suits!" Since the mid-1970s, there have been more prisoners, but fewer of them litigate.

A second explanation, legalistic in character, is the permissive judiciary theory. Adherents of this view locate the primary cause of increased filings in the decisions of "activist judges" who have provided prisoners with both the means and the motivation by intruding in affairs best left to states. In this view, prisoner filings increase proportional to the favorable decisions that expand prisoner rights, and one would expect increased litigation following decisions that further recognize and protect prisoners' rights.

A third explanation borrows from demography, and might be called the expanding at-risk population theory, in which the number of prisoner suits reflects a growing population of persons with a higher probability of having their rights violated than other populations. Hence, the increase in prisoner suits should be roughly proportional to the increase in the nation's prison population.

The final explanation is the social resistance thesis, in which litigation is interpreted as opposition to particularly objectionable conditions of prison existence. This position locates the primary sources of litigation in problems endemic in the criminal justice system, particularly prison conditions and policies. Prisoner suits are interpreted as a form of social action rather than as simply a dependent variable.

Each of these conceptions and implied theories has some merit, but not all are equally supported by data. The remainder of this study will compare these issues and explanations to national prisoner filing data in federal district courts.

Conceptions Versus Reality: A Critique

Many of the misconceptions of prisoner litigation have their sources in how discussions are conceptualized. Several preliminary problems should be clarified. First, despite federal classification distinctions, the categories of federal and state prisoners are commonly conflated, thus confounding the nature of filings. Second, civil rights and *habeas corpus* cases tend not to be distinguished, thus distorting the filing differences among each category. Third, the grounds of litigation by state and federal prisons have shifted over the years. It thus becomes necessary to distinguish between the various categories of prisoner suits filed by each group. Finally, using a base year from the early 1960s by which to compare later filing rates is misleading. Because relatively few suits were filed in the early 1960s, a small number of additional filings substantially affects the proportion of increase. For example, in criticizing the "excessive" use of the *habeas corpus* writ by prisoners, Reed (1980) has used the base year of 1953, in which only 541 *habeas corpus* petitions were filed, to dramatize the "swelling" of prisoner *habeas corpus* petitions. She also commits the common error of assuming that all prisoner litigation is *habeas corpus* litigation, using state prisoners' total filing figures from 1979 (18,502) rather than only the *habeas corpus* filings (7,123) to dramatize excessive *habeas corpus* filings.

By distinguishing between the grounds of filing and who files what, one can better understand Galanter's (1983: 61) claim that litigation occurs in a social context, and is not simply a "figure" waiting passively to be counted.

Federal Prisoner Filings

Federal prisoner filing data indicate that, despite gradual increases, there has been no dramatic explosion in any single category and, in fact, filings may be in decline. Both the numbers and the nature of suits filed by federal prisoners have shifted since the 1960s. There was no sudden increase in *habeas corpus* petitions by federal prisoners following the 1963 trilogy of cases expanding *habeas corpus* review. Post-trilogy *habeas corpus* filings remained relatively stable between 1963–1965, but gradually increased after 1966, and increased more rapidly from 1969–1974. Despite modest fluctuations, the filing trend in federal suits overall has been one of slow but rather steady decline since the peak filing year of 1975, although federal prisoner suits have begun to climb slightly since 1981. This suggests that for federal prisoners, at least, the explanation of "judicial permissiveness" may be overstated because the aggregate pattern of filings seems unrelated to judicial decisions in any single year.

Federal prisoners' civil rights complaints have never been particularly numerous. Prior to 1970, they annually comprised less than 3% of all federal prisoner filings. After 1970, however, they gradually increased from 3% to a high of 20% in 1981. Since 1981 they have tapered off. Such low activity in contrast to motions to vacate sentence and petitions for writs of *habeas corpus* suggests that federal prisoners may be less interested in changing the conditions of confinement and more interested in avoiding continued confinement. Parole, classified as "other" after 1971, constituted less than 10% of annual filings through the 1960s, and federal legislation abolishing parole will presumably phase out this category completely.

Civilian and Federal Prisoner U.S. Filings

Comparing the proportion of prisoner to civilian litigation provides a useful indicator of the relationship between prisoner and nonprisoner suits. If it is true that the U.S. is a litigious society (Lieberman, 1981), then prisoner litigation may simply reflect a broader social trend. One would therefore expect that the proportion of federal prisoner to nonprisoner filings would be fairly stable, since both would reflect similar social forces impelling litigiousness. Civilian litigation has increased five-fold between 1960 and 1984, while total prisoner filings have "only" quadrupled. From the early 1960s through the mid-1970s, the percentage of federal prisoner to nonprisoner filings slowly grew and peaked at 18% in 1974. After 1975, the proportion has steadily decreased and since 1979, federal prisoner suits have constituted less than 10% of all U.S. filings. By 1984 they dropped to 5%. The proportionate decrease of prisoner to civilian suits suggests that federal prisoners are, as a group, becoming less litigious than the general population. These data, then, do not support the contention that federal prisoner filings are "exploding" at an abnormal rate, or that federal prisoners are squeezing out civilian suits with a plethora of complaints. The curvilinear trend in the proportion of federal prisoner filings also suggests that their filings are not strongly correlated with civilian filings.

State Prisoner Filings

In contrast to multiple filing categories available to federal prisoners, state prisoners have generally filed under two categories: *habeas corpus* petitions and civil rights complaints. Together, these two categories have historically constituted nearly all private prisoner litigation (about 99% after 1976).

Looking only at total filings by state prisoners, which have increased nearly 30-fold between 1960 and 1984, it is tempting to accept critics' contentions that an epidemic of litigation is spreading from prisons. But simple tabulation conceals several important patterns.

Petitions for writs of *habeas corpus,* the most numerous of state prisoner suits from the 1960s through the mid-1970s, have declined dramatically in recent years, while civil rights complaints, especially since 1967, have increased. Three significant trends emerge. First, the decrease in *habeas corpus* filings challenging confinement indicates that state prisoners, unlike their federal counterparts, are not using federal courts simply as a "key to the front door." In contrast to federal prisoner filings, state prisoners' requests for writs of *habeas corpus* increased substantially immediately after the 1963 Supreme Court trilogy, indicating that these decisions may have had a more profound impact on state prisoner activity. However, the number of *habeas corpus* petitions began tapering off after 1970 and have continued to decrease dramatically as a proportion of all state prisoner filings. Second, civil rights suits, by contrast, did not increase substantially immediately following early civil rights decisions of the 1960s expanding prisoners' rights to petition federal courts. But they did rise immediately following the 1969 *Johnson* v. *Avery* decision, which expanded the power of jailhouse lawyers and availability of legal resources to prisoners. Third, the increase in civil rights suits, which challenge prison conditions and policies, suggests that most prisoners have accepted their confinement status and are more interested in making their environment more habitable than in overturning their original conviction. Because prisoners are filing fewer "let me out of here" complaints, it is difficult to sustain the "key to the front door" thesis.

Civilian and State Prisoner Filings

In the early 1960s, state prisoner filings as a percentage of all private filings sharply increased, from 2% in 1960 to 13% in 1966. This was in part the result of initial federal court decisions which provided access to courts, and in part the result of increasing public attention to the problems of prison conditions. There was a stability in the percentage of federal prisoner to all filings. This proportion did, to be sure, increase dramatically

between 1960 and 1965. But, since 1967, the proportion of prisoner to civil suits has remained reasonably constant, ranging between 16% and 20%. Because state prisoners and civilians are filing at a stable proportional rate, this is interpreted to mean that prisoners may import into the institution broader attitudes toward litigation as a means of dispute resolution. Hence, unlike federal prisoners, who file at dissimilar rates to both civilian and state prisoners, state prisoners and civilians may be responding to similar social factors. If true, this means the sources of prisoner litigation may be shaped by social pressures originating beyond the walls.

Annual Change in Prisoner and Civilian Filings

Another way to look at the data is to compare the changes in filing rates of federal and state prisoners with those of civilians. This provides a better picture of the relationship between prisoner litigation as a societal phenomenon. On the whole, prisoner litigation has not kept up with the civilian increase. Despite periodic fluctuations, U.S. civilian litigation has steadily increased by about 11% annually since 1966. Federal prisoner filings increased most rapidly between 1964 and 1970. On the whole, then, federal prisoner filings have in recent years been dramatically less than those of civilians. Since the peak prisoner filing year of 1975, the number of U.S.-classified civilian suits about tripled between 1976 and 1984, while the number of similar federal prisoner suits actually decreased by about 5% during the same period. In only three years since 1971 have federal prisoner suits risen at a greater rate than those of civilians. In four of those years there was a drop in filings over the previous year for prisoners, while civilian filings decreased only twice. Further, since 1971, in only one year (1981) did federal prisoner filings increase by more than 10%.

State prisoners, too, have exhibited a lower annual increase than their civilian counterparts, although the difference is not as dramatic. The greatest disparity in the filing rates between the two groups occurred in

the 1960s. Between 1960 and 1970, civilian filings increased by about one-third, while state prisoner filings increased nearly 13-fold. Between 1970 and 1984, however, this was reversed; civilian filings increased by 144%, compared with a 125% increase for prisoners. Between 1980 and 1984, civilian suits have increased far more rapidly, 44%, to only 36% for prisoners. Since 1971, the annual increase in state prisoner filings exceeded civilian suits only four times, and in only three of those years (1978, 1979, and 1981) did filings increase by more than 6% over the previous year. While the data do indicate a steady but slow increase, they provide no strong evidence to suggest that prisoners are more apt than civilians to take complaints to the courts.

Litigation and Prison Population

The demographic explanation of prisoner litigation suggests that increased prisoner filings reflect the increase in the nation's prison population. The federal prison population actually decreased by 16% between 1960 and 1969, while the number of filings nearly tripled. Hence, the population explanation does not explain the surge of filings in the 1960s. Conversely, between 1970 and 1984, federal prisoners increased by 71% while their filings increased by only 8%. If filings were directly related to an increase in the number of potential litigants, one would expect filings to roughly correspond to the increase in the population. This did not occur. Hence, filings and federal prison population are counter-cyclical.

Fact is, a similar pattern for state prisoners in the 1960s exists. The population of state prisoners gradually decreased between 1960 and 1969 by 7%. During the same period, litigation increased by 968%. After 1970, however, the number of state prisoners exploded rapidly, increasing by 144% between 1970 and 1984. The number of prisoner filings during the same period increased slightly less, by 125%. As the state prisoner population increased between 1970 and 1984, so too did prisoner filings, and at about the same rate. The demographic view, then, seems better suited to explain filing by state prisoners in the past 15 years than it does to filings by federal prisoners.

Perhaps the most powerful way to assess the so-called litigation explosion is by examining the proportion of suits filed per prisoner. This provides an indicator of the frequency of litigation relative to the entire prisoner population. The data reveal that the combined filings of state and federal prisoners tripled from about 1 to about 3 filings per 100 inmates between 1960 and 1964. After 1965, the per-prisoner filing rate rapidly expanded from nearly 4 per 100 prisoners in 1965 to about 8.5 in 1974. Since 1975, however, the combined rate, despite slight fluctuations, has decreased slightly, to less than 7% in 1984. The fact remains that, despite the increase in the national prison population, there are fewer suits per prisoner in 1984 than there were in 1969. In other words, although there are more prisoners, they are filing proportionately few suits. Hence, the increase in petitions in recent years may reflect, among other things, a larger at-risk population eligible to litigate.

Examining state and federal prisoners separately, however, shows dramatic differences. Federal prisoners are proportionately far more active in the courts than state prisoners. In 1984, federal prisoners filed over 13 suits per 100 prisoners, a substantial decrease from the early 1970s when they filed about 20 suits per 100. It is nonetheless considerably higher than the rate of state prisoners. In 1960, state prisoners filed about 1 suit for every 200 prisoners. By 1964, the year after the Monroe decision, this had quadrupled to over two suits per 100 prisoners. This ratio reached its highest level in 1981, when 7 suits per 100 prisoners were filed, but despite this single-year ratio, the trend since the mid-1970s has been one of decline in the proportion of state prisoners going to court. By 1984, about one prisoner in 20 litigated, the lowest rate since 1969. While this trend does not necessarily mean that prisoner filings and prison population are unrelated, it strongly indicates that there are other factors operating that influence filing rates.

Discussion

There can be no disputing the fact that prisoners seek relief for their problems in federal courts. The significance and causes of their litigation, however, are less certain. Several inferences may be drawn from the data presented above.

First, the factors impelling prisoners to sue are complex, and cannot easily be subsumed under a simplistic mono-causal explanation. There is no support here for psychological explanations. If this view were correct, one would have expected filings to match the increase of prisoners. There is strong evidence that most suits possess substantive, if not judicial, merit (Thomas, in press). This, coupled with shifting filing grounds, suggests that prisoners are responding to specific grievances rather than blindly following some preconditioned filing reflex. Further, since there are dramatically fewer "turn-me-loose" suits, the "front door" thesis seems simply wrong. State prisoners especially are filing fewer *habeas corpus* petitions, and are increasingly challenging such perceived problems as disciplinary proceedings, medical care, or prison violence.

The data do suggest some, albeit marginal, support for the judicial permissiveness thesis. The number of filings for both state and federal prisoners did rise dramatically in the 1960s following landmark prisoners' rights decisions. State prisoners' civil rights filings also increased dramatically after both the Cooper and the Johnson decisions in the 1960s. However, the increases began well before the decisions, indicating that the decisions may be epiphenomenal, and a contributing but not a causal factor in the increase. The past 25 years have been a time of dramatic social change, and these changes have included the manner in which rights are defined and wrongs corrected. Protest permeated virtually all levels of social life, and made itself felt in prisons. Prison protest was originally led by black Muslims, and later by jailhouse lawyers who first challenged their lack of access to law, and once access was won, then turned their energies on prison conditions. The courts have become increasingly

utilized as a means for dispute resolution: lacking internal forums, prisoners have turned to external agencies for relief. Further, despite the continued protection of prisoners' rights, there has been no surge of filings since important federal decisions of the 1970s expanded rights to health care, equal protection, access to law, limited due process in disciplinary hearings, and other broad categories. In fact, the rate of increase seems to have been stemmed, and the number of filings per prisoner decreasing. Hence, one cannot lay the "blame" for increased litigation simply on judicial expansion of prisoner rights, because the evidence generally does not corroborate dramatic increases following crucial decisions of the past 15 years. It has clearly been a factor, however, both in establishing rights to be protected and in protecting the avenues for redress.

The demographic argument also lacks support. The decrease in the national population in the 1960s led to increased suits, and the rise in the national population after 1970 resulted in fewer suits per prisoner. Hence, there must be other factors impelling litigation that are hidden behind population shifts. Because of the fluctuations in filing trends, the shifting legal theories on which prisoners sue, the expansion of specific rights through federal decisions, and the shifts in the rates of suits per prisoner, it seems that prisoners are responding to singular issues that may shift periodically.

As suggested by Kates (1984) and Thomas (1984), it appears that prisoners use suits as a form of social resistance to perceived problems in either the criminal justice system (trial or sentencing procedures, discretionary revocation of goodtime) or prison conditions (overcrowding, violence). Granted, federal courts have assisted this resistance by recognizing the need to protect the constitutional rights of prisoners, but the deeper genesis of litigation lies in broader social acceptance of civil rights for a variety of "unconventional" social groups, in the willingness of support groups to aid prisoners, and in the general social acceptance of law as a means of dispute resolution when all else fails. The shifts in the causes of action and legal theories on which litigation is based suggest as well periodic changes in the nature of complaints. This, in turn, indicates that litigation is discrete in that it is not consistently addressing a single issue, but challenges particular problems that periodically wax and wane. While the data do not fully support this view, they do seem to present sufficient evidence to suggest further research.

The data have shown that there is no evidence for continued use of the "explosion" metaphor. They also suggest that the "hyperlexis" of prisoners has been greatly exaggerated, since relatively few prisoners sue. One should also bear in mind that prisoners are a high-risk population, one whose liberty has been curtailed by law, and law thus becomes the weapon of response.

The roots of prisoner litigation are complex and not easily reduced to a single simple explanation. In rejecting the hyperlexis view, it has been suggested above that prisoner litigation might best be interpreted as a form of social resistance to prison problems. To further examine this thesis, further research should examine the specific grievances impelling prisoners to sue, and compare these complaints with the nature of the institution from which they come. It is crucial to retain the distinction between state and federal prisoners and to distinguish also between the various legal theories on which suits rest. Further, future research must examine state filing rates rather than limit analysis to aggregate national filing data. Different states may have different problems, and aggregating data at state level allows for comparing the conditions, filings, and outcomes as they vary across states and institutions.

When prisoners' rights are perceived to be violated, the courts offer an alternative to less acceptable forms of problem solving. In this paper, it has been suggested that prisoner litigation is not a pathological epidemic to be condemned. Instead, it should be viewed as a nonviolent and legitimate attempt to address specific grievances. As a consequence, prisoner litigation should be examined within the context of prison existence, sociolegal changes that expand and protect rights, and dispute resolution.

References

Administrative Office of the United States Courts. 1984. *Civil and Trials Statistical Tables, Twelve Month Periods (1960–1984)*. Washington: U.S. Department of Justice.

Allen, Karen M., Nathan A. Schactman, and David R. Wilson. 1982. Federal habeas corpus and its reform: An empirical assessment. *Rutgers Law Journal* 13: 675–772.

Alpert, Geoffrey P. 1978. The determinants of prisoners' decisions to seek legal aid. *New England Journal of Prison Law* 4: 304–325.

———. 1982. Women prisoners and the law: Which way will the pendulum swing? *Journal of Criminal Justice* 10: 37–44.

Alpert, Geoffrey P. and John Wiorkowski. 1977. Female prisoners and legal services. *Quarterly Journal of Corrections* 1: 28–33.

Anonymous. 1982. Mediating inmate lawsuits gets mixed results. *Corrections Magazine*: 46–48.

Aylward, Anmarie and Jim Thomas. 1984. Quiescence in women's prison litigation. Some explanatory issues. *Justice Quarterly* 1: 253–276.

Bator, Paul M. 1963. Finality in criminal law and federal habeas corpus for state prisoners. *Harvard Law Review* 76: 441–528.

Bedau, Hugo A. 1981. How to argue about prisoners' rights: Some simple ways. *Rutgers Law Review* 33: 687–705.

Burger, Warren J. 1976. *American Bar Association Journal* 62: 189.

Camp, George M. and Camille G. Camp. 1985. *The Corrections YearBook*. South Salem, NY: Criminal Justice Institute.

Federal Judicial Center. 1980. *Recommended Procedures for Handling Prisoner Civil Rights Cases in the Federal Courts*. Washington: The Federal Judicial Center.

Friendly, Henry J. 1970. Is innocence irrelevant? Collateral attack on criminal judgments. *University of Chicago Law Review* 38: 142–172.

Galanter, Marc. 1974. Why the "haves" come out ahead: Speculations on the limits of legal change. *Law and Society Review* 9: 95–160.

———. 1983. Reading the landscape of disputes: What we know and don't know (and think we know) about our allegedly contentious and litigious society. *UCLA Law Review* 31: 4–71.

Harriman, Linda and Jeffrey D. Straussman. 1983. Do judges determine budgets? Federal court decisions in prison reform and state spending for corrections. *Public Administration Review* 43: 343–351.

Jackson, Robert H. 1952. *Brown v. Allen*, 344 U.S. 443.

Jacobs, James B. 1982. *New Perspectives on Prisons and Imprisonment*. Ithaca: Cornell University Press.

Justice, William W. 1973. Prisoners' litigation in the federal courts. *Texas Law Review* 51: 707–720.

Kates, Erika. 1984. *Litigation as a Means of Achieving Social Change: A Case-Study of Women in Prison*. Ann Arbor: University Microfilms.

Lieberman, Jethro K. 1981. *The Litigious Society*. New York: Basic Books.

Locin, Mitchell. 1981. Prisoners filing away with suits. *Chicago Tribune*, October 18: 1–6.

Manning, Bayless. 1977. Hyperlexis: Our national disease. *Northwestern University Law Review* 71: 767–782.

Meese, Edwin. 1985a. Address of the Honorable Edwin Meese III Attorney General of the United States before the American Bar Foundation. July 9. Washington, D.C.: U.S. Department of Justice.

———. 1985b. Address of the Honorable Edwin Meese III Attorney General of the United States before Old Dominion. September. Washington, D.C.: U.S. Department of Justice.

———. 1985c. Interview: Reagan seeks judges with traditional approach. *U.S. News and World Report*, October 14: 67.

———. 1986. The law of the constitution: A bicentennial lecture. Address before the University Citizen's Forum on the Bicentennial of the Constitution. October 21.

Palmer, John W. 1986. Constitutional Rights of Prisoners. Cincinnati: Anderson.

Possley, Maurice. 1980. Inmates using an out—They sue. *Chicago Sun Times*, October 15: 20.

———. 1984. Federal trivia cases try judge's patience. *Chicago Tribune*, March 28: 1.

Reed, Anne Willis. 1980. Guilt, innocence, and federalism in *habeas corpus*. *Cornell Law Review* 65: 1,123–1,147.

Shapiro, David. 1973. Federal habeas corpus: A study in Massachusetts. *Harvard Law Review* 87: 321–372.

Suchner, Robert W., Anmarie Aylward, and Jim Thomas. 1986. Ideology and cue theory: Decision making in federal courts. Presented at the Law and Society Association annual meetings.

Thomas, Jim. 1984. Law and social praxis: Prisoner civil rights litigation and structural mediations. In S. Spitzer and A. Scull (eds.), *Research in Law, Deviance and Social Control* (Vol. VI). Greenwich, CT: Jai Press.

———. In Press. *Prisoner Litigation and Social Change*. Totowa, NJ: Allanheld.

Thomas, Jim, A. Aylward, M. Oldham, M. L. Casey, D. Moton, and G. W. Wheetley. 1985. Rethinking prisoner litigation: Some preliminary distinctions between habeas corpus and civil rights. *The Prison Journal* 65: 83–106.

Turner, William B. 1979. When prisoners sue: A study of prisoner section 1983 suits in the federal courts. *Harvard Law Journal* 92: 610–663.

U.S. Department of Justice. 1980. *Sourcebook of Criminal Justice Statistics—1984*. Washington: National Criminal Justice Information and Statistics Service.

———. 1980. *Prisoners in State and Federal Institutions on December 31, 1984*. Washington: Bureau of Justice Statistics.

Article Review Form at end of book.

135

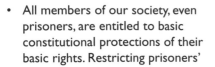

WiseGuide Wrap-Up

- All members of our society, even prisoners, are entitled to basic constitutional protections of their basic rights. Restricting prisoners'
rights and access to resources may make both prisons and society less safe while costing taxpayers more money in the long run.
- Jailhouse lawyers and other prisoner litigants provide a peaceful means of dispute resolution and a safety valve for tension and stress.

R.E.A.L. Sites

This list provides a print preview of typical **Coursewise** R.E.A.L. sites. There are over 100 such sites at the **Courselinks**™ site. The danger in printing URLs is that web sites can change overnight. As we went to press, these sites were functional using the URLs provided. If you come across one that isn't, please let us know via email to: webmaster@coursewise.com. Use your Passport to access the most current list of R.E.A.L. sites at the **Courselinks** site.

Site name: Death Row Inmate Webring

URL: http://www.geocities.com/CapitolHill/Senate/5831/

Why is it R.E.A.L.? This site is a link to sites such as Families Outside the Walls, Norwegians Against Death Penalty, NuHearts & Another Side of Justice, and Members in Spirit.

Key topics: battered women's syndrome, capital punishment, miscarriages of justice, overcrowding

Try this: See if the families outside the walls of prison are presenting accounts that any reasonable person could accept or are they making things up?

....

Site name: FindLaw—U.S. Supreme Court Decisions

URL: http://www.findlaw.com/casecode/supreme.html

Why is it R.E.A.L? Most U.S. Supreme Court decisions of this century can be found here, including civil rights decisions affecting prisons and prisoners, and law firm offices across the country. A powerful search engine simplifies finding cases by key words. Pretend you have a friend who needs a criminal lawyer.

Key topics: battered women's syndrome, interrogation, law, prisoner rights, prosecution, miscarriages of justice

Try this: Click on this site and find the name and address of the criminal lawyer nearest you.

....

Site name: Critical Criminology Division of the American Society of Criminology (ASC)

URL: http://www.soci.niu.edu/~critcrim/prisons/prisons.html

Why is it R.E.A.L.? This site has many statistics for U.S. jails and prisons, but for the most part, Illinois prisons and minority prison populations are discussed. There are many Illinois links to items like wrongful convictions of individuals on death row.

Key Topics: capital punishment, miscarriages of justice, prisoner rights, victimization

....

section

5

Key Points

- Rehabilitation is an aim of many criminal justice programs.

- Most rehabilitation programs punish offenders while providing treatment.

- It is difficult to gauge the needs of various offenders.

- Treating offenders is in the best interest of society, the offender, and the offender's family.

- A society's overriding belief about punishment will dictate the types of programs available for offenders.

Rehabilitation and Treatment

Brian Payne Ph.D. Department of Sociology & Criminal Justice; Old Dominion University; Norfork, VA USA [bpayne@odu.edu]

Rehabilitation conjures up various images to various people. This is due in part to the controversies surrounding rehabilitation programs as well as the way the concept itself is interpreted. Basically, rehabilitation can be one of three things. First, it can be viewed as a process in which specific treatment programs are applied to offenders throughout the world in an attempt to treat the cause of the offenders' misconduct. Second, it is a discipline of study in that social workers, counselors, and social scientists participate in determining the programs that work best for various offenders. Third, it is a goal of the justice processes along with other goals: deterrence, retribution, incapacitation, and restitution.

Though it is a distinct goal, it is one that overlaps with the other goals. That is, people who are successfully treated will be deterred from future crimes, in an environment in which the offender is punished, and perhaps even removed from society. Or, one who is successfully treated will not commit future offenses and likely "paid for" the offenses during the treatment process. This ambiguity often makes it difficult to evaluate the effectiveness of various treatment programs. Also, it is important to note that reliance on treatment and rehabilitation programs directly relates to a culture's overriding philosophy of punishment. In the United States, for example, rehabilitation and treatment ideologies permeated policies throughout the sixties until the Martinson report challenged the effectiveness of such programs despite his retraction. A conservative shift in the political arena then led to less confidence in and reliance on these programs until recently. Other cultures show similar cycles.

The pervasive theme that permeates rehabilitation policies and research is that certain rehabilitation and treatment programs will work under the right conditions. Indeed, as will be shown in this section, different programs work better for different offenders. What works best for whom is an important question addressed by Immarigeon. The need to address women's treatment needs is considered by Atkinson and McLean, who illustrate that until recently this area has received relatively little attention. Zaitzow's article addresses this gap in the correction's literature by examining specific needs of female inmates and shows that attention to these needs increases the likelihood of successful rehabilitation. The Association for the Treatment of Sexual Abusers suggests that utilizing hormonal agents, anti-androgens, and surgical castration in the management of sexual abusers continues to be an area of concern and attention for many, including sexual abusers and the general public, while Stevens addresses the issue of education as one method of reducing

How do we know if a rehabilitation program has been successful?

Compare and contrast the treatment needs of sexual and violent offenders?

How are women's treatment needs different from men's treatment needs?

Describe the type of treatment program you would design for juvenile offenders.

Should society be concerned with rehabilitating offenders? Why? Why not?

recidivism levels among prisoners. Serin and Brown examine the rehabilitation needs of violent offenders in the next article. Finally, the need to include rehabilitation programs for juveniles is addressed in a separate reading by Krisberg. The important point to keep in mind is that although all programs may not work for all offenders, the programs can succeed in assisting the justice system in meeting the rehabilitative, retributive, and deterrent ideals of justice.

? Questions ?

Reading 26. Which treatment programs have been the most successful? Why don't some programs work?

Reading 27. What program was used to treat women convicted of fraud? How were the women selected for the program?

Reading 28. What are the treatment needs of women? How are women's needs different from men's needs?

Reading 29. Can sexual offenders be treated? Why should we treat sexual offenders?

Reading 30. In what way would education impact recidivism levels among prisoners? Why?

Reading 31. Can violent offenders be treated? Should the victim be involved in the treatment?

Reading 32. How are juvenile programs different from adult programs? What is it about a culture's history that leads to the development of juvenile corrections programs?

Which treatment programs have been the most successful?
Why don't some programs work?

What Works?

Russ Immarigeon

Russ Immarigeon lives in Hillsdale, N.Y., and writes on criminal justice and child welfare issues. He co-edits the SUNY Press book series, "Women, Crime and Criminology."

The 1990s are restless, often despairing times in criminal justice. Sensational newspaper and television stories can topple promising innovations. Misleading headlines can also give impetus to political movements that hamper meaningful criminal justice operations. The specter of unsupervised parolees committing horrendous crimes or allegations that prison inmates are lounging in luxury at taxpayers' expense are never helpful to rational criminal justice policy-making.

Political leaders routinely fight one another to see who is the toughest on crime. Little media attention is given to how criminal justice agencies actually operate or what they need to accomplish their mission. Instead, piecemeal, ill-considered "remedies" are imposed on criminal justice systems; systems then adapt to these mandates.

Academic and popular commentary on the state of criminal justice in America is eerily congruent. Sociologist Herbert Gans argues that the threat of crime in our communities has created, among the lower and working classes as well as the middle class, a public mood that supports increasingly punitive criminal sanctions that promise little

more than criminal displacement or isolation.

David C. Anderson, former editorial page writer for *The New York Times* and *The Wall Street Journal*, is decidedly more despondent about the public mood. Anderson argues that expressive justice ("laws, policies, and practices that are designed more to vent communal outrage than to reduce crime") has grasped control of criminal justice in the United States. Another journalist, Wendy Kaminer, agrees that, as far as crime policy and practice are concerned, substance seems irrelevant.

Searching for What Works

"There ain't no success stories in prison," says an inmate in Jerome Washington's *Iron House: Stories from the Yard*. That also can be the case for most of the men and women sentenced to incarceration or community corrections in the United States. Yet, how many success stories emerge from these confined or otherwise often punitive experiences? Almost 20 years ago, a research group hired by the New York state Legislature claimed that Washington's maxim holds as true for intervention programs as for inmates. Robert Martinson, one member of the research team, boldly stated that "Nothing works!"

Martinson's salvo gave the media a mask to hide behind when it failed to examine firsthand the work-

ings of correctional rehabilitation programs, and it abetted the political retrenchment of public funds from rehabilitation programs behind as well as beyond prison walls. It also propelled the correctional research community into action. Several researchers, with Stuart Adams and Ted Palmer leading the counterattack, issued important challenges to Martinson's imprecise assertion. Within several years, Martinson himself would retreat from his original statement. Later, Francis Cullen and Karen Gilbert would argue that rehabilitation is valuable because it is the only justification for humane state intervention, its purpose is supported regularly by public opinion polls and it counters harsher approaches to criminal sanctioning.

But the damage was done. Thereafter, little attention was given to the question, "What works?" Throughout the 1980s and early 1990s, however, as penal populations and community corrections caseloads grew, the "What works?" question attracted increasing attention from researchers and policymakers alike. An impressive literature has been published by Canadians such as Don Andrews, James Bonta and Paul Gendreau and by Americans such as Alan Harland, Phil Harris and Peter Jones. New Zealander Kaye McLaren has examined extensively the characteristics of programs that reduce reoffending. Last year, National Development and Research Institutes (NDRI), a New York City-based research group, began a three-year

What Works? by Russ Immarigeon. *Corrections Today*, December 1995, 57(7), 8. Reprinted with permission of the American Correctional Association, Lanham, MD.

project to complete a comprehensive review of all evaluations conducted since 1968 assessing the effectiveness of jail, prison, and community corrections interventions. In short, NDRI will review what has happened since Martinson's exaggerated assault on correctional programming.

What We Know

The "What works?" literature is quite extensive and is growing at a rapid pace. Generally, more meta-analysis of the existing research literature is occurring than original research on the impact of particular program or penalty interventions. Recent literature reviews, however, are extremely relevant for program development, and practitioners and policymakers are, at best, neglectful if they do not consider the findings of these reviews. Often, they reveal that much of current correctional policy is simply headed in the wrong—and ultimately costly—direction.

Kaye McLaren's and Paul Gendreau's research indicates some of what is known about what works in correctional interventions. McLaren, a policy and research analyst with the New Zealand Department of Justice, reports that "there is a significant body of evidence for the existence of a small but significant group of correctional interventions which have been effective in reducing re-offending. "Successful interventions," she says, "share certain common components, and together these components form a set of principles of effectiveness which can be applied to many types of intervention." These principles, she adds, are useful in community and residential settings.

McLaren identifies "principles of effectiveness" that include the following factors:

- a social learning approach that assumes attitudes and behavior can change if noncriminal attitudes and behaviors are introduced and reinforced;

- clear, consistent rules and sanctions to make legal sanctions certain and understandable;

- illustration of and support for noncriminal attitudes and behaviors;

- practical problem-solving skills;

- positive links between community and program resources;

- relationships between staff and offenders that are open, emphatic, warm, trusting and encouraging of noncriminal attitudes and behaviors;

- advocacy for offenders and brokerage with community resources;

- use of ex-offenders as positive role models;

- offenders' involvement with the design of specific interventions;

- staff focus on strengthening pro-social and noncriminal behavior rather than stopping antisocial and criminal behavior;

- offender peer groups directed toward reinforcing antisocial and noncriminal behavior;

- sound theoretical knowledge and adequate resources to apply appropriate principles of effectiveness;

- multiple methods of intervention rather than reliance on narrowly based interventions;

- emphasis on relapse prevention and self-efficacy; and

- matching individual offenders with specific interventions.

McLaren notes that none of these principles are set in stone, yet they do provide direction for program design that is based on experience and has passed some evaluative muster. Understanding of what works is evolving and, in fact, the ability of a program to reevaluate and revise its forms of intervention also is critical for program success.

Paul Gendreau, a professor of psychology at the University of New Brunswick, also has reviewed the literature and, like McLaren, he adds that it is as important to identify what does not work as it is to clarify what does work, at least in certain circumstances.

Gendreau agrees with McLaren about the positive influence of directing intensive services to high-risk offenders, the matching of offenders and interventions, the importance of disrupting criminal networks and providing relapse prevention, and

the value of advocacy and brokerage services. However, Gendreau also identifies "principles of ineffective intervention," which include traditional psychodynamic therapies, non-directive relationship-oriented therapies, radical non-intervention and traditional medical model approaches, the use of intensive services with low-risk offenders, and clinical approaches that encourage externalizing blame to parents and others, venting anger or ignoring the impact of their crimes on the victims.

Significantly, Gendreau finds that many of the so-called "punishing smarter" strategies do not work. Such interventions include boot camps, electronic monitoring, longer periods of incarceration, urinalysis, humiliation and shock incarceration. Many of these options are politically popular and more likely to receive scarce state or federal funding, but Gendreau's findings, which are supported by other research, colorfully illustrate the frustration of many observers that programs receive political support more for the appearance than the reality of working.

"When it comes to putting offenders in programs," says McLaren, "it's a case of one size doesn't fit all." McLaren recommends three approaches to offender placement— "put offenders in programs that address problems they actually have, put offenders with more severe problems into more intensive programs, and choose programs that fit into what's known about the most effective way to impact a given problem."

Making Things Work

Certainly, measuring recidivism is important. Offenders who do not recidivate commit no further crimes, or at least no detected crimes. However, measurements of recidivism too frequently assume that the interventions they assess were properly designed, skillfully implemented or actually determined behavioral change. Design, implementation and causal factors suggest that it is important to look beyond recidivism to qualitative aspects of the processes that produce behavioral change. Indeed, it is important to look beyond criminal justice interventions to see whether any other life-course events were responsible for the changed behavior.

The factors for what makes programs work outlined by McLaren, Gendreau, and others can be found in interventions associated with correctional options programs. In the following pages: (1) a New York community service program illustrates the effectiveness of limiting correctional intervention to clear and concise requirements that staff and offenders can work together to achieve; (2) a review of programming for female offenders suggests the utility of matching individual offender needs with specific program interventions; and (3) a review of two states' approaches to restorative justice demonstrates that victim, offender, and community involvement in criminal justice decision-making helps create a strong, supportive environment for the use and growth of correctional options.

Community Service

Community service sentences are options that impose unpaid hours of labor on offenders who work for government or private, not-for-profit community or neighborhood groups. In the United States, community service sentences were first used in 1968 for offenders convicted of driving violations. More than 25 years later, no statistics are available in this country that give an accurate overview of the extent and nature of use of these penalties. Moreover, the use of community service usually is enmeshed in poorly focused or overly optimistic statements of purpose. Little evaluation has been done to see what impact community service sentences have on the offenders serving them, the communities obtaining free penal labor or the criminal justice systems that increasingly impose them.

Community service sentences initially were viewed with caution as well as with enthusiasm. Critics were as likely to support the option as they were to raise questions about its application. Some critics claimed that community service was a form of penal servitude; others worried, with good reason as it turns out, that community service sentences were widening the net of social control. More recently, critics have raised questions about the utility of commu-

nity service as a method of achieving offender accountability, a concept that is rarely defined with much cogency. Also, critics say that the term "community service" is a misnomer that belittles the voluntary community service performed by millions of Americans not involved with the criminal justice system. In other words, community service should be restricted to the worthy, not the unworthy, among us. Community service has nonetheless become a routine judicial sentencing option in most jurisdictions.

The Center for Alternative Sentencing and Employment Services (CASES) in New York City runs one of the country's best-known community service programs, the Community Service Sentencing Project (CSSP). CASES was founded in 1989 when community service and court employment programs operated and evaluated by the Vera Institute of Justice merged to form the new agency. CASES handles lower-end felons who complete 70 hours of community service over two-week periods at work sites throughout the city. Most of these sentences were imposed in lieu of 30 to 90 days of jail time.

The CSSP, recently cited in *USA Today* as "a model of the way it ought to be run," is distinguished by its concise use of community sentence work and the clarity of its operations. Unlike most community service penalties or programs, CSSP manages and supervises the same 70-hour work period for all clients in the program. Throughout the program's history, supervisors have regularly informed judges about the program's selection criteria, supervision process, and enforcement mechanisms. The program takes a "just deserts" approach, matching a specific penalty to a particular goal, reducing the incarceration of petty, persistent property offenders.

"In order to maintain the integrity of the sanction," says Joseph Singleton, an associate director at CASES, "CSSP's intake criteria is selective and the sentence is enforced through compliance activities, a warrant execution capacity and re-sentencing procedures." What makes this program work is a combination of formal and informal operating procedures.

The CSSP places court representatives in courtrooms in four boroughs of New York City. Each day, these representatives size up the daily court docket, looking for eligible offenders. After offenders are identified, they are interviewed briefly. Then, the court representative appears at sentencing to let the court know the program is willing to accept offenders sentenced to 70 hours of community service. The program does not accept clients with other formal conditions of probation.

"Compliance monitors start each day at the same time our enforcement officers start," Singleton says. "They call all participants in the program at seven o'clock in the morning, wake them up, remind them of their obligations and make sure there are no problems hindering their arriving at their work site."

"It doesn't take too much for many of them to not go in," Singleton observes, mindful of the limited work habits and histories of program participants. The program provides offenders with bus or subway tokens to travel to and from the work site each day, and the program has an 800 number for participants to call if problems arise or they cannot appear. If offenders have substance abuse, housing, child care or other problems that put them at risk of not showing up, support service coordinators ask them what they need and bring them to where they can get help.

Correctional Options for Female Offenders

Several years ago, Meda Chesney-Lind and the author reviewed available statistics, program descriptions and research evaluations for a report, "Women's Prisons: Overcrowded and Overused," published by the National Council on Crime and Delinquency. What we found then holds regrettably true today: The population in women's prisons is rising at a rate greater than increases in the male population, most of the new women entering prisons are nonviolent property and drug crime offenders, and relatively few programs are available in the community to effectively divert women from incarceration. We also found, with a few exceptions, that women offenders receive little attention from probation and parole agencies, corrections departments, and legislative or judicial review committees when it comes to developing community-based sanctioning programs or prison overcrowding remedies.

A major step in developing programs that work for female offenders is recognizing the need for such programming. One stumbling block is the lack of empirical evaluations of the few programs that are working with female offenders and their families. The author spoke to a half dozen leading practitioners and researchers, and all expressed concern about the paucity of evaluation in the field of female offender programming.

A second important step is understanding why it is useful to establish female-specific programming. Nearly all practitioners who work with female offenders say that one fault of many of these programs is that they are based on models that are used with men. Often this is done because administrators, perhaps leery of an equal protection law suit, mistake difference for discrimination, equity with equality. A key lesson, program operators assert, is that women are different from men and require different forms of programming that address their needs and situations. Programs must know who they are working with and design interventions that directly address their individual situations.

Barbara Bloom, a California-based criminal justice consultant and author of *Why Punish the Children?*, reports that programs for female offenders often fail because they do not conduct assessment studies to identify the needs of these women and the services that are available to them. Programs that address perceived rather than real needs may be gender-specific, she says, but they are not individually specific; therefore, they run the risk of being duplicative, irrelevant or otherwise unnecessary.

Lessons learned from specific programs often can be helpful to others. Bloom notes, for instance, that if programs have insufficient autonomy over such matters as which offenders can be selected for their treatment intervention and which behaviors will be defined as rule violations, then these programs likely will lose sight of their original goals and objectives.

Parenting and other programs for women located in women's prisons run the risk, she says, of being identified by female offenders as part of prison management, thereby erecting a significant barrier to the desired delivery of services.

Creating the opportunity structure for interventions that work with and for female offenders requires a supportive policy environment and carefully designed programs. Two years ago, Sherry Haller, executive director of a Hartford, Conn., advocacy and public policy group, pulled together six practitioners and policy analysts to identify "the critical experiences of the female offender population (particularly as victims of sexual abuse and domestic violence), and the relationship between these experiences [and] their criminal behaviors, addictions, and abilities to serve as the primary caregivers to their children." In an unpublished report, Hallet and her colleagues identify not only a continuum of sanctions for female offenders, but also an array of supportive roles that can be played by policymakers, criminal justice administrators, municipal leaders, citizens, and social service providers.

Finally, and perhaps most important, programs designed for female offenders must confront a conundrum rarely faced squarely: Women often are physically and mentally healthier and safer inside prison than they are in the community. But women are not imprisoned for protection; their incarceration is meted out as punishment. And punishment, studies by Gendreau and others seem to show, is what works least, especially for women. So, the challenge for program designers is to create community-based programs that address the myriad needs of female offenders in a safe and nurturing environment.

Restorative Justice

Restorative justice is rapidly paving paths into the mainstream of not only sanctioning theory, but sanctioning practice, as well. Restorative justice practices, such as victim-offender reconciliation, the use of community boards and restitution programming, originate in biblical traditions. In recent years, however, religion-based organizations such as the Mennonite Central Committee Office of Criminal Justice and the Justice Fellowship have written extensively about the foundations of restorative justice, and they have managed programs based on restorative justice principles, the most notable of which are victim-offender reconciliations programs.

A central dynamic of restorative justice is that most punishment-oriented practices—the widespread use of imprisonment, for example—have failed because they do not meaningfully include victims and offenders in making decisions about criminal sentences. In essence, restorative justice builds on several principles of effective intervention, including self-management and control, problem-solving, and attitude changes.

"Restorative justice," notes Kay Pranis, the Minnesota Department of Corrections' restorative justice planner, "is not a program or a specific set of programs. It is a way of thinking about how to approach the problem of responding to crime, a set of values which guides decisions on policy, programs, and practice. Restorative justice is based on a re-definition of crime as injury to the victim and community rather than affront to the power of the state. The primary purpose of the criminal justice system in the restorative justice model is to repair the harm of the crime to the degree possible."

Mark Umbreit, among others, has conducted important research on restorative justice interventions. Specifically, in juvenile offender cases, Umbreit found that victim-offender mediation was experienced as a demanding sanction, satisfying to victim and offender alike. Use of this sanction seemed to reduce victims' fears and, at least slightly, reduce offender recidivism within one year of the victim-offender meeting.

Communities are now organizing around restorative justice in two states. In Minnesota, the Department of Corrections has a restorative justice planner who is working with communities, victims groups, and corrections managers to inform them about the nature and implementation of restorative justice. In Vermont, with support from a Correctional Options grant, the Department of Corrections is now implementing statewide use of reparative sanctions.

In 1990, the Minnesota Citizens Council on Crime and Justice and several religious groups organized a conference to explore the restorative justice concept. Shortly thereafter, the council conducted a public opinion survey that found sizeable support for reparative sanctions. A public education campaign reached out to inform key community leaders. Independently, the Minnesota Department of Corrections also was examining restorative justice. In 1991, the Department of Corrections and the Citizens Council joined together in their efforts. Late in 1992, a statewide conference drew the attention of many middle-level correctional managers. Feedback from this conference encouraged further state pursuit of restorative justice options.

The Vermont Department of Corrections recently restructured its mission to increase community participation in the development and operation of sentencing options. A major tenet of this restructuring is that the role of state government is to serve and support local communities, and local communities, in turn, are to serve and support individuals and families. Restorative justice, through the work of community reparative boards, is intended to act as the "lynch-pin" of this significant reform.

Reparative probation brings offenders face to face with community members at a meeting that is designed to establish a negotiated agreement detailing a plan for offenders to repay victims and the community. A public opinion survey laid a firm foundation for the program: 75 percent of those surveyed wanted an overhauling of the criminal justice system; 92 percent wanted property offenders to repay their victims; strong support was evident for giving community work assignments instead of jail time for drunk drivers, drug users, shoplifters, and others; strong support also existed for using community reparation boards to monitor such sentences; and support was even evident for using community sanctions with repeat offenders.

"Vermonters want to be actively involved," says Project Director Michael J. Dooley. "They want punishment to focus on opportunities and means for offenders to repair injuries and damages they caused."

Reparative probation is one method Vermont has designed to sanction low-risk offenders who commit crimes of lesser severity. Whereas high-risk, violent offenders are channeled into a risk-management track that incorporates intensive interventions, reparative probation is designed to "repair the damage done to victims." Once adjudicated guilty, offenders in this program are given a probation sentence that is suspended using an administrative probation order that imposes the condition of completing the Reparative Probation program. Offenders appear before community reparation boards, which are composed of five local citizens. Together, the board and the offender devise a plan to restore and make whole the victims of crime, make amends to the community, learn about the impact of crime on victims and communities, and learn ways of avoiding new offenses. Aspects of these plans can include community service work, restitution, victim-offender mediation, decision-making programs, skills development and others. All conditions must be completed within 90 days, when the board can discharge successfully completed cases.

Despite seemingly utopian brush strokes, restorative justice options are susceptible to both monitoring and evaluation. The Minnesota effort, for example, has already identified "benchmarks" for the effective use of restorative justice intervention. These benchmarks include the degree of available victim services, the opportunities for victim and offender participation, the encouragement of offenders to take personal responsibility for their actions, the extent of community involvement in decision-making and the development of connections between citizens and criminal justice professionals. Some care must be given to the forms of monitoring and the methods of evaluation, but restorative justice interventions can nonetheless be measured and reviewed in an accountable fashion.

Conclusion

Correctional options programs offer the promise of a broad range of alternatives for criminal justice systems historically lacking choices among

In 1990, the U.S. Congress authorized the Correctional Options Program in response to the pervasive problem of prison and jail crowding and the high recidivism rate of youthful offenders incarcerated in traditional correctional institutions. With this authorization, the Bureau of Justice Assistance (BJA) was charged with providing financial and technical assistance to public agencies and nonprofit organizations to deal with these issues.

The BJA has defined correctional options as cost-effective interventions that reduce reliance on traditional modes of incarceration while, at the same time, enhancing the reintegration of offenders into the community. These interventions include community-based alternatives to incarceration, institution-based treatment or training programs, early release for offenders with intensive re-entry services and supervision or a combination of such programs.

The BJA has structured the program in three parts. Part I grants encourage the development and implementation of innovative correctional options within existing correctional systems. Part 2 grants support nonprofit organizations providing research, training, and technical assistance in coordination with correctional options projects. Part 3 grants support innovative boot camps that further the program's goals.

the penalties they mete out to criminal offenders. However, concentration on politically popular options is short-sighted unless greater attention is given to a broader conceptualization of not just the range of available alternatives, but also the use of specific forms of intervention with individual offenders. No intervention, however well designed and implemented, is appropriate for everyone. Moreover, as research shows, it is frequently the case that less restrictive interventions are more effective than sanctions that sound tougher and more punitive.

Two points require emphasis. First, no effort to establish effective programs or sanctions can thrive without meaningful assessment and evaluation research. Research is necessary not only to determine specific outcome measures, but also to design program services and determine who is eligible for particular programs. The Vera Institute of Justice regularly compiled and reviewed arrest history and other data on jail-bound offenders in New York City before it opened the doors to its community-service program. Research continued as the program was implemented, and program administrators were given up-to-date information on such matters as the average number of prior offenses held by offenders before they are given jail time. This information determines the program's selection criteria.

Finally, a policy development process is essential if a jurisdiction hopes to maximize its use of correctional options by creating a supportive environment for these programs. Recently, in Vermont, Gov. Howard Dean told a gathering of corrections professionals of his concern that one bad experience with an offender in a community-based program could destroy the state's entire reparative justice initiative.

The Center for Effective Public Policy has pioneered an intermediate sanctions process that includes creating a group of high-level policy-makers; establishing educational, data-gathering and decision-making processes to guide the group's deliberations; emphasizing the use of local resources to meet specific policy objectives; and implementing determined policies and sanctions. Crucial to this process, the center affirms, is the commitment of policymakers to become and remain a part of the decision-making and implementation, and the availability of the staff, time, and fiscal resources to properly support the actions and agenda of the policy group. Whether states follow these guidelines or they inform all concerned constituencies before implementing programs and policies, as Vermont has done, there are clear-cut ways to ensure that correctional options not only can work but that they also can be allowed to improve over time.

References

Anderson, David C. 1995. *Crime and the politics of hysteria: How the Willie Horton story changed American Justice.* New York: Times Books.

Cullen, Francis and Karen Gilbert. 1982. *Reaffirming rehabilitation.* Cincinnati: Anderson Publishing Co.

Gans, Herbert. 1995. *The war against the poor: The underclass and antipoverty policy.* New York: Basic Books.

Kaminer, Wendy. 1995. *It's all the rage: Crime and culture.* Reading, Mass.: Addison-Wesley.

McKnight, John. 1995. *The careless society: Community and its counterfeits.* New York: Basic Books.

Washington, Jerome. 1994. *Iron house: Stories from the yard.* Fort Bragg, Calif: QED Press.

This project was supported by Grant No. 94-DD-CX-K007 awarded by the Bureau of Justice Assistance, Office of Justice Programs, U.S. Department of Justice. The Assistant Attorney General, Office of Justice Programs, coordinates the activities of the following program offices and bureaus: Bureau of Justice Assistance, Bureau of Justice Statistics, National Institute of Justice, Office of Juvenile Justice and Delinquency Prevention, and Office for Victims of Crime. Points of view in this article are those of the author and do not necessarily represent the official positions or policies of the U.S. Department of Justice or the American Correctional Association.

 Article Review Form at end of book.

What program was used to treat women convicted of fraud? How were the women selected for the program?

Women and Fraud:

Results of a Program at the Prison for Women

Jill Atkinson[1]
and Heather McLean[1]

Psychology Department, Prison for Women

Although there is much literature on group programs for women in prison,[2] little is known about the effect of such programs on recidivism. Most studies show differences in measures of self-esteem, institutional behaviour, alienation, and trust in others before and after treatment.[3] Only a handful of studies have followed their participants to determine effects on recidivism. Of these, one failed to find differences between control and experimental groups,[4] one had a follow-up period of only 90 days,[5] and one used an inadequate measure of recidivism (parole officers' estimates of recidivism over seven years).[6]

There are a few published reports of group programs for women convicted of shoplifting and theft. These, however, are fraught with the same problems noted above: they show no treatment effectiveness, use no objective measures, or have inadequate or no follow-up.[7] Finally, there is no published literature on the treatment of fraud offenders.

Why a Program Specific to Fraud Offenders?

The impetus for the program came in part from the women themselves, who voiced concern that their needs were not being met by regular psychological services. Because most of these women neither created institu-

tional difficulties nor had much need for crisis intervention, few received individual counselling.

In addition, group programs dealing with anger control, substance abuse, cognitive skills and educational or vocational training, while designed to meet the needs of many women, are not appropriate for most female fraud offenders, who are more likely to be educated, drug-free, socially skilled, stably employed and of average to above-average intelligence.[8]

Nevertheless, these women pose a significant problem—their fraud is typically chronic and results in multiple incarcerations. The costliest of property crimes, fraud is also the fastest growing offence in Canada for both men and women. While receiving only 17% of all charges in Canada, women account for 27% of all fraud charges.[9]

Given the unique needs of fraud offenders, their growing numbers and our limited resources, a short-term group program was chosen as the most cost-effective intervention.

The Program

According to clinical assessments, female federal fraud offenders differ from other federally incarcerated women. Using these clinical data, the Psychology Department at the Prison for Women developed a model of the historic or familial development of chronic fraud, as well as the current

functional relationships that maintained the behaviour. The curriculum was based on the principles used in relapse-prevention programs for people with addictions as well as on the tenets and process guidelines of feminist therapy. However, the model of feminist therapy was expanded to incorporate the history of the participants because many had not been abused by men, but virtually all had been abused by their mothers.

A more detailed description of the curriculum, model, homework assignments, group objectives and related materials is available.[10]

Program Parameters

Three groups were conducted at approximately six-month intervals. In all, 19 women attended: 6 in the first group, 8 in the second, and 5 in the third. One woman did not complete the sessions because of an untimely transfer; thus 18 women completed the program.

The program was initially designed as eight sessions but was expanded to nine for the first group. Subsequent groups attended 10 sessions, each lasting two hours.

The women signed consent forms so that we could use pre- and post-test data for research. The women were also informed that they would be contacted discreetly for follow-up information 6, 12 and 18 months after the program was completed, but they could decline to participate in that phase.

Women and Fraud: Results of a Program at the Prison for Women, J. Atkinson and H. McLean. *Forum on Corrections Research*, 6(7), 1994, 39–41.
Reprinted by permission of the Correctional Service of Canada.

Program Evaluation

We hypothesized that, as a result of the fraud group program, the women would improve their assertiveness and self-efficacy. To assess this, we administered two psychometric measures before and after the program. One was the Interpersonal Behavior Survey,[11] which samples subclasses of assertive behaviours. This survey is useful in outcome evaluation because it measures change. The second measure was the Subjective Rating of Likelihood to Reoffend Scale, which samples participants' sense of self-efficacy in avoiding reoffending. It is a single seven-point scale that participants use to rate the likelihood of their reoffending.

To obtain family background and demographic information, we administered two measures before the first session. One was the Parental Bonding Instrument,[12] which measures parental care and overprotection in childhood. We used this instrument to test our hypothesis that female fraud offenders would describe their mothers as cold and overly concerned with appearances. The second measure was a Background Information Questionnaire, which records demographic variables such as age, race, number of children, number of offences, educational attainment and marital status.

Finally, after completing the program, women filled out a Program Evaluation Questionnaire, which rates the program's curriculum and relevance, as well as the performance of the group leaders.

General Findings

The results from the three groups participating in the fraud program were mixed. While group one showed reliable treatment gains, the two subsequent groups did not. When data on the measures of assertiveness and likelihood to reoffend were combined across all three groups, however, treatment effects were evident: women showed significant improvements in assertiveness and increased confidence in their ability to avoid reoffending.

On the measure of parental bonding, participants rated their mothers as significantly more reject-ing and controlling than community norms for women.

On the Program Evaluation Questionnaire, women rated their satisfaction with, and the usefulness of, the program as very high. Many women commented, however, that the program should be longer.

Longitudinal Follow-Up Information

The women were contacted at 6- and 12-month intervals after completing the program. We collected information on reoffending and then compared the scores of women who reoffended with those of women who did not. None of the pre-program, post-program or change measures discriminated between recidivists and non-recidivists at any point after release.

Although there are several possible explanations for this failure to show treatment-related reductions in recidivism, three seem particularly plausible. First, 10 sessions is likely not intensive enough an intervention for repeat federal offenders without follow-up sessions in the community.

Second, group one, which showed the greatest treatment gains, was the most homogeneous group: all of the women had histories of fraud offences only. Some of the women in groups two and three, however, had committed other offences as well to sustain a drug habit.

Third, the failure to find a treatment effect could have been due to the general nature of the measures used. To explore the latter possibility in future research, we added a test before group three to assess how well the women could apply the course content to their own offence patterns, identify their individual high-risk situations, and think of alternatives to criminal behaviour. This knowledge-acquisition test is similar to those currently used in the evaluation of relapse-prevention programs.

Unfortunately, we are presently unable to determine whether the recidivism rates for participants were lower than recidivism rates for other female fraud offenders with similar chronic histories. If and when recidivism data for female offenders become available by offence, the recidivism rates of women who par-ticipated in the fraud program could be compared with those of similar women who did not.

The absence of recidivism data for female offenders presents a serious obstacle to an evaluation of any group program for women in prison. It is likely, however, that this problem will be resolved by current Canadian efforts to obtain these data, at both the federal and provincial levels.[13]

Conclusion

The Women and Fraud program at the Prison for Women has generated new information about the dynamics of women's fraud offending. The program was useful to the women themselves and an exciting step forward in gathering knowledge about a specific subgroup of incarcerated women.

Notes

1. Jill Atkinson and Heather McLean, Psychology Department, Prison for Women, Correctional Service of Canada, P.O. Box 515, Kingston, Ontario K7L 4W7.
2. For a review see K. Kendall, *Literature Review of Therapeutic Services for Women in Prison,* Companion Volume 1 to *Program Evaluation of the Therapeutic Services at the Prison for Women* (Ottawa: Correctional Service of Canada, 1993).
3. R. J. Homant, "Ten Years After: A Follow-up of Therapy Effectiveness," *Journal of Offender Counseling, Services, and Rehabilitation,* 10 (1986): 51–57. See also F. E. Sultan and G. T. Long, "Treatment of the Sexually/Physically Abused Female Inmate: Evaluation of an Intensive Short-term Intervention Program," *Journal of Offender Counseling, Services, and Rehabilitation,* 12 (1988):131–141.
4. Homant, Ten Years After: A Follow-Up of Therapy Effectiveness.
5. D. W. Edwards and G. A. Roundtree, "Assessment of Short-term Treatment Groups with Adjudicated First Offender Shoplifters," *Journal of Offender Counseling, Services, and Rehabilitation,* 6 (1981): 89–102.
6. J. W. MacDevitt and G. D. Kedzierzawski, "A Structured Group Format for First Offense Shoplifters," *International Journal of Offender Therapy and Comparative Criminology,* 34 (1990): 155–164.
7. Sultan and Long, Treatment of the Sexually/Physically Abused Female Inmate: Evaluation of an Intensive Short-term Intervention Program. See also Edwards and Roundtree, Assessment of Short-term Treatment

Groups with Adjudicated First
Offender Shoplifters. And MacDevitt
and Kedzierzawski, A Structured
Group Format for First Offense
Shoplifters.

8. D. Zietz, *Women Who Embezzle or
Defraud: A Study of Convicted Felons*
(New York: Praeger Publishers, 1981).
See also J. L. Atkinson and H. McLean,
"Women and Fraud: The Prison for
Women's Treatment Program for
Female Federal Fraud Offenders,"
unpublished manuscript, Prison for
Women, Kingston, Ontario.

9. A. Hatch and K. Faith, "The Female
Offender in Canada: A Statistical
Profile," *Canadian Journal of Women and
the Law*, 3 (1989): 432–456.

10. Atkinson and McLean, Women and
Fraud: The Prison for Women's
Treatment Program for Female Federal
Fraud Offenders.

11. P. Mauger, D. Adkinson, S. Zoss, G.
Firestone and D. Hook, *The Interpersonal
Behavior Survey* (IBS) (Los Angeles:
Western Psychological Services, 1980).

12. G. Parker, H. Tupling and L. B. Brown,
"A Parental Bonding Instrument,"
British Journal of Medical Psychology, 52
(1979): 1–10.

13. Jim Bonta of the Policy Branch, Public
Security Canada, is completing a
database for federally sentenced
women. Grant Coulson and Verna
Nutbrown of the Vanier Correctional
Centre for Women have developed a
provincial database for female
offenders.

 **Article Review
Form at end of
book.**

What are the treatment needs of women? How are women's needs different from men's needs?

Treatment Needs of Women in Prison

Barbara H. Zaitzow

Appalachian State University

Introduction

Ideally, jailing or imprisoning women is meant to exact retribution for their crimes and rehabilitation of their character; the majority of these women eventually return to society. In practice, however, the problems prevalent in most women's correctional facilities negate any real effectiveness in their stated goals. On the contrary, the one thing incarcerated women can look forward to once the door closes behind them is being transformed from offenders into victims. This chapter focuses on the paradox of incarcerated women as criminals and victims. Issues related to the programmatic needs and availability of treatment programs for women offenders are discussed. Recommendations for change are put forth in which treatment is advocated as a viable option for offenders who are interested in positive change in their lives.

Sykes (1958) described the pains of imprisonment for men as the deprivation of liberty, the deprivation of goods and services, the deprivation of heterosexual relationships, the deprivation of autonomy, and the deprivation of security. All these deprivations apply equally to female prisoners, and some may be more severe for women (Carlen, 1994). An obvious example is separation from

one's family. Women may also suffer from receiving fewer leisure, work, and educational opportunities and closer surveillance than men.

Women's prisons increase women's dependency, stress women's domestic rather than employment role, aggravate women's emotional and physical isolation, jeopardize family and other relationships, engender a sense of injustice (because women are denied many of the opportunities available to male prisoners), and may indirectly intensify the pains of imprisonment. The irony of this situation is that the majority of women currently housed in institutions throughout the United States will be released from confinement and expected to fit in to mainstream society. Without providing these women the necessary social skills with which they may become viable contributors to society, their chances for successful assimilation as well as day-to-day survival will be impeded. Thus, a reevaluation of the purpose(s) of imprisonment as well as consideration of the unique needs of women offenders is long overdue.

Historical Overview of the Treatment of Women in Prison

The history of penology in this country presents a dismal picture of the treatment of all criminal offenders. Until penal reforms were instituted in the mid-nineteenth century, men, women, children, mentally ill per-

sons, and every form of degenerate were frequently locked up together. No consideration was given to age, type of offense, or circumstance (Pollock-Byrne, 1990). Since women's crimes were predominantly restricted to sex offenses and drunkenness, a criminal woman was considered disgraced, dishonored, and pathetic (Giallombardo, 1966:7). Women involved in criminal offenses were not considered dangerous, and often their male partners took the total blame, thus precluding their imprisonment (Chandler, 1973:3). Prisons were seen as places to exact retribution or restitution for misdeeds. The concept of rehabilitation—making positive changes in offenders in order to restore them to society as useful members—was late in coming.

This notion of rehabilitation has undoubtedly been the single most damaging influence on female corrections, largely because the idea of "treatment" for women entailed the fostering of sexual morality, the imposition of sobriety, the instilling of obedience, and the prescribing of the sex-role stereotype of mother and homemaker, rather than addressing treatment needs (Chandler, 1973:7; Freedman, 1981).

Social-Sexual Environment

The reformists demonstrated their philosophy in the architecture of prisons for women. Instead of the massive fortress-like penitentiary housing used for men that had high concrete walls, armed personnel, and gun towers, the "domestic model" for women provided each woman her own room in "the home":

"The home" planned for women was a cottage that was built to house twenty to thirty women, who could cook their own food in a "cottage kitchen." Several similar cottages would be arranged in quadrangles on green, tree-filled lawns. The cottages in most states were built to contain a living room, dining room and one or two small reading rooms. The idea was that a domestic atmosphere would help the women learn the essential skills of running a home and family. (Burkhart, 1973:367)

This was the first "cottage" penal facility for women. Since that time three additional types of women's prisons have developed. The "campus" plan is designed to resemble a college campus. Grass and trees surround numerous buildings, each with separate functions and separated by grassy court areas. In the "complex" model, several buildings that may contain one or more functions such as living areas, dining halls, vocational training facilities, or classrooms cluster around the central administration building. The "single-building" style consists of one major facility that houses all of the prison functions (Glick and Neto, 1977:20).

Deception in Prison Appearance

On the surface, most women's prisons are more attractive than men's. Some have been converted from country mansions or children's homes, and the obvious aspects of security (such as gun towers) are often lacking. Indeed, prison departments have recognized that for women, security considerations do not loom so large because there is less public anxiety and fear when women escape from custody. Most women's institutions retain the traditional categories of minimum, medium, and maximum security differentiated by the degree of surveillance, the number of security-check body counts, the frequency of room searches or "shake downs," freedom of movement, and architectural design. The most desirable type of incarceration, minimum security, allows freedom for a number of activities within the prison

schedule and rules. However, most women's prisons are medium security, which are more restrictive than minimum security institutions but permit more freedom than close custody or maximum security facilities (Stephan, 1992). Close custody means that inmates must be escorted at all times by a custody officer for daytime activities such as meals, group sessions, and counseling, and they are barred from participation in night activities. The small proportion of dangerous women, estimated at 5 percent to 8 percent, is found in strict custody under the highly controlled environment known as maximum security. In addition to the more dangerous inmates, women under death sentences are also confined to maximum security. Temporary maximum security may be imposed on women who are dangerous to themselves or others because of emotional disturbance. This status is also used to punish rule breaking.

Although women can wear their own clothes and decorate their rooms, facades are deceptive. In many ways female prisoners are worse off than their male counterparts. As the inmates point out, there is only the appearance of a campus. Repression is every bit as strong as in men's prisons; it is simply more subtle. In fact, inmates have referred to the social control in women's prisons as "pastel fascism," control glossed over and concealed by a superficial facade of false benevolence and concern for the lives of inmates. What few possessions they have are often confiscated or destroyed, and they are subject to arbitrary body searches at any time (Velimesis, 1972; personal communications with women inmates housed in a maximum security prison in the southeast, 1994 and 1995). When women in prison fail to conform to expectations, physical control is quickly instituted. For example, on Christmas day, 1975, all 700 women inside the California Institute for Women were locked in their cottages and not allowed on the grounds. The majority were denied holiday visits from family and friends. All tours of the institution were also canceled. A rebellion had occurred a week earlier in response to the cancellation of prison holiday plans and a special Woman's Day. So-

called instigators of the rebellion were put in solitary confinement ("An Inside View," 1976:2).

In recent years, women inmates have begun to use litigation to remedy the institutional abuses that they have been subjected to. For example, indictments were filed against ten male and four female employees at the Georgia Women's Prison in 1992 after ninety inmates alleged that they had been victims of a variety of forms of sexual abuse (including rape, exchange of sex for favors and/or retaliation for refusal to participate, coerced into prostitution as well as forced to have abortions when sexual activity between officers and women inmates resulted in pregnancy). The Georgia case is not uncommon, and serious cases have been brought to the attention of the media and the courts in a number of states (Wilson, 1992).

Entry into Prison

The objectives of the correctional system and the crimes of female offenders notwithstanding, once women enter institutions they often go from being victims of justice to victims of injustice. Cruel and unusual punishment is not supposed to exist today; however, one would never know it by observing life in a women's penal facility.

After arriving at her assigned correctional home, the new female prisoner must go through a series of orientation or "get-acquainted" procedures. She may come in handcuffed and be refingerprinted and photographed for institutional records. She soon loses all remaining dignity when she is stripped and searched for contraband, showered, and issued prison attire and bedding. Over the next two to six weeks the incarcerated woman, who is segregated during this period, goes through medical and psychiatric examinations for everything from venereal disease to mental illness.

By the time she joins the general prison population, she has been instilled with the extensive rules and regulations of her confinement, including her new status of "institutional dependency." Although women's prisons are usually not the maximum security fortresses that men's prisons are, some suggest that the rules women must abide by are stricter (Carlen, 1994). These rules and regulations, as well as disciplinary actions for infractions, vary from one institution to another.

Many female inmates view the rules and regulations of prisons as willful efforts to "diminish their maturity" by "treating them like children and fostering dependency" (Mann, 1984:210). An example of such a rule is found at the Pennsylvania State Correctional Institution for Women, where inmates are required to "recite the Lord's Prayer in unison at bedtime" (Deming, 1977:159). The reality of women's prisons is that they create just as much frustration and pain as men's prisons (Giallombardo, 1966:Ch. 7; Freedman, 1981; Rafter, 1990).

The Perpetuation of Dependency Among Women Inmates

Much of the treatment and control of women in prison is premised on the individualization of women's problems. The women are typically characterized as having in some way "failed" to meet their adult responsibilities. While the prison administrators and staff recognize that many of the problems experienced by the women are endemic to their social situation outside prison, they argue, perhaps quite reasonably, that there is little they can do about the wider social problems of poverty, inadequate housing, and unemployment. On the other hand, many stress that a number of the problems presented by the women reflect personal limitations that could be effected by staff intervention, either by means of education and training or by personal interaction and informal counseling. Here, a shared objective of staff is to encourage a degree of self-confidence among the women and to help them cope with the difficult decisions they face in their outside lives.

There is, however, an inevitable contradiction here, in that the ordered regimes governing prison life inevitably deny women choice over even the most trivial aspects of day-to-day living. They are told what time they will get out of bed; what time they will take their meals; when they will read, write letters, or watch television; and at what time they will again be in bed with their lights out. Indeed, there are few areas of prison life in which the women are encouraged, or indeed able, to take responsibility for making decisions (Clark, 1995:312). Regardless of their age, women prisoners have the status of schoolgirls. This is powerfully brought home by the practice in some establishments of calling all women "girls," irrespective of their age, and of addressing female staff members as "miss." Many inmates are not allowed to see their children or families and, in fact, often lose custody of their children. At some places, children under eighteen are not allowed to visit at all. Furthermore, just as in male prisons, the arbitrary and capricious nature of parole boards wears down inmates' ability to be self-reliant and to plan a constructive program for themselves that would lead to their release.

Historically, the dominant model of training was domestic: the socialization of women to their traditionally accepted roles. The emphasis, therefore, was on gardening and housework, and instruction was provided in needlework, cookery, child care, and dressmaking. Rafter (1985:174) makes an interesting point in this context. She refers to the work of such writers as Foucault (1977), who argue that imprisonment was economically useful to capitalism. But whereas imprisoned men did provide a source of cheap labor, the institutions for women functioned to keep women *out* of the industrial labor force. When training was given to women, it paralleled as nearly as possible the work that the women would do on release—namely, domestic work. The prison commissioners, in their report for 1945, summed up this objective well: Training should be directed toward "better housewives rather than better housemaids. Every aspect of domestic work, whether in shops or in the service of prison, should be made to serve one idea—that of instilling into the women the ideas of a good home and how they may best be achieved" (Commissioners of Prisons, 1947:73). The objective was to turn female inmates into decent housewives and good mothers. This emphasis continues today (Fletcher, Shaver, and Moon, 1993).

Programs

Since there are so few women's prisons, women of all ages and all crimes are thrown together. The population is also much more heterogeneous than in men's prisons, where there is the opportunity for some degree of classification. Classification systems serve two purposes: to provide the type of security arrangements necessary to protect society, and to consider the personal characteristics of the individual insofar as these may reflect possibilities for training. But most jurisdictions have few institutions for women, and so in effect women remain unclassified. In contrast, an effort is made to separate experienced male offenders from the less dangerous. Hence the majority of women experience the rules and restrictions necessary only for the minority (Feinman, 1994).

In women's prisons there is little provision for work or education, primarily because of the domestic ideology that permeates the regimes. In the words of Dobash, Dobash, and Gutteridge, "the emphasis which predominates implies that the failure of women prisoners is their failure as wives, mothers and housekeepers" (1986:182). In practice, work is geared to the maintenance of the institution and seems to have little positive purpose. This is not to say that work is good in men's prisons, but there are clear differences in emphasis.

Vocational Programs

Vocational education and training for women in many women's institutions or women's divisions of men's prisons are very limited (Moyer, 1992). Female inmates who already have advanced education have little use for the educational programs that may be offered, and there is no avenue for them to make use of their academic skills (for example, as teachers). Conversely, no special programs or incentives are available for female prisoners who are educationally handicapped, mentally retarded, or simply uninterested, assuming such women could be identified.

Vocational training programs that do exist usually are in such traditionally female areas as sewing, clerical skills, food services, and cosmetology. Even in the larger women's institutions, no more than two or three programs are offered, and these are virtually always geared toward preparing women in a domestic or otherwise "women's" capacity. While such training may result in the cost-efficient maintenance of the prison, it does not address or prepare women inmates' need to be self-supporting upon release (Durham, 1994).

The scarcity of vocational and rehabilitation programs for female prisoners can usually be attributed to one of the following:

- Such programs are not cost-effective as there are so few female prisoners.

- Financial expenditures are unwarranted for female inmates who pose less of a threat to society than their male counterparts.

- There is a low rate of women's participation in such programs.

- Many female correctional facilities are inaccessible.

- Women are still regarded foremost in the traditional roles of housewife and mother.

Consequently, legislators and corrections officials continue to give full priority to men's vocational programs while teaching women merely to cook, sew, and clean (Haft, 1974; Feinman, 1994). Unfortunately, this gives women, especially those serving long sentences, few or no opportunities to learn new skills or earn enough money to aid their families on the outside.

Vocational programs in correctional institutions are not impressive in overall quality. For the most part, the instructors are poorly trained, use out-of-date equipment, and teach nonmarketable skills. Several factors deter the development of more effective vocational programs: The equipment necessary for many of the programs is considered too costly in most correctional systems; the inmate's average term of two or three years is too short for the completion of apprenticeship require-

ments for most trades; overcrowded conditions often result in waiting lists for training programs; and the debilitating conditions of prison life discourage offenders from participating in training until it is too late for them to learn enough to make participation worthwhile (Conrad, 1983). But even with up-to-date equipment and good instructors, inmates often have difficulty in gaining admission into labor unions in the free community and in persuading private industry to hire them.

Educational Programs

Academic education is offered in most women's prisons. Remedial education is prevalent, and basic courses leading to an elementary education or a high school diploma are commonly provided. Some prisons offer college curricula leading to the associate of arts degree or, more rarely, to the bachelor of arts. Most states offer college courses to women inmates either through correspondence courses or in conjunction with nearby colleges (Pollock-Byrne, 1990).

Adult education courses that are offered include subjects such as consumer education, family life education, child development, and personal grooming. While such courses are undoubtedly useful, they also indicate sexual stereotyping. Evidence that such courses are associated with the traditional roles of housewife and mother is seen when these educational courses for women are compared with the social education programs common to men's educational curriculum. These recent trends in correctional education for men are "specifically geared to reorienting the incarcerated or community treated offender with the normative and socially acceptable attitudes and values of free society" and include major areas such as "improving communication skills, personal management, personality development, social and family relationships, laws, and economic issues" (Roberts, 1971:131). Social values are instilled with a goal of restructuring an inmate's attitudes, values, and orientations to societal institutions and undoing years of "negative acculturation."

However, no mention is made of efforts toward these ends in the

studies of women's prisons. Instead, the roles of mother, homemaker, and successful shopper are perpetuated in the few adult education courses available in women's institutions.

Defining Correctional Treatment

When correctional treatment is discussed, terms such as *humanitarian reform, corrections, rehabilitation,* and *treatment* are often used interchangeably, creating some confusion as to exactly what correctional treatment involves. Also at issue is the part played by incarceration and mandatory supervision in the correctional treatment process. However, for the sake of simplicity, correctional treatment may be defined as any planned and monitored program of activity that has the goal of rehabilitating or "habilitating" the offender so that she or he will avoid criminal activity in the future. Unfortunately, the implementation of various rehabilitative programs has typically involved only the male population; women offender's unique needs have been ignored.

Rehabilitation of Offenders

Perhaps more studies have been directed toward determining the effect of prison rehabilitation programs than any of the other justifications for imprisonment. The accumulated empirical evaluations of these programs have proved disappointing for advocates of rehabilitation. The widely circulated assessment by Martinson and his colleagues (1974) has been verified in large measure by a subsequent Panel on Research on Rehabilitation Techniques organized by the National Research Council of the National Academy of Sciences (Lipton, Martinson, and Wilkes, 1975; Sechrest, White, and Brown, 1979). The panel drew the following conclusions:

The current state of knowledge about rehabilitation of criminal offenders is cause for grave concern, particularly in view of the obvious importance of the problem. After 40 years of research and literally hundreds of studies, almost all the conclusions that can be reached have to be formulated in terms of what we do not know. The one positive conclusion is discouraging: the research methodology that has been brought to bear on the problem of finding ways to rehabilitate criminal offenders has been generally so inadequate that only a relatively few studies warrant any unequivocal interpretations. The entire body of research appears to justify only the conclusion that we do not know of any program or method of rehabilitation that could be guaranteed to reduce the criminal activity of released offenders. Although a generous reviewer of the literature might discern some glimmers of hope, those glimmers are so few, so scattered, and so inconsistent that they do not serve as a basis for any recommendation other than continued research.

Furthermore, a more penetrating inquiry into the nature of the problem of rehabilitation and the programs and methods that have been tried leads to the conclusion that there is even less in the research than meets the eye. The techniques that have been tested seem rarely to have been devised to be strong enough to offer realistic hope that they would rehabilitate offenders, especially imprisoned felons. In general, techniques have been tested as isolated treatments rather than as complex combinations, which would seem more suited to the task. And even when techniques have been tested in good designs, insufficient attention has been paid to maintaining their integrity, so that often the treatment to be tested was delivered in a substantially weakened form. It is also not clear that all the theoretical power and the individual imagination that could be invoked in the planning of rehabilitative efforts have ever been capitalized on. Thus, the recommendation in this report that has the strongest support is that more and better thinking and research should be invested in efforts to devise programs for offender rehabilitation. (Sechrest et al., 1979:3–4)

Faced with such discouraging assessments, many policy analysts urged abandonment of rehabilitation as an organizing objective of the prison system. In most maximum security prisons, of course, the small number of programs designed to deal with the rehabilitative needs of the inmates often served as showpiece programs that cast a rhetorical gloss of rehabilitation over a basically punitive custodial system. A national survey of correctional administrators, however, indicates that the vast majority are not prepared to give up rehabilitative programs altogether (Cullen, Latessa, Burton, and

Lombardo, 1993). They appear convinced that such programs will work for subgroups of offenders with both the need and motivation to take advantage of them. Furthermore, such programs offer some relief from the personally destructive features of prison life: the debilitating idleness; loss of autonomy and ability to exercise initiative; the latent and overt threats of force and violence; and the routinization, monotony, and regimentation of activities and relationships.

The efforts to create academic and vocational training opportunities, self-help programs for drug abusers, individual and group therapy and counseling possibilities, and paid work in prison industries also serve an important symbolic function. They express confidence and hope in the ability of people to change when they become motivated to seek new directions in their lives. They embody a continuing faith that such directions are never fully determined by the past. Prison administrators now appear more inclined to make participation in such programs voluntary rather than mandatory as a condition for release on parole. It appears that in the prison world, the rehabilitative ideal is not dead so much as reduced in expectation to accord more fully with the realities and limitations of the prison experience.

We are left then with many questions about such programs: What types of programs are likely to be most successful? What types of inmates respond effectively to the different types of programs that can be made available? What types of measures best reveal the changes attributable to the programs? What effect do such changes have on recidivism rates or other indicators of postprison adjustment? What kinds of continuing support during the postrelease period are needed to sustain the changes achieved and their effect on future criminality? What types of research procedures must be instituted to determine what works and what does not?

Individual Counseling

There have been two studies of the effects of individual psychotherapy on young incarcerated female offenders, and both of them (Adams, 1959; Adams, 1961) report no signifi-

cant effects from the therapy. But one of the Adams studies (1959) does contain a suggestive, although not clearly interpretable, finding: If this individual therapy was administered by a psychiatrist or a psychologist, the resulting parole suspension rate was almost two-and-a-half times *higher* than if it was administered by a social worker without this specialized training. Thus, social workers were significant contributors to the administration of individual psychotherapy.

Group Counseling

Group counseling has indeed been attempted in correctional institutions, both with and without a specifically psychotherapeutic orientation. Most research on the use of psychotherapy within a correctional setting has been conducted with male samples. The few and dated studies with females, however, are worth noting.

Adams's (1959) research on individualized treatment for women inmates found that there was nothing gained from treating females by group rather than individual methods. A study by Taylor of borstal (reformatory) inmates in New Zealand (1967) found a similar lack of any great improvement for group therapy as opposed to individual therapy or even to no therapy at all. But the Taylor study does offer one positive finding: When the "group therapy" participants *did* commit new offenses, these offenses were less serious than the ones for which they had originally been incarcerated.

There is a third study that does report an overall positive finding as opposed to a partial one. Truax, Wargo, and Silber (1966) found that females subjected to group psychotherapy and then released were likely to spend less time reincarcerated in the future. But what is most interesting about this improvement is the very special and important circumstance under which it occurred. The therapists chosen for this program did not merely have to have the proper analytic training; they were specially chosen for their "empathy" and "nonpossessive warmth." In other words, it may well have been the therapists' special personal gifts rather than the fact of treatment itself that produced the favorable result.

Common Elements of Effective Programs

The most effective treatment programs appear to have a number of common elements. First, many of these programs are set up by inspired and dedicated leaders. Second, the programs commonly transmit a philosophy of life that generates a sense of mission or purpose among offenders. Third, they usually have a unified treatment team. Fourth, they generally entrust offenders with some decision-making responsibilities. Fifth, they usually help offenders develop skills that make them believe they can do something or that they have mastered some important insights about themselves or life. Sixth, the most effective programs are often unique. Seventh, successful community-based institutional programs avoid alienating formal decision makers. Resistance to administrators is usually costly to institutional programs, and good public relations is a critical factor in the survival and development of community-based programs. Finally, effective programs have adequate community support networks.

Sometimes the basic element in an effective program is thought to be the charismatic and inspired leader who can persuade others to accept whatever he or she has to offer, regardless of the program structure. This viewpoint reflects a psychological reductionism that claims that effective programs are established and sustained only through the initiative and commitment of such inspired persons. Effective programs, however, depend on a variety of interrelated factors in addition to effective leaders, such as receptive clients, adequate funding, compliant organizational-environmental structures, and acceptance within the larger political and correctional community.

The task of correctional research today is to determine the effect of the interrelationship between leadership and program structure in various types of settings, to ascertain whether different styles of leadership are needed to implement and conduct effective programs in community-based and institutional settings, to identify the components that are intrinsic to effective programs, and to weigh the effect of the interrelationships among the common elements of effective programs.

Recommendations for Correctional Treatment

To expand the role of, and to improve the services of, correctional treatment in the future, several recommendations are in order:

1. Involvement in treatment should be entirely voluntary. Participation, or the lack of participation, in these programs should not be related to the length of institutional stay or to the length of supervision in community programs.

2. Adult inmates should have the opportunity to become involved in meaningful and adequately paid work during incarceration.

3. Both juvenile and adult inmates should have the opportunity for some degree of self-governance during confinement.

4. Safe environments must be provided for institutionalized offenders. Only when inmates feel safe can they be concerned about much more than personal survival.

5. A variety of programs should be offered in correctional institutions. These interventions should be grounded on good program design, implemented with program integrity, and evaluated on an ongoing basis with sophisticated research methods.

6. More care must be taken to ensure that common elements of effective programs thrive in correctional environments.

7. A progressive array of services must be established for offenders in the community. Such a network of support services, as therapeutic communities have demonstrated, is imperative to improve the positive impact of correctional treatment.

8. Career and economic incentives must be made available for persons who have the motivation and skills to become effective treatment agents so that they will be persuaded to seek out such employment and to stay involved in correctional service.

9. Only through well-planned and soundly executed research can further development of treatment concepts and practices take place; therefore, research on correctional treatment must be given a much higher priority than it is presently accorded.

The future of correctional treatment ultimately depends on three factors: funding research, so that more effective technologies can be developed for the treatment process; the identification of what works for which group of offenders, so that offenders interested in treatment can be given the interventions most compatible with their needs and interests; and the creation of more humane correctional contexts, so that the environment will not interfere with the treatment process.

The United States is not a pacesetter for corrections and has not been for a long time; contentment with warehousing offenders will put our nation back in the Dark Ages of corrections. Considerable fanfare went into the burial of treatment in the mid-1970s, although treatment programs continue to exist in community and institutional settings. We need to put the same burst of energy into reemphasizing treatment, not as a panacea or as a condition of release, but as a viable option for those who are interested in change, growth, and positive movement in their lives. Anything less will be cruel and unusual punishment.

Toward Change

Changes in women's prisons are more apparent in the United States than in other countries. In 1964, the Supreme Court ruled that state prisoners could sue state officials in federal courts for the denial of their constitutional rights. Since then, the courts have upheld prisoners' rights in such areas as the need to maintain a law library, limits on censorship of mail, and procedural fairness in prison discipline. Most of the litigation has been based on two constitutional amendments: the Fourteenth, which guarantees equal protection of the law, and the Eighth, which prohibits cruel and unusual punishment. For example, the court held that prisoners in a women's jail in San Francisco must be allowed to participate in a work furlough program from which they had been excluded. Other cases have given reasonable parity with male prisoners in vocational training, apprenticeship programs, medical care, educational programs, work-release opportunities, and access to legal materials. A class action suit by women in a New York county jail resulted in a judgment that it was unconstitutional for the conditions of imprisonment for women to be inferior to those of male prisoners.

It is questionable, however that achieving parity with men's prisons is the best solution. These institutions are themselves in considerable need of reform. Nor would complete equality be entirely beneficial for women. To attempt to eradicate gender differences within prisons while they persist in the outside world makes little sense. For example, the fact that women continue to be responsible for child care means that prison programs should be designed to take this into account (see Baunach, 1985, for examples of programs that are geared toward female prisoners increasing contact with their children).

An alternative approach in the United States was the establishment of co-correctional institutions. In the mid-1970s, there were over twenty co-correctional state and federal institutions, but, since then, more than half have reverted to one-sex institutions. Co-correctional institutions have a variety of objectives: to reduce the dehumanizing and destructive aspects of confinement, to reduce institutional control problems (that is, to reduce assaultive homosexuality and violent behavior), to provide a more normal atmosphere, to aid the prisoner's adjustment on release, to obtain economies in staffing and in the provision of training programs for both male and female prisoners, and to expand the career opportunities for female correctional officers. Although coed prisons increase social opportunities for male prisoners, they have yet to generate similar advantages for female inmates because they offer no additional program resources or operational adaptations (Smykla and Williams, 1995).

Co-correctional institutions are not without their critics. Crawford (1980), for example, draws attention to the fact that they still have a disproportionately male population. This has two consequences: It destroys any separate programming for women and forces them into programs designed to meet the needs of male prisoners, and the atmosphere in co-correctional prisons continues the exploitation by men that many of the women in institutions previously experienced in the outside world. According to Crawford, the real reasons behind the move to co-corrections are money, overcrowding, and the need to smooth out the operation of *men's* institutions. They do not meet the unique and special needs of female offenders. Instead, she proposes mother-child institutions. Another critic (Schweber, 1984) makes much the same point. She believes that men continue to dominate higher status positions and occupational courses in the institutions and proposes instead what she calls the "co-ordinate" prison. This means that the women's prison is separate but shares programs and services with a nearby male facility.

Heidensohn (1985) has argued that the prison system was designed to deal with men, but discussions of, for example, the merits of the "classic" silent versus the separate system were not geared toward one particular sex. Rather, their adoption resulted from beliefs about the best way to mold the *human* spirit. Also the domestic and psychiatric ideologies that have permeated the regimes of women's prisons indicate that special account was taken of female prisoners. The real difficulty is that stereotypical assumptions have been made about the characteristics of female prisoners and hence about their "needs." We clearly need to know much more about who these women are. Only then can we design a coherent policy for dealing with them.

No one can argue with the necessity of prisons and jails for people who commit crimes, even women. However, although incarceration is not a picnic for anyone (nor, some argue, should it be), clearly on a collective basis female inmates are a great deal worse off than male inmates. For one thing, it is arguable that many of these women should be in prison at all. Often their biggest crime seems to be trying to feed their families or having the misfortune to be pregnant or nonwhite. Outdated rules and regulations, poor diet, neglectful health care, degradation, lack of vocational training and recreational facilities, exploitation, abuse, and unsanitary conditions typify the conditions in many prisons and jails that house women. Reform is needed both within the correctional system and in a society that condones inhumane treatment of women prisoners.

References

Adams, S. (1959, March 6). "Effectiveness of the Youth Authority Special Treatment Program: First Interim Report." *Research Report No. 5*. California Youth Authority.

Adams, S. (1961, January 31). "Assessment of the Psychiatric Treatment Program, Phase I: Third Interim Report." *Research Report No. 21*. California Youth Authority.

Baunach, P. (1985). *Mothers in Prison*. New Brunswick, NJ: Transaction Books.

Burkhart, K (1973). *Women in Prison*. Garden City, NY: Doubleday.

Carlen, R (1994). "Why Study Women's Imprisonment? Or Anyone Else's?" *British Journal of Criminology*, 34:131–139.

Chandler, E. W. (1973). Women in Prison. Indianapolis: Bobbs Merrill.

Clark, J. (1995). "The Impact of the Prison Environment on Mothers." *Prison Journal*, 75:306–329.

Commissioners of Prisons. (1947). *Report for the Year 1945*. London: HMSO.

Conrad, J. (1983). "Correctional Treatment." *Encyclopedia of Crime and Justice*. New York: Macmillan.

Crawford, J. (1980). "Two Losers Don't Make a Winner: The Case Against the Co-Correctional Institution." In J. Smykla (ed.), *Co-ed Prison*. New York: Human Sciences Press.

Cullen, F. T., Latessa, E. J., Burton, V. S., and Lombardo, L. X. (1993). "The Correctional Orientation of Prison Wardens: Is the Rehabilitative Ideal Supported?" *Criminology*, 31:85.

Deming, R. (1977). *Women: The New Criminals*. Nashville, TN: Thomas Nelson.

Dobash, R., Dobash, R., and Gutteridge S. (1986). *The Imprisonment of Women*. Oxford: Basil Blackwell.

Durham, A. M. (1994). *Crisis and Reform: Current Issues in American Punishment*. Boston: Little, Brown and Co.

Feinman, C. (1994). *Women in the Criminal Justice System*. Westport, CT: Praeger Publishers.

Fletcher, B. R., Shaver, L. D., and Moon, D. G. (1993). *Women Prisoners: A Forgotten Population*. Westport, CT: Praeger Publishers.

Foucault, M. (1977). *Discipline and Punish: The Birth of the Prison*. London: Penguin Press.

Freedman, E. (1981). *Their Sister's Keepers: Women's Prison Reform in America, 1830–1930*. Ann Arbor: University of Michigan Press.

Giallombardo, R. (1966). *Society of Women. A Study of a Women's Prison*. New York: Wiley.

Glick, R. and Neto, V. (1977). *National Study of Women's Correctional, Programs*. Washington, D.C.: U.S. Government Printing Office.

Haft, M. (1974). "Women in Prison: Discriminatory Practices and Some Legal Solutions." *Clearinghouse Review*, 8:1–3.

Heidensohn, F. (1985). *Women and Crime: The Life of the Female Offender*. New York: New York University Press.

"An Inside View of CIW." (1976, February). *Sister Newspaper*. Venice, CA: The Women's Center.

Leonard, E. (1983). "Judicial Decisions and Prison Reform: The Impact of Litigation on Women Prisoners." *Social Problems*, 31:1, 45.

Lipton, D., Martinson, R. M., and Wilkes, J. (1975). *The Effectiveness of Correctional Treatment: A Survey of Treatment Evaluation Studies*. New York: Praeger.

Mann, C. R. (1984). *Female Crime and Delinquency*. University, AL: University of Alabama Press.

Martinson, R. (1974). "What Works: Questions and Answers About Prison Reform." *Public Interest*, 35:22–54.

Moyer, I. L. (1992). *The Changing Roles of Women in the Criminal Justice System* (2d. ed.). Prospect Heights, IL: Waveland Press.

Pollock-Byrne, J. M. (1990). *Women, Prison, and Crime*. Belmont, CA: Wadsworth.

Rafter, N. (1985). *Partial Justice: Women in State Prisons 1800–1935*. Boston: Northeastern University Press.

Rafter, N. (1990). *Partial Justice: Women, Prisons and Social Control* (2d. ed.). New Brunswick, NJ: Transaction.

Roberts, A. S. (1971). *Sourcebook on Prison Education*. Springfield, IL: Charles C. Thomas.

Schweber, C. (1984). "Beauty Marks and Blemishes: The Co-Ed Prison as a Microcosm of Integrated Society." *The Prison Journal*, 46:1, 3.

Sechrest, L., White, S., and Brown E. (1979). *The Rehabilitation of Criminal Offenders: Problems and Prospects*. Washington, D.C.: The National Academy of Sciences.

Smykla, J., and Williams, J. (1995). "Co-Corrections in the United States of America, 1970–1990." In J. Smykla and J.

Williams (eds.), *Women and Criminal Justice*.

Stephan, J. (1992). "Census of State and Federal Correctional Facilities, 1990." Washington, D.C.: Bureau of Justice Statistics:8.

Sykes, G. (1958). *The Society of Captives*. Princeton, NJ: Princeton University Press.

Taylor, A. J. W. (1967). "An Evaluation of Group Psychotherapy in a Girls' Borstal." *International Journal of Group Psychotherapy*, 2:168–177.

Truax, C. B., Wargo, D. G., and Silber, L. D. (1966). "Effects of Group Psychotherapy with High Adequate Empathy and Nonpossessive Warmth upon Female Institutionalized Delinquents." *Journal of Abnormal Psychology*, 4:267–274.

Velimesis, M. (1972). *Women in County Jails and Prisons*. Philadelphia: Pennsylvania Program for Women and Girl Offenders.

Wilson, T. (1992, November 16). "Ga. Indictments Charge Abuse of Female Inmates." *USA Today*:3A.

 Article Review Form at end of book.

Can sexual offenders be treated? Why should we treat sexual offenders?

Anti-Androgen Therapy and Surgical Castration

Adopted by the ATSA Executive Board of Directors on February 7, 1997

Utilizing hormonal agents, anti-androgens and surgical castration in the management of sexual abusers continues to be an area of concern and attention for many including re-searchers, clinicians, program admin-istrators, legislators, sexual abusers, victims of sexual abuse, as well as the general public. The Association for the Treatment of Sexual Abusers holds that:

- Organic treatments have been used to reduce the sexual drive of some sexually aggressive males and other paraphiliacs whose inability to control their behavior leads to repeated occurrences of sexually deviant behavior.

- The role of sexual motivation varies among abusers; therefore, the reduction of sexual drive would be of limited usefulness for some abusers.

- Anti-androgen therapy should be prescribed by a physician only after an extensive offense-specific evaluation has been completed.

- Not all abusers are the same and anti-androgen therapy is not appropriate for use with all sexual abusers. It is important to develop ordered and reasonable criteria based on diagnosis, history, motivation, and risk when prescribing the medical intervention.

- Anti-androgen medications carry some medical risk; therefore, the treatment should only be administered under ongoing medical supervision.

- Anti-androgen treatment should be coupled with appropriate monitoring and counseling within a comprehensive treatment plan. An abuser should be involved in concurrent cognitive-behavioral treatment designed to address other aspects of the deviant behavior in addition to sexual interests. These medications should never be used as a sole method of treatment.

- As with any treatment intervention, appropriate informed consent must be obtained when anti-androgen therapy is implemented.

- The effect of surgical castration is to reduce the availability of androgen by removing the testes where approximately 95% of the testosterone is produced. Although it seems reasonable and has, in fact, been shown that surgical castration may reduce paraphiliac fantasies and behaviors, there are alternative and less invasive treatments available.

- ATSA is opposed to surgical castration procedures based on the availability of anti-androgen medications which can achieve the same, if not better, results.

- A substantial percentage of surgical castrates retain sexual functioning. Even if an abuser's capacity to have an erection or ejaculate is permanently inhibited, the act of sexual aggression many times involves more than the use of the penis and those behaviors would not be affected.

- Replacement androgens can be obtained after the surgical castration procedure, taken as a supplement to restore testosterone levels to pre-castration levels, thus nullifying the effects of the surgical castration.

Anti-Androgen Therapy and Surgical Castration. Adopted by the ATSA Executive Board of Directors, 1998. Association for the Treatment of Sexual Abusers, 10700 SW Beaverton-Hillsdale Highway, Suite #26, Beaverton, Oregon 97005–3035. Phone 503–643–1023. e-mail: atsa@atsa.com

Bibliography

Berlin F. S. & Meinecke C. G. (1981). Treatment of Sex Offenders with Antiandrogenic Medication: Conceptualization, Review of Treatment Modalities and Preliminary Findings. *American Journal of Psychiatry* 138, 601–607.

Bradford, J. M. W. (1995). Pharmacological Treatment of the Paraphilias. In J. M. Oldham & M. B. Riba (Eds.), *Review of Psychiatry* (pp. 755–778). Washington D.C.: American Psychiatric Press.

Bradford, J. M. W. (1985). Organic Treatments for the Male Sexual Offender. *Behavioral Sciences and the Law*, 3, 355–375.

Bremer, J. (1959). *Asexualization: A Followup Study of 244 Cases.* New York: MacMillan.

Cooper, A. J., Sandau S., Losztyn S. & Cernovsky, Z. (1992). A Double-blind Placebo Controlled Trial of Mexdroxyprogesterone Acetate and Cyproterone Acetate with Seven Pedophiles. *Canadian Journal of Psychiatry,* 37, 687–693.

Cooper, A. J. (1986). Progesterone in the Treatment of Male Sex Offenders: A Review. *Canadian Journal of Psychiatry,* 31, 73–79.

Heim, N. & Hursch, C. J. (1979). Castration For Sexual Offenders: Treatment or Punishment? A Review and Critique of Recent European Literature. *Archives of Sexual Behavior,* 8, 281–304.

Kafka, M. P. (1994). Sertaline Pharmacotheraphy for Paraphilias and Paraphilia-related Disorders: An Open Trial. *Annals of Clinical Psychiatry,* 6, 189–195.

Meyer, W. J., Cole, C., & Emory, E. (1992). Depo-provera Treatment for Sex Offending Behavior: An Evaluation of Outcome. *Bulletin of the American Academy of Psychiatry and the Law,* 20, 249–259.

Ortmann, J. (1980). The Treatment of Sexual Offenders, Castration and Antihormonal Therapy. *International Journal of Law and Psychiatry,* 3, 443–451.

Stermac, L. & Hucker, S. (1988). Combining Cognitive-Behavioral Therapy and Pharmacotheraphy in the Treatment of Pedophile Incest Offenders. *Behavioral Sciences & the Law,* 6, 257–266.

Sturup, G. K (1972). Castration: The Total Treatment. In H. L. P. Resnik & M. E. Wolfgang (Eds.), *Sexual Behaviors: Social, Clinical and Legal Aspects* (pp. 361–382). New York: Little, Brown.

 Article Review Form at end of book.

In what way would education impact recidivism levels among prisoners? Why?

Educating Offenders

Dennis J. Stevens[1]

To examine the effects of education on incarcerated offenders, 60 inmates who had earned a baccalaureate degree while incarcerated were tracked after their release from the North Carolina Department of Corrections. Their recidivism rates were compared with inmates who had not pursued education while incarcerated. The data for this study were gathered from education and recidivism studies of 30 U.S. states. The results show that inmates who earned baccalaureate degrees while incarcerated became law-abiding individuals significantly more often than inmates who had not advanced their education while incarcerated. Since it is less expensive to educate inmates than to reincarcerate them, lowering recidivism rates should become a mission of the correctional community, and college degree programs must be an intrinsic part of that mission.

American prison experts concern themselves with correctional population yet seem to neglect correctional outcomes. That is, 425,409 inmates were released from American institutions in 1993 and, once released, many of those inmates received no significant opportunity to change their lifestyle.[2] Although the American public is decidedly punitive toward criminals, it is more lenient toward inmates because they are not an immediate threat. And while the public does not expect correctional organizations to control crime, people believe that incarceration alone will stop crime.[3] That is,

people expect incarceration to teach the offender a lesson.

Therefore, it could reasonably be argued that, from the public's perspective, reducing recidivism is the responsibility of the community into which convicts are released, not the prisons from which they are released. Nonetheless, placing unprepared, uneducated, unusually bitter individuals in the community could increase the threat to public safety and increase recidivism, because many Americans see violence as an appropriate response to danger.[4] (For the purpose of this article, recidivism is defined as a return to prison for a criminal offence other than a technical violation of parole.)[5] Many released inmates, however, commit crimes and elude detection or receive penalties other than incarceration for their crimes.

Correctional education has three functions: first, it acts as an agent of change for both the inmate and the system; second, it remains committed to freedom of inquiry; and third, it provides an opportunity to study, evaluate and respond to all variables in the individual, the system and society that are to benefit from the educational concerns with process, product and social reform.[6] Correctional education will reduce unproductive prison time, help inmates understand society, give noncustody professionals an opportunity to monitor correctional operations, and reduce recidivism. Although some researchers see academic progress as the primary purpose of

education, it does confer secondary benefits such as employability.

The Controversy

Does correctional education reduce recidivism? Most of the evidence appears to be inconclusive.[7] Some writers argue that the evidence does not correlate correction education with reduced recidivism, while others go further and suggest that nothing can alter criminally violent behaviour.[8] These opponents argue that criminal tendencies learned on the outside cannot be unlearned on the inside. Martison[9] argues that, except for some isolated cases, the rehabilitation efforts of advanced education reported so far (1947–1967) have done nothing appreciable to reduce recidivism. Martison's influence in corrections has frequently been associated with the shift from a treatment/rehabilitation orientation to a just-deserts/justice orientation.

Methodology

All degree-granting institutions participating in North Carolina inmate education were asked to submit data about male and female inmates to whom they granted degrees. Additionally, 10 years' worth of criminal records of North Carolina non-degree-inmates were examined.

Specifically, 320 inmates earned 373 post-secondary degrees in North Carolina prisons from one private university and four community

"Educating Offenders" by Dennis J. Stevens, *Forum on Corrections Research*, January 1998, 10(1), 33–36. Reprinted by permission.

colleges between 1981 and 1991. The participants in this study originally resided in one female prison and five male prisons, largely in the southeastern region of North Carolina. All were high-security prisons serving high-risk offenders.

Findings

When the North Carolina data were pooled with data from other U.S. states, the results clearly showed that earning a degree while incarcerated significantly reduced recidivism in both male and female offenders. More specifically, 60 educated men and women prisoners who earned a four-year degree in prison were not reincarcerated during the three years after their release, and all but one of these individuals found employment relating to their degree. The degree-earning offenders earned more than they did before their incarceration (if employed—most were unemployed at the time of their arrest and conviction). These findings support the position of Ryan and Mauldin[10] and are consistent with Jenkins, Pendry and Steurer,[11] who report that inmates released from prison who had completed a two- or four-year degree while incarcerated earned far more money than they had before going to prison.

State statistics show that approximately 40% of North Carolina's general prison population was reincarcerated within three years of release.[12] Applying this statistic to the study sample (assuming that the degree-earning offenders were typical of the general inmate population of North Carolina) would mean that 24 former inmates (40% × 60) instead of three would have been reincarcerated. The difference of 21 inmates saved North Carolina taxpayers $1,942.29 per day (at $92.49 per inmate) or $708,935.85 for the first year of reincarceration and each year thereafter.[13] This fact is consistent with calculations from a state auditor who projected a saving of US$6.6 million for every 1% reduction in recidivism.[14]

It should be noted that, although all states were asked to submit data, only 30 correctional educational directors responded and only eight of those were from states that had studied the correctional education and recidivism question. After evaluating their data, it appears that the earning of two-year and four-year college degrees by inmates lowers recidivism rates. The following are examples of the data received.

Alabama

In Alabama, adult correctional education is provided through the Department of Post-Secondary Education. The Alabama two-year college system is responsible for delivering correctional education programs to inmates throughout the state. One community college was established to serve seven correctional institutions. Of Alabama's 19,492 inmates, approximately 11% are enrolled full time in correctional education. The general prison population recidivism rate in any given 12-month period averages 35%, compared with 1% for inmates who complete post-secondary degrees.[15]

Florida

Florida's correctional system has approximately 60,000 inmates. Of these, 23% (14,000) participated in diverse academic, vocational and special education programs delivered by the Correctional Education School Authority (CESA). More than 7,000 diplomas and certificates of achievement or completion were awarded. CESA-educated inmates were 19% more likely to find employment after release than inmates who were not CESA-trained. Clearly, employment opportunities reduce recidivism. However, CESA had not conducted any recidivism tests based on education.[16]

Illinois

In 1988, the Illinois Department of Corrections studied 760 releases including: inmates who completed academic education programs only; inmates who completed vocational programs only; inmates who completed both academic and vocational programs; and a control group. Results show that releasees[17] who completed academic secondary or post-secondary programs or non-accredited community college vocational programs were less likely to re-offend and more likely be employed than the control group, who did not complete either vocational or post-secondary school education while incarcerated.

Oklahoma

Oklahoma researchers examined 360 inmates who, while incarcerated in Oklahoma, participated in college-level courses offered through the Televised Instructional System (TIS). TIS participants were matched with a cohort of non-participants. Results show that TIS participants had lower recidivism rates than the matching group.[18]

Maryland

In Maryland, Jenkins and his colleagues reported that inmates released from prison who had completed a two- or a four-year degree while incarcerated were most likely to be employed. Of further importance, 46% of the inmates released from the general prison population of Maryland's 19,014 inmates were returned to prison within three years of their release, compared with none of the 120 inmates who received degrees while in prison.

New York

In 1992, New York's Correctional Service reported that 24 colleges and universities throughout the state provide college programming for approximately 3,500 inmates in 66 correctional institutions. Of the inmates who earned a college degree (academic or vocational) while incarcerated, 36% were returned to prison, compared with the 45% who returned from New York's general prison population.

Texas

In Texas, 44,282 of the state's 120,000 inmates (38%) received educational services. The criminal justice center at Sam Houston State University conducted a two-year recidivism study of inmates in the Texas system. Of the

> The results clearly showed that earning a degree while incarcerated significantly reduced recidivism in both male and female offenders.

60 men and women who had earned degrees and were released, 10% (6) returned to prison. Generally, the recidivism rate in Texas is 36%.

Other data were analyzed to determine recidivism rates for various types of degree earners who left Texas prisons between September 1990 and August 1991. Two years after release, the overall recidivism rate for degree holders was only 12% and inversely differentiated by type of degree (associate 14%, baccalaureate 6%, masters 0%). The projected savings to Texas taxpayers for the reductions in recidivism described above range from US$11.6 million to as high as US$130.7 million.

Conclusion

The consistency in the study results demands acknowledgment—that is, positive educational intervention for inmates is necessary because it is practical, ethical and effective at reducing crime. When the costs of accredited correctional education are compared with the costs of reincarceration, results support funding for correctional education. Conservatively, of 425,409 inmates released in 1993, 45% will reoffend within three years.

> The consistency in the study result demands acknowledgment—that is, positive educational intervention for inmates is necessary because it is practical, ethical and effective at reducing crime.

It is recommended that the correctional system do whatever is necessary to keep the public safe from recurring criminal behaviour. One of the most cost-effective methods of accomplishing this objective is to educate criminals. An effective education, including a holistic educational experience, can be provided by experienced educators through accredited institutions of higher learning. It is important to note that short-sighted or poorly managed educational experiences are inappropriate in the prison classroom, and unlikely to contribute to the results reported in this article.

In sum, high-quality education is the least-expensive model of recidivism reduction. With certain offenders, education will work. Other offenders are unlikely to be deterred from committing crime by anything the correction system has to offer. The results of this study clearly identify a link between correctional education and reduction of recidivism by means of employment.

Notes

1. Dr. Dennis J. Stevens, 102 South Randolph, Goldsboro, NC 27530, is a professor who teaches academic courses in the college classroom and to law enforcement officers at North Carolina's Justice Academy. He also teaches felons at high-security penitentiaries like Attica in New York, Eastern and Women's Correctional in North Carolina, Stateville and Joliet near Chicago, and CCI in Columbia, South Carolina. The author must acknowledge the help of Dr. Charles S. Ward, Director of Education, Eastern Corrections, who collected the data for the North Carolina Bar Association's Task Force on Alternatives to the Present Punishment System.

2. For specific data, see the U.S. Bureau of Justice Statistics (1996). D. J. Stevens, "The Impact of Time Served and Regime on Prisoners' Anticipation of Crime: Female Prisonisation Effects," *The Howard Journal of Criminal Justice*, in press 1998. See also "The impact of time served and custody level on offender attitudes," *Forum on Corrections Research*, 7, 3 (1995): 12–14. And see "The Depth of Imprisonment and Prisonisation: Levels of Security and Prisoners' Anticipation of Future Violence," *The Howard Journal of Criminal Justice*, 33, 2 (1994):137–157.

3. C. A. Innes, "Recent Public Opinion in the United States Toward Punishment and Corrections," *The Prison Journal*, 73, 2 (1993): 220–236. See also J. Q. Wilson, *Thinking About Crime* (New York, NY: Basic Books, 1975).

4. D. J. Stevens, "Prison Regime and Drugs," *The Howard Journal of Criminal Justice*, 36, 1 (1997): 14–27. See also "Communities and Homicide: Why Blacks Resort to Murder," *Police & Society* (summer, 1997). And see "Explanations of Homicide: Interviews with Female Killers," paper presented at the annual conference of the Academy of Criminal Justice Sciences, Las Vegas, NV, 1996.

5. Recidivism has many definitions, including "repetition of criminal behaviour." Another definition includes "fingerprinted rearrests for alleged crimes." See S. Clarke and A. L. Harrison, *Recidivism of Criminal Offenders Assigned to Community Correctional Programs or Released from Prison in North Carolina in 1989*, report prepared for the North Carolina Sentencing and Policy Advisory Commission, Institute of Government (Chapel Hill, NC: University of North Carolina at Chapel Hill, 1992).

6. M. V. Reagen and D. M. Stoughton, *School Behind Bars: A Descriptive Overview of Correctional Education in the American Prison System* (Metuchen, NJ: Scarecrow Press, 1976): 15.

7. S. P. Lab and J. T. Whitehead, "From Nothing Works to the Appropriate Works. The Latest Stop on the Search for the Secular Grail," *Criminology*, 28 (1990): 405–419. And see K. P. Morrison, "Reading, Writing, and Recidivism," *CEA News and Notes*, 15, 2 (1993): 11.

8. M. K. Cary, "How States Can Fight Violent Crime. Two Dozen Steps to a Safer America," Backgrounder (The Heritage Foundation, 1993). And see F. T. Cullen and K. E. Gilbert, *Reaffirming Rehabilitation* (Cincinnati, OH: Anderson, 1988).

9. R. Martison, "What Works? Questions and Answers About Prison Reform," *The Public Interest* (Spring 1974): 22–50.

10. T. A. Ryan and B. J. Mauldin, "Correctional Education and Recidivism: A Historical Analysis" (Report available from University of South Carolina, College of Criminal Justice, Columbia, SC, 1994).

11. D. Jenkins, J. Pendry and S. J. Steurer, *A Post-Release Follow-up of Correctional Education Program Completers Released in 1990–1991* (Baltimore, MD: Maryland Division of Correction, 1992).

12. North Carolina Department of Corrections, *Report on Inmate Incarceration Cost Per Day for the Year Ended June 30, 1995* (Raleigh, NC: 1995).

13. North Carolina Department of Corrections, *Report on Inmate Incarceration Cost Per Day for the Year Ended June 30, 1995*.

14. Windham School System, *Three-Year Outcome Study of the Relationship Between Participation in Windham School System Programs and Reduced Levels of Recidivism* (Huntsville, TX: Windham School System, 1994).

15. M. Gregg, *Education and Recidivism Report* (Deatsville, AL: Ingram State Community College, 1995).

16. CESA, CESA *Annual Report 1994–1995* (Tallahassee, FL: CESA 1995).

17. Illinois Council on Vocational Education (ICVE), *Correctional reeducation: A way to stay out*. Recommendations for Illinois and a report of the Anderson Study (Springfield, IL: Illinois Department of Corrections, 1988).

18. M. Langenbach, M. North, L. Aagaard and W. Chown, "Televised Instruction in Oklahoma Prisons: A Study of Recidivism and Disciplinary Actions," *Journal of Correctional Education*, 41, 2 (1990): 87–94.

Article Review Form at end of book.

Can violent offenders be treated? Should the victim be involved in the treatment?

Treatment Programs for Offenders with Violent Histories:

A National Survey

Ralph Serin and Shelley Brown

Research Branch, Correctional Service of Canada

While the evaluation of program efficacy is critical to good correctional and fiscal management, other considerations also have merit. This article highlights findings from a recently completed national survey of treatment programs for offenders with violent histories. Prior reviews of published programs for violent offenders have been disappointing,[1] yet discussions with field staff suggested there were many programs in existence. A major purpose of this review was to delineate the nature and quantity of these programs provided in the Service. This review is deliberately qualitative and descriptive, as the goal was to provide information to consumers, rather than formal program evaluation. It was our belief that the review of all programs presently being delivered to violent offenders would yield important information for those interested in the integration of programs for violent offenders. For this survey, Anger and Emotions Management (AEM) and

Living Without Violence (LWV) represented 31.1% and 17.6% of the programs, respectively. Interestingly, approximately half (51.4%) of the programs reviewed were other programs. Apparently, specific sites developed them to meet their particular needs. These data, then, should inform the Service about a range of issues related to meeting the treatment needs of violent offenders. Also, as a compilation of existing treatment programs, the data represent a compendium for staff to review when making recommendations for transfer and release of violent offenders for whom treatment needs remain.

Types of Programs

Those surveys completed in January 1997, were coded and entered into the present review. Overall, the national completion rate (number of returns divided by the number of sites) was 37.7% (52 responses from 138 sites). Regionally, the completion rates were Atlantic, 28.1%; Quebec, 51.6%; Ontario, 34.2%; Prairies, 38.5% and Pacific, 33.3%. Similarly, the completion rates by security level were minimum, 53.9%; medium, 72.2%; maximum, 66.7% and commu-

nity 22.5%. Given the limited time frame, the completion rate was fairly good. An additional 16 surveys received after the deadline for data entry were) not included. Further, several sites, particularly community sites, not offering programs may simply have failed to provide a nil response. . . .

Targeted Groups

The survey listed a number of potential target groups, or types of offenders, for whom the program was intended. These target groups were: persistently violent, criminal violence, anger, institutional violence, domestic violence and domestic exclusive. This was principally to determine whether programs were restrictive in their selection of offenders. Many programs reported using several of the targets, potentially leading to quite heterogeneous groups regarding treatment needs. Other targets such as suicidal, mentally disordered, victims of domestic abuse and lifers were also reported, but accounted for less than 7% of the total targets. These data allow us to consider whether existing programs are targeting those offenders for

Treatment Programs for Offenders with Violent Histories: A National Survey, R. Serin and S. Brown, *Research Branch, Correctional Service of Canada*, May 1997, 9(2). Reprinted by permission of the Correctional Service of Canada.

whom the program was originally intended and where additional programming efforts might be required in light of the prevalence of these "types" of offenders.

Selection and Exclusion Criteria

The survey also asked respondents to indicate specific selection criteria used to accept offenders into their program. Staff can review these results to confirm that the specific treatment needs of offenders selected to their programs are addressed in the program content. There appears to be considerable regional variation in selection criteria. On average, most programs consider current offences, but relatively few consider prior assaults or incorporate pretreatment test results into selection. Similar breakdowns are available by security level, on request.

With respect to exclusion, over 75% of the programs exclude offenders with active psychotic symptoms. Similarly, 30% exclude offenders with low motivation, 12% exclude those who deny they require treatment, and 18% exclude offenders because of low intelligence. This latter decision makes intuitive sense given the emphasis on cognitive treatment strategies in these programs. It is also understandable that poorly motivated and resistant offenders will be disruptive in groups. However, with nearly 40% of programs excluding such offenders, this identifies an emerging new treatment target group. Breakdowns by region, security level and setting are available and will be detailed in the final report.

Waiting Lists

One measure of treatment needs is the number of offenders who have been referred for a particular program, but who have been placed on a waiting list until space permits their participation. Nationally, 78.9% of those programs surveyed maintain a waiting list. The average number of offenders waiting for admission to a violent offender program is 40, although the range is from 3 to 169. Regional breakdowns of offenders on waiting lists

are Atlantic (8), Quebec (17), Ontario (61), Prairies (33) and Pacific (54). Further, the number of offenders waiting differs according to security level: minimum (14), medium (64), maximum (36). Setting is also important regarding waiting lists: community (11), institutional (45).

Group Versus Individual Programs

Consistent with direction over the last decade to provide treatment in group format, 72.6% of programs are exclusively group. Since the survey only sampled programs, individual therapy was not included, but 27.4% of the programs surveyed augment group programming with individual sessions. There are regional and setting differences, with the Pacific region only reporting group sessions, whereas the Prairies offer individual sessions in 57.1% of their programs. The other regions offer individual sessions in 13% to 32% of their programs. There are no major differences among security levels, nor community versus institution-based programs.

Program Orientation and Components

Not surprisingly, 85% of the programs surveyed nationally provide a cognitive behavioural model of intervention. Psychotherapeutic approaches are reported in 20.5% of the programs, suggesting that these approaches are integrated into a complementary model. Similarly, 20.5% of the programs reported their theoretical orientation as psychoeducational. Program components indicate the content presented in the various treatment programs. As with the issue of target groups, it is important for program deliverers to confirm that the content of their program addresses the needs of those offenders selected.

Treatment Targets

Respondents were to indicate whether specific treatment targets reflected in the literature were included

in their program. For these data, the "other" category includes symptom management, dealing with remorse, confronting denial, dealing with stress, self-esteem, relationships or social reintegration. The percentage of programs addressing these targets in treatment are presented in Table 1.

Program Length

The average program length, combined with waiting list information, should help staff review resources and plan strategies for best meeting the treatment needs of violent offenders. On average, programs included 22 sessions, averaging 2.5 hours each over the course of 13 weeks. This means that a maximum of three programs could be delivered at a site if a program deliverer was dedicated to only one program. Nationally, it appears that, on average, these programs have been in place for 36 months, with only minor variation across the regions and security levels.

Changes to Programs

Unfortunately, most respondents (70%) were unable to comment on the degree of change their program has undergone. However, the remaining 30% reported changes regarding program content (72.1%) and report format (34.3%). Few programs (7.2%) reported changes to admission criteria. Other changes such as procedures and scheduling were also reported (37.5%).

Methodology

Many of the programs reported maintaining a control group (37%) and database (73.2%). Similarly, 67.1% reported having an advisory committee. Interestingly, only 17% reported a formal evaluation, with 30% reporting published findings (10.8 formal, 18.5 informal), yet most (53.8%) indicated that evaluations were in progress. The majority of programs (87.7%) have treatment manuals which reflect content (100%), rules (92%), admission criteria (94%), expulsion criteria (88%), report format (86%), homework assignments (84%) and a test battery

Table 1 Treatment Target by Location

Treatment Target	Institutional %	n/52	Community %	n/20	National %	n/72
Arousal reduction	63.5	(33)	35.0	(7)	55.6	(40)
Problem solving	80.8	(42)	90.0	(18)	83.3	(60)
Communication skills	88.5	(46)	85.0	(17)	87.5	(63)
Assertiveness	78.8	(41)	75.0	(15)	77.8	(56)
Insight	92.3	(48)	90.0	(18)	91.7	(66)
Cognitive distortions	88.5	(46)	80.0	(16)	86.1	(62)
Relapse prevention	63.5	(44)	60.0	(12)	62.5	(45)
Other	13.5	(7)	20.0	(4)	15.3	(11)

Note: percentages do not sum to 100 given that the response categories were not mutually exclusive.

Table 2 Assessment Method by Location

Assessment Method	Institutional %	n/53	Community %	n/19	National %	n/72
Interview	96.2	(51)	100.0	(19)	97.2	(70)
File review	77.4	(41)	68.4	(13)	75.0	(54)
CTP	58.5	(31)	68.4	(13)	61.1	(44)
Collateral informal	30.2	(16)	47.4	(9)	34.7	(35)
Testing	62.3	(33)	47.4	(9)	58.3	(42)

Notes: CTP = correctional treatment plan; percentages do not sum to 100 given that the response categories were not mutually exclusive.

(78%). Additional information contained in the treatment manuals, such as participant contracts, session goals, session summaries and guidelines for staff, were also reported, albeit infrequently.

Assessment of Treatment Needs

Various strategies for the assessment of treatment needs were recorded by program deliverers. The endorsement frequency of these methods is presented in Table 2.

These data provide evidence that program staff use multimethod assessment in identifying treatment needs. It is disappointing, however, that these data suggest that correctional treatment plans appear to be only modestly linked to the identification of treatment needs for violent offenders.

Assessment of Treatment Gain

Respondents were provided with eight choices for assessing treatment gain. In order of most frequently to least frequently endorsed, these were: offender satisfaction, role plays, knowledge questionnaire, test battery interactions with staff, behavioural rating, institutional performance and institutional charges. By combining these categories into a composite score, we can conclude that, on average, programs use four different methods for the assessment of treatment gain.

Risk Assessment

Incorporation of risk considerations into programs for violent offenders was reviewed in several ways. First,

respondents were asked to indicate whether a risk assessment is conducted; 83.6% reported it was. Fewer respondents (63.3%), however, indicated a risk assessment was part of the initial assessment. Risk was rarely considered as part of the admission criteria for the program (16.7%). Further, assessments of risk were often (53.3%) not considered in post-treatment reports.

Summary

The findings of this survey are informative and encouraging. First, even allowing for modest completion rates because of time constraints, there are a significant number and variety of programs offered to violent offenders. Second, the majority of programs report relevant treatment targets, multimethod assessments of treatment need and treatment gain. Surprisingly, almost half of the programs surveyed were not core programs, indicating considerable initiative in the field to meet treatment needs. Offenders admitted to these surveyed programs are likely heterogeneous regarding type of offences. However, program content and treatment targets are diverse, optimally providing responsive intervention. For most of the questions considered, there were minor regional variations. Since offender profiles also vary among the regions, this is not necessarily problematic. Finally, these results suggest the need for improved integration with correctional treatment plans and greater emphasis on risk assessments by program staff.

Note

1. R. C. Serin, *Treating Violent Offenders: A Review of Current Practices,* Research Report R-38 (Ottawa: Correctional Services of Canada, 1994). And see R. C. Serin and S. L. Brown, "Strategies for Enhancing the Treatment of Violent Offenders," *Forum on Corrections Research,* 8, 3 (1996); 45–48.

 Article Review Form at end of book.

How are juvenile programs different from adult programs? What is it about a culture's history that leads to the development of juvenile corrections programs?

The Legacy of Juvenile Corrections

Barry Krisberg

Barry Krisberg is the executive director of the National Council on Crime and Delinquency.

As the field of juvenile corrections prepares itself for the next century, practitioners need to understand the historical legacy that continues to influence contemporary policy and practice. As historian William Appleman Williams reminds us, "History offers no answers per se, it only offers a way of encouraging people to use their own minds to make their history." Few areas of the justice system are more in need of critical reexamination than juvenile justice.

This past year, the states introduced more than 700 bills to move more troubled youngsters from specialized juvenile facilities to adult prisons. To some, juvenile corrections has come to symbolize soft-headed liberalism. Others see that juvenile facilities are becoming severely crowded, with many juvenile institutions failing to meet even basic professional standards of child protection. At this stage, public officials seem reluctant to spend taxpayers' dollars to reform juvenile corrections—even as they continue to pour billions of dollars into adult prisons. For example, the 1994 crime bill will give states nearly $9 billion for prison construction and several more billion for boot camps, but juvenile corrections was little more than an afterthought in those congressional deliberations.

The Childsavers

Although religious philanthropic organizations established the first specialized juvenile facilities in the United States in 1825, the most significant growth in public juvenile corrections commenced in the second half of the 19th century. For instance, the very first state juvenile reform school, the Lyman School, opened in 1846.

At that time, growing fears about immigration and the potential for class warfare led government officials to centralize the administration of juvenile facilities. In 1876, there were 51 reform schools or houses of refuge nationwide—of these, nearly three-quarters were run by state or local governments. By 1890, almost every state outside the South had a reform school, and many states had separate facilities for males and females, as well as separate facilities allowing for racial segregation. Youths were admitted to these facilities for a broad range of behaviors, including criminal offenses, status offenses and dependency. The length of stay was regulated by facility administrators, who also could exercise broad discretion to transfer disruptive young detainees to adult prisons.

The new reform schools came under attack by advocates who often are referred to as "the childsavers." This group, which included urban clergy, such as Charles Loring Brace, emphasized the need for prevention services in cities. The group founded children's aid societies to distribute food and clothing and to provide temporary shelter and employment for destitute youths. Brace often attended juvenile facilities managers conferences to argue that the longer the period of confinement, the less likely the youth would be reformed. He and his followers implemented an alternative strategy of placing urban youngsters in apprenticeships with farm families in the West and Midwest. The childsavers had great faith in the curative powers of rural family life. Brace declared these families "God's reformatories" for wayward youths.

Reacting to the childsavers' criticism of reform schools, institutional managers began to locate these facilities in rural areas where it was assumed that agricultural labor would aid the reform process. Many institutions initiated a "cottage system" to create the appearance that youths were living with surrogate parents in home-like environments. In fact, the cottages actually functioned as a classification system to separate children by age, race and "criminal sophistication."

The Impact of the Civil War

The Civil War deeply affected the world of juvenile corrections. Many

The Legacy of Juvenile Corrections, Barry Krisberg, *Corrections Today*, August 1995, 57(5), 122. Reprinted with permission of the American Correctional Association, Lanham, MD.

Southern reform schools were destroyed in battles. The participation of juveniles in the Northern draft riots led to a significant increase in incarcerated juveniles. In the South, white officials arrested thousands of emancipated slaves and sent them to segregated Southern prisons and reform schools—places of savage brutality that rivaled the worst abuses of slavery.

The high inflation rates following the Civil War sharply reduced the funds that were spent on institutional upkeep, and conditions of confinement deteriorated. Many institutions resorted to contracting out the labor of their young charges to increase revenues for the reform schools. Critics of the contract labor system charged that making profits, rather than reformation, was becoming the prime function of juvenile facilities. Reports abounded of cruel and vicious exploitation of these captive child laborers. Newspaper accounts told of stabbings, fights, arson and attacks on staff at these institutions.

Growing criticism by organized labor, religious groups and the child-savers led many states to investigate juvenile facilities and to establish state boards to oversee the operation of juvenile correctional institutions. These oversight groups uncovered horrid conditions, massive corruption and abusive practices. In this era, the National Prison Association (now ACA) was established, in part, to promulgate enlightened professional standards for the operation of these reform schools. It was hoped that the new regulatory bodies would curb these problems, but little real progress was made. Reform schools continued to proliferate, housing even greater numbers of troubled youths.

The Juvenile Court Movement

The early decades of the 20th century witnessed the growth of the juvenile court movement. The new children's court also ushered in the expansion of probation services and diagnostic clinics for juvenile offenders. There was increased optimism in juvenile corrections that delinquents could be reformed by applying emerging scientific knowledge. One innovation was the introduction of physical exercise, along with special massage and nutritional regimens. Many felt that neglect of the body led to depraved behavior. Also popular: military drill, the precursor of the today's correctional boot camps.

None of these innovations led to reduced rates of recidivism, but institutional managers were eager to find alternatives to inmate idleness, which worsened as the contract labor system was abandoned. Public criticism of training schools continued and resulted in several states excluding children under 12 from these facilities.

One of the most interesting ideas of this era was the model of offender self-government. One such institution, the George Junior Republic, was organized to be a virtual microcosm of the outside world. Self-government meant that youths were involved in the definition and enforcement of rules, under the close supervision of staff. This concept still is seen today in the popular treatment methods known as guided-group interaction or positive peer culture.

The Move Toward Community-Based Services

Juvenile corrections facilities continued to function almost impervious to change throughout the next 50 years. It was not until the late 1950s that a few states, such as New Jersey, began to experiment with alternatives to traditional incarceration. Periodic media coverage of escapes, riots and brutality in facilities deepened public skepticism over the efficacy of juvenile corrections. Legal decisions in the 1960s established that juveniles possessed basic rights to due process and equal protection under the law. The President's Crime Commission in 1967 called for diverting as many youngsters as possible from the failed systems of juvenile corrections. "Deinstitutionalization" became a buzz word. However, large-scale reform rarely matched liberal rhetoric.

Then, in the early 1970s, Massachusetts sent shock waves across the nation when it closed all of its state training schools. The Lyman School, the first training school opened in the United States, was the first to be closed. In short order, Massachusetts replaced its large traditional juvenile institutions with a network of very small, secure facilities and a wide array of community-based services. Nearly 1,000 youths were quickly removed from brutal and corrupt institutions to innovative and humane community programs.

The Massachusetts reforms were met with intense opposition by the corrections establishment; however, youth advocates used the Massachusetts model to draft the federal Juvenile Justice and Delinquency Prevention Act (JJDPA) of 1974. This landmark legislation offered grants to states that were willing to remove status offenders from secure custody, to separate adult and juvenile offenders and to promote "advanced juvenile justice practices." Despite these federal resources, only three states—Missouri, Utah and Vermont—tried to faithfully replicate the Massachusetts approach.

The reform thrust of the JJDPA was soon blunted by 12 years of the Reagan and Bush administrations that fundamentally opposed the concept of deinstitutionalization. Moreover, the juvenile reform movement was confronted with growing political rhetoric aimed at "cracking down on juvenile criminals." Through most of the 1980s and '90s, the public response to juvenile offenders was decidedly unsympathetic. This period witnessed a wave of legislative reforms designed to make it easier to adjudicate youths in adult courts. States mandated automatic waiver to the criminal justice system for a new range of offenses. A national war against drugs produced an unprecedented increase in the number of youths entering adult penal facilities. States such as Colorado, Georgia and Minnesota passed laws permitting juvenile corrections officials broad latitude in administratively transferring young people to "youthful offender" facilities operated by adult corrections departments.

Today, juvenile facilities face severe conditions of crowding. Lengths of stay in juvenile facilities have increased steadily in the past 15 years. Despite this expanded use of incarceration, public officials have not invested much in new facilities or increased agency budgets. The larger crisis of crowding in adult facilities is consuming a lion's share of public resources. As a result of increasing caseloads and restricted budgets, many juvenile corrections facilities have experienced deteriorating conditions of confinement and basic lapses in meeting professional standards. Not surprisingly, many state and local juvenile facilities have faced lawsuits that challenge the constitutionality of conditions of confinement.

Back to the Future

Responding to political enthusiasm and the availability of federal funds, many jurisdictions are opening boot camps that are reminiscent of the fad of military drill at the turn of the 20th century. The previously discredited practice of sentencing offenders to detention centers is back in fashion. The new national congressional leadership has expressed its nostalgic support for juvenile corrections practices such as Boys Town of the 1930s.

Once again, private groups, both for profit and nonprofit, are claiming an increasingly larger market share of the $3 billion a year juvenile incarceration industry. Although not by conscious design, many public juvenile facilities are as racially segregated today as they were 100 years ago. Moreover, given the public antipathy toward the alleged leniency of the juvenile justice system, one wonders if juvenile corrections has a viable future in the United States.

At the 1994 International Congress of Juvenile Court Judges, representatives from 62 nations expressed their firm commitment to the value of a humane and rational system of care for troubled youths. These nations are struggling to achieve the American ideal of individualized treatment, education and rehabilitation. Many of the conferees were shocked at reports that, in the United States, juvenile justice was rushing to embrace a punitive model. This international perspective should provide a "wake-up call" to those of us committed to an enlightened view of juvenile corrections.

The picture is, by no means, all bleak. Ironically, a few jurisdictions are expressing great interest in the Massachusetts model. Positive steps forward can be seen in Arizona, Indiana, Missouri, Nebraska, New Jersey and Ohio. Further, the Office of Juvenile Justice and Delinquency Program's (OJJDP) Comprehensive Strategy on Serious, Violent and Chronic Juvenile Offenders places major focus on blending treatment and public safety concerns. Indeed, OJJDP is exercising the national leadership role in juvenile corrections that its founders envisioned for it.

There is renewed interest in upgrading professional standards in juvenile corrections. Professional groups—such as the American Correctional Association, American Probation and Parole Association and National Juvenile Detention Association—are actively speaking out against the punitive rhetoric that is so popular in Washington, D.C., and in state capitals across the nation. Private philanthropy also is supporting progressive juvenile justice reform. For example, the Edna McConnell Clark Foundation is working to encourage leadership development within juvenile corrections, the Robert Wood Johnson Foundation is funding juvenile corrections reform in a number of states, and the Annie E. Casey Foundation has launched a major program to reform juvenile detention practices.

It is too soon to tell if these small, yet positive, steps forward can withstand the chilling political climate the juvenile corrections field faces. Although the battle for an enlightened vision of juvenile justice may not be lost, the struggle ahead appears long and arduous. Professionals in juvenile corrections will be tested. The history of juvenile corrections teaches us that true champions for children—such as Charles Loring Brace; Julia Lathrop, one of the founders of the Illinois juvenile court; Jane Addams, founder of Hull House in Chicago; and Jerome Miller, architect of the Massachusetts reform—have previously stepped forward to make a difference. Today, more than ever, we need such heroes.

 Article Review Form at end of book.

WiseGuide Wrap-Up

- Rehabilitation and treatment programs can be successful under the right conditions. One problem that has occurred is that program placement is sometimes determined by the needs of the program rather than the needs of the offender. Such practices potentially undermine the effectiveness of many treatment programs.

- Successful treatment requires a commitment on the part of program administrators and participants in the treatment. Unfortunately, some offenders are forced to participate in programs without realizing why they should be there. If a person does not want to be treated or rehabilitated, chances of success are virtually nonexistent.

- For many, the desire to improve their living conditions helps them make the decision to participate fully and actively in the treatment program. The desire to get better is often what is needed to allow rehabilitation to succeed. It is often difficult to determine exactly what caused the offender's behavior. It is not impossible, however, to determine his or her needs.

R.E.A.L. Sites

This list provides a print preview of typical **Coursewise** R.E.A.L. sites. There over 100 such sites at the **Courselinks**™ site. The danger in printing URLs is that web sites can change overnight. As we went to press, these sites were functional using the URLs provided. If you come across one that isn't, please let us know via email to: webmaster@coursewise.com. Use your Passport to access the most current list of R.E.A.L. sites at the **Courselinks** site.

Site name: South Forty Corporation: An Avenue from Prison to Society

URL: http://members.aol.com/south40x/page4.htm

Why is it R.E.A.L.? This is a homepage of a non-profit criminal justice agency that has been cutting edge in developing vocational, counseling, and educational programs for offenders and ex-offenders to prepare them for the world of work before they leave prison.

Key topics: education, reintegration

Try this: See if you can guess why employers should hire former prisoners presented by the South Forty Corporation. Click on the site to see how close your answers are to their answers.

Site name: Delancey Street Foundation

URL: http://www.igc.apc.org/justice/cjc/delancey.html

Why is it R.E.A.L.? Delancey Street is considered the nation's leading self-help residential education center for former substance abusers and ex-convicts. It currently has about a thousand residents located in five facilities throughout the country: New Mexico, New York, North Carolina, Los Angeles, and headquartered in San Francisco.

Key topics: alternatives to incarceration, effects on families, probation, reintegration

Try this: The average resident has been a hard-core drug addict for ten years. Go to this site and see if you can find how many times the average Delancey Street client has been to prison.

section 6

Correctional Officers and Correctional Systems

Michael D. Rothwell
MSDART Cherry Program; PO Box 812; Goldsboro, NC 27533—
(ncs0571@interpath.com)

Kate King, Ph.D.
West Texas A&M University; Canton, Texas 79016—(kking@WTMAIL.EDU)

Key Points

- Prison populations continue to grow.

- The cost of prison construction is increasing.

- Alternatives to incarceration are more cost effective.

- Alternatives to incarceration can serve as punishment while enhancing public safety.

- The prison environment is becoming more complex. Officers can choose how to respond to the problems that arise in prison.

- The approach the officers choose determines their personal job satisfaction and efficiency.

WiseGuide Intro

The Western world continues to experience a growth in prison populations. As those populations increase, the competition for resources among agencies escalates. Correctional managers face a delicate balancing act, juggling the need for punishment with the need for community alternatives that are cost effective and that enhance public safety.

Alternatives to incarceration, such as boot camps, shock probation, residential community correction facilities, day reporting centers, and intensive supervised probation, are popular strategies that have been developed to combat the surging growth in prison populations. However, innovative management strategies, such as unit management techniques, seem to be replacing traditional methods of prison management, explains Houston in his search for excellence. Greene examines the idea of increasing prison bed capacity to efficiently deal with overcrowding but argues that legal sanctions must also aid in the overcrowding problem. Payne and Gainey look at electronic monitoring of offenders as a method of dealing with overcrowding and examine some of the societal opportunities to be gained from this method of correctional supervision.

Then, too, correctional officers, like the prisoners they supervise, must cope with the institutional environment. Prison policies are often contradictory, vague, or simply impossible to fulfill in the real prison world. When some people hear the words "prison guard," they often think of hacks, screws, bulls, turnkeys, and tower guards. But prison staff members not only supervise inmates inside the walls, they also make their careers there, and are called "correctional officers." The prison world is a complex and changing society, containing many different personalities, approaches to the job, obstacles, and opportunities with which the officers must deal. In addition to the typical inmate, correctional officers must now deal with juveniles being sentenced as adults, elderly inmates, and those with full-blown AIDS. Special needs of inmates call for special responses from staff.

How might the officers in today's prisons fulfill the varied expectations of their job and further their own careers? Hepburn and Knepper's article on human services workers suggests that job satisfaction is enhanced when prison workers see themselves as helping professionals rather than custodians. King discusses coping mechanisms created by correctional officers who must guard inmates suffering from advanced stages of AIDS in a community hospital. Cadwaladr reports that female officers approach the job differently, relying on negotiation and persuasion to defuse potentially violent situations. Finally, Adler reveals how officers in England feel about cross gender supervision in male prisons. As alternatives to incarceration expand, researchers will need to continue to evaluate the overall effectiveness of these programs in terms of cost, recidivism rates, job satisfaction levels, and public safety.

❓ Questions ❓

Reading 33. What other managerial strategies other than traditional methods can help promote institutional tranquility in modern penitentiaries?

Reading 34. In what way can community partnerships and sanctions aid in the control of prison overcrowding? Is bed capacity the only answer to efficient crime control?

Reading 35. Why would the general public think that electronic monitoring of offenders is soft on crime? Are there societal opportunities to be gained by leaving some offenders in the home?

Reading 36. In what way might human services work help improve the prison environment for both prisoners and officers?

Reading 37. How is the changing inmate population affecting the correctional officers' role?

Reading 38. In contrast to a male officer, how would a female correctional officer conduct herself differently with a male prisoner?

Reading 39. What happens when female correctional officers are deployed in a men's prison?

Section 6 Questions

What can be done to control the population growth in prisons?

Do community corrections programs provide less costly alternatives to incarceration?

Does placing an offender in a community corrections program fulfill the notion of punishment?

Is public safety enhanced or jeopardized by placing offenders in alternative programs?

In what ways might approaching the job of correctional officer as a human services worker benefit both staff and inmates?

What special problems do correctional officers face when guarding inmates outside the prison environment?

Why might women approach the job of correctional officer differently than men?

How might the security level of the facility impact correctional officers' options?

What other managerial strategies other than traditional methods can help promote institutional tranquility in modern penitentiaries?

Unit Management and the Search for Excellence

James Houston

Appalachian State University

Introduction

The task of corrections is becoming ever more difficult. This chapter delineates a more rational way of ensuring the security and delivery of services in a correctional institution. Unit management has proved to be an effective way to enhance staff job satisfaction and promote institutional tranquility. Finally, a model unit program is proposed to illustrate the flexibility of unit management as an approach to managing a correctional institution.

Today there are approximately 1 million people incarcerated in U.S. prisons (Allen and Simonsen, 1998). Many of these prisons are overcrowded, dangerous warehouses; on the other hand, others are well-managed institutions that are a credit to the community. Nevertheless, one conservative estimate is that U.S. prisons siphon off in excess of $20 billion a year (McDonald, 1989). Such an investment demands a prudent and just return for each dollar spent. However, that return is questionable not only in terms of how well the inmate population is served, but also in regard to staff needs and the efficient allocation of resources.

The effective management of a complex organization such as a prison requires the implementation of an approach to management that recognizes the multidimensionality of the organization. As a consequence, correctional executives must implement a system that effectively integrates inmate supervision and service delivery to a diverse and often violent inmate population while recognizing the needs of employees.

Traditionally, prisons have relied on a pyramidal type of organizational structure, with most decisions and policy moving from top to bottom. Little has been written about the management style of early prison administrators, but historical anecdotes document a paramilitary organizational structure to accomplish stated objectives, keeping convicts segregated from the rest of society.

As European feudal society began to break up in the twelfth century, "many people were cut loose from the land and from the two basic social organizations of the agricultural society, the family and the tribe" (Irwin, 1985). These increasing numbers of "rabble" needed to be controlled, and that task was left to the sheriff and the military.

The prison system in America reflected its European roots. The military continued controlling the masses and was given responsibility for implementing the 1717 Act of Parliament. This law authorized the transportation of convicts from England to the American colonies for the purpose of being sold as bond servants to colonial planters (see Tappan, 1960; for a discussion of early U.S. federal prisons, see Keve 1991). The colonists also brought with them the tradition of the sheriff and his responsibility for operating the gaol (jail). With the sheriff came the paramilitary approach to prison management.

Prior to the U.S. Civil War, jails were organized haphazardly, and the punishment of criminals was considered primarily a local matter. Prisons that serve a large area such as a state are an American invention. As more traditional methods of punishment such as flogging declined, the prison in America gained in popularity. The paramilitary approach to management was an attractive and efficient way to allocate scarce resources in these institutions. For example, in the early nineteenth century, de Beaumont and de Toqueville found a paramilitary management structure in the U.S. prisons they visited. *The Rules and Regulations for the Connecticut State Prison* clearly illustrates this structure with the warden at the top of the management pyramid and the deputy warden, overseers, and watchmen performing all duties and tasks as may be directed by the warden (de Beaumont and de Toqueville, 1833).

Eventually, however, corruption, administrative abuses, and patronage led to reforms and the establishment of boards of administration charged with the responsibil-

Unit Management and the Search for Excellence, J. Houston. Excerpt from *Correctional Management: Functions, Skills, and Systems* (1994). Reprinted by permission of Nelson-Hall Publishers.

ity to control and manage all state prisons (Tappan, 1960). The National Congress on Penitentiary and Reformatory Discipline held at Cincinnati, Ohio, in 1870 stated:

It is now commonly acknowledged that no prison system can be successful, to the broadest and most desirable extent, without some central authority at the helm, to give unity and efficiency to the whole prison administration of the state. (E.C. Wines, ed.)

Zebulon Brockway believed that there should be unity of spirit and identity of aim (1871/1970). He advocated an organization that was pyramidal in shape, with final authority residing at the top of the structure. Ultimately, boards of correction delegated management responsibility to the respective wardens and superintendents, and it was they who developed the various policies and procedures. This highly centralized form of management lent itself well to the paramilitary structure that efficiently carried out the orders of the warden or superintendent.

In 1946, the American Correctional Association issued its *Manual for Correctional Standards*, which stated there and through its subsequent editions that each agency should be headed by a chief executive, implying a paramilitary structure fanning out below each state director of corrections (ACA, 1966).

Thus, while there have been many changes in American prison institutional discipline, classification, sentencing structure, and programming, little has changed in the approach to management of prisons during the last 150 years. It was not until the 1970s that the U.S. Bureau of Prisons pioneered a new approach to management and revolutionized the way many corrections executives view correctional management today.

Traditional Models of Organizational Management

Scientific management, based on Frederick Taylor's system for achieving the maximum possible efficiency of machines and workers, gave way to the classical school of management. The classical school focused on organization structure and how best to structure resources and personnel to achieve organizational goals. The classical school gave way to the human relationists and their emphasis on relationships. Their primary contribution was recognition of the workplace as a social experience just as it is a vehicle to attain organizational objectives. The systems approach appeared during World War II and viewed the organization as the sum total of its parts. A problem in one part of the system affected the rest of the organization.

Managers discarded very little of the various models of organization, as each had its merits. However, they all seem to have come together during the 1960s when, it was believed, Rensis Likert (1967) discovered that the informal structure of the organization was more important than the formal structure. He suggested some important aspects of the informal structure that can modify, supplement, or replace the more traditional structural designs used in business and government (Figure 7.1).

Likert found that the lowest producing departments fall to the left of the continuum and that the departments falling to the right of the continuum are the highest producing departments; that is, they can be described as system three or four organizations, in which employees participate more. Further, when employees were asked what kind of organization they worked in, they usually described two or three, a more authoritarian structure. When asked to describe the kind of organization they would like to work in, they usually described a system four.

According to Likert, three things appear to explain the success of system four management: supportive relationships, group decision making and group methods of supervision, and high performance goals for the organization. The success of system four organizations demonstrates that the organization is a tightly knit, effectively functioning social system. This system is composed of interlocking work groups with a high degree of group loyalty among members and favorable attitudes and trust between superiors and subordinates. A system four work group includes a superior and all of his or her subordinates. Each subordinate, in turn, is a superior for subordinates at the next lower level in the organization. This linking pin function is necessary for the effective functioning of the organization. Clearly, the functional unit fits neatly into the system four scheme.

Unit Management Defined

The decision by the U.S. Bureau of Prisons to adopt unit management as a management structure and operating philosophy reflected a general trend in the 1970s to decentralize organization. Many private companies as well as organizations in the public sector learned that their structure was too rigid to quickly adapt to market conditions or public need. During this period, there also began a movement toward the adoption of work teams to improve service delivery and to allow greater input into decision making by the rank and file.

Unit management springs from notions about decentralization; its adherents point to two central arguments (White, 1936):

- Certain matters may be handled better at the local level and should remain there.

- Administrative officials at the center may act in an arbitrary and capricious manner.

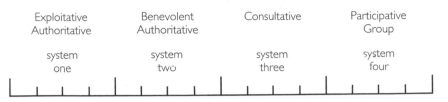

Figure 7.1 Likert's management systems. (*Source:* Adapted from R. Likert. (1967). *The Human Organization: Its Management and Value.* New York: Harper and Row.)

Since its inception, the U.S. Bureau of Prisons had been a traditional pyramidal agency, with the director sitting at the top and the layers of the organization spreading out beneath him or her. Policy and budgetary decisions reflected a top-down approach that often failed to allow for input from lower levels.

By 1970, the U.S. Bureau of Prisons (BOP) recognized two needs that would drive the adoption of unit management (Toch, 1992). One was to reduce tension and violence in many institutions and to protect weaker inmates who are prone to more predatory inmates. The second need was to deliver effective programs for those inmates with a history of substance abuse. The Narcotic Addict Rehabilitation Act (NARA) units were already proving to be successful, and the BOP recognized a need to devise programs that effectively delivered services to those inmates who had histories of substance abuse but did not qualify for a NARA unit.

Unit management was an idea whose time had come. It was time for a paradigm shift. Roy Gerard, Robert B. Levinson, and then director of the U.S. Bureau of Prisons Norman Carlson embarked on a journey that has revolutionized prison management (Gerard, 1991). The result had been an approach to prison management that incorporates the basics of sound management principles. Staff are allowed more input into organizational decision making and direct contact with inmates, which results in a more humane prison environment.

According to the U.S. Bureau of Prisons, a *unit* is defined as a small, self-contained inmate living and staff office area, which operates semiautonomously within the confines of the larger institution (Unit Management Manual, 1977). The essential components of a unit are

- A smaller number of inmates (50–120) who are assigned together permanently.

- A multidisciplinary staff (unit manager, case manager[s], correctional counselor[s], full- or part-time psychologist, clerk typist, and correctional officers) whose offices are located within the inmate housing unit and are permanently assigned to work with the inmates of that unit.

- A unit manager with administrative authority and supervisory responsibility for the unit staff.

- A unit staff with administrative authority for all within-unit aspects of inmate living and programming.

- Assignments of inmates to units based on age, prior record, specific behavior, specific behavior typologies, need for specific type of correctional program (such as drug abuse counseling), or on a random-assignment basis.

- A schedule that includes work in the unit evenings and weekends, on a rotating basis, in addition to the presence of the unit correctional officer.

Prior to the implementation of unit management, Bureau of Prison's institutions, similar to most state correctional institutions today, were arranged hierarchically with functions arranged by department. That is, a separate department head supervised similar functions. Faulty communications between departments were often the result. The Federal Correctional Institution (FCI) at Terminal Island, California, is a good example of how organizational functioning was improved by the implementation of unit management.

In 1976, the Bureau of Prisons decided to implement unit management at FCI, a unique institution that was actually two institutions under one warden. The northern part of the institution housed approximately 600 men, and the southern end of the institution about 150 women inmates. As a consequence, there were duplicate services and departments for both men and women. One advantage of the implementation of unit management was the consolidation of all services.

The warden appointed a committee comprised of two units for women and four units for men to implement unit management. Included was a drug program unit for men and one for women under one unit manager. The remaining units were for general population inmates with no special services other than those normally required for all inmates of the institution. There were a number of personnel problems to be worked out,

but once those were decided, unit managers were selected, dormitories were rehabilitated and converted into cubicles for inmate privacy, and office space for staff was constructed.

Inmates with histories of drug abuse or serving NARA sentences were assigned to a drug program unit. The men's drug program unit housed approximately 100 male inmates; the female drug unit housed approximately 80 inmates. Otherwise, there were approximately 120 inmates assigned to each unit by alphabet. Each unit contained two case managers, four correctional counselors, a secretary, and one unit manager who was responsible for supervision of all activities in the unit. While no official data were collected, the general view of staff in the institution at the time was that supervision was more effective, staff appreciated the opportunity to be proactive, disciplinary reports decreased, staff morale rose, and rapport with inmates increased.

Classification and History of Unit Management

Unit management is the evolutionary product of the classification process in prisons. Classification is defined as "a method by which diagnosis, treatment planning, and the execution of the treatment program are coordinated in the individual case" (Loveland, 1960:623). Classification grew slowly, first with the segregation of the sexes and children from adults. Gradually, institutions began to add educational and spiritual programs along with vocational training. Many states had relatively sophisticated classification systems by the 1930s, when the U.S. Bureau of Prisons instituted classification as a central intake procedure.

As the BOP grew, classification was introduced as the primary prisoner management tool (Keve, 1991). Until the 1930s, the Bureau of Prisons utilized only rudimentary classification procedures. By that time, new institutions had been constructed so that prisoners of varying age groups could be designated to different institutions, with female prisoners going to Alderson, West Virginia. By the 1950s, the Classification Committee —composed of the associate warden, captain, superintendent of education, chaplain, superintendent of industries, and the chief of classification and parole—was the vehicle for inmate classification. Undoubtedly, many inmates agreed to program participation because of intimidation fostered by the amount of "brass" in the room.

Treatment Team

During the early to mid-1960s, the concept of the *treatment team* began to take shape. The treatment team consisted of a group of staff (case manager, liaison officer, and teacher) who were responsible for the classification, periodic program review, and all other inmate case management matters. The liaison officer, a position developed from the research of Glaser (1964), was assigned to work with the case manager to handle much inmate contact and was also required to work with the correctional officers in the inmates' cell house or dormitory. From that position evolved the correctional counselor, a nondegreed position assigned to work directly with the team, the inmate, and the inmates' work and housing supervisor.

Unit management and the treatment team appeared to be made for each other. However, unit management as a concept in the Bureau of Prisons had an even earlier beginning (BOP, 1977) at the National Training School for Boys (NTS) in Washington, D.C., where inmates on one caseload were moved into one housing unit, and an interdisciplinary staff worked with them as they implemented a counseling and recreational program. Based on the success of this effort, the entire institution was reorganized according to this model.

In 1963, the Federal Youth Center at Englewood, Colorado, established a unit system featuring unit officers and a separate case manager for each unit. However, it wasn't until the Kennedy Youth Center at Morgantown, West Virginia, opened in 1969 that unit management got off the ground as a means to organize an entire institution.

The earliest units were specialized entities designed to handle substance abusers and difficult-to-manage inmates. For example, the Narcotic Addict Rehabilitation Act

Team Meetings

Team meetings are informal meetings with the case manager, correctional counselor, a representative of the education department, and often a psychologist and the unit manager sitting in. Prior to the meeting, the correctional counselor meets with the inmate and develops a visiting list and discusses other areas of concern. In the meantime, the inmate is subjected to a variety of psychological, medical, and educational tests to aid the team in developing a program for the inmate at the time of initial classification.

Before the meeting the case manager obtains a printout of all inmates due for action that week. On the day of the meeting, the case manager sees that inmates are able to meet with the team and that they will arrive at the meeting site at the designated time. The informality of the session promotes cooperation between inmates and staff, and all program decisions are arrived at jointly; other matters, such as custody level, are not an issue for negotiation. It is not uncommon for a team to spend all day in session meeting with inmates and conducting discussions. After inmates are through with their session, they return to their work assignment or cell house.

A record of all decisions is maintained by a member of the team and the decisions are later entered into the management information system for later retrieval. The advantage of the team approach is that staff listen to the inmate in all matters of importance to him or her, the decisions are explained, and even if the inmate does not agree, hostility is likely to be blunted.

of 1966 (NARA) delegated to the U.S. Bureau of Prisons the responsibility for drug treatment of certain eligible felons who had committed their offenses in order to support serious heroin habits. Those units established the basic rules for unit functioning.

In 1968, the first NARA unit was established at the Federal Correctional Institution (FCI), *Danbury, Connecticut.* Shortly afterward, other units were established at the FCIs at Terminal Island, California, and Milan, Michigan, and in the early 1970s, Fort Worth, Texas, and Lexington, Kentucky. Additionally, a number of drug abuse programs were established in a number of FCIs and penitentiaries, followed by an alcoholism unit at FCI Fort Worth and the S.T.A.R.T. unit at the U.S. Penitentiary at Marion, Illinois, for the most intractable inmates.

The experience at the Kennedy Youth Center that had been preceded by the Narcotic Addict Rehabilitation Act (NARA) units and followed by the various drug abuse programs established by the Bureau of Prisons in the 1970s proved that the idea of unit management would work. It ultimately worked in a variety of settings—penitentiaries and the less-secure federal correctional institutions (FCIs). Treatment teams replaced the old classification committees and inmates came to be viewed as members of the team and

allowed input. Previously, inmates were faced by all top managers in the institution; now they were included as team members with the staff who were supposed to know them best.

How Unit Management Works

In a *unitized* institution, newly arriving inmates meet with a unit correctional counselor within twenty-four hours of their arrival to compose a preliminary visiting list and discuss any concerns and fears. During the initial orientation period, medical, psychological, and educational testing is completed and inmates are moved into their units. Within a short time (usually one to two weeks), inmates meet with their team to develop programs that attempt to meet their needs relative to education, counseling, and employment upon release. Other concerns such as custody and institutional work assignment are also addressed. Periodically, inmates are brought before the team for review of their program and custody classification. There may be some variation depending on the institution, but the process has remained basically the same for at least fifteen years.

The advantage of unit management is that staff are able to follow inmates closely, physically see them daily, and interact on a more equal level as individuals and human beings. In addition, decisions are made on the unit, inmates have a say in those decisions, and there is the added flexibility of programming. This proactive approach has, in many instances, brought unruly and mutinous institutions under control.

Roy Gerard (1991), one of the originators of unit management, offers what he calls "commandments" for the successful implementation and operation of units:

1. *The concept of unit management must be understood by and have the support of top-level administration.* Unit management threatens the established hierarchical order. Many executives and supervisors do not want their position or authority challenged or changed and see unit management as a threat. In many ways it is a threat. Power is redistributed, information flows to the unit manager, and security and case management decisions are made by unit staff members. Executives and supervisors need to be able to see the advantages without worrying about their role. Such a view requires commitment to the organization and a strong sense of personal security.

2. *There must be a table of organization that has unit managers at a "department head" level, giving them responsibility for staff and inmates assigned to their unit.* On this table the unit managers and the head of security report to the same supervisor.

3. *The unit's population size should be based on its mission; that is, a general unit can house from 150 to 250 inmates and a special unit can house from 75 to 125 inmates without negatively affecting the unit mission.* Ideally, staffing should reflect the following:

	General Unit	Special Unit
Unit Manager	1	1
Case Manager	2	2
Correctional Counselor	2	2
Secretary	1	1
Mental Health	1/2	1
Part-time education, recreation, and volunteer staff.		
Twenty-four-hour coverage of correctional officers.		

4. *Inmates and unit staff should be permanently assigned to the unit; correctional officers should be stationed on the unit for a minimum of nine months.* The administration of an institution is tempted to move inmates around for a number of reasons. However, anecdotal evidence reflects that when inmates are responsible to the same staff over a prolonged period of time, the staff and inmates come to know each other well enough that inmates exhibit fewer problems. Unit management divides the large number of inmates into small, well-defined, and manageable groups whose members develop a common identity and close association with each other and their unit staff.

5. *In addition to correctional officer coverage, unit staff should provide twelve-hour supervision Monday through Friday and eight hours on each weekend day.* At the FCI, Terminal Island, the warden established a work schedule that required case managers and correctional counselors to work two evenings per week. In addition, all unit managers were required to work at least one evening per week and one weekend per month. The advantage of this schedule is that case managers, counselors, and unit managers are available to meet the needs and work schedules of inmates in their unit. A tertiary advantage is that more staff are available for supervision of inmates. This work schedule is in use in nearly all U.S. Bureau of Prisons' institutions as well as many state institutions that have implemented unit management.

6. *Staff offices should be located on the unit or as near to it as possible.* Access is the key to success. Availability of unit staff to inmates reflects the decentralized nature of the institution and increases the accessibility of staff. It increases the frequency of contacts and the intensity of the relationship between staff and inmates, resulting in

1. Better communication and understanding between individuals

2. More individualized classification and program planning

3. More valuable program reviews and program adjustments

4. Better observation of inmates, enabling early detection of problems before they reach critical proportions

5. Development of common goals that encourage positive unit cohesiveness

6. Generally a more positive living and working environment for inmates and staff

A Model Unit Management Program

The establishment of unit programs is a policy matter left up to the warden, assistant wardens, and the respective unit managers (in consultation with staff). Some units may offer only required services relative to case management needs and minimal individual counseling as called for by individual circumstances. It is likely that these types of units will be found in institutions for older, more sophisticated inmates. However, for younger inmates and for inmates with special needs such as substance abuse, a program can be devised that attends to the needs of the inmates.

A successful unit program is hinged on a unit plan, and it is important that all staff participate in developing the unit plan. This is much like a master plan that defines "unit missions and goals, describes programs, defining (sic) responsibilities, prescribes how the unit will evaluate its operation" (BOP, 1977). One approach is to divide the day into equal segments from 8:00 A.M. to 9:00 P.M. Assuming adequate space for group counseling and executive approval of the program, the inmate can be required to fill each segment of the day constructively. The following sample program illustrates the options available to unit staff:

8:00–10:00 A.M.	Work (industries)
10:00–12:00 noon	Work (industries)
12:00– 1:00 P.M.	Lunch (cell time)

1:00–3:00 P.M.	School (GED)
3:00–4:30 P.M.	Group counseling
4:30–6:00 P.M.	Count, cell time, supper
6:00–7:30 P.M.	Group counseling
7:30–9:00 P.M.	Self-help group (tutoring, parent effectiveness training [P.E.T.], etc.)

This schedule is arrived at in consultation with inmates at the time of classification and periodic reviews, and it allows unit staff to maintain close watch over the activities of inmates. In addition, as one segment of the program is completed (e.g., GED), another activity can be inserted into the vacant time slot.

Some critics may point out that programs and security do not go well together and as a consequence, programs are given short shrift in favor of security. The problem is not that programs and security are incompatible, but rather that programs are imposed on the security framework. The advantage of unit management is that security is part of the approach, and programs and security are viewed from the same side of the fence. In this plan, unit staff are full partners in security efforts by demanding accountability from inmates regarding their conduct for eleven hours out of the day.

The Effectiveness of Unit Management

It is difficult to state exactly how many systems have implemented unit management, as there have been no nationwide surveys. However, Table 7.1 illustrates which sates are believed to have implemented unit management.[1] The table includes the states of Connecticut, Georgia, Iowa, Missouri, and New York, all of which have provided no information.

The impact of unit management on institutions has been spectacular in some instances and more subtle in

others. Staff generally believe that they are included in the decision-making and planning processes. Inmates, on the other hand, believe that they have close interaction with staff and are given the opportunity to participate in unit processes. Overall, in those institutions that have implemented unit management, it has been found that few areas are unaffected by its use.

The U.S. Bureau of Prisons assessed the impact of unit management as it is implemented in many institutions. Bureau of Prisons' researchers found that inmate assaults on other inmates in intermediate adult institutions decreased, and that overtime pay decreased, not only during disturbances but during other more tranquil periods. In addition, abuse of sick days declined (Rowe et al., 1977). Further research was conducted by the U.S. Bureau of Prisons (BOP, no date) using Rudolf Moos's Correctional Institutions Environmental Scale (CIES). The CIES was administered to staff and inmates at the Federal Correctional Institution, Milan, Michigan, both prior to implementation and afterwards, revealing remarkable *favorable results*, including greater inmate satisfaction with programs and increased job satisfaction by staff.

Unit management has also been implemented in Australian prisons. Robson (1989) reports that the implementation of unit management has been found to be more efficient and cost effective in one institution. He also notes that unit management appears to have reduced vandalism, negative behavior, and assaults. Pierson (1991) reports that Missouri implemented unit management with success, but there have been modifications in the concept to allow for budget constraints; for example, units house from 150 to 300 inmates instead of the number advocated by Levinson and Gerard. Nevertheless, Pierson reports the same advantages of unit management as does the U.S. Bureau of Prisons.

The latest and most recent evaluation of unit management was completed by the Ohio Department of Corrections in 1991 (Executive Summary, Ohio DOC, 1991). Central office staff conducted interviews and onsite reviews at twenty of the de-

partment's twenty-two institutions. With few exceptions, the report concludes that

We have found it [unit management] to be both an effective and efficient means of addressing the concerns of managing an expanding inmate population while remaining sensitive to community expectations and the responsibilities we share with our legal system. Since the transition to unit management, we have observed a marked improvement in the overall operation of our institutions. The report found improvement in a variety of areas. (p. 3)

The authors of the report note the proactive approach of unit management and conclude that escapes drop significantly, inmates are held more responsible for their behavior, nonsecurity staff are more involved and more knowledgeable of security measures, the multidisciplinary team approach responds to inmate needs more quickly, and the overall delivery of services is improved. In addition, line staff are more aware of management's expectations, the custody-treatment staff dichotomy is reduced, and in general the overall experience of staff is expanded.

The Ohio experience is an excellent example of the commitment necessary by executive staff if unit management is to succeed. Obviously, initial interest is in the area of inmate management, but as the U.S. Bureau of Prisons and the Ohio Department of Corrections found, the importance of involving staff in "everything" is just as important as good inmate management.

Summary

Corrections today is faced with seemingly insurmountable problems. Over-crowding, gangs, shrinking budgets, a better educated workforce, and a more difficult to manage inmate population are just a few of the issues that must be faced by the corrections manager. Unit management is an approach to managing a correctional institution that takes advantage of sound management principles and efficiently delivers services to the inmate population.

Involving staff in policy decisions, recognizing their achievements, and building a climate that

Table 7.1 Unit Management in the United States

State	Date Begun	Facilities—Number and Percentage in Unit Management		Size Range (avg.) Ideal	Staffing Pattern	Staff/Inmate Ratio
Connecticut	—	—	—	— —	—	—
Georgia	—	—	—	— —	—	—
Iowa	—	—	—	— —	—	—
Michigan	1973	24/24	100%	120/450/175/200	3	1:58
Missouri[a]	—	—	—	— —	—	—
Nebraska	1979	6/6	100%	82/130/100/100	7	1:14
New York City (June)	—	—	—	— —	—	—
New Hampshire	1986	1/1	100%	25/200/150/175	4.5	1:33
North Carolina	1982	2/11	18%	93/120/110/100	4	1:28
Ohio	1986	13/17	75%	150/400/250/300	6	1:42
Oklahoma	1986	13/13	100%	120/180/150/150	6	1:25
South Carolina	1982	4/10	40%	126/312/150/150	5	1:30
Tennessee[b]	1988	0/14	—	—160—	6	1:27
Virginia	1985	1/10	10%	72/100/72—	3	1:24
Bureau of Prisons	1965[c]	47/47	100%	150/400/250/200	6	1:42

[a]Obtained from other sources.

[b]The NIC provided the information with no explanation as to how Tennessee could claim to have units, but show no institutions involved.

[c]The 1965 date reflects the BOP's first experiments with the forerunner of Unit Management at the National Training School.

Note: In 1996, the Wisconsin Department of Corrections conducted a national survey and found 27 states using unit management (Wisconsin Department of Corrections National Survey, 1996).

Source: Correspondence with the National Institute of Corrections (April 1992).

fosters camaraderie and excellence are the qualities that serve the public and promote quality control. Communication, classification, program planning, inmate observation, and other activities are more easily monitored for quality.

Unit management is both a management approach and a service delivery vehicle. It grew out of the U.S. Bureau of Prisons' need to reduce tension and protect weaker inmates as well as to provide a vehicle to deliver substance abuse programs. Early units such as the NARA and the Drug Abuse Program units proved that the concept would work and provided the impetus to expand unit management throughout the U.S. Bureau of Prisons.

Today, fourteen states, besides the BOP, claim to use unit management, and the concept appears to be growing internationally as well. The success of unit management, where implemented, can be attributed to the ability of staff to better relate to inmates, increased staff job satisfaction, and increased program flexibility.

Note

1. Until the publication of *Correctional Management: Functions, Skills, and Systems* (Nelson-Hall), no information was available on how many jurisdictions claimed to utilize unit management. A call to the National Institute of Corrections revealed that no one had made an effort to determine how widespread the use of unit management had become. I am grateful to Patricia Scholes for her work in putting together most of the information that appears in Table 7.1. However, the reader is cautioned to view the table with some skepticism because some jurisdictions may be using something they call unit management, but it may not conform to the definition of Gerard et al.

References

Allen, H.E. and Simonsen, C.E. (1998). *Corrections in America* (8th ed.). Upper Saddle River, NJ: Prentice Hall.

American Correctional Association. (1966). *Manual of Correctional Standards*. College Park, ND: Author.

de Beaumont, G. and de Toqueville, A. (1833, 1970). *On the Penitentiary System in the United States and Its Application in France.* Philadelphia: Carey, Lea & Blanchard. Reprinted by A.M. Kelly.

Brockway, Z.H. (1871/1970). "The Ideal of a True Prison System for a State." In E.C. Wines, D.D., LL.D., (ed.), *Transactions of the National Congress on Penitentiary and Reformatory Discipline*, Albany: Weed, Parsons and Co., Printers. Reprinted by the American Correctional Association.

Business Week. (1970, June 8). "The Push for Quality":130–144.

Executive Summary. (1991, December). "A Report Prepared Pursuant to Amended Substitute House Bill 298." Columbus: Ohio Department of Corrections.

Gerard, R.E. (1991, April). "The Ten Commandments of Unit Management." *Corrections Today*:32, 34, 36.

Glaser, D. (1964). *The Effectiveness of a Prison and Parole System*. Indianapolis: Bobbs-Merrill.

Irwin, J. (1985). *The Jail: Managing the Underclass in American Society*. Berkeley: University of California Press.

Keve, P.W. (1991). *Prisons and the American Conscience: A History of U.S. Federal Corrections*. Carbondale, IL: Southern Illinois University Press.

Levinson, R.B. and Gerard, R.E. (1973). "Functional Units: A Different Correctional Approach." *Federal Probation*, 37(4):8–15.

Likert, R. (1967). *The Human Organization: Its Management and Value*. New York: Harper and Row.

Loveland, F. (1960). "Classification in the Prison System." In P. Tappan (ed.) *Crime, Justice, and Correction*. New York: McGraw-Hill.

McDonald, D.C. (1989). "The Cost of Corrections: In Search of the Bottom Line." In National Institute of Corrections, *Research in Corrections*. Boulder, CO: National Institute of Corrections 2(1).

McGregor, D. (1960). "Theory X and Theory Y." In D.S. Pugh. (1984). *Organization Theory* (2d ed.). New York: Penguin Books.

Pierson, T.A. (1991, April). "One State's Success with Unit Management." *Corrections Today*:24, 26, 28, 30

Robson, R. (1989). "Managing the Long Term Prisoner: A Report on an Australian Innovation in Unit Management." *The Howard Journal* 28(3):187–203.

Rowe, R., Foster, E., Byerly, K., Laird, N., and Prather, J. (1977). *The Impact of Functional Unit Management on Indicies of Inmate Incidents*. (Unpublished research report by the U.S. Bureau of Prisons.)

Skolnick, J. (1993). *Justice Without Trial: Law Enforcement in Democratic Society* (3d ed.). New York: John Wiley and Sons, Inc. Skolnick discusses the elements of authority and danger relative to the role of the police officer, but his notions of solidarity among police officers also have merit in a discussion of staff solidarity vis-a-vis inmates. The existence of potential danger and the inherent authority of staff members creates a press to look to each other for mutual support. See also Kauffman, K. (1988). *Prison Offices and Their World* Cambridge, MA: Harvard University Press; and Lombardo, L.X. (1981). *Guards Imprisoned*. New York: Elsevier.

Tappan, P.W. (1960). *Crime, Justice, and Correction*. New York: McGraw-Hill.

Toch, H. (1992, Winter). "Functional Unit Management: An Unsung Achievement." *Federal Prisons Journal* 2(4):15–19.

U.S. Bureau of Prisons. (1977). *Unit Management Manual*. Washington, D.C.: U.S.B.O.P.

U.S. Bureau of Prisons (1975, September). *Preliminary Evaluation of the Functional Unit Approach to Correctional Management* (Unpublished report by the U.S. Bureau of Prisons.)

U.S. Bureau of Prisons (no date). *Position Paper on Functional Units*. (Unpublished document.)

Webster, J.H. (April, 1991). "Designing Facilities for Effective Unit Management." *Corrections Today*:38, 40, 42.

White, L.D. (1936). "The Meaning of Principles in Public Administration." In J.M. Gaus, L.B. White, and M.E. Demock (eds.), *The Frontiers of Public Administration*. Chicago: University of Chicago Press.

Wines, E.C., D.D., LL.D. (ed.). (1871). "The Present Outlook of Prison Discipline in the United States." In E.C. Wines, D.D., LL.D. (ed.), *Transactions of the National Congress on Penitentiary and Reformatory Discipline*, Albany: Weed, Parsons and Co., Printers. Reprinted by the American Correctional Association, Washington, D.C., 1970.

 Article Review Form at end of book.

In what way can community partnerships and sanctions aid in the control of prison overcrowding? Is bed capacity the only answer to efficient crime control?

Controlling Prison Crowding

Judith Greene

Judith Greene is program director of the State Partnership for Criminal Justice, which offers technical assistant to states trying to control population growth.

Faced with growing jail and prison populations fueled by the "War on Drugs," U.S. correctional systems have invested heavily in expanding their bed capacities. Yet, the construction boom has not caught up with the population boom in most states. Despite spending more than $5 billion on new prison beds since the early '80s, California still was operating at 181 percent of capacity in 1985. Incarceration rates have skyrocketed in the past decade, from 313 per 100,000 in 1985, to 600 per 100,000 in 1995—and the 1,585,401 inmates held in the nation's jails and prisons at the end of 1995 was nearly triple the number held in 1980. Double celling and augmenting capacity with temporary "emergency" beds have not sufficed to manage the overflow. Consequently, increasing numbers of inmates are shipped from state to state wherever empty beds can be found.

Structured Sentencing Programs

A few states are struggling to gain control of correctional population levels through "structured sentencing" measures: sentencing guidelines designed to spare prison beds for more serious and violent offenders.

In 1988, the Edna McConnell Clark Foundation initiated a program to help criminal justice policymakers plan and implement reforms such as these. Now based in newly formed Institute on Criminal Justice at the University of Minnesota Law School, the State Partnership for Criminal Justice (SPCJ) helps convene policymakers in selected states and supports a process by which key state leaders form a steering committee including legislators, corrections and probation commissioners, judges and prosecutors. The SPCJ process assists each steering committee in implementing strategies tailored to each state's needs.

The following look at the experiences with prison crowding and population control in two of the nine states which have participated in SPCJ illustrates the challenges policymakers face as they balance the burgeoning cost of operating expanding correctional systems and the need to sustain other vital systems (e.g., education, housing and health care) which can produce more fundamental, long-term improvements in public safety.

Oregon's Effective Incarceration Project

In partnership with SPCJ, Oregon's Citizens Crime Commission, an affiliate of the Portland Chamber of Commerce, launched the Effective Incarceration Project in the summer of 1996. The project is geared toward improving state criminal justice policy-

making by providing citizens with better and more complete information on criminal justice issues. The project's steering committee is co-chaired by Dave Cook, director of the Oregon Department of Corrections, and Paul Lorenzini, senior vice president at PacifiCorp, who chairs the Crime Commission board of directors.

With a longstanding tradition of reliance on community corrections, Oregon has maintained a rate of incarceration well below the national average since 1971. Yet, despite growing population pressures, prison bond measures had been soundly rejected by Oregon voters in 1980, 1983 and 1986. By 1987, the prison system was operating at almost double its capacity. Gov. Neil Goldschmidt began an $85 million effort to double the size of the prison system.

At the same time, the Oregon legislature mandated that the Oregon Criminal Justice Council devise strict sentencing guidelines to manage increasing population levels. The resulting sentencing structure aimed to toughen sanctions for serious violent crimes. Its implementation produced dramatic increases in both admissions and average time served for such offenses. But, because the guidelines also created a strong presumption favoring probation and intermediate sanctions for less serious offenders, overall prison populations were held within capacity for five years.

In 1994, however, the state's voters gave overwhelming approval to a ballot initiative which imposed harsh mandatory prison terms for 16

Controlling Prison Crowding, Judith Greene. *Corrections Today,* January 1997, 59(1), 50–56. Reprinted with permission of the American Correctional Association, Lanham, MD.

serious felony crimes, trumping the guidelines and catapulting the state toward a new crowding crisis. Early estimates projected that the number of inmates in Oregon would double by the year 2000, but Cook thinks that the actual growth curve may prove to be somewhat less sharp. "Our district attorneys are trying to be discerning in the use of their discretionary powers under the new law, so the specific impact should be smaller than we originally thought," he says.

Even so, since passage of the "get tough" ballot measure, the prison population has jumped. According to an article by Bogan and Factor in the April 1995 issue of *Overcrowded Times*, the prison population has increased by 25 percent— from 6,844 in December 1994 to 8,550 two years later. A series of fiscal ballot initiatives passed since 1990 has constricted Oregon's tax base, and policymakers are worried that mandatory sentences embraced by voters could force cuts in health care, education and other vital state services.

Faced with the prospect of renewed crowding, Oregon's current governor, John Kitzhaber, has launched a new construction effort to expand the prison system to 17,500 beds by 2005. This plan is coupled with an ambitious effort to reserve new beds for the state's more serious, violent or career offenders. Kitzhaber won authorization during the 1995 legislative season to give responsibility back to the counties for all offenders sentenced to 12 months or less. His legislative package has provided a greatly increased state funding stream for local jails, community corrections and substance abuse treatment programs, and given communities control of the allocation of these monies.

Public Misconceptions and the "Get Tough" Mentality

Since these mandatory sentencing provisions were voted in 1994, SPCJ has sponsored two public opinion polls regarding crime problems and correctional policies in Oregon. The first was conducted by a national research firm in April 1995, and the second by a Portland-based firm in June 1996. Results from both polls confirm a solid base of public support for using community corrections and intermediate sanctions to help nonviolent offenders.

But, research also suggests that public misconceptions about the operation of the state's criminal justice system may have fueled the "get tough" mood expressed in the vote for mandatory sentences. While overall crime rates have been stable in Oregon for many years, with violent crime showing recent decreases, more than two-thirds of those polled said they thought crime was on the rise. And, while sentencing guidelines had stabilized prison population levels within capacity and abolished parole release, most Oregonians nonetheless believe that violent offenders routinely are set free due to prison crowding.

"The 'disconnects' between some of the public's beliefs and the realities of the criminal justice system point to the importance of the Effective Incarceration Project," says Ray Mathis, executive director of the Citizens Crime Commission. "If the public has current information on what is actually happening in public safety, that could certainly affect how they vote and what they demand of their elected officials."

Cook agrees. "The problem has been lack of knowledge," he says. "I believe that once people come to know the facts about what the system is accomplishing and what is effective, they'll act accordingly. They'll want to know if we're using their tax money wisely, and whether there are ways to use it even more effectively."

North Carolina's Criminal Justice Partnership Act

In 1994, North Carolina joined the SPCJ partnership with the goal of implementing major legislative initiatives which paralleled Oregon's reforms. Two measures already had been enacted by the legislature and were about to be launched when an SPCJ steering committee was formed:

- The Structured Sentencing Act introduced sentencing guidelines to "truth in sentencing" while gaining front-end control of the criminal justice to balance

sentencing policy with correctional resources.

- The State County Criminal Justice Partnership Act established a comprehensive statewide community corrections system to provide cost-effective intermediate sanctions for nonviolent offenders in the community.

These two measures followed decades of sentencing policy struggles which had made management of the correctional system difficult. Prior to 1982, North Carolina's judges had enjoyed wide discretion under an indeterminate sentencing system, and there were few constraints on release decision-making by the state's parole commission. Despite such broad latitude, North Carolina frequently led the nation in per capita incarceration rates.

In 1979, a legislative commission on corrections voiced concerns about sentencing disparities and recommended the establishment of a system of presumptive prison terms based on the classification of each offense. Judges would deviate only if they found aggravating or mitigating factors, and parole release would be abolished. However, when the Fair Sentencing Act was passed in 1981, plea bargains were exempt from these restraints and provisions of liberal "good time" and "gain time" were incorporated. For a while, sentences were shorter and more uniform, but upward deviations soon increased and prison crowding worsened. Discretionary parole was reinstated and the time served on prison sentences imposed by judges began to fall.

By the mid 1980s, although a statewide network of "client-specific planners" had been established to advocate for alternative sentences for nonviolent offenders, prison crowding continued to escalate. Another legislative study recommended expansion of correctional capacity— both prison beds and sentencing alternatives—and the creation of a sentencing commission charged with the development of a comprehensive sentencing policy. In the meantime, under a 1987 settlement in a lawsuit challenging crowded prison conditions, the legislature enacted a cap on prison populations which triggered early release of offenders when populations rose to 98 percent of capacity. This measure slowed the growth of the state's incarceration rate by throwing the proportion of time actually served by imprisoned offenders into a downward spiral—from 40 percent in 1986 to 18 percent by 1993—fueling, in turn, demands for tougher penalties by an incensed public.

In settling the lawsuit, the state had committed itself to a $275 million prison building plan which gained public endorsement through a prison bond referendum passed in 1990. The North Carolina Sentencing and Policy Advisory Commission was established by the legislature that same year to revamp the state's sentencing structure. After spending two years devising a sentencing guidelines grid, the commission submitted two separate options to the legislature. The first would have required significant prison expansion beyond the prison construction effort already underway. This option was rejected. The second option has been designed to bring population levels into balance with the projected future capacity, and would not require commitment of additional capital expenditures. This sentencing grid structure, adopted in July 1993, covers both misdemeanors and felonies. Each felony conviction can be classified according to the grid structure, and each grid cell contains a specific prescription for sentencing: a presumptive prison or jail sentence range for serious cases, or, for less serious offenders, a judge can choose incarceration or select an intermediate sanction such as day reporting or drug treatment. In a few grid cells representing the least serious felony cases, a judge's choices are restricted to nonincarcerative options. Parole release was eliminated again.

Sentencing data from 1995 show that the primary goals are being reached: to reduce the overall proportion of offenders sentenced to prison, while (as in Oregon) sharply increasing the proportion of violent and career offenders incarcerated and lengthening the time these offenders serve. In 1995, 29 percent of felons sentenced under the new law were imprisoned, compared with 48 percent of those sentenced in 1993 under the old law. But felons released from prison in 1993 had only

served an average of 15.7 months. Sentencing Commission projections indicate that felony offenders sentenced under the new law in 1995 will, on average, serve within a range of 34 to 44 months.

The State-County Criminal Justice Partnership Act was enacted in tandem with the new structured sentencing law to provide more effective sentencing options for the increased numbers of low-level felons sentenced to intermediate sanctions and community punishments. During a legislative session on crime convened by Gov. Jim Hunt early in 1994, additional probation budget funds were appropriated to support the expected increased use of intermediate and community punishments. Partnership Act grant funds also were earmarked by the Department of Corrections for contracting by local jurisdictions for community corrections programs.

When in Doubt . . . Build?

At the end of November 1996, North Carolina's prisons held almost 29,000 inmates and operated at 118 percent of capacity. By the end of next year, enough new prison beds will be added so that housing inmates in leased beds out of state no longer will be required. When the building program is complete, North Carolina expects to have 35,500 prison beds on-line. According to Corrections Secretary Franklin Freeman, the prison population should come into balance with a 33,000-bed capacity by 1998, and will remain at or below capacity until at least 2003.

But Secretary Freeman believes that just having the bed capacity is not enough to ensure the success of the state's population control efforts. "Structured sentencing will not work unless you have strong community sanctions in place," Freeman says. "If you only build prison beds, the reform will fail. Without community partnerships providing intermediate sanctions and the intensive supervision which are both vital to proper management of the people we're redirecting to community sanctions, it all will be undermined."

Freeman believes that a recent SPCJ-sponsored public opinion poll

has been an essential element in the state's effort to strengthen the community sanctions system. "We learned that there was strong support for certain intermediate sanctions," he says. "The poll results helped us identify which ones they were, and to get them 'framed right' so we could continue to build even stronger support for our strategy."

The opinion research also has added political credibility to the reform package. "It helped us build and sustain these intermediate sanctioning programs during the crucial early months, when the concept came under repeated attack in the legislature," Freeman adds. "And it has served as a springboard for our public education effort, reinforcing the role of intermediate sanctions as an integral part of structured sentencing."

Judge Thomas Ross, who chairs the North Carolina Sentencing Commission and co-chairs the state's SPCJ steering committee with Secretary Freeman, agrees. "The public opinion poll gave us concrete information we could use to demonstrate that our policy reforms were supported," he says. The steering committee sees public education about the reforms as the central element necessary to sustaining success and warding off setbacks. Judge Ross has become a tireless campaigner in this regard—crisscrossing the state to share information about editorial boards and citizen groups.

A second aspect of the SPCJ partnership which, according to Ross, has greatly strengthened implementation of the state's sentencing reform agenda, has been the structure of the SPCJ steering committee itself: low-profile but high-powered, with joint leadership from both corrections and the courts. "We have brought other elements to the table which were not there before," he says. "We've been able to forge a coherent, consistent legislative approach to replace competition between the DOC and the Department of Human Resources. We've been able to go directly to the treatment folks and say 'Join in with us . . . help us to design community programs that really work.' "

 Article Review Form at end of book.

Why would the general public think that electronic monitoring of offenders is soft on crime? Are there societal opportunities to be gained by leaving some offenders in the home?

A Typology for Assessing the Electronic Monitoring Experience

B. K. Payne and R. R. Gainey

Introduction

Numerous sanctions to deal with criminal offenders have evolved with our rapidly changing society. Indeed, in the mid-1800s, probation and parole evolved to fill the need of treating offenders in ways viewed as more humane during that time period. A detailed analysis of sentencing policies over the past decade would also support the claim that methods of punishing offenders change as society changes. Electronic monitoring is a particularly important recent sanction that came as a result of the needs of society and technological advancement.

Both the American public and public officials seem to have varied perceptions of electronic monitoring. On the one hand, electronic monitoring has technological appeal and appears to many to be less costly than imprisonment, and a useful way of controlling at least some offenders. On the other hand, during this period of renewed interest in retribution and a discounting of rehabilitation, many view electronic monitoring as soft on crime (Larivee,

1993). In this paper we describe a typology that outlines the potential costs of electronic monitoring as they are experienced by the offender.

Review of Literature

In the United States, electronic monitoring programs were first implemented in 1984 in West Palm Beach, Florida (Maxfield & Baumer, 1990), and were "designed as a punishment alternative to help build accountability and responsibility" (Papy & Nimer, 1991, p. 31). Starting with only 94 offenders on electronic monitoring, by the early 1990s, it was estimated that more than 12,000 offenders were on electronic monitoring (Clark, 1994, p. 99; Renzema & Skeleton, 1991, p. 6).

Electronic monitoring programs are administered using different monitoring devices (Lilly et al., 1992; Nellis, 1991, Papy, 1994; Rackmill, 1994). The two most common devices are typically referred to as "passive" and "continuous signalling systems." In the passive system, a computer calls the home at various times when the offender is ordered there and the offender places a signalling device in the phone, or answers the phone, to show that he or she is there. In the

continuous signalling system, the offender's whereabouts are constantly monitored by transmitters and receivers placed on the offender and the telephone. If the offender moves too far away from the phone when he or she is not supposed to, the telephone will immediately notify enforcement officials (Nellis, 1991, p. 166; Lilly et al., 1992, p. 43).

Not only are different devices used in the electronic monitoring programs, they are also administered for different reasons at different parts of the criminal justice process including pretrial release (Cadigan, 1991; Cooprider, 1992; Cooprider & Kerby, 1989; Gowen, 1995), as a sanction imposed by the courts, and as a condition of release from jail or prison (Cohn, 1996; Maxfield & Baumer, 1990; Rackmill, 1994). Regardless of where electronic monitoring occurs in the system, ethical, legal, political, and social questions arise (Schmidt, 1991; Walker, 1990). As Lilly (1989, p. 89) points out, electronic monitoring is criticized "as a tool of Big Brotherism because it uses electronic equipment to turn homes into prisons and can widen the criminal justice net." Building on this, other scholars question whether electronic monitoring simply widens the net of

From "How Monitoring Punishes," *Journal of Offender Monitoring*, Winter 1998, pp. 23–25, Vol. 12, No. 1. Reprinted by permission.

the criminal justice system increasing its overall costs to taxpayers (Maineprize, 1992). Still others view intermediate sanctions, including electronic monitoring as an "effective and economical alternative to incarceration" (Lilly & Ball, 1989, p. 89).

The debate on effectiveness actually centers on the way that electronic monitoring programs fulfill the goals of punishment—deterrence, retribution, rehabilitation, incapacitation (van Hirsch, 1976). The deterrent power of electronic monitoring has not yet been assessed (Siegel, 1997). The very nature of these programs removes the offender from society for a duration of their sentence. More importantly, however, the goals typically associated with electronic monitoring programs are rehabilitation and control/surveillance (Ball, 1989). Building on the control aspect, Rackmill (1994) says that "the purposes of home confinement are diverse and the specific restrictions imposed through it determine how intrusive and punitive the sanction is" (p. 49). Realizing, as Kant suggests, that retribution is a natural human emotion, we have developed a typology describing ways that electronic monitoring sanctions actually punish offenders.

Punishment Typology

The typology we developed is, in part, based on Durkheim's ideas. For example, our typology focuses on the way that the sanction controls the behavior of the offender. Further, the sanction, as a social fact, is suggested to fulfill many functions for society, the criminal justice system, and the offender. Third, the sanction is viewed as a result of technological changes in an organic society. Finally, the sanction is based on the premise that control over the offender's life is needed in order to maintain order in society. Without such controls, anomie and disorder would spread at rates more quickly than the subsequent response of policymakers, legislatures, and practitioners.

It is important to note that our typology is based on general aspects of the probation and parole disposition. That is, those who are on probation or parole generally must abide by what are called conditions of probation/parole in an environment

full of rules restricting the behavior of the offender. Utilizing these ideas, our typology suggests that the conditions and restrictions associated with the electronic monitoring sanction make it punitive.

Conditions are activities that the electronic monitoring offender is forced to do as a result of the punishment. Broadly speaking, two types of conditions seem to relate to the electronic monitoring sanction: controlling conditions and technological conditions.

Controlling conditions are activities that the offenders have to do as a condition of the sentence that are designed primarily to control offenders. Several examples are noteworthy. Offenders on electronic monitoring usually have to provide urine for alcohol and drug tests. Therefore, they are forced to refrain from alcohol use which is legal for the rest of the adult population. Also, offenders have their work, leisure time, and sleep interrupted by law enforcement calls to ensure that the offender is where he or she is supposed to be. Further, some of the offenders feel that they have to keep their houses in order (e.g., clean and straighten) at all times in case the probation officer visits the residence (Payne & Gainey, 1997).

There are also technological conditions associated with electronic monitoring. Obviously, having to wear a monitor is one such condition. Research suggests that this can be uncomfortable, embarrassing, or otherwise problematic, particularly for females (Payne & Gainey, 1997). Hooking the equipment up to the phone yields other potential costs for the offender. Beyond the simple need to explain the equipment to visitors, the way the equipment limits phone services for the offender and his/her co-habitants also raises concerns (Schmidt, 1991). That is, some may not be able to have call waiting or answering machines. Finally, the offender, in many jurisdictions, has to pay a fee to offset the costs of the sanction. As one offender said, "Jail costs the public a lot, electronic monitoring costs the offender a lot" (Payne & Gainey, 1997).

Restrictions

Whereas conditions are concerned with what the offender has to do as a

result of the sanction, restrictions entail activities that the offender cannot do because of the electronic monitoring sanction. There are three types of restrictions: controlling restrictions, technological restrictions, and passive restrictions.

Controlling restrictions are activities that the offender is unable to engage in that control various aspects of the offender's life. Generally, those on electronic monitoring do not have weekends free—something most people look forward to. Those on electronic monitoring cannot go to the store or for a walk if they feel the desire. Likewise, they do not have the ability to go out with friends or family members. Further, they can not stay late at work or meet their friends after work. Perhaps more problematic for the offender may be the suggestion that they may not be able to get away from their roommates should they ever want time alone.

Technological restrictions are activities that the offender cannot do as a result of the technology associated with the sanction. For example, the offender and their family/co-occupants cannot ignore the phone or turn the ringer off on their phone—something others may do regularly. They may be restricted from talking too long on the phone in case their electronic monitoring supervisor tries to call. Likewise, they are responsible for the equipment, which they often have to pay for and may be blamed for technical problems over which they have little or no control. Imagine the concern one might feel if the electricity goes off and they have no way of contacting their supervisor to let them know they are where they should be.

Passive restrictions are experiences of the offender that restrict various aspects of the offender's life, but do not necessarily control the offender and aren't associated with the technological aspect of the sanction. For example, offenders sanctioned to electronic monitoring must watch as others do things the offender is unable to do. Or, the offender's whereabouts will always be known to his or her friends, which may be troublesome to some. Further, offenders might worry about getting into trouble because of things their family or friends might do (e.g., bringing drugs into the home). Finally, the embarrassment or shame of not being able to leave the house and having to tell others about the situation likely presents some anguish for some offenders.

Concluding Remarks

What is clearly needed is more electronic monitoring research focusing on offenders' experiences and the public's attitudes about this sanction. This typology is by no means a definitive typology. Rather, it is a foundation from which more research on electronic monitoring can begin. To understand the actual costs of the sanction, those who have experienced the sanction need to be studied. While our typology may respond to the past data well, it needs to be tested on the sanction about which it is designed. The degree and importance of each cost can best be assessed through examinations of those sentenced to electronic monitoring programs.

Also, increased awareness among the public is needed in order to convince legislatures of the need to continue to implement, fund, and rely on alternative sentences (Brown & Elrod, 1995; Crouch, 1995; Turner et al., 1997). If the public opposes such programs, legislatures will continue their attack on alternative sanctions. However, if the sanctions are found to meet the needs of the retributive public, and the public becomes aware of the punitive aspect of the sanction, anomic conditions will lessen and the public will come to trust this new sanction. Until greater awareness occurs in four areas, the public will likely continue to distrust electronic monitoring.

First, the public needs to know whether the sanction punishes offenders. Second, the public needs to know whether the sanction rehabilitates offenders. Third, the public needs to know that the sanction is generally proportionate to the offense, meaning that for the most part, only less serious offenders are given this sanction. Fourth, the public must come to see the sanction as cost-effective.

Where the public stands on these issues is unclear. Through the offender and public opinion research we suggest, steps toward increased understanding and awareness about electronic monitoring will be taken. Further, researchers will hopefully be able to use this information "to effect planned change."

References

Apospori, E. & Alpert, G. (1993). Research Note: The role of differential experience with the criminal justice system in changes in perceptions of severity of legal sanctions over time. *Crime and Delinquency* 39(2): 184–194.

Brown, Michael, P. & Elrod, Preston. (1995). Electronic house arrest: An examination of citizen attitudes. *Crime and Delinquency* 41 (3): 332–346.

Cadigan, Timothy P. (1991). Electronic monitoring in federal pretrial release. *Federal Probation* 55 (2): 26–30.

Charles, Michael T. (1989). The development of a juvenile electronic monitoring program. *Federal Probation* 53 (2): 3–11.

Clark, Charles S. (1994). Prison overcrowding: Will building more prisons cut the crime rate? *CQ Researcher* 4 (5): 99–106.

Cohn, Alvin. (1996). The evaluation of electronic monitoring programs. *Perspectives*, Fall: 28–35.

Colson, Charles & Van Ness, Daniel W. (1989). Alternative to incarceration: A conservative perspective. *Journal of State Government* 62 (2): 59–64.

Cooprider, Keith W. (1992). Pretrial bond supervision: An empirical analysis with policy implications. *Federal Probation* 56 (3): 41–49.

Cooprider, Keith W. & Kerby, Judith. (1990). A practical application of electronic monitoring at the pretrial stage. *Federal Probation* 54 (1): 28–35.

Crouch, Ben M. (1993). Is incarceration really worse: Analysis of offenders' preferences for prison over probation. *Justice Quarterly* 10 (1): 67–88.

Gowen, Darren. (1995). Electronic monitoring in the Southern District of Mississippi. *Federal Probation* 59 (1): 10–13.

Inciardi, James. (1996). *Criminal Justice*, 5th ed. New York: Harcourt Brace.

Larivee, John J. (1993). Community programs: A risky business. *Corrections Today* 55 (6): 20–24.

Lilly, J. Robert. (1989). What about house arrest? *Journal of State Government* 62: 89–91.

Lilly, J. Robert, Ball, Richard A., Curry, G. David, & Smith, Richard C. (1992). The Pride, Inc., Program: An evaluation of 5 years of electronic monitoring. *Federal Probation* 56 (4): 42–33.

Maineprize, Stephen. (1992). Electronic monitoring in corrections: Assessing cost effectiveness and the potential for widening the net of social control. *Canadian Journal of Criminology*, April, p. 161–180.

Martin, Randy, Mutchnick, Robert, & Austin, W. Timothy. (1990). *Criminological*

Thought: Pioneers Past and Present. New York: MacMillan.

Maxfield, Michael J., & Baumer, Terry L. (1990). Home detention with electronic monitoring. *Crime and Delinquency* 36 (4): 521–536.

McClelland, K. A., & Alpert, G. P. (1985). Factor analysis applied to magnitude estimates of punishment seriousness: Pattern of individual differences. *Journal of Quantitative Criminology* 1 (3): 307–318.

Nellis, Mike. (1991). The electronic monitoring of offenders in England and Wales: Recent developments and future prospects. *British Journal of Criminology* 31 (2): 165–185.

Papy, Joseph E. (1994). Electronic monitoring poses myriad of challenges for correctional agencies. *Corrections Today* 56 (4): 132–135.

Papy, Joseph E., & Nimer, Richard. (1991). Electronic monitoring in Florida. *Federal Probation* 55 (1): 31–33.

Payne, Brian K., & Gainey, Randy R. (1997). Electronic monitoring: What those on it have to say about it. A paper presented at the annual meeting of the Southern Criminal Justice Association. Richmond, VA.

Petersilia, Joan, & Deschenes, Elizabeth Piper. (1994a). What punishes? Inmates rank the severity of prison vs. intermediate sanctions. *Federal Probation* 58 (1): 3–8.

———. (1994b). Perceptions of punishment: Inmates and staff rank severity of prison versus intermediate sanctions. *Prison Journal* 74 (3): 306–329.

Rackmill, Stephen J. (1994). An analysis of home confinement as a sanction. *Federal Probation* 58 (1): 45–52.

Renzema, Marc, & Skeleton, David. (1991). The scope of electronic monitoring today. *Journal of Offender Monitoring* 4 (4): 6–11.

Schmidt, Annesley K. (1991). Electronic monitors: Realistically, what can be expected? *Federal Probation* 55 (2): 47–53.

Siegel, Larry. (1995). *Criminology,* 5th ed. St. Paul, Minnesota: West.

Sigler, Robert T., & Lamb, David. (1995). Community-based alternatives to prison: How the public and court personnel view them. *Federal Probation* 59 (2): 3–9.

Spelman, William. (1995). The severity of intermediate sanctions. *Journal of Research in Crime and Delinquency* 32 (2): 107–135.

Turner, Michael G., Cullen, Francis T., Sundt, Jody L., & Applegate, Brandon. (1997). Public tolerance for community-based sanctions. *The Prison Journal* 77 (1): 6–26.

von Hirsch, Andrew. (1976). *Doing Justice.* New York: Hill & Wang.

Walker, James L. (1990). Sharing the credit, sharing the blame: Managing political risks in electronically monitored house arrest. *Federal Probation* 54 (2): 16–20.

 Article Review Form at end of book.

In what way might human services work help improve the prison environment for both prisoners and officers?

Correctional Officers as Human Services Workers:

The Effect on Job Satisfaction

John R. Hepburn
Arizona State University

Paul E. Knepper
Northern Kentucky University

Increasing attention has focused on how prison guards adjust to working in prison (Crouch 1980; Cullen et al., 1989; Hepburn 1985; Lombardo 1981a; Philliber 1987). A major product of recent research is the observation that correctional workers are responsible for what prisoners experience because they create and maintain the human environment within the walls. This observation has prompted a proposal for redefining the correctional officers' role from that of a traditional "correctional security officer" to that of a "human services worker." Toch (1978), Lombardo (1981b, 1985), and Johnson (1987) argue that the "support-oriented guard" would assist prisoners with institutional problems and would act as a referral agent or advocate in the prison bureaucracy. Given the appropriate training and support systems, each officer would be not only a rule enforcer but also a lay counselor, a dispute mediator, an administrative ombudsperson, and a treatment aide. Specifically, Johnson and Price argue as follows:

> Correctional officers must evolve roles that blend, merge, or balance custodial and treatment functions. Human service roles offer one means to this end. Officers who play human service roles seek to advise, support, console, refer, or otherwise assist inmates with the problems and crises of adjustment produced by imprisonment (1981:344).

Human services work, these writers maintain, will improve the prison environment for prisoners and officers alike. Officers engaged in human services activities will be more satisfied with their jobs as a result of greater variety, increased autonomy, and other intrinsic aspects of their work. As Lombardo (1982) points out, human services officers may pursue direct and routine contact with prisoners, thereby creating a more active, more self-directive job in which they can exercise their skill and abilities in working with people.

The human services model holds the promise of more humane environments in correctional institu-

tions. Yet its promise has not been tested. Do correctional officers with the human services orientation enjoy greater job satisfaction than do traditional security officers? Do they have greater intrinsic rewards and less role ambiguity, which contribute directly to this higher level of satisfaction? Our study focuses on the differences in job satisfaction between human services officers and correctional security officers. More specifically, we examine the effect of intrinsic and extrinsic rewards, authority, and role ambiguity on the job satisfaction of human services and correctional security officers.

Correctional Officers and Human Services Roles

The subjective quality of work experience, as measured by employees' job satisfaction, is a frequent topic of both psychological and sociological research in occupations. Early literature in this area concentrated on explaining differences in workers' attitudes and behavior by referring to the pre-employment characteristics

Correctional Officers as Human Services Workers: The Effect on Job Satisfaction, John R. Hepburn and P. E. Knepper. *Justice Quarterly,* 10(2), 1993, 315–337. Reprinted by permission of Academy of Criminal Justice Sciences.

of workers (e.g., gender, age, educational level, employment background). More recently, however, researchers have found that organizational conditions and aspects of the job are far more important than individual attributes for explaining job satisfaction (Coverman 1989; Gruenberg 1980; Kalleberg 1977; Mottaz 1985, 1986b, 1987; Tuch and Martin 1991; Voydanoff 1978).

One relevant line of research focuses on the relationship between extrinsic and intrinsic aspects of work and job satisfaction (Bateman and Strasser 1984; Brooke, Russell, and Price 1988; Mottaz 1985, 1986a, 1987, 1988; Wright and Hamilton 1979). Extrinsic aspects of the job include such factors as the amount of pay, job security, fringe benefits, and opportunities for advancement; the intrinsic aspect include the freedom to plan one's work activities, the chance to use one's skills and talents, and the likelihood of personal growth on the job. Of the two, intrinsic aspects of the job generally are found to be more important in explaining job satisfaction (Gruenberg 1980; Kalleberg 1977; Mottaz 1987).

Little is known about the relative effects of intrinsic and extrinsic rewards on job satisfaction among correctional officers. Jurik et al. (1986) and Jurik and Winn (1987) concluded that the greater the intrinsic rewards of the job, the greater the job satisfaction. The regimentation, social isolation, and security orientation of the officer's work, however, can limit the degree to which intrinsic rewards are obtainable. Even so, the movement to human services roles may increase officers' range of activity, authority, and autonomy, and thus may improve the level of their job satisfaction.

Human Services Work and Authority

One possible effect of the human services model is on officers' level of authority over the prisoners. Because an officer's authority may be questioned by uncooperative and hostile prisoners at any time, officers must enter even the most routine encounters cautiously. Yet recent studies report that officers feel they do not have enough authority over prisoners to perform their jobs effectively; the lower the sense of authority over prisoners, the lower the job satisfaction (Fox 1982; Hepburn 1987; Irwin 1980).

The effect of human services work on officers' level of authority is unclear. One possible outcome of officers' increased involvement in prisoners' everyday activities may be an increase in the conflictual and manipulative relations between prisoners and officers. Prisoners use "cons," "games," and other schemes to resist or manipulate officers; such manipulative actions are likely to increase as the officers' sphere of influence over prisoners' routine activities is enlarged. If, indeed, such challenges and manipulations increase, the officers may feel that their authority is being tested and undermined. As a result, human services work would decrease the officers' sense of authority, thereby reducing their job satisfaction.

A more likely outcome is an increase in both authority and job satisfaction. Broadening the range of involvements by officers in prisoners' activities would extend and diversify their authority over prisoners. Not only would officers be involved in a wider sphere of activities, but their legitimate authority over prisoners would be augmented by developing special skills, knowledge, and expertise and by establishing personal relationships with prisoners (Hepburn 1985; Lombardo 1981a). Johnson (1987), for example, distinguishes between the authoritarian stance of the custody officer and the authoritative position of the human services worker. It appears likely, then, that human services work would increase the officers' authority, thereby increasing their job satisfaction.

Human Services Work and Role Strain

A second possible consequence of the transformation to human services work is a change in the degree of role strain among officers. Role strain arises when one's responsibilities and duties are vague, ill-defined, and ambiguous, or when administrative directives are inconsistent or contradictory (Cheek and Miller 1983; Fox 1982; Johnson 1987; Lasky, Gordon, and Srebalus 1986; Lombardo 1981a). Because role strain is related in-versely to job satisfaction (Brooke et al., 1988; Coverman 1989; Reichers 1986), it is important to examine the effects of human services work on role strain.

Advocates of the human services model assert that human services workers will have a lower level of role strain than do traditional correctional officers. If human services work can mitigate the prison's rigid organizational structure, increase the officers' autonomy and control over their activities, and decrease direct personal supervision over officers' work performance, human services work may reduce the role strain experienced by correctional officers (Johnson and Price 1981; Lombardo 1981b; 1982).

Yet findings from previous research suggest that human services work actually will produce a higher level of role strain than that produced by the traditional duties of custody and control. When officers are called on to serve the treatment needs of the facility, they are expected to form personal relationships with prisoners, to display helping behaviors, and to exercise professional judgment and flexibility in performing their job and in enforcing discipline. Yet custody and control remain their primary duties, and the custodial needs of the facility require impersonal relationships, full enforcement of rules, and controlling behaviors (Cressey 1959, 1965). When confronted by such contradictory expectations, officers usually "fall back" to the more highly structured role of the custody functions (Poole and Regoli 1980). A recent study by Cullen et al. (1989:39), for example, noted that "officers seek to resolve the conflicts and ambiguities of their occupational role by responding to inmates rigidly and impersonally, rather than in a flexible and individual manner as encouraged by a human services model."

Job satisfaction generally is higher in more highly structured roles (Zeitz 1983); this has been found to be the case in research with correctional officers (see Philliber 1987). Because human services delivery will produce a less structured and more ambiguous role, it appears likely that human services work will increase role strain, thereby reducing job satisfaction.

The Research Problem

Our research examines the relationship between human services work and job satisfaction. The literature advocating the transformation to human services work suggests clearly that correctional officers assigned to human services duties enjoy greater intrinsic and extrinsic rewards than correctional officers assigned to the more traditional duties of custody and control; therefore they will have greater job satisfaction.

Hypothesis 1: The intrinsic and extrinsic aspects of the job will be more rewarding for human services officers than for correctional security officers.

Hypothesis 2: The greater the intrinsic and extrinsic rewards, the higher the level of job satisfaction.

It is not clear, however, what effect (if any) human services work will have on the officers' perceived authority over prisoners and on role strain. For research purposes we hypothesize that human services work is related positively to the officers' perceived degree of authority over prisoners and negatively to the officers' level of role strain.

Hypothesis 3: The perceived degree of authority over prisoners will be greater among human services officers than among correctional security officers.

Hypothesis 4: The greater the perceived degree of authority over prisoners, the higher the level of job satisfaction.

Hypothesis 5: The level of role strain will be lower among human services officers than among correctional security officers.

Hypothesis 6: The less the role strain, the higher the level of job satisfaction.

The first six hypotheses examine strategic bivariate relationships; they postulate that differences in job satisfaction between human services officers and correctional security officers are due to differences in rewards, perceived authority, and role strain. This explanation of the basic relationship between type of work and job satisfaction leads us to the following hypothesis:

Hypothesis 7: Human services officers will have a higher level of job satisfaction than correctional security officers.

At the more general level, we focus on the determinants of job satisfaction among correctional officers: how do the characteristics of the officer's work affect his or her overall satisfaction with the job? Prior research suggests that individual attributes (e.g., age, race, gender, education) and features of the prison (e.g., security level, adult or juvenile prison, male or female prison) may have a significant bivariate association with job satisfaction; yet these factors should have no direct effect on job satisfaction when important characteristics of the work are controlled. That is, job satisfaction among both human services officers and correctional security officers is affected significantly by those characteristics of their work which differentiate these two "types" of correctional officers.

Hypothesis 8: Job satisfaction among human services officers and correctional security officers is a direct effect of the intrinsic and extrinsic rewards of their work, their perceived authority over prisoners, and the degree of role strain experienced.

Findings

Correctional program officers are found to have a significantly greater sense of authority over prisoners and a significantly lower level of role strain than correctional service officers. The *t*-test results also reveal that the CPOs find greater rewards in the intrinsic and extrinsic aspects of the job than do the CSOs and have greater overall job satisfaction.

Support for Hypotheses 2, 4, and 6 is found, which presents the correlation matrix of bivariate coefficients among all variables examined.[4] Job satisfaction is associated positively with the intrinsic rewards of the work, the extrinsic social rewards of the work, and the extrinsic monetary rewards of the work. Also, the greater the degree of perceived authority over prisoners, the greater the job satisfaction. Finally, role strain is found to be related inversely to job satisfaction.

These significant bivariate relationships are suggestive, but a multiple regression analysis is more informative inasmuch as it provides the net effect of each independent variable on the dependent variable. For this analysis we assume a causal model in which (1) the work characteristics of authority over prisoners, role strain, intrinsic rewards, and extrinsic rewards are affected directly by each of the antecedent variables and by the type of job; and (2) job satisfaction is affected causally by the eight antecedent and five job characteristic variables. . . .

Also, we see that the combined effects of the antecedent variables on authority are significant; they explain 10 percent of the total variation in authority. The effects of age and job type are significant: increased age and CPO status increase one's sense of authority over prisoners.

Similar results exist for the other work characteristics. The antecedent variables have a significant direct and additive effect on role strain, intrinsic rewards, extrinsic social rewards, and extrinsic monetary rewards. Age has a positive effect on intrinsic rewards and extrinsic social rewards; gender has a significant effect on extrinsic monetary rewards (higher for females). As hypothesized, job type is related significantly to sense of authority, role strain, and the intrinsic and extrinsic rewards of the job when the independent effects of the antecedent factors are controlled. . . .

The additive effect of 13 variables is significant, explaining nearly 49 percent of the variation in job satisfaction. Net the effects of the other variables in the regression equation, only role strain and intrinsic rewards have a significant independent effect on job satisfaction. Role strain decreases ($B = -.2066; p < .001$) and intrinsic rewards increase ($B = .4867; p < .001$) job satisfaction among correctional officers. Neither job type nor any of the other antecedent variables has a significant main effect on job satisfaction.

Taken together, the findings from six equations suggest the need for a further analysis of job satisfaction among correctional officers—one that explores the relationship between job type and job rewards, role strain, and sense of authority in determining job satisfaction. In particular, the statistically significant effect of job type on intrinsic rewards and role strain, as well as the failure of job type to produce a significant main effect on job satisfaction, suggests that the effect of job type on job satisfaction may be *mediated* by both intrinsic rewards and role strain.

The interaction between job type and role strain and between job type and intrinsic rewards in determining job satisfaction, only hinted at in earlier research, becomes the focus of the following analysis. Although job type fails to have a direct effect on job satisfaction, it clearly exerts a negative effect on role strain and a positive effect on intrinsic rewards. This observation suggests that the position and responsibilities of being a CPO appear to increase the intrinsic rewards of the job and to reduce role strain, thereby increasing the officer's job satisfaction. Given our interest in uncovering the difference between CSOs and CPOs in regard to job satisfaction, we reestimate the job satisfaction equation separately for CSOs and for CPOs.

Job type *conditions* the effect of role strain on job satisfaction. For CSOs, role strain significantly decreases ($b = -.1107; p < .001$) job satisfaction. For CPOs, however, role strain fails to produce a statistically significant effect. The significant t-value ($t = 13.12; p < .001$) supports the interactive relationship between job type and role strain in determining job satisfaction. In simple terms, the effect of role strain on job satisfaction depends on whether the officer is a correctional security officer or a correctional program officer.

These data also show that intrinsic rewards are a major positive influence on job satisfaction for both CSOs ($b = .2914; p < .001$) and CPOs ($b = .4321; p < .001$), but the effect among CPOs is significantly larger than among CPOs ($t = 13.12; p < .001$). Clearly, correctional program officers place greater importance on intrinsic rewards of the job in determining their level of job satisfaction than do correctional service officers.

Finally, the effect of perceived authority on job satisfaction is *conditioned* by job type. For CSOs, the effect is negative and trivial ($b = -.0143$), and fails to achieve statistical significance. For CPOs, the effect of authority on job satisfaction is positive, nontrivial ($b = .2080; p < .05$), and statistically significant. The ability to maintain control over prisoners is more important to reported job satisfaction among CPOs than among CSOs ($t = 12.16; p < .001$).

Conclusions

This study centers on the relationship between type of job and job satisfaction among correctional officers. Toch (1978), Lombardo (1981b, 1985), and Johnson (1987) propose that human services roles for correctional officers will result in greater job satisfaction. We find that job satisfaction is significantly greater among Arizona's human services-oriented correctional program officers than among the traditional custody-oriented correctional security officers. Even so, we note the complexity in the relationship between job type and job satisfaction. When other important factors are controlled, job type does not have a significant main effect on job satisfaction. Job satisfaction among correctional officers is explained by the intrinsic rewards of their work and by the degree of their perceived authority over prisoners.

Yet it would be premature to conclude that job type is unrelated to job satisfaction. Rather, job type is found to condition the effects of intrinsic rewards, perceived authority, and role strain on job satisfaction. Among *correctional program officers*, both intrinsic rewards and perceived authority affect job satisfaction positively; role strain has no significant relation to job satisfaction. Among *correctional security officers*, in contrast, role strain affects job satisfaction negatively, intrinsic rewards affect job satisfaction positively (albeit less so than among correctional service officers), and perceived authority over prisoners is not related significantly to job satisfaction.

Because job type appears to condition the effect of these variables on job satisfaction, further research should explore additional distinctions between human services officers and correctional security officers. Perhaps this research will clarify the complex relationship between job type and job satisfaction suggested here. Researchers may wish, for instance, to examine more closely why perceived authority remains important for human services workers but not for security officers. We surmise that this difference is due to the difference between the forms of authority used by the two groups.

The everyday duties of human services officers requires a high level of informality, friendliness, and interpersonal skills. Human services officers must display a willingness and an ability to solve prisoners' problems. Their authority is based on interpersonal relations and expertise, and they use it to help prisoners cope with the problems of prison life (Johnson 1987). For these officers, authority over prisoners means possessing the personal skills and expertise necessary to maintain order and solve problems (Lombardo 1987).

In contrast, security officers are admonished by management to avoid social relationships with prisoners or involvement in their personal problems. Their custodial and rule-enforcing duties require more formal relationships and greater social distance. Their authority derives from the uniform they wear—legitimate authority—and from the limited sanctions and rewards at their disposal. These officers use their authority to control prisoners and to suppress the prisoners' problems. For security officers, then, authority means having adequate support from the administration and the legal system to repress prisoners (Johnson 1987; Lombardo 1987). These and other differences in the meaning of authority may well explain the observed difference in officers' relationship of perceived authority to job satisfaction.

Additional research also will help to clarify the relationship between role strain and job satisfaction. If role strain is related to job satisfaction only for security officers, we must elaborate this interactive relationship. Perhaps our measure of role strain (which focuses on role ambiguity and role contradictions) is not germane for human services officers. Why is the security officers' job satisfaction influenced by these dimensions of role strain, whereas human services officers (for whom such ambiguities and contradictions are anticipated to be even more prevalent) are not affected? One possible explanation is that human services officers have greater autonomy in the workplace, which insulates them from the negative effects of role strain reported by security officers.

Intrinsic rewards are found to be an important determinant of job satisfaction for both groups, but the effect is greater for human services officers than for security officers. Because the measure of intrinsic rewards used here is operationalized by items that reflect autonomy on the job, this observed difference in the effect of intrinsic rewards on job satisfaction further suggests a possible link between job type, autonomy, and job satisfaction.

These data do not allow us to exclude the possibility that the relationships observed are due to a selectivity factor. As mentioned above, each officer begins as a correctional security officer. Only those who request reclassification and score very well on a written certification test are eligible to assume one of the few positions in the Department as a correctional program officer. Possibly those who request and receive reassignment as correctional program officers are those who already perceive a greater sense of authority over prisoners, lower role strain, higher intrinsic and extrinsic rewards, and greater job satisfaction. Conceivably the nature of the role attracts certain "types" of correctional officers. Without random assignment or longitudinal data, we cannot address such possibilities or exclude such alternative explanations for our findings.

Although the findings are not definitive, they address two important issues. First, organizational conditions and aspects of the job are found to be far more important than individual attributes in explaining job satisfaction. Even if a self-selection factor is operating here, it is clear that the individual attributes of the officers studied do not explain much of the observed variation in the job satisfaction of either the correctional program officers or the correctional security officers. Second, the data give quantitative support to the movement toward a human services model for correctional officers. Taken together, these findings suggest that efforts to enhance and enrich the duties of correctional officers, to extend their control over, and their involvement in, prisoners' activities, and to redefine their roles as service workers than as control agents deserve

additional attention. Such a transformation could benefit the prisoners; it appears to benefit the officers.

Notes

Note: Footnotes 1–3 are not included in this publication.

4. The relationships among the antecedent variables deserve brief comment. First, the significant, positive association of age with race, gender, and education suggests that younger officers are more likely than older officers to be nonwhite, female, and better educated—a finding that is consistent with recent recruitment objectives (see Jurik and Musheno 1987). Second, the male officers surveyed are more likely than their female counterparts to be working in higher-security prisons and in prisons housing male offenders. Third, the inverse association of SECURITY and OFFAGE reflects the fact that each of the four juvenile facilities has a rather high level of security, whereas the range of adult facilities includes several units with low levels of security (including two adult facilities exclusively for DWI offenders). Fourth, the covariation of EDUC and JOB-TYPE shows that CSOs have a lower level of education than do CPOs.

References

Bateman, T. and S. Strasser (1984) "A Longitudinal Analysis of the Antecedents of Organizational Commitment." *Academy of Management Journal* 27:95–112.

Brooke, P., D. Russell, and J. Price (1988) "Discriminant Validation of Measures of Job Satisfaction, Job Involvement, and Organizational Commitment." *Journal of Applied Psychology* 73:139–45.

Cheek, F. and M. Miller (1983) "The Experiences of Stress for Correctional Officers: A Double-Bind Theory of Correctional Stress." *Journal of Criminal Justice* 11:105–20.

Cohen, J. and P. Cohen (1975) *Applied Multiple Regression/Correlation Analysis for the Behavioral Sciences* 2nd ed. Hillsdale, NJ: Erlbaum.

Coverman, S. (1989) "Role Overload, Conflict, and Stress: Addressing Consequences of Multiple Role Demands." *Social Forces* 67:965–82.

Cressey, D. (1959) "Contradictory Directives in Complex Organizations: The Case of the Prison." *Administrative Science Quarterly* 4:1–19.

——— (1965) "Prison Organizations." In J. March (ed.), *Handbook of Organizations*, pp. 1023–70. Chicago: Rand McNally.

Crouch, B., ed. (1980) *The Keepers*. Springfield, IL: Thomas.

Cullen, F., F. Lutze, B. Link, and N. Wolfe (1989) "The Correctional Orientation of

Prison Guards: Do Officers Support Rehabilitation?" *Federal Probation* 53:33–42.

Fox, J. (1982) *Organizational and Racial Conflict in Maximum Security Prisons.* Boston: Heath.

Gruenberg, B. (1980) "The Happy Worker: An Analysis of Educational and Occupational Differences in Determinants of Job Satisfaction." *American Journal of Sociology* 86:247–71.

Hepburn, J. (1985) "The Exercise of Power in Coercive Organizations: A Study of Prison Guards." *Criminology* 23:146–64.

——— (1987) "The Prison Control Structure and Its Effects on Work Attitudes: The Perceptions and Attitudes of Prison Guards." *Journal of Criminal Justice* 16:49–64.

Hepburn, J. and A. Crepin (1984) "Relationship Strategies in a Coercive Institution: A Study of Dependence Among Prison Guards." *Journal of Social and Personal Relationships* 1:139–57.

Hepburn, J. and C. Albonetti (1980) "Role Conflict in Correctional Institutions." *Criminology* 17:445–59.

Irwin, J. (1980) *Prisons in Turmoil.* Boston: Little, Brown.

Johnson, R. (1987) *Hard Time.* Monterey: Brooks/Cole.

Johnson, R. and S. Price (1981) "The Complete Correctional Officer: Human Services and the Human Environment of Prison." *Criminal Justice and Behavior* 8:343–73.

Jurik, N., G. Halemba, M. Musheno, and B. Boyle (1986) "Education, Working Conditions and the Job Satisfaction of Correctional Officers." *Work and Occupations* 14:106–25.

Jurik, N. and M. Musheno (1987) "The Internal Crisis of Corrections: Professionalization and the Work Environment." *Justice Quarterly* 3:457–80.

Jurik, N. and R. Winn (1987) "Describing Correctional Security Dropouts and Rejects: An Individual or Organizational Profile." *Criminal Justice and Behavior* 14:5–25.

Kalleberg, A. (1977) "Work Values and Job Rewards: A Theory of Job Satisfaction." *American Sociological Review* 42:124–43.

Lasky, G., B. C. Gordon, and D. Srebalus (1986) "Occupational Stressors among Federal Correctional Officers Working Different Security Levels." *Criminal Justice and Behavior* 13:317–27.

Lombardo, L. (1981a) *Guards Imprisoned.* New York: Elsevier.

——— (1981b) "Occupational Stress in Correctional Officers: Sources, Coping Strategies, and Implications." In S. Zimmerman and H. Miller (eds.), *Correction at the Crossroads: Designing Policy*, pp. 129–49. Beverly Hills: Sage.

——— (1982) "Stress, Change and Collective Violence in Prison." In R. Johnson and H. Toch (eds.), *The Pains of Imprisonment*, pp. 77–93. Beverly Hills: Sage.

——— (1985) "Mental Health Work in Prisons and Jails: Inmate Adjustment and

Indigenous Correctional Personnel."
Criminal Justice and Behavior 12:17–28.
——— (1987) *Guards Imprisoned.* 2nd ed.
Cincinnati: Anderson.
Mottaz, C. (1985) "The Relative Importance
of Intrinsic and Extrinsic Rewards as
Determinants of Work Satisfaction."
Sociological Quarterly 26:365–86.
——— (1986a) "An Analysis of the
Relationship between Education and
Organizational Commitment in a Variety
of Occupational Groups." *Journal of
Vocational Behavior* 28:214–28.
——— (1986b) "Gender Differences in Work
Satisfaction, Work-Related Rewards and
Values, and the Determinants of Work
Satisfaction." *Human Relations* 39:359–78.
——— (1987) "An Analysis of the
Relationship between Work Satisfaction
and Organizational Commitment."
Sociological Quarterly 28:541–58.

——— (1988) "Determinants of
Organizational Commitment." *Human
Relations* 41:467–82.
Philliber, S. (19887) "Thy Brother's Keeper: A
Review of the Literature on Correctional
Officers." *Justice Quarterly* 4:9–37.
Poole, E. and R. Regoli (1980) "Role Stress,
Custody Orientation, and Disciplinary
Actions." *Criminology* 18:225–36.
Reichers, A. (1986) "Conflict and
Organizational Commitment." *Journal of
Applied Psychology* 71:508–14.
Toch, H. (1978) "Is a 'Correctional Officer' by
Any Other name a 'Screw'?" *Criminal
Justice Review* 3:19–35.
Tuch, S. and J. Martin (1991) "Race in the
Workplace: Black/White Differences in
the Sources of Job Satisfaction."
Sociological Quarterly 32:103–16.

Voydanoff, P. (1978) "The Relationship
between Perceived Job Characteristics
and Job Satisfaction among
Occupational-Status Groups." *Sociology of
Work and Occupations* 5:179–92.
Wright, J. and R. Hamilton (1979)
"Education and Job Attitudes among
Blue Collar Workers." *Sociology of Work
and Occupations* 6:59–83.
Zeitz, G. (1983) "Structural and Individual
Determinants of Organization Morale
and Dissatisfaction." *Social Forces*
61:1088–1108.

Article Review Form at end of book.

How is the changing inmate population affecting the correctional officers' role?

Coping in Alien Territory:

Corrections Officers in the AIDS Ward

Kate King

West Texas A&M University

The mandate to provide medical care for inmates suffering from extraordinary diseases such as AIDS has created a paradoxical situation where correctional regulations directly contradict the rules and needs of health care providers. In order to deal with this dilemma, corrections officers working in health care facilities have been forced to devise a number of coping mechanisms.

The prison has a Constitutional obligation to provide adequate medical care to inmates. When an inmate with AIDS becomes seriously ill with an opportunistic infection, he must be given medical care. *Estelle* v. *Gamble* (1976) established a Constitutional right to adequate medical care for inmates. The Court held that "deliberate indifference to serious medical needs" violates the Eighth Amendment.

Prison health care delivery systems are designed to provide primary health care, not to meet the complex needs of inmates with HIV-related diseases. Because the prison must obtain adequate medical care for inmates in its custody, for AIDS infected inmates, frequently, that care comes from a community hospital. Prisons have traditionally been exempt from many of the demands of interorganizational cooperation. Correctional managers, as well as line officers, find themselves ill prepared for the unprecedented ongoing

relationships now developing between prisons and community hospitals. True, prisons have often utilized community hospitals, but the needs and relationships are changing because of AIDS. Because inmates with end-stage AIDS have recurring serious infections, corrections officers take the same inmates back and forth between the prison and hospital time and again. The environment becomes more complex as prisons must interact with hospitals in long-term relationships.

The corrections officers who guard inmates at the community hospital are placed in a difficult position. They are expected to follow the directives of the prison in keeping their charges, and yet they are in a very different environment from the prison. Due to the public nature of the hospital environment and the sheer number of persons having daily access to the inmates, it is virtually impossible for the officers to follow all of the prison's rules with regard to those inmates. Because of this different environment, often the old rules do not fit the new situation. Faced with a changing organizational environment, the traditional coping methods of the officers may become dysfunctional.

When specific correctional mandates conflict with hospital rules or with the officer's best judgment of how to handle a particular situation, the officer will experience some discomfort. There are many things officers must cope with in the

community hospital environment. Maintaining custody and control over the inmates is one concern. Having their authority challenged in front of the inmates is difficult for officers to deal with. Orders given by corrections officers may be overruled by hospital staff. Coping with the monotony of waiting in the halls of the hospital is a challenge, especially when the officers must be alert to the possibilities of danger and escape which always exist when inmates are being treated in a community setting. Lack of respect and consideration from some hospital employees is another element corrections officers must cope with as they attempt to do their jobs in the community hospital setting. Finally, officers must cope with the spectre of AIDS. Inmates in this environment are suffering from a devastating debilitating disease which transforms healthy, hearty men and women into frightened, often demented and physically tortured souls. The secondary diseases which attack AIDS patients disfigure and deform them, often leaving them helpless and abhorrent to observe. These factors combine to make the work environment stressful for the corrections officers in the hospital setting. New coping mechanisms must be developed to do the job and protect themselves physically, professionally, and emotionally.

This paper describes the coping mechanisms employed by state corrections officers called on to provide secure custody for inmates being treated for HIV-related illnesses in a large teaching hospital in a northeastern city. The data were collected over a six-month time frame using direct observation, informal interviews, and extended fieldwork in the ethnographic tradition. . . .

The officers claimed they felt like fish out of water in the hospital environment. They complained of daily security infractions and felt they would be held responsible if something went wrong, but, in fact, believed they had no control over the situation. The officers pointed out that, in contrast to the prison, in the hospital many different people have access to the inmate. Physicians, physicians' assistants, medical students, nurses, nurses' aids, medical technicians, therapists, social workers, dieticians, counselors, hospital administrators, clergy, food service workers, housekeeping staff, volunteers, and those who transport patients from their rooms to various parts of the hospital for services and treatment have easy access to all patients, including inmates. That these people might be questioned or searched before entering and upon leaving the inmate's room is untenable in the hospital setting.

Corrections officers said they must also deal with doctor's orders which clearly conflict with security concerns. In the traditional prison setting, officers feel they have some control over where the inmates go and when they can go there. Through the use of strict schedules and locked gates, inmate whereabouts are controlled by security staff. In the hospital setting, where there are multiple inmates, corrections officers may be the last to know when and where an inmate patient will be at anytime during the day. Hospital employees may come to get inmates to take them for X-rays, eye exams, surgery, appointments in nuclear medicine, and dental exams without checking with security personnel. Patients are scheduled for treatments by doctors and technicians who may not consider the security aspects of their patients. As a result, different inmates may be scheduled for treatment throughout the hospital complex simultaneously, creating hardship for the officers who must provide security coverage for all inmates at all times.

The officers pointed out that prison directives state an officer must accompany an inmate whenever he or she leaves the unit. In the hospital studied, in the infectious diseases ward, there are five officers plus a supervisor on duty during the day and evening shifts, and four officers and a supervisor during the night shift. An additional officer provides telephone coverage in the office, does paperwork, counts supplies, weapons, and bullets, and acts as the officer in charge while the supervisor conducts his rounds, checking on officers watching inmate patients in rooms throughout the hospital. This arrangement allows one officer from the day and evening shifts to escort inmate patients to and from their various appointments. If a second escort is needed there is no one available to provide coverage for officers needing to use the restroom or break for lunch until one of these officers returns. State law guarantees corrections employees lunch and break time, but these considerations are forfeited to appease hospital scheduling demands.

When more than two inmate patients are scheduled for appointments at one time the officers must tell the hospital employees that one of the inmates cannot go because there is no security coverage. This frequently causes conflict between the hospital employees who have been sent to retrieve the patient and the officers who cannot let him go.

Another factor the officers must cope with is visitation. In the prison environment, visitation is strictly controlled. In the hospital, visitors are allowed from mid-afternoon to 8 P.M. Visitors can come and go all day, seven days a week. Visitors can utilize the kitchen and the lounge and can go down to the cafeteria in the hospital and bring food and drink back up with them. Because of the fatal nature of AIDS, visitors are given more leeway on this unit and often stay all day and night. Large groups of people and entire families have "camped out" in the lounge for days when it was obvious that their loved one with AIDS would not live much longer. Indeed, this sort of caring and "being there" is encouraged by the hospital staff, especially by the social workers and clergy.

In this environment, it is difficult for the corrections officers to regulate visitation in the traditional manner. Inmates, on the whole, receive far fewer visitors than noninmate patients. Because the hospital is over 100 miles from the nearest major city, many family members are unable to make the trip with any frequency. For some, the cost is prohibitive. When visitors do come to the AIDS unit, corrections officers frequently allow more visitors in the room than the directives state, and if someone comes to visit an inmate who is not on the visitation list a "courtesy visit" is allowed "just this once. . . ."

If a sergeant is on duty, most corrections officers will refer a visitor to the supervisor, thus being relieved of the duty to make a decision. In one observed instance, an officer made the decision himself to not allow outside food brought by a visitor in to the patient. The family member complained loudly, stating that the nurse had specifically told her to go to McDonald's because that's what the patient had asked for. The officer on the post remained firm, stating that outside food was not allowed. The family member went to the sergeant to complain. The sergeant permitted the food to be given to the patient, in order to avoid a scene, and the officer felt as though he had not been supported. The officer stated bitterly, "In this place, you just can't win. You are truly damned if you do and damned if you don't. Well, fine. Just know that when some convict gets some junk (drugs) and flips out, it won't be my ass hanging on the line."

Telephone calls to and from inmates are also handled differently in the hospital than in the prison. Correctional directives state that inmates are allowed to make one collect phone call per day, and are not allowed to receive incoming calls. In-room telephone service is not allowed, so inmates must use the pay phone at the end of the hallway, near the entrance to the AIDS ward. Because the phone is outside the area covered by the correctional staff, an officer must accompany the inmate to the phone and wait there until the inmate finishes his conversation. . . .

In the hospital studied, corrections officers are relegated to the hallway in the AIDS ward. They are allowed to stay, but only if they behave themselves. Because many of the patients are quite ill and stay in their rooms much of the time, the officers assigned to watch those rooms may simply sit out in the hallway and watch the doors. Monotony and boredom are common complaints. The escort officer and the rover officer move about for the duration of their shift, the escort officer traveling all about the hospital with various inmate patients and the rover giving breaks to the officers stationed at all posts. For those officers assigned to one post, however, their eight hour shift consists of sitting in one chair and watching one set of doors. To cope with the monotony, the officers carry on conversations with each other and with anyone who stops to visit. Some sing softly to themselves, pace back and forth, play automated chess with a computer, study for college classes, and read. The officers assigned to regular duty on the AIDS ward sometimes finish a novel a day and several magazines. . . .

Most inmates behave themselves and follow the rules of the hospital because they are told at the beginning of their stay that any inappropriate conduct will be punished severely. In addition to correctional sanctions, the hospital usually discharges troublesome inmates immediately, so the inmate not only incurs additional punishment, he is forced to go back to the prison, sick or not. For most, this is incentive enough to follow the rules.

A different, but just as dangerous factor corrections officers face in this duty is exposure to infection. The officers are constantly exposed to pneumonia, tuberculosis, and other infectious diseases. Occasionally, a patient with tuberculosis is not diagnosed immediately as being infectious and so is not confined to his room. In fact, during the period of observation for this study, there were five instances of patients with tuberculosis who were not diagnosed immediately and so walked freely through the halls or left the doors to their rooms open. Officers also were concerned with lax quarantine procedures for those who were diagnosed as infectious. Nurses occasionally entered the rooms without the mandatory masks on and neglected to close the patient's door, angering the officers stationed outside those doors, who felt imperiled by the nurses' careless behavior. Some officers expressed anger and resentment toward the hospital employees' behavior, but other officers seemed resigned to the fact that they were being exposed to health risks in the AIDS unit. One officer commented "I guess I should be worried, but I figure, if I haven't come down with anything by now, I'm probably not going to, and besides, it beats getting shot or stabbed. . . ."

Lack of respect and consideration from hospital employees is a marked feature of the environment for corrections officers. There are, of course, exceptions. It was observed that certain nurses, nurses' aides, medical technicians, and food service personnel are obviously fond of and have respect for the officers. As a group, however, the corrections officers seem to believe that the hospital personnel dislike them and wish they were not there. The officers claim that the majority of hospital personnel cannot be trusted and must be watched carefully. The officers state that certain hospital personnel are actively monitoring their conduct and waiting for a chance to point out any correctional shortcomings.

This contention is buttressed by the fact that certain hospital employees continue to mention the behavior of the officers who provided coverage from the maximum security facility before the current officers came to the hospital. They point out that the prior officers behaved as if the hospital were simply an extension of the prison with all rules and regulations intact. Specific examples of misdeeds committed by these officers are repeated, like how they commandeered the unit, taking furniture from the patients' rooms for personal use, how they verbally harassed and insulted non-inmate patients and visitors (calling patients and their visitors "faggots"), how they insulted hospital staff, how they tore coatracks off the walls to put up in their office, engaged in horseplay in the hallways (e.g., crutch races and "farting contests"), how they gambled in the hallway, and occasionally resorted to fisticuffs as a means of dispute resolution. In one instance, a firearm was discharged with the bullet going through the ceiling into the patient's room upstairs. These stories are recounted in scathing tones and given as proof that "prison guards can't be trusted."

When the arrangements were made with the medium security facility currently providing officers, the officers were given strict orders to comply with all hospital demands. Corrections officers stated that their superintendent's "head was on the block," meaning, if there were any complaints about officer behavior, consequences would be severe. This message was transmitted in no uncertain terms to the officers assigned to the hospital. It was in this environment that the officers who were observed in this study began their tenure. Entering into a hostile environment, commanded to defer to hospital procedure in case of conflict between institutional rules, yet legally held accountable for correctional regulations, the officers felt themselves to be unwelcome and unsupported.

Officers repeatedly stated that if the hospital had its way, there would be no security personnel allowed. The officers openly stated that hospital employees disliked the corrections officers and went out of their way to make their jobs more difficult.

Feeling that they are not given their due respect as professionals in their field, and feeling that they are being held accountable for the past misdeeds of others, the officers react in several ways. One method of coping is by discontinuing the importance of the hospital employees' opinions. One officer commented that "It doesn't really bother me that they don't like us. After all, what do they know about prison work?" Another stated that "The ones who really know us like us. They know we're doing a good job. The others . . . who gives a shit what they think?" Some officers respond by mimicking certain employees who are overtly hostile toward the officers. One woman who especially despises the correctional personnel on the unit physically slumps and sticks out her lower lip when she approaches the back portion of the unit where the officers are positioned. As she passes by, one or two officers will slouch and push out their lips, imitating the woman.

Many officers dismiss the hospital employees' disrespect by pointing out that "They're just jealous. They bust their butts all day for pennies and we sit here reading science fiction for twice their salary. That's why they don't like us. We've got better cars, motorcycles, boats, houses, everything. They're just jealous. . . ."

Another element corrections officers must deal with is being exposed to the deterioration and disintegration of people dying with AIDS-induced diseases. Many officers admitted that they had been changed by this duty. Some said their whole attitude towards inmates had changed. "Before this job at the hospital, I used to think inmates were all scum. Now I feel sorry for some of them. I guess they're just doing the best that they can. I guess it depends on what crimes they commit, too. I used to think that whatever happened to them, they deserved. But nobody deserves this AIDS thing. I wouldn't wish it on anybody. . . ."

In addition, when a previously cooperative inmate's behavior became problematic, officers leaving one shift took pains to explain to oncoming officers that the inmate was experiencing dementia and was not responsible for his outbursts. The oncoming officers were urged not to respond harshly, because "He can't help himself. It's the AIDS." Aside from making allowances for sickness-related behavior and permitting inmates more privileges, corrections officers seemed to protect themselves from deterioration and pain they were exposed to daily by the use of gallows humor. . . .

The corrections officers who provide secure custody for inmates in community hospitals face daily dilemmas. In the hospital studied, the officers see themselves, first and foremost as guards. Their number one priority is maintaining security. However, they are also representatives of the prison to the community and must therefore be careful to present a professional image to the public. The officers are called upon to act as counselors to inmates and their families, and to act as resource locators to help family members find lodging near the hospital. The officers are required to play the part of diplomat, appeaser and conciliator, always making sure hospital personnel are happy. The burden of cooperation is on their shoulders; after all, the prison needs the hospital's services far more than the hospital needs the prisoners. Not "rocking the boat" requires the officers' constant energy, creativity and attention. Because virtually every aspect of the officers' on-the-job behavior can be described as appeasement, accommodation, or atonement for past bad acts by other officers, these officers experience anxiety about not doing their "real" job of providing secure custody "by the rules. . . ."

 Article Review Form at end of book.

In contrast to a male officer, how would a female correctional officer conduct herself differently with a male prisoner?

Women Working in a Men's Jail

M. I. Cadwaladr

M. I. Cadwaladr, "Breaking into Jail: Women Working in a Men's Jail," M.A. thesis, Department of Sociology and Anthropology, The University of British Columbia, 1993.

When you think about a correctional officer (prison guard) in a men's prison, what image comes to mind? Burly, "no-nonsense" men? A man with a gun standing in a sentry tower? Whatever your image (accurate or otherwise), it probably does not include women, because the majority of correctional officers in prisons for men are men.

Nevertheless, many women do work in correctional institutions—all Canadian federal prisons have included female guards since 1983.

Like most women working in male-dominated professions, female correctional officers must deal with problems and barriers rooted in sexism. In fact, the perception of working in a non-traditional workplace for women is intensified in prisons for men: not only is most of the staff male, but the focus of the job is the care and control of men.

A recent study attempted to present a detailed picture of what it is like to be a woman working as a correctional officer in a jail for men. If nothing else, it revealed that female guards in men's jails find themselves in a confusing position.

On the one hand, to be female is to be different, an outsider. On the other hand, female guards have much in common with, and are sympathetic to, their male peers as a result of their shared job experience.

Methodology

The research site was a modern, urban Canadian jail (where the author formerly worked as a correctional officer), which houses 150 men awaiting trial or bail. The institution was designed to accommodate women as correctional officers—the inmates' shower stalls and toilets were enclosed, and there were separate change facilities for female correctional officers. With the exception of one post requiring "skin frisks," women were assigned to perform all duties within the jail.

In 1990–1991, in-depth interviews were conducted with 21 female guards (approximately half the number of women who have ever worked as guards in the jail), 17 women working in jobs traditionally held by women in a jail (nurses, clerks, librarians), and 6 correctional managers. Numerous informal discussions were also conducted with male and female correctional officers and former inmates.

The average age (at the time of hiring) of the correctional officers interviewed was 24. Of the 21 female guards, 6 had a university degree and all but 2 had some post-secondary education.

Working Styles of Male and Female Guards

Most of the female correctional officers said they performed the job with a less aggressive style than men, not necessarily out of preference, but because of different life experiences and physical limitations. Most women are smaller than men, and women are socialized to fulfil helping rather then aggressive roles.

Therefore, the female guards used different skills than the men. By relying heavily on verbal skills and intuition, the women were able to get the inmates to co-operate and were more likely to talk out problems and perhaps diffuse potential violence.

Another indication that women perform their job differently is that the female guards relied more heavily than men on the internal disciplinary procedure. This suggests that female officers may be more likely to rely on established and legitimized means of discipline than to bully or threaten.

The skills employed by men and women therefore complement each other. Women may humanize the workplace in small ways by establishing less aggressive relationships with inmates. As well, if issues are resolved by negotiation rather than by force, there is less chance of injury to either inmates or staff.

By and large, the respondents felt that male guards believe female guards competently perform the day-to-day tasks of the job. But the respondents also reported that many men expressed concerns that women would not be able to back them up in a crisis situation. At this point, the men feel the job becomes real "men's work."

Women Working in a Men's Jail, M. I. Cadwaladr. *Forum on Corrections Research,* 6(1), 1994, 46–48. Reprinted by permission of the Correctional Service of Canada.

It is important to note that the use of force in a jail is the exception and that officers do not respond to dangerous situations alone. In fact, guards spend hours practicing a unified response to an emergency because in crisis situations the individual size and strength of the officer are not as important as the discipline and co-ordination of the group.

But the female correctional officers reported that in emergency situations some men adopt a protective, chivalrous attitude toward them. The women resented this treatment, feeling that they are seen as a liability and that the male officers place themselves in danger by not concentrating fully on the situation at hand.

Physical prowess and a willingness to enter into physical confrontations are also a way of generating esteem and peer acceptance. When women are kept out of crisis situations, they are denied a crucial means of gaining peer acceptance.

Personal and Sexual Harassment

Most of the women reported that they did not personally experience unwanted touching or suggestions (sexual harassment in the narrowest sense). When asked if sexual harassment was a problem, many replied, "not for me." The same women then went on to describe "other harassment" (from male peers), which included physical assaults, threats, unfounded graphic sexual rumours about individual women, and daily doses of demeaning remarks from peers, inmates and supervisors.

Although some women did describe dramatic episodes of harassment, they most often referred to an undercurrent of sexism and inequality.

One form of sexual harassment involves rumours about female correctional officers, primarily speculation about their sexual orientation or sex lives. For example, many female correctional officers reported that they are assumed to be lesbians by people both inside and outside the criminal justice system.

Women are also frequently rumoured to be sexually involved with both supervisors and inmates.

Further, one of the main social activities for correctional officers is to go out drinking after work. But if women go out and drink with the men, they are often assumed to be promiscuous; a favourite myth among men is that loose women get what they deserve, like harassment.

Harassment from inmates was not reported to be a big problem. Inmates were said to be generally favourable or neutral toward women's employment in prisons. Inmates reported that female guards treat them better than men, as the women are less confrontational and more willing to carry out requests. As such, the prisoners have much to gain by ensuring that women remain.

Female correctional officers also have more direct and effective options for dealing with the harassing behaviour of inmates. They can simply charge the inmate with a disciplinary infraction.

However, most women don't complain about harassment from staff. Harassment is seen as normal in the male culture of the jail, so it becomes customary and is viewed as having little importance. It is also assumed to be inevitable and the price women have to pay for working in a jail.

Most important, the burden of dealing with harassment is placed squarely on the shoulders of the victims. They can either tolerate it or face even worse problems if they report it. The women expressed a real fear of being isolated if they were to complain. They would almost certainly be ostracized, blamed, and accused of overreacting.

Why?

Prisons have a strong subculture, and this creates a great deal of pressure to remain loyal to other officers. Guards have a code of behaviour that strongly prohibits informing or "ratting" on one's peer group—a "rat" is despised and isolated for his or her disloyalty to the group.

As well, the women reported that the most significant consequence for the "harasser" would be a transfer to another institution, where he would be free to harass again. The likely outcome of a complaint would be merely a reprimand or a short suspension.

In a nutshell, women don't complain about harassment because it is a no-win situation. The costs of complaining simply outweighs the benefits.

Coping in the Men's World of the Jail

To cope, most of the women simply accepted what they felt they could not change. They sought male approval and endured the difficulties of the job without protest. It seems most female correctional officers try to maintain harmonious relationships with their male peers and not draw attention to themselves, hoping to be left alone to do their jobs.

The women also dealt with the difficult working environment through some form of withdrawal. This could mean taking stress leave, becoming apathetic or emotionally detached, refraining from unnecessary social contact with colleagues, or even quitting.

Other women found a set of "sympathetic others" in the workplace, who provided moral support, acceptance and feelings of being a normal person because they shared both the experiences of the job and the sense of isolation.

Recommendations

The study found that female correctional officers see themselves as competent on the job, but with a less aggressive manner of carrying out their duties than some of their male peers. Yet, they receive unwanted paternalistic protection that devalues them in the correctional organization. Female guards also experience both personal and sexual harassment, which becomes normalized and accepted by both men and women.

Female guards cope with the challenges and frustrations of their jobs by either gaining some measure of acceptance in the workplace, simply tolerating difficulties (including personal or sexual harassment), or somehow withdrawing from the workplace.

Considering this, the study recommended that (1) managers and guards undergo training to sensitize them to the problems of women working in prisons; (2) strong policy prohibiting sexual and personal harassment—with mechanisms for complaints existing outside the para-military chain—be established, with significant consequences for "harassers"; and (3) job candidates be screened for their ability and willingness to develop relationships built on mutual respect with female colleagues.

 Article Review Form at end of book.

What happens when female correctional officers are deployed in a men's prison?

Cross Gender Supervision and Control in Male Prisons in England:

A Summary of Officers' Perspectives

Joanna Ruth Adler

This article reports findings from interviews conducted with 120 officers working within medium to high security prisons in England. It presents part of a project designed to test whether the impact of women officers in male prisons was similar in England to that described elsewhere. In total, 120 officers and 120 prisoners participated. Results indicate that marginally more female officers (65%) reported problems with their colleagues than with prisoners (50%). Almost half of the women reported interpersonal problems with their colleagues whereas only 10% of the men reported such problems. The women are perceived as calming influences yet as being less able to control violent situations.

Introduction

In the English and Welsh Prison Service, women constitute between 10% and 4% of officers and governors depending on rank. Before the introduction of female officers into male prisons, it was predicted that within the Prison Service, male officers would react to their new female co-workers as did those in Australia, Canada and the United States. There, male officers generally viewed the coming of women as one more liberal change imposed from on high. Women threatened the basic premise that they held that "masculinity" was what was needed to do the job properly. Men closed ranks and women did not receive the assistance or support of the men with whom they shared basic working conditions.

The debate has centered on a number of different areas. In favour of the introduction of female officers into male prisons, it has been argued by that women have a calming effect on male prisoners. By emphasizing women's interactive abilities, it has been argued that they may produce a better response from male prisoners, possibly avoiding confrontation.

Opposition to the posting of women questions their abilities to maintain and restore control.

In an ideal situation, relationships within and between groups of officers and prisoners should be professional and findings have indicated that women are more likely than men to develop friendly relationships with prisoners. However, the nature of the relationship between the prisoners and officers is not simple and there are potential security implications of over friendly interactions.

It should also be remembered that female deployment in male prisons was an enforced result of equal opportunities' law. Thus, it should not be too surprising that it is reported that the reaction of most North American prison administrators was mostly negative yet research has demonstrated the prevalence of paternalistic (over) protection of women in potentially dangerous situations. Bowersox's (1981) and Bryn Jones' (1996) findings suggest that men try to shield women from possible assault

Cross Gender Supervision and Control in Male Prisons in England: A Summary of Officers' Perspectives, J. R. Adler. First published by Pavilion Publishing (Brighton, UK) Ltd. in *The British Journal of Forensic Practice*, Volume 1, Issue 1, February 1998.

and women find it unnecessary. Willerton and Patterson (1995) report anecdotal evidence suggesting that female members of staff were prevented by male colleagues from dealing with incidents that would require the use of Control and Restraint techniques. In turn, this "protection" served to reinforce the prejudice that women could not handle certain situations with "violent and refractory prisoners" (p. 3).

Another way of manipulating the image of female officers could be by the use of rumour and innuendo. For example, Clayton (1995) reports that 26% of women and 10% of men reported that stories had been spread about them in the previous six months. Also, 17% of women and 7% of men reported being intimidated or bullied at work. This relates to one of the most pressing fears in prisons which is that personal safety of both officers and prisoners can be compromised. In America, Flynn (1982) and Alpert (1984) cite the Supreme Court Case of *Dothard* v. *Rawlinson, 1977,* where the court ruled that women in maximum security settings were at risk and could cause a loss of order. However, Flynn also cites the California Supreme Court which concluded that "the desire to protect women from the general hazards inherent in many occupations cannot be a valid ground for excluding them from those occupations. . . . Women must be permitted to take their chances along with men when they are otherwise qualified and capable of meeting the requirements of their employment. . . . We can no more justify denial of the means of earning a livelihood on such a basis than we could deny all women drivers' licenses."

Methodology

To summarize the present study, 120 prisoners and 120 officers from two category B (medium to high security) prisons ("Mars" and "Saturn") participated in the research. The project was designed to explore male and female officers' means of control and management of fear in themselves and in prisoners. This paper is concerned only with the quantitative findings from the officers who participated.

In both prisons, every wing-based female officer agreed to take part. In total, 120 officers participated of whom 26 were women; 5 participants were members of ethnic minorities; the average age was 35.4 with the youngest officer being 22 and the oldest being 58; the average length of service was 5.2 years with the shortest serving officer having been in post for two months and the longest for 29 years. Four principal officers, 19 senior officers and 97 basic grade officers participated. The prison wings included one for vulnerable prisoners; one for "lifers"; three "Category B" wings; one "Category C"—medium to low security wing; one "Category B" wing with some prisoners going through "basic regime" and one "Category B wing" with a drug rehabilitation section.

Results

For reasons of space, only some of the results are reported here. Overall, officers concluded that they worked within "good regimes" yet, they made comments that displayed concern about the future direction of the Prison Service. Those officers who felt that they had some influence within the wing were more positive about the regime than those who did not. This was tested statistically using χ^2 which yielded a "λ" of 0.20 (p < 0.05) This would imply that 20% of the variance in assessments of the regime is accounted for by differences in perceived influence over that regime. Forty-five percent of the officers did not feel influential enough and 68% of them felt that the job was not appropriately structured.

Officer-Prisoner Relationships

Seventy-five percent of the officers reported that they did not trust the prisoners at all; forty-four (37%) of the officers reported that it depended on either the prisoner or the situation involved and only one (1%) officer reported trusting prisoners. When asked if the prisoners trusted them, sixty-eight (57%) of the officers reported that it depended either on the prisoner concerned or on the task in hand; thirty-four (29%) of the officers believed that the prisoners did not trust them at all; twelve (10%) re-

ported that they "think so" and five (4%) of the officers thought that the prisoners trusted them completely.[1]

Sixty-eight (57%) of the officers reported problems with the prisoners, however, most of them were related to the environment rather than the individual officers concerned and relatively few were physically dangerous. There was no significant difference between men and women in reporting whether they experienced problems with the prisoners. However, a χ^2 analysis indicates that there is a difference in the type of problems experienced by men and women. Women seem to face both system (such as arguments over food) and interpersonal problems from the prisoners whereas the men are more likely to face system problems (Pearson = 9.92, df 3, p < 0.05). However, a "λ" test failed to demonstrate that the variance was significantly explained by gender. This is perhaps due to the low numbers in all but one of the "cells." It is worth noting that male officers tend to experience problems with the prisoners more frequently than do female officers (Pearson = 18.03, df 9, p < 0.05) but again, "λ" is negligible.

Staff Relationships

Prison officers are traditionally portrayed as a closely knit group, however, little assessment has been made of their feelings regarding the teams with which they work. The current research indicates that firstly, 98% of officers feel that it is important or very important to be a member of a team; secondly that 92% of them do feel part of a team. The third finding of relevance is that there is a degree of ambivalence over colleagues' performances. Just over half (52%) were ambivalent or negative about other team members yet when asked directly about their colleagues, the participants were largely positive. Eighty-two (67%) reported that their colleagues were either good or very good. Thirty (25%) reported that it depended on the officers, or that they were okay in general; only five (4%) officers reported that their colleagues were bad or very bad. Although not satisfactorily significant, it is worth mentioning two findings: that the older officers tend to be more positive about their colleagues and, surprisingly, that the female officers also tend to be more positive about their colleagues than are the male officers. This finding seems to point to a worse relationship amongst male officers than between female and male officers but it is also worth noting that 33% of the male officers report that their attitudes towards their colleagues depend on their colleagues' sex. When specifically asked if they had confidence in their colleagues, 73% of the officers do, only 5% have no confidence in their colleagues and the rest have varying levels of confidence depending on the colleagues concerned.

All one hundred twenty officers report that they generally "get on with" their colleagues but half of the sample reported problems with them. A λ^2 comparison demonstrated that female officers are significantly more likely to report problems with their colleagues than are male officers, (Pearson = 4.26, df 1, p < 0.05). Further comparisons were made between the type of problems experienced. They point to findings that are consistent with the previous literature, namely, that women are more likely to experience interpersonal problems with their colleagues than are the male officers (Pearson = 15.55, df 1, p < 0.01).

Control and Maintenance of Good Order

Although there were no statistically significant differences between the means of maintaining control favoured by male and female officers, it is worth stating that the female officers only reported making use of three of the methods reported in table 1. Eleven female officers reported using interpersonal skills to maintain control, six reported that the system maintains control rather than individual officers, and five reported that the prisoners were in control. It appears that both men and women use techniques that have been traditionally associated with women.

When analysing the interviews, it became clear that the officers were combining two of the questions in their answers, namely how they would handle a situation that looks like it might become nasty and how they would handle a situation that has

turned nasty. Their answers have been collapsed and are shown in table 2. There were no statistically significant differences between male and female officers' preferred means of control nor were there statistically significant differences between the methods favoured in either prison or wing (despite their different "clientele").

There is little difference between those encounters identified as being potentially nasty and those actually experienced. One hundred officers (83%) reported that they had been involved in such encounters and there was a wide pattern in the frequency of involvement in such encounters. Thirty (25%) of the officers reported involvement more than four times a year, with fifteen officers stating that they were involved in nasty situations all the time.

Given the nature of this research, it was also particularly important to attempt to assess whether the officers had come into conflict with each other. Thirty-eight (32%) of the officers had been involved in unpleasant situations with other offi-

cers. There were no significant differences in the numbers of male and female officers reporting previous involvement in unpleasant situations with other officers. The frequency of such events varied but was largely rare. There were no significant differences between the types of situation reported by men and women, nor, in the proportions reporting such involvement (39% of the women reported involvement in such situations and 33% of the men) and physical confrontation was rare. Women tended to worry about doing their job whereas men tended not to worry (Pearson = 3.36, df 1, p = 0.07).

Sixty-five (55%) of the officers reported that there were situations which made them feel uncomfortable. There were some gender differences that tend towards statistical significance relating to the type of situation that made officers feel uncomfortable (Pearson = 19.137, df 19, p = 0.059). Only one woman reported being made uncomfortable by general violence, none reported discomfort from a lack of control, changes to

Table 1 Means of Control Employed by Officers

Means of Control	Number of Officers	Percentage of Officers
Interpersonal skills	45	39
The system maintains control	25	22
The prisoners are in control	20	18
Experience	8	7
It varies	7	6
Respect or authority or presence	6	5
Control and restraint	1	1

Table 2 Means of Managing Potential and Actual Violence Broken Down by Gender

Female Officers	Means of Control	Male Officers
19 (73%)	A stage approach from use of interpersonal skills through to control and restraint	58 (62%)
3 (12%)	Control and restraint	12 (13%)
2 (8%)	Calming the situation	10 (11%)
—	It depends on the situation	7 (7%)
—	By talking to the prisoners	3 (3%)
1 (4%)	Through knowledge of prisoners	1 (1%)
—	Use of nonverbal cues	1 (1%)

the regime, from the hierarchy, or from the actions taken by other officers whereas no men reported problems with prisoners becoming too personal. Women are proportionately *more* likely to report problems in their working environment, discomfort when searching prisoners or over privacy and related to offence types.

Sixty-four (54%) of the officers reported that they sometimes felt fearful whilst carrying out their duties and in contrast to Gomme's findings (1988), there were no statistically significant differences in the incidence of fear between male and female officers. There were also no differences between officers from different wings and officers from different prisons. Although just over half of the officers appear to feel fearful, this is somewhat mediated by previous involvement in "nasty situations." Of those officers who had not previously experienced "nasty situations," fewer reported feeling fear (Pearson = 5.47, df 1, p < 0.05). Officers who do not tend to worry at work generally, also tended to be those who did not report fear (Pearson = 9.62, df 1, p < 0.01). Another unsurprising finding is that the same officers tend to worry about their safety and report feeling fear (Pearson = 11.92, df 1, p < 0.01).

One hundred five officers (88%) reported that their answers relating to fear were based on personal experience and there was a low correlation between experience and level of fear (r = 0.27, p < 0.05). This provides tentative support for the suggestion that officers with more experience are more likely to have been involved in worse situations. They can report having felt fearful under certain conditions because they have had time to find themselves in those conditions.

Professional Support

Eighty-eight (73%) of the officers reported that they had the support of their colleagues. Thirty-one (26%) said that it depended on which colleagues or situation and one officer reported no support from colleagues. There were no significant differences between male and female officers' reports of support from their colleagues.

Fifty-seven (48%) of the officers said that they felt they had the complete support of their supervisors;

fifty-nine (50%) reported that it depended on the supervisor concerned and three (2%) said that they did not feel supported by their supervisors. Of those three, two were women. There were no significant differences between different wings or prisons. There was a degree of ambivalence expressed by the female officers, however, when tested, this was statistically insignificant as a number of male officers were also ambivalent about official sources of support.

The most visible Prison Service sources of support after an incident may be the (post incident) care teams. One hundred thirteen officers were aware of the existence of the care teams in their prison. Only seventeen (14%) of the officers reported that they had previously used the services of the care team. When asked whether they thought that they might use the services in the future, sixty-three (53%) of the officers said that they would, fifty-one (43%) said that they would not and one officer was unsure. Thus, almost half of the sample either foresaw no likelihood of difficulties ahead, or were unwilling to disclose their potential needs for support to their colleagues on the care teams or simply felt that they could cope with whatever came their way without the aid of a formal support service. There were no significant differences between men and women, officers from different wings or prisons in whether they had previously used the care team or whether they would in the future.

Conclusions

Marginally more female officers (65%) reported problems with their colleagues than with prisoners (50%) and this is in line with literature from various countries. Also in line with previous literature is that the female officers' problems with colleagues is in marked contrast to the experiences of the male officers. Almost half of the women reported interpersonal problems with their colleagues whereas only 10% of the men reported such problems. Similarly, male officers seem to be more likely to report environmental problems with the prisoners than interpersonal ones whereas female officers are as likely to report interpersonal problems as environmental problems.

Male officers seem to report experiencing problems with prisoners more frequently than do the female officers. Associated with this finding, male officers are more likely to report more frequent "unpleasant situations with other officers."

Despite predictions to the contrary, men and women officers do not report favouring different methods of maintaining control. There are a number of possible interpretations of this finding but all require further research. The first is that the participants tended to give "text book" answers in an attempt to fulfill perceived experimenter demands. It is unlikely that such an effect would only manifest itself in relation to some, but not all, of the "awkward" questions. Most officers were keen to portray their view and to have them heard. Such views were not always in line with Prison Service policy nor were they "politically correct." Therefore, social desirability is probably not an adequate explanation.

The two most plausible interpretations are either that there really is no difference in means of control or that male and female officers are using different terms of reference. The reported reliance on a stage approach to (potential) conflict resolution implies that both men and women use techniques that are demanded by the situation.

The second main interpretation of the finding that men and women favour the same techniques relates to their terms of reference. For example, it is possible that both male and female officers favour trying to negotiate before using physical restraint. However, the points at which they decide to change approaches and their techniques within each approach may be different. It was not possible to test this contention in the current data set therefore it is suggested that this would be a useful area of future research.

One key component to specific interpersonal interactions is the quality of any existing relationship. Female officers seem to have better relationships with prisoners than do male officers. There is, though, a need to assess what makes a "good relationship." The Learmont (1995) and Woodcock (1994) reports both mention the problems caused by officers who did not believe that the prisoners would actually go as far as killing them. Although many would argue that a significant proportion of the prison population does not need to be there, there is no dispute that there are a number of prisoners who have previously shown their aptitude for violent confrontation. It is commonly accepted that competent coping with such prisoners involves teamwork from officers. Whilst the picture is generally positive in this regard, it should be noted that there were a number of qualms expressed about support from line managers and governors for actions taken by the teams or individuals on them.

Also in common with previous literature, female officers recognised that if they were "over protected," they may be put at risk through either lack of practice of protective skills or lack of information from their colleagues. Although these views were mentioned by some of the female officers, others reported receiving protection from some of the prisoners and mentioned the utility of protective male colleagues. In a similar vein, there was some ambiguity regarding supervisor support. It is possible to conclude that all officers felt in need of more support. The vast majority of officers were aware of the existence of the Care Teams but there was much ambivalence expressed over their efficacy, confidentiality, and accessibility.

On moving to a consideration of feelings of acceptance, the picture becomes less clear but when the officers were asked directly whether they felt accepted, there were no differences between the perceived levels of acceptance of male and female officers. This is not what was predicted but may be explained by the relatively low level of colleague social interaction generally. In other words, the officers, be they male or female, are not as bonded together as those described by Clemmer (1940), Mathieson (1965), Jacobs (1977), or Zimmer (1986). Given the associated violent confrontations that were reported by all of the above, the current finding is not necessarily problematic.

When asked to provide examples of "a nasty situation," 81% of the officers mentioned one or another form of violent confrontation. When recalling previous nasty experiences, 74% of the officers reported that they had been involved in one or more

such incidents. There were no significant differences between male and female officers' experiences of such events despite reports that the women were protected or prevented from attending them. This apparent anomaly may have arisen because in attempting to shield them, male officers inadvertently put them at risk.

It seems fair to acknowledge that women do have different interpersonal relationships and problems when compared with male officers. Although there was no significant difference between the numbers of male and female officers who reported experiencing problems with prisoners, male officers were more likely to report more frequent problems than were female officers. However, there is a difference in the type of problem experienced. Male officers' problems with prisoners tended to be related to the environment whereas female officers' problems with prisoners were as likely to be interpersonal as environmental.

In a similar manner, a significantly greater proportion of female officers reported problems with their colleagues. Of those officers who reported such problems, there was no difference in the frequencies of difficulties reported by male and female officers. Female officers were more likely to experience interpersonal problems than were the male officers. A similar picture appears in regard to worries about the job. A little over half of the women reported aspects of the job that worry them whereas the proportion of men who worried is a little over a third.

As has been demonstrated, women officers were perceived as calming influences by the male officers concordant with previous research findings (Cormier, 1975; Flynn, 1982; Jurik, 1988; Szockyj, 1989, and DPF2, 1994). However, the women are also seen as being less able to control violent situations and this is in line with Zimmer (1987) and Szockyj (1989).

It has been noted that the introduction of female officers may provide a calming influence and better interpersonal skills. However, it is also noted that the female officers themselves may experience problems interacting with both prisoners and officers. Such problems would be predictable within an environ-

ment traditionally characterised as very masculine or "macho." It is possible that the generally good staff-prisoner relationships are associated with the deployment of female officers. They may have influenced male officers to the extent that the male officers adopt traditionally female responses to conflict. In other words, calming rather than exacerbating. However, this may be less likely than the notion that Prison Service training in interpersonal skills use is actually showing signs of beginning to work.

Note

1. In a prison, trust is an ambiguous concept. Distrust must be a common sense approach of the one group towards the other yet trust is vital for the maintenance of daily routines. Part of the difficulty inherent within an understanding of trust is demonstrated in the finding that there are more officers who distrust the prisoners than there are those who believe the prisoners distrust them. Whilst it may be true that prisoners have to rely on officers to do things for them, whether prisoners would "trust" them is a question that needs to be addressed. It is likely that prisoners' responses would be negative.

References

Adler, J. R. (1994). *Fear in Prisons*. London: Prison Reform Trust Occasional Paper.

Alpert, G. P. (1984). "The Needs of the Judiciary and Misapplications of Social Research: The case of female guards in men's prisons." *Criminology*, 22, 3, 441–456.

Becker, A. (1975). "Women in Corrections: A process of change." *Resolutions*, 1, 19–21.

Bowersox, M. S. (1981). "Women in Corrections: Competence, competition, and the social responsibility norm." *Criminal Justice and Behavior*, 8, 4, 491–499.

Bryn Jones, C (1996—personal communications from Home Office) (Unpublished Report for Criminal Justice Studies). A Woman's Place . . . Cross Sex Postings and Problems of Acceptance in the Prison Service.

Clayton, M. (1995). *Male/Female Working Relationships in Five Prison Service Establishments*. Kent: Psychological Services.

Clemmer, D. (1940). *The Prison Community*. New York: Holt, Rinehart & Winston.

Cormier, B. M. (1975). *The Watcher and The Watched*. New York: Tundra.

DPF2 (1994). *Equal Opportunities in the Prison Service: Working in Cross Postings*. London: HM Prison Service.

Figgie, H. E. (1980). *The Figgie Report on Fear of Crime: America Afraid.* Ohio: ATO Inc.

Flynn, E. E. (1982). "Women as Criminal Justice Professionals: A challenge to change tradition." In Rafter, N. H. & Stanko, E. A. (Eds.) *Judge, Lawyer, Victim, Thief: Women, gender roles and criminal justice.* Northeastern University Press.

Gerstein, L. H., Topp, C. G. and Correll, G. (1987). "The Role of the Environment and Person When Predicting Burnout Among Correctional Personnel." *Criminal Justice and Behavior,* 14, 3, 352–369.

Gomme, I. (1988). "The Role of Experience in the Production of Fear of Crime: A Test of a Causal Model." *Canadian Journal of Criminology,* 30, 1, 67–76.

Graham, C. (1981). "Women are Succeeding in Male Institutions." *American Correctional Association Monographs,* 1, 27–36.

Horne, P. (1985). "Female Correction Officers." *Federal Probation,* 59, 3, 46–54.

Jacobs, J. (1977). *Stateville—The Penitentiary in Mass Society.* London: University of Chicago Press.

Jurik, N. (1985). "Individual and Organizational Determinants of Correctional Officer Attitudes Toward Inmates." *Criminology,* 23, 523–539.

———. (1988). "Striking a Balance: Female Correctional Officers, Gender Role Stereotypes, and Male Prisons." *Sociological Inquiry,* 58, 3, 318–330.

Learmont, J. (1995). Review of Prison Service Security in England and Wales and the Escape from Parkhurst Prison on Tuesday 3rd January 1995. Cm 3020 London: HMSO.

Lennon, M. C. and Rosenfeld, S. (1992). "Women and Mental Health: The interaction of job and family conditions." *Journal of Health and Social Behavior,* 33, 4, 316–327.

Mathiesen, T. (1965). *The Defences of the Weak.* London: Tavistock.

Personnel Planning Group. (1995). Equal Opportunities in the Prison Service: Progress Report, 1st October 1993, 31st March 1995. London: HM Prison Service.

Prison Service. (1994). Briefing 74, 6th June 1994. London: HMSO

Szockyj, E. (1989). "Working in a Man's World: Women Correctional Officers in an Institution for Men." *Canadian Journal of Criminology,* 31, 3, 319–328.

Toch, H. (1977). *Police, Prisons, and the Problem of Violence.* Washington, D.C.: U.S. Government Printing Office.

Willerton, C. & Patterson, P. (1995). Study of Women in Prison Officer Grades. Management Consultancy Service, Reference M044.

Woodcock, J. (1994). Report of the Enquiry into the Escape of Six Prisoners from the Special Secure Unit at Whitemoor Prison, Cambridgeshire on Friday 9th September 1994. Cm 2741 London: HMSO.

Zimmer, L. E. (1986). *Women Guarding Men.* London: University of Chicago Press.

———. (1987). "How Women Reshape the Prison Guard Role." *Gender and Society,* 1, 4, 415–431.

Zupan, L. S. (1986). "Gender-related Differences in Correctional Officers' Perceptions and Attitude." *Journal of Criminal Justice,* 14, 4, 349–361.

 Article Review Form at end of book.

WiseGuide Wrap-Up

Clearly, the debate over whether to "lock 'em up" or explore alternatives to incarceration will continue. Public policy and the competition among social service agencies for taxpayer dollars demand that this issue be explored. Prisons are social worlds where staff members must establish means of interacting with inmates and each other, adapt to changes in the environment, and find some measure of dignity and satisfaction in their careers.

R.E.A.L. Sites

This list provides a print preview of typical **Coursewise** R.E.A.L. sites. There are over 100 such sites at the **Courselinks**™ site. The danger in printing URLs is that web sites can change overnight. As we went to press, these sites were functional using the URLs provided. If you come across one that isn't, please let us know via email to: webmaster@coursewise.com. Use your Passport to access the most current list of R.E.A.L. sites at the **Courselinks** site.

Site name: American Correctional Association (ACA)

URL: http://www.corrections.com/aca/index.html

Why is it R.E.A.L.? American Correctional Association reflects the expanding philosophy of corrections and its increasingly important role within the community and society as a whole. It has many publications and has an accreditation department that examines prisons across the U.S.

Key topics: correctional facilities and systems, overcrowding, privatization of prisons, shock incarceration, unit management

Try this: This organization has 20,000 members and reduced membership charges for students. Guess how much membership costs students; then click on this site to see if you are correct.

Site name: Corrections Connection Network

URL: http://www.corrections.com/main/about.htm

Why is it R.E.A.L.? This site claims to be the largest online corrections resource with over 2,500 web pages of information covering 1,500 products and services listings and over 10,000 links to corrections-related information. There are links to criminal justice academic programs, news about corrections, chat rooms, and a jobs list.

Key topics: correctional officers, student attitudes

Try this: When you go to this site, go to the job guide and see how many openings there are that pay college tuition for individuals who join certain organizations. Hint: One job pays up to $30,000 toward tuition, and it isn't the military.

Site name: U.S. Government Jobs/Correctional Officers

URL: http://www.usajobs.opm.gov/wfjic/jobs/BQ6899.HTM

Why is it R.E.A.L.? Correctional jobs and other federal employment opportunities are offered by the U.S. government on this site.

Key topics: correctional officers

Try this: Click on the site. Go to the federal job scams section. Have you ever seen an ad in the newspaper or interviewed with a company representative that resembles the scam described at this site?

Index

Note: Names and page numbers in **bold** type indicate authors and their readings.

Putting it in *Perspectives*
-Review Form-

Your name:_____   Date: _____

Reading title: _____

Summarize: Provide a one-sentence summary of this reading: _____

_____

_____

_____

Follow the Thinking: How does the author back the main premise of the reading? Are the facts/opinions appropriately supported by research or available data? Is the author's thinking logical?

_____

_____

_____

_____

_____

Develop a Context (answer one or both questions): How does this reading contrast or compliment your professor's lecture treatment of the subject matter? How does this reading compare to your textbook's coverage?

_____

_____

_____

_____

_____

_____

Question Authority: Explain why you agree/disagree with the author's main premise.

_____

_____

_____

_____

_____

_____

_____

COPY ME! Copy this form as needed. This form is also available at http://www.coursewise.com
Click on: *Perspectives*.